Lecture Notes in Artificial Intelligence 9825

Subseries of Lecture Notes in Computer Science

More information about this series at http://www.springer.com/series/1244

Elio Tuci · Alexandros Giagkos
Myra Wilson · John Hallam (Eds.)

From Animals to Animats 14

14th International Conference
on Simulation of Adaptive Behavior, SAB 2016
Aberystwyth, UK, August 23–26, 2016
Proceedings

 Springer

Editors
Elio Tuci
Aberystwyth University
Aberystwyth
UK

Myra Wilson
Aberystwyth University
Aberystwyth
UK

Alexandros Giagkos
Aberystwyth University
Aberystwyth
UK

John Hallam
University of Southern Denmark
Odense
Denmark

ISSN 0302-9743   ISSN 1611-3349 (electronic)
Lecture Notes in Artificial Intelligence
ISBN 978-3-319-43487-2   ISBN 978-3-319-43488-9 (eBook)
DOI 10.1007/978-3-319-43488-9

Library of Congress Control Number: 2016946319

LNCS Sublibrary: SL7 – Artificial Intelligence

© Cover illustration: Jean Solé

Printed on acid-free paper

This Springer imprint is published by Springer Nature
The registered company is Springer International Publishing AG Switzerland

Preface

This book contains the articles presented at the 14th International Conference on the Simulation of Adaptive Behavior (SAB 2016), held in Aberystwyth at Aberystwyth University, Wales, in August 2016.

The objective of the biennial SAB conference is to bring together researchers in computer science, artificial intelligence, artificial life, complex systems, robotics, neuroscience, ethology, evolutionary biology, and related fields in order to further our understanding of the behaviours and underlying mechanisms that allow natural and artificial animals to adapt and survive in uncertain environments.

Adaptive behaviour research is distinguished by its focus on the modelling and creation of complete animal-like systems, which – however simple at the moment – may be one of the best routes to understanding intelligence in natural and artificial systems. The conference is part of a long series that started with the first SAB conference held in Paris in September 1990, which was followed by conferences in Honolulu (1992), Brighton (1994), Cape Cod (1996), Zürich (1998), Paris (2000), Edinburgh (2002), Los Angeles (2004), Rome (2006), Osaka (2008), Paris (2010), Odense (2012), and Castellón (2014).

In 1992, MIT Press introduced the quarterly journal *Adaptive Behavior*, now published by SAGE Publications. The establishment of the International Society of Adaptive Behavior (ISAB) in 1995 further underlined the emergence of adaptive behaviour as a fully fledged scientific discipline. The present proceedings provide a comprehensive and up-to-date resource for the future development of this exciting field.

The articles cover the main areas in animat research, including the animat approach and methodology, perception and motor control, evolution, learning, and adaptation, and collective and social behaviour. The authors focus on well-defined models, computer simulations, or robotic models that help to characterise and compare various organisational principles, architectures, and adaptation processes capable of including adaptive behaviour in real animals or synthetic agents, the animats.

This conference and its proceedings would not exist without the substantial help of a wide range of people. Foremost, we would like to thank the members of the Program Committee, who thoughtfully reviewed all the submissions and provided detailed suggestions on how to improve the articles. We are also indebted to our sponsors. And, once again, we warmly thank Jean Solé for the artistic conception of the SAB 2016 poster and the proceedings cover.

We invite readers to enjoy and profit from the papers in this book, and look forward to the next SAB conference in 2018.

August 2016

Elio Tuci
Alexandros Giagkos
Myra Wilson
John Hallam

Organisation

From Animals to Animats 14, the 14th International Conference on the Simulation of Adaptive Behavior (SAB 2016), was organised by the Department of Computer Science, Aberystwyth University, UK, and the International Society for Adaptive Behavior (ISAB).

Conference Chairs

Myra Wilson   Aberystwyth University, Aberystwyth, UK
John Hallam   University of Southern Denmark, Odense, Denmark

Program Chairs

Elio Tuci   Aberystwyth University, Aberystwyth, UK
Alexandros Giagkos   Aberystwyth University, Aberystwyth, UK

Local Organization

Frédéric Labrosse   Aberystwyth University, Aberystwyth, UK
Patricia Shaw   Aberystwyth University, Aberystwyth, UK
Marek Ososinski   Aberystwyth University, Aberystwyth, UK
Suresh Kumar   Aberystwyth University, Aberystwyth, UK
Daniel Lewkowicz   Aberystwyth University, Aberystwyth, UK
James Finnis   Aberystwyth University, Aberystwyth, UK
Peter Scully   Aberystwyth University, Aberystwyth, UK
Laurence Tyler   Aberystwyth University, Aberystwyth, UK

Program Committee

Francois Michaud	Richard Duro	Angelo Arleo
Anders Christensen	Luca Gambardella	Luís Correia
Paul Graham	Luc Berthouze	Roderich Gross
Seth Bullock	Josh Bongard	Naoto Iwahashi
Jean-Baptiste Mouret	Julien Diard	Ryohei Nakano
Lola Cañamero	Philippe Gaussier	Mikhail Prokopenko
Takashi Ikegami	Marc Schoenauer	Davide Marocco
Michail Maniadakis	Marco Dorigo	Tom Ziemke
Carlo Pinciroli	Inaki Rano	Christian Balkenius
Marco Mirolli	Nikolaus Correll	Stefano Nolfi
Serge Thill	Frédéric Alexandre	Andreagiovanni Reina
Inman Harvey	Andrew Philippides	Phil Husbands

Onofrio Gigliotta
Benoît Girard
Vito Trianni
Ali Turgut
Swen Gaudl
Eliseo Ferrante
André Santos
Alastair Channon

Eris Chinellato
Ester Martínez-Martín
Antonio Morales
Enric Cervera
Hugo Vieira Neto
Angel Pascual Del Pobil
Álvaro Gutiérrez
Stéphane Doncieux

Angelo Cangelosi
Tomassino Ferrauto
Daeeun Kim
Marek Ososinski
John Hallam
Peter Scully
Patricia Shaw

Sponsoring Institutions

ISAB
Webots (robot simulation)
Aberystwyth University

University of Southern Denmark
https://www.cyberbotics.com
http://www.aber.ac.uk

Contents

Circumnutation: From Plants to Robots

Michael B. Wooten and Ian D. Walker[✉]

Department of Electrical and Computer Engineering, Clemson University,
Clemson, SC 29634, USA
{mbwoote,iwalker}@clemson.edu

Abstract. We discuss and demonstrate how an approach used by plants can be adapted as a useful algorithm for motion planning in robotics. Specifically, we review the process of circumnutation, which is used by numerous plants, and particularly climbing vines, to explore and contact their environments. We show how circumnutation can be adapted to generate practical algorithms for motion planning for continuum tendril robots. The analysis and discussion is supported by experimental results using a robot tendril. Using circumnutation, performance of the robot is enhanced by efficiently enabling environmental contact, which helps guide and stabilize the robot.

Keywords: Robotics · Continuum robots · Vines · Circumnutation

1 Introduction

Biology has frequently served as an inspiration for robotics researchers [1]. In particular, the creation of androids, and their endowment with human-inspired algorithms enabling these humanoid robots to exhibit human-like behavior, has long been a holy grail for robotics. Additionally, robots and algorithms inspired by the form and function of such widely disparate biological forms as dogs, snakes, lizards, flies, birds, and fish have been developed and studied [2].

Almost all biological inspiration in robotics has come from animals, and most of this from vertebrates. This appears a natural consequence of the fact that conventional robot structures (e.g. manipulators and legs) have been constructed from rigid links, and so their movements and capabilities are well-matched to those of vertebrate animals.

Animals are not the only living and moving forms in nature however. Plants, although sessile (fixed base) demonstrate an amazing variety of structures and movements. These movements are typically slow relative to the usual expectations for robots, but they nevertheless demonstrate a remarkable range of adaptive behavior.

Until recently, apart from some high-concept thought experiments [3], few robotics researchers have considered plants as inspiration for their work [4]. However, in recent years efforts have produced a new generation of soft and compliant continuum trunk and tentacle robots [5]. These new robots have much in common with continuous biological morphologies, inviting comparisons with plant

© Springer International Publishing Switzerland 2016
E. Tuci et al. (Eds.): SAB 2016, LNAI 9825, pp. 1–11, 2016.
DOI: 10.1007/978-3-319-43488-9_1

stems and roots in addition to invertebrate animals. Recent work has considered the development of robots inspired by plant roots [6,7], but there appears to have been little attention paid thus far to the strategies plants use for motion generation to explore and exploit their environments.

Circumnutation is the term given in biology to a motion pattern commonly observed in plants, notably vines, in exploring (growing into) their environments [8,9]. In circumnutation, the stem simultaneously grows (extends) and bends, with the tip tracing an elliptical pattern. Charles Darwin first recorded this behavior and described it as a continuous self-bowing of the whole shoot, successively directed to all points of the compass [10]. This strategy is seen to increase the probability of encountering a support [11]. The movement thus represents a biologically optimal strategy for motion planning of plants to explore their a priori unknown environments, with the goal of encountering environmental objects as soon as possible, given the constraint of the long, thin flexible structure of the plants.

In this paper, we show how, by adapting circumnutation for robot motion planning, new and useful robot behaviors can be synthesized. In particular, we show how thin continuum robot tendrils can more efficiently explore their environments using circumnutation-based movements. In the process, new insight into the potential of tendril robots is gained. Continuum tendril robots and their capabilities are discussed in the following section. Section 3 details novel robot circumnutation algorithms and their implementation on a robot tendril. Section 4 presents conclusions.

2 Continuum and Tendril Robots

In the past few years, a new type of robot structure, that of continuum robots, has emerged [5]. Continuum robots, like plant stems, have continuous backbone structures that can bend and often extend at any point along the structure. They are significantly more compliant then their rigid-link counterparts. This gives them unique advantages over conventional rigid link robots, notably the ability to gently penetrate tight spaces and adaptively wrap around and grasp environmental objects [1,12,13]. Exploitation of the first of these capabilities has seen continuum robots find a niche in a variety of medical procedures [14].

Design of continuum robots has been strongly influenced by similar structures in biology, notably elephant trunks and octopus arms [1]. However, a long, thin (relatively high length to diameter ratio) variant of continuum robots, directly inspired by plant tendrils [15] has been proposed for remote inspection operations [16].

An example of a long, thin continuum robot tendril is shown in Fig. 1. Based on a spring-loaded concentric tube design [17], the tendril has three serially connected, independently controllable sections. Each section can be bent in two dimensions, via three remotely actuated tendons running along the backbone and terminated at the end of the section. The backbone core is comprised of three concentric carbon-fiber tubes (largest diameter at the base end). External compression springs are fitted to allow the tendon actuation to provide relative extension and contraction between the tubes, and thus the sections [18].

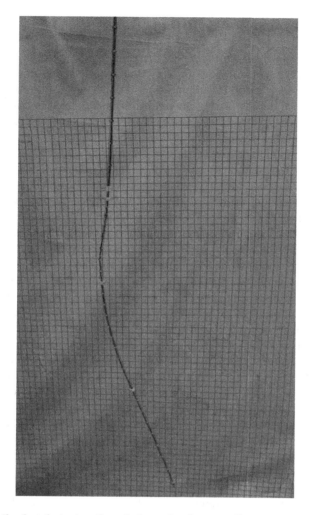

Fig. 1. Tendril robot featuring three independently controlled sections, each with two degrees of freedom in bending, and local extension and contraction between sections.

The resulting robot is highly flexible, with physical properties resembling many plant stems. The maximum length of the tendril is approximately 1.8 m, with a total length to width ration of 130 to 1 [18].

Due to the thin physical form and correspondingly flexible motion characteristics of tendril robots, development of strategies for operating them presents significant challenges. While kinematics for continuum robots are well established [19], motion planning for continuum robots remains an active research area [20]. Tendril robots are significantly thinner than previously deployed continuum-style robots [21], and lack the structural stiffness to adopt their follow the leader (tip) motion planning strategies. Their intended role in remote inspection requires more sophisticated motion planning than for simple robot plant stems [22].

3 Circumnutation with Robot Tendrils

Examination of plant behaviors provides alternative and useful insight into how to plan and execute motion plans for long thin robotic structures. The physics of plants in general [23], and circumnutation in particular [24], have been extensively studied. The details of the kinematics of circumnutation varies between plants [24], but the pattern of generally elliptical tip motion is consistent, providing a model of how to efficiently move a thin backbone.

The robot tendril illustrated in Fig. 1 was used to investigate the effectiveness of circumnutation-based algorithms. The key aspect of adapting circumnutation to the robot was in scheduling the actuators to rotate bending about the backbone, while also enabling backbone extension, to produce the somewhat irregular helix [24] traced by plant tips.

In order to implement robot circumnutation, we initially choose the desired section to perform the action. This is done for the tendril in Fig. 1 by changing a variable for the operating mode in real time via the existing graphical user interface. Next, the numbers for the motors to be moved are loaded into an array and a second variable is set to the length of that array. This allows the function to perform circumnutation in any one or in multiple sections. For example, in the case of a single section, the array holds the numbers of the three motors attached to that section, and the second variable is equal to three.

To achieve circumnutation in a single section, the first motor in the array is signaled to pull its tendon. This is arbitrarily chosen to be the first motor in the sequence: 0 for the base, 3 for the middle, and 6 for the distal section. After this initial move, the next motor in the sequence activates and pulls its tendon until the tension equals or surpasses the tension in the first motor's tendon. Then the previous motor unwinds to relieve the tension in its line. This process repeats through the sequence until one full revolution occurs. The number of these full revolutions is predefined in the program and arbitrarily selected.

Circumnutation in multiple sections is performed in a similar way to that of a single section. The key difference is that, for multiple sections, the number of array entries increases. In the case of all three sections the array is formed as 0, 3, 6, 1, 4, 7, 2, 5, and 8. The total number of motors to move in this case is nine. The most important change is that instead of winding or unwinding one tendon at a time, the action is performed in sets of three. In the case of circumnutation in all three sections at once, motors 0, 3, and 6 pull on their tendons at the same time, since these tendons are down the same side of the device. Otherwise, the algorithm repeats as though for a single section but in sets of two or three depending on the operating mode.

An example movement of the robot using the above approach is illustrated in Fig. 2.

Figure 2 shows the side by side time evolution (top to bottom) of a hop vine performing (biological) circumnutation, with the tendril robot of Fig. 1 evolving correspondingly on the right, according to the actuation strategy described above.

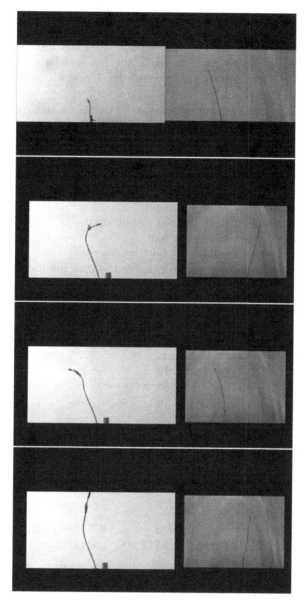

Fig. 2. Circumnuation. Top to bottom: increasing time. Left: hop vine. Right: tendril robot.

It can be seen that the robot tip follows an approximately similar trajectory to that of the plant. The real-time speed of the motion is significantly greater for the robot (the plant motion was scaled up to match). However, the basic kinematics of circumnutation were achieved. The full video can be viewed at: https://www.youtube.com/watch?v=3fbgUxE0V8o&feature=youtu.be.

The underlying algorithm for the robot circumnutation is given below.

1. Depending on selection variable (user input), store motor designations in an array and store how many are to move in another variable.
    (a) i.e. Distal section is controlled by motors 6, 7, and 8, 3 motors, and so on
2. Wind the first motor(s) in the set
3. Enter nested loop until predefined number of iterations achieved
    (a) Until we have moved all tendons included in the current set to move (usually 3)
        i. Wind the next motor(s) in the sequence until the tension of the previously wound tendon is achieved
            A. Wind until the tension is greater than or equal to tension on tendon prior in the sequence
        ii. Unwind the previously wound tendon once
        iii. Go to 3-a until condition is met
    (b) Increment counter variable
    (c) Go to 3 unless increment counter equals the max iterations

The corresponding program (Arduino) code for the robot circumnutation is reproduced below.

```
// =================================================================
Circumnutation subroutine
if(id == ButtonID_Circumnutation)   {
if (MotorSelection == 9) // ====================
Distal section
{ // Counter-Clockwise
// =======================  Wind 6 -> 7 -> 8 -> 6 and re-peat
motorstomove[0] = 6; motorstomove[1] = 7; motorstomove[2] = 8;
numbertomove = 3;
}else if (MotorSelection == 10) // =================
Middle Section
{ // Counter-Clockwise
// =======================  Wind 3 -> 4 -> 5 -> 3 and re-peat
motorstomove[0] = 3; motorstomove[1] = 4; motorstomove[2] = 5;
numbertomove = 3;
}else if (MotorSelection == 11) // =====================
Base Section
{ // Counter-Clockwise
// =======================  Wind 0 -> 1 -> 2 -> 0 and re-peat
motorstomove[0] = 0; motorstomove[1] = 1; motorstomove[2] = 2;
numbertomove = 3;
}else if (MotorSelection == 12) // =====================
Multi - Section Circumnutation
{ // Counter-Clockwise
// =======================  Wind 0,3,6 -> 1,4,7 -> 2,5,8 -> 0,3,6
 and repeat
```

```
motorstomove[0] = 0; motorstomove[1] = 3; motorstomove[2] = 6;
motorstomove[3] = 1; motorstomove[4] = 4; motorstomove[5] = 7;
motorstomove[6] = 2; motorstomove[7] = 5; motorstomove[8] = 8;
numbertomove = 9;
}else if (MotorSelection == 13) // ===========================
    Multi Section (2) Circumnutation
{ // Counter-Clockwise
// =======================  Wind 3,6 -> 4,7 -> 5,8 -> 3,6
  and repeat
motorstomove[0] = 6; motorstomove[1] = 3;
motorstomove[3] = 7; motorstomove[4] = 4;
motorstomove[6] = 8; motorstomove[7] = 5;
numbertomove = 6;
}
move_motors(motorstomove,numbertomove/3,SERVO_WIND);
delay(DELAY_TIME);
sensor_update();
for (ndx = 0; ndx < CIRCUMNUTATION_DURATION && !Emergen-cyState;
 ndx++)
{
for (i = 1; i <= 3; i++)
{
for (j = (numbertomove/3)*(i%3), k = (numberto-move/3)*((i-1)%3);
j < (numbertomove/3)*(i%3)+(numbertomove/3); j++, k++)
wind_to_threshold(motorstomove[j],SensorWeight[motorstomove[k]]);
delay(DELAY_TIME);
sensor_update();
move_motors(&motorstomove[(numbertomove/3)*((i-1)%3)],
(numbertomove/3),SERVO_UNWIND);
delay(DELAY_TIME);
sensor_update();
}
}
}
```

3.1   Discussion

The benefits (and a key motivation for the approach in this paper) for the robot mirror those gained by the plants themselves. While the high flexibility of a long thin stem offers the advantages of being able to enter and thread through tight spaces, it also presents the corresponding disadvantage of low structural stability. The robot tendril, like many plant stems, suffers from sag due to gravitational loading, and buckling due to applied external forces. Many long thin plants, especially vines, devote most of their energy to growth rather than structural support [8,9]. To compensate for this, a key part of their growth strategy is to actively use the environment for support. By connecting to fixed points in the environment, plants (and robots) can partly or fully decouple the parts of their structure between contact points, reducing the effects of disturbance forces, and using the environment for support against gravity [8].

Different climbing plants use a variety of contact and attachment mechanisms (twining, pads, roots, specialized tendrils, thorns, prickles, etc.) to attach to the environment [8], but a common strategy for the free space tip motion is to use circumnutation to search the environment for environmental contacts. An excellent example can be seen in the video at: https://www.youtube.com/watch?v=erNNiVwZXv8. Tendril robots can benefit from a corresponding strategy. In [18], the authors demonstrated how the active use of environmental support using passive thorns on the backbone of the tendril of Fig. 2 significantly improved the

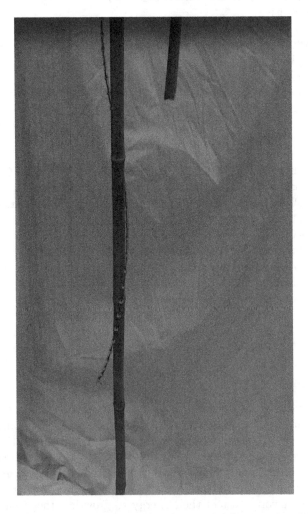

Fig. 3. Tendril robot coiling around bamboo post following circumnutation.

achievable workspace of the robot. The key advantage of hooking to fixed points in the environment is that coupling of forces (due to tendon actuation as well as externally applied) within the backbone is significantly reduced, resulting in greater control authority over the robot [18].

However, to adopt this strategy, particularly in the a priori partially known environments anticipated for robot tendril inspection operations, a methodology for efficiently moving to contact the environment is required. Note that at this time the field of tendril robots is sufficiently new that no formal algorithms for their motion planning has been established in the literature. Circumnutation offers a convenient existence proof from nature for similar robotic structures engaged in analogous explorations. Adaptation of the approach for robot tendril motion planning, as in this paper, provides the robot with a systematic approach to first find, then engage, environmental objects of interest (see Fig. 3).

Figure 3 shows the tendril robot engaging in twining behavior, wrapping around a static environmental object (a bamboo pole). In this operation circumnutation can be used as a motion primitive to efficiently move the robot to contact the pole. Subsequently a second motion primitive (twining) can be used to exploit the contact. We conducted multiple version of the experiment, and found the process robust to variations in initial pole placement and tendril geometry. In our experiments, no local sensing was used. If local contact sensing was available, the circumnutation and twining movements could be combined into a larger motion primitive.

In the future, we anticipate circumnutation-based algorithms forming a key part of a suite of algorithms (possibly forming part of larger motion primitives) enabling the practical operation of long thin robotic structures.

4   Conclusions

In this paper, we show how circumnutation, a movement strategy commonly observed in plants, can be adapted to synthesize a successful algorithm for robot motion planning. Circumnutation involves elliptical motion of the tip of a plant stem, and is used by plants to increase the likelihood of finding environmental support. We show that, and detail how, circumnutation can be used as the basis for algorithms for motion planning in thin continuum robots, which similarly benefit from environmental contact and support. The discussion is supported by experimental results with a tendril robot performing circumnutation to more efficiently achieve environmental contact.

Acknowledgments. This work is supported in part by the U.S. National Science Foundation under grant IIS-1527165, and in part by NASA under contract NNX12AM01G.

References

1. Trivedi, D., Rahn, C.D., Kier, W.M., Walker, I.D.: Soft robotics: biological inspiration, state of the art, and future research. Appl. Bionics Biomech. **5**(2), 99–117 (2008)
2. Meyer, J.-A., Guillot, A.: Biologically inspired robots, Chap. 60. In: Siciliano, B., Khatib, O. (eds.) Springer Handbook of Robotics, pp. 1395–1418. Springer, Berlin (2008)
3. Moravec, H.: Mind Children: The Future of Robot and Human Intelligence. Harvard University Press, Cambridge (1988)
4. Martone, P.T., Boller, M., Burgert, I., Dumais, J., Edwards, J., Mach, K., Rowe, N., Rueggeberg, M., Seidel, R., Speck, T.: Mechanics without muscle: biomechanical inspiration from the plant world. Integr. Comp. Biol. **50**(5), 888–907 (2010)
5. Robinson, G., Davies, J.B.C.: Continuum robots - a state of the art. In: Proceedings of IEEE International Conference on Robotics and Automation, Detroit, Michigan, pp. 2849–2854 (1999)
6. Mazzolai, B., Beccai, L., Mattoli, V.: Plants as model in biomimetics and biorobotics: new perspectives. Front. Bioeng. Biotechnol. **2**, 1–5 (2014). doi:10.3389/fbioe.2014.00002
7. Sadeghi, A., Tonazzini, A., Popova, I., Mazzolai, B.: Robotic mechanism for soil penetration inspired by plant root. In: Proceedings of IEEE International Conference on Robotics and Automation, Karlsruhe, Germany, pp. 3457–3462 (2013)
8. Goriely, A., Neukirch, S.: Mechanics of climbing and attachment in twining plants. Phys. Rev. Lett. **97**(18), 1–4 (2006)
9. Putz, F.E., Mooney, H.A.: The Biology of Vines. Cambridge University Press, New York (1991)
10. Darwin, C.: The Movements and Habits of Climbing Plants. John Murray, London (1875)
11. Isnard, S., Silk, W.K.: Moving with climbing plants from charles Darwin's time into the 21st century. Am. J. Bot. **96**(7), 1205–1221 (2009)
12. Walker, I.D.: Continuous backbone continuum robot manipulators: a review. ISRN Robot. 1–19 (2013)
13. Webster III, R.J., Jones, B.A.: Design and kinematic modeling of constant curvature continuum robots: a review. Int. J. Robot. Res. **29**(13), 1661–1683 (2010)
14. Burgner-Kars, J., Rucker, D.C., Choset, H.: Continuum robots for medical applications: a survey. IEEE Trans. Robot. **31**(6), 1261–1280 (2015)
15. Walker, I.D.: Robot strings: long, thin continuum robots. In: Proceedings IEEE Aerospace Conference, Big Sky, MT, pp. 1–12 (2013)
16. Mehling, J.S., Diftler, M.A., Chu, M., Valvo, M.: A minimally invasive tendril robot for in-space inspection. In: Proceedings of BioRobotics 2006 Conference, pp. 690–695 (2006)
17. Tonapi, M., Godage, I.S., Vijaykumar, A.M., Walker, I.D.: Spatial kinematic modeling of a long and thin continuum robotic cable. In: Proceedings IEEE International Conference on Robotics and Automation, Seattle, WA, pp. 3755–3761 (2015)
18. Wooten, M.B., Walker, I.D.: A novel vine-like robot for in-orbit inspection. In: Proceedings of 45th International Conference on Environmental Systems, Bellevue, WA, pp. 1–11 (2015)
19. Jones, B.A., Walker, I.D.: Kinematics for multisection continuum robots. IEEE Trans. Robot. **22**(1), 43–55 (2006)

20. Li, J., Teng, Z., Xiao, J., Kapadia, A., Bartow, A., Walker, I.D.: Autonomous continuum grasping. In: Proceedings of IEEE/RSJ International Conference on Intelligent Robots and Systems, Tokyo, Japan, pp. 4569–4576 (2013)
21. Buckingham, R.: Snake arm robots. Ind. Robot Int. J. **29**(3), 242–245 (2002)
22. Truong-Thinh, N., Ngoc-Phuong, N.: Design and development of a continuum structure for robotic flower. In: Proceeding of IEEE Conference on Robotics and Bi-omimetics, Phuket, Thailand, pp. 118–123 (2011)
23. Brown, A.H.: Circumnutations from darwin to space flights. Plant Physiol. **101**, 345–348 (1993)
24. Niklas, K.J., Spatz, H.-C.: Plant Physics. University of Chicago Press, Chicago (2012)

Using Marker-Based Motion Capture to Develop a Head Bobbing Robotic Lizard

Anna Frohnwieser[1]([✉]), Alexander P. Willmott[2], John C. Murray[3],
Thomas W. Pike[1], and Anna Wilkinson[1]([✉])

[1] School of Life Sciences, University of Lincoln, Lincoln, UK
{afrohnwieser,awilkinson}@lincoln.ac.uk
[2] School of Sport and Exercise Science, University of Lincoln, Lincoln, UK
[3] School of Computer Science, University of Lincoln, Lincoln, UK

Abstract. Robotic animals are regularly used in behavioral experiments, typically in experimental interactions with individuals of the species they were modelled on. In order to do so successfully, these robots need to be designed carefully, taking into consideration the specific perceptual system of the model species. We used marker-based motion capture to measure head bobbing in a widely popular lizard species, bearded dragons, and found that head bobbing is highly stereotypic yet differs subtly when displayed towards males and females. These results were then used for the construction of a robotic lizard, with the aim to use it in behavioral and cognitive studies, focusing on social cognition. This is the first study to use motion capture of head bobbing in lizards to inform the design of a robotic animal.

Keywords: Motion capture · Robotic lizard · Bearded dragon · Head bobbing

1 Introduction

Recreating realistic animals is a difficult task. Particularly in studies involving the interaction between a robot and real animals, care has to be taken as to how the robot is perceived by the animals. This includes, among other factors the robot's size, coloration, odor and motion characteristics. It is important to consider that each species has a different perceptual system, and therefore human perception alone is not a sufficient indicator of the realism of a robotic animal (see [1]). For example, color perception often differs substantially between different species, and so colors recreated for the human eye may not elicit realistic perceptual responses in the animal species being studied [2]. Careful, well-designed studies should be undertaken to examine the animals' perception of the robot to ensure that it appears as realistic as possible. When developing a robotic animal to mimic the species it is modelled after, even small aberrations in speed, angle or combination of movements may make it seem unrealistic. Depending on the task the robot is being created for, this can be detrimental. Even when the anatomy,

© Springer International Publishing Switzerland 2016
E. Tuci et al. (Eds.): SAB 2016, LNAI 9825, pp. 12–21, 2016.
DOI: 10.1007/978-3-319-43488-9_2

including bone structures, joints and muscles, is understood, it remains challenging to know how specific movements take place. In this paper we explain how we used motion capture to create a robotic bearded dragon (*Pogona vitticeps*) that moves in a realistic manner, which will be used in experiments focusing on social cognition (i.e., the study of how animals interact, acquire information and learn from each other). We chose bearded dragons as our model species because their behavioral repertoire is relatively simple and therefore comparatively easy to replicate and interpret [3]. The aim is to create a robot that is able to mimic some of the species' most characteristic behaviors. This will allow us to investigate these behaviors, and specifically other animals' response to them, in more detail, and ultimately to use robotic "demonstrators" in social learning experiments. Animal social cognition is a field that can vastly profit from using robotic animals, as they allow for greater reliability and control over the many factors outside the experimenter's power when using live animals (see [1]). Using robots for this type of work enables us to study social cognition in animals in much greater depth, providing full control over the presented stimuli and making it possible to vary them precisely, while excluding "noise" in the information provided, influenced for example by motivation and reliability of the demonstrator animal and interactions between demonstrators and subject animals [1]. Bearded dragons are responsive to social cues and show sophisticated social learning abilities [4]; these experiments will therefore provide valuable insights into reptile social behaviors and the perceptual mechanisms that underlie them.

1.1   Motion Capture of Animals

The most common use of marker-based motion capture in animals is with horses. They are mainly recorded for the film and games industry to recreate realistic models. Abson and Palmer [5] showed how biomechanical knowledge, including painting of the internal anatomy onto the skin of the horse, combined with well thought out marker and camera placement can lead to efficient recordings that require minimal post-processing. Other groups have used motion capture to improve the locomotion of quadruped robots. For example, Moro and colleagues [6] used motion capture of a horse walking on a treadmill to improve types of locomotion typical for horses in a small robot. Few other species have been used in motion capture studies. To understand the characteristic hopping motion and body posture of kangaroos, markers were placed on a kangaroo's joints [7]. Motion capture has also been used to record lizards, including bearded dragons [8–10], with the aim of informing war robots. These studies focus on walking behavior to generate data that is used for building walking robots capable of navigating difficult terrain, however none of them consider other behaviors of the lizards.

1.2   Head Bobbing in Lizards

One of bearded dragons' most characteristic behaviors is head bobbing—rapidly moving the head up and down, which can be supported by expansion of the skin on the neck and changes in coloration. This behavior is thought to be produced as an aggressive signal, showing dominance over a conspecific or during their mating ritual, and will often be responded to with arm waving, which is a submissive signal [3]. Because it is a very common behavior, carries a lot of communicative value and is relatively easy to replicate in a robot we chose head bobbing as our main focus for this study.

Behavioral studies investigating head bobbing have been conducted in several lizard species, some of which have used robotic lizards. Jenssen [11] investigated the influence of different behavioral modifiers on head bobbing in the Jamaican lizard (*Anolis opalinus*), while Lovern and Jenssen [12] showed that different types of head bobs emerge at different ontogenetic stages in green anoles (*Anolis carolinensis*). Martins and colleagues [13] used a robotic sagebrush lizard (*Sceloporus graciosus*) to investi-gate the influence of different types of head bobs on male and female conspecifics, showing that males attend more to the overall posture while for females the number of head bobs is important in evaluating other lizards. Macedonia and colleagues [14,15] showed how different anoles species can recognize members of their own species via their head bobs and how altering the dewlap color or head bob motion of a robotic anoles lizard influences species recognition. Other studies looked at inter species variation in head bobs (*Sceloporus graciosus* and *Anolis sagrei*), using robotic lizards to elicit head bobbing in live animals [16,17]. Ord and Stamps [18] investigated which factors of displays in Anolis lizards (*Anolis gundlachi*) influence perception in noisy environments by using robotic lizards that showed these displays in different combinations. To our knowledge, these robots were built to match a lizard perceived by the human sensory system, and no specific studies were carried out into how they were perceived by the animals they were modelling. While this seems sufficient in most cases, subtle differences in coloration, motion or odor, that might not be detectable by humans, can potentially influence the responses of other animals and thus the results of these experiments (see [1]). Head bobbing in lizards has previously been measured from video recordings [19]. Depending on the quality of the videos data recorded this way usually lacks detail, as movements that are too small and too fast to be visible to the human eye are missed. Furthermore, three dimensional data cannot be recorded if only one camera is used, and the animals have to be perfectly aligned with the camera, as any rotation of the head or body will lead to inaccurate results. To our knowledge, no studies have been conducted on head bobbing in bearded dragons. Therefore, the present experiment was designed to gain insight into the specific motion of head bobbing in bearded dragons to inform the design of a robotic lizard that will be used in behavioral and cognitive studies with these animals.

2   Methods

2.1   Motion Capture

Animals. Three male and two female bearded dragons (*Pogona vitticeps*) were used for motion capture. All animals were habituated to being handled by

humans on a daily basis. They were housed at the cold-blooded cognition laboratory at the University of Lincoln in groups of two to three animals per vivarium,
with males being held separately to avoid aggression. The room temperature
was kept at 28°C (±3) with additional heat lamps provided in each vivarium.
All animals received water ad libitum, vegetables and fruit once per day and
live food three times per week. None of the animals had previously been housed
together and they were of different ages, with two males and one female being
at least four years old and one male and one female being two years old.

System. Kinematic data were collected at 150 Hz using the Cortex software
package (v. 5.3, Motion Analysis Corporation (MAC), Santa Rosa, CA) running
on a PC coupled to twelve MAC Raptor motion capture cameras. The cameras were placed around a platform (120 cm x 60 cm) that was partitioned into
two equal halves by a glass plate (Fig. 1a) in such a way that both sides could
be recorded individually. This gave us the opportunity to record two interacting animals individually and simultaneously. Each animal was equipped with

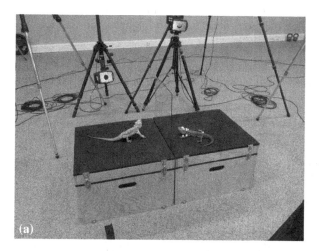

Fig. 1. (a) Set up of the experiment, showing the platform, divided by a glass plate,
the digital cameras and two bearded dragons with markers (b) Bearded dragon with
18 retroreflective markers attached to its skin

18 6.4 mm diameter retroreflective markers: three on its head, two on each leg, two on the shoulders, two on the hips, one at the center of the back and two on the tail (Fig. 1b). Marker locations were chosen to correspond with joints and anatomical points important for modelling the movements we were interested in, while taking into account the small size of the animals. The markers were applied using toupée tape, which is commonly used in human studies and proved to work well with bearded dragon skin, attaching securely while being easy to remove. The animals were habituated to the markers and did not attempt to remove them or pay any attention to them. Therefore, we believe they did not influence their behavior.

Procedure and Trials. An animal was placed on either side of the platform, with a cloth covering the glass partition. The animals were left to habituate for a few minutes, during which food was used to elicit movement. Animals were considered habituated when they moved freely on the platform to explore it. The cloth was then lifted and the recording started. During recordings animals were allowed to move freely on the platform. Each recording lasted 5 min, and 21 recordings were taken in total. The animals were recorded in several different pairings depending on their motivation and behavior in previous trials (Table 1).

Table 1. List of combinations of animals recorded, number of 5 minute trials each combination was recorded for and number of head bobs recorded for each combination.

Animal 1	Animal 2	Number of trials	Number of head bobs
Male 1	Male 2	3	1
Male 1	Female 1	3	12
Male 2	Female 1	3	0
Male 2	Female 2	2	0
Male 1	Female 2	2	6
Male 3	Female 2	4	0
Male 1	Male 3	4	8

Post-Processing. Data was post-processed using Cortex software. Post-processing consisted of assigning marker IDs and manual clean-up of switched markers, which was necessary due to the small size of the animals and relative closeness of the markers.

2.2 Construction of the Robot

To construct the robot, 3D scans of bearded dragons were taken using an iSense scanner attached to an iPad with a Z-resolution of 0.5 mm. These scans were then imported into Google Sketchup and modified to allow for articulation of

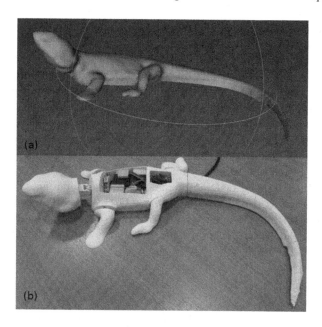

Fig. 2. (a) 3D scan of a bearded dragon that was used for the construction of the robot; (b) first prototype of the robot.

the head and front legs. This modified model was then 3D printed and two servo motors placed inside it. A Femtoduino Arduino clone board was used to control the servos to provide the movement of the head and arms (Fig. 2).

Several additional studies were undertaken to ensure the robot was realistic. 3D print-ed models of bearded dragons were used to investigate the importance of color, shape and eyes (Frohnwieser, Pike, Murray &Wilkinson in prep). Bearded dragons were presented with a white model lit in different colors for one minute each, the same model with or without eyes attached to it and several white objects with or without eyes. We found that bearded dragons responded more to a model if it was presented in bearded dragon skin color than grey, more to the model than objects of different shapes, and more to the model and the objects when they had eyes attached to them.

3   Results

In this study, three male and two female bearded dragons were recorded interacting with each other (see Table 1). Out of these, one male (Male 1) showed the desired head bobbing behavior. He was therefore paired with all other animals, to allow for a comparison between head bobbing towards males and females. In total, 27 instances of head bobbing were recorded, 18 towards females and 9 towards males. Two of them had to be excluded due to missing markers and artefacts. We focused our analysis on the marker at the tip of the head (Fig. 1b) and recorded its movement on the vertical axis. This allowed us to look at the sequence and speed of head bobbing. The results showed that head bobbing is highly stereotypic. All head bobs showed the same sequence of five dips and five raises of the head, with oscillations of decreasing amplitude. Each head bob sequence lasted for about 4.3 s, with the first dip being the longest (Fig. 3a). This was remarkably consistent across all head bobs that were recorded.

There was a difference in head bobs towards male and female lizards (Fig. 3b). When head bobbing at a male, the focus animal's head stayed significantly higher than when head bobbing at a female (autoregressive integrated moving average [ARIMA] models, incorporating both moving average and seasonal components, were fitted to the averaged male and female data, and differences between them compared using a Cox test: $z = -13.85$, $p < 0.001$). This difference was evident for all five bobs within a sequence, and was most prominent for the first head bob, with the head being 11.2 mm higher at the lowest point of the bob and 10 mm higher at the highest.

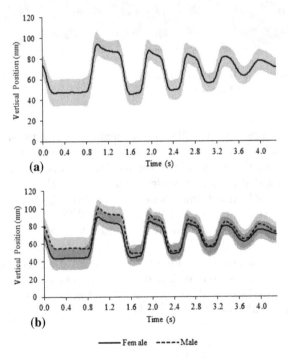

Fig. 3. (a) Mean ± standard deviation (shaded area) vertical head position over all 25 recorded head bobs. (b) Comparison of head bobs towards male and female lizards, showing mean vertical head position (lines) ± standard deviation (shaded areas).

4   Conclusion and Future Work

Our results show that head bobbing in bearded dragons is highly stereo-typed with each sequence containing five characteristic head bobs. Furthermore, these sequences differ in the height of the head when displayed towards male or female lizards. Motion capture provides an easy and efficient way to measure this type of data, ensuring that all behaviors are recorded and that no data is missed. Furthermore, it reduces the occurrence of artefacts that manual coding of video data might cause. Marker-less approaches of capturing motion from synchronized video cameras are being developed, which can be useful for animals that cannot be recorded in a laboratory setting or that do not tolerate the attachment of markers [20]. However, this technique relies on textural differences within the animal and is not as efficient or detailed as marker-based approaches. As we did not find any aversive effects of the markers to the bearded dragons and they can easily be moved to a laboratory, we think marker-based motion capture is an excellent tool to record their behaviors.

The data recorded in this experiment was translated onto the robot using individual data points, i.e., the number of head bobs per sequence, the maximum and minimum vertical position of each head bob and the time span the head remained in each position. Therefore, the motion of our robot is highly realistic and recreates the head bobs with a very high level of detail. Since we found differences in head bobbing towards males and females we can use the robotic bearded dragon to investigate these behaviors in more detail, asking questions such as "Are the two types of head bobs perceived differently by the animal watching the robot?", "Do the two types of head bobs elicit different reactions, such as aggressive or mating behaviors?" or "Does exaggerating the differences between the two types of head bobs elicit greater responses than the original ones?".

We propose that more detailed studies should be undertaken into the exact motion of animals before creating robots to represent them. This is especially important when designing a robot to be used in interaction studies with live animals, as these might perceive and attend to factors invisible to the human eye. While for robots interacting with humans it may be sufficient to use human perception alone as a measure of how realistic they are, this is surely not the case for robots interacting with animals, as perception differs greatly between species. It is therefore instrumental to use subjective measures of features such as color, odor or motion in the creation of these robots. When planning and constructing our robotic lizard we have undertaken such studies, specifically to investigate the importance of color, shape and eyes, to make it possible to create a robotic lizard that is able to interact with real animals.

The data presented in this article shows how motion capture can improve the construction of robotic animals by measuring detailed movements and translating them onto a robot, which can be invaluable information for improving the study of robotics, animal behavior and animal cognition. We showed that with this method subtle differences that might otherwise be missed, such as the height difference in displays towards males or females, can be measured easily and in great detail.

Acknowledgements. The authors would like to thank Franky Mulloy, Joe Moore, Anthony Gorman and Sophie Moszuti for their help with data recording; Suzie Li Wan Po, Meredith Tise, Annali Beese, Matthew Walker and Manuel Jara for their involvement with creating the models and robot; and Dawn Simpson, Emma Huntbach and Hannah Thompson for animal care; and three anonymous reviewers for valuable input.

References

1. Frohnwieser, A., Murray, J., Pike, T., Wilkinson, A.: Using robots to understand animal cognition. J. Exp. Anal. Behav. **105**, 14–22 (2016)
2. Fleishman, L.J., Endler, J.A.: Some comments on visual perception and the use of video playback in animal behavior studies. Acta Ethol. **3**, 15–27 (2000)
3. Brattstrom, B.H.: Social and thermoregulatory behavior of the bearded dragon Amphibolurus barbatus. Copeia **1971**(3), 484–497 (1971)
4. Kis, A., Huber, L., Wilkinson, A.: Social learning by imitation in a reptile (Pogona vitticeps). Anim. Cogn. **8**(1), 325–331 (2014)
5. Abson, K., Palmer, I.: Motion capture: capturing interaction between human and animal. Vis. Comput. **31**, 341–353 (2014)
6. Moro, F.L., Spröwitz, A., Tuleu, A., Vespignani, M., Tsagarakis, N.G., Ijspeert, A.J., Caldwell, D.G.: Horse-like walking, trotting, and galloping derived from kinematic motion primitives (kMPs) and their application to walk/trot transitions in a compliant quadruped robot. Biol. Cybern. **107**, 309–320 (2013)
7. Hutchinson, J.: Outdoor Motion capture helps analyse kangaroo posture and hopping mechanisms (2010). http://www.vicon.com. Accessed 1 Mar 2016
8. Kim, C., Shin, H., Lee, H.: Trotting gait analysis of a lizard using motion capture. In: 2013 13th International Conference on Control, Automation and Systems (ICCAS 2013), pp. 1247–1251 (2013)
9. Kim, C., Shin, H., Jeong, T.: Motion analysis of lizard locomotion using motion capture. In: 2012 12th International Conference on Control, Automation and Systems, pp. 2143–2147 (2012)
10. Kim, H., Shin, H., Lee, H.: Trotting gait generation based on the lizard biometric data. Trans. Korean Inst. Electr. Eng. **62**(10), 1436–1443 (2013)
11. Jenssen, T.A.: Display modifiers of Anolis Opalinus (Lacertilia: Iguanidae). Herpetologica **35**(1), 21–30 (1979)
12. Lovern, M.B., Jenssen, T.A.: Form emergence and fixation of head bobbing displays in the green anole lizard (Anolis carolinensis): a reptilian model of signal ontogeny. J. Comp. Psychol. **117**(2), 133–141 (2003)
13. Martins, E.P., Ord, T.J., Davenport, S.W.: Combining motions into complex displays: playbacks with a robotic lizard. Behav. Ecol. Sociobiol. **58**, 351–360 (2005)
14. Macedonia, J.M., Stamps, J.A.: Species recognition in Anolis grahami (Sauria: Iguanidae): evidence from responses to video playbacks of conspecific and heterospecific displays. Ethology **98**, 246–264 (1994)
15. Macedonia, J.M., Clark, D.L., Riley, R.G., Kemp, D.J.: Species recognition of color and motion signals in Anolis grahami: evidence from responses to lizard robots. Behav. Ecol. **24**, 846–852 (2013)
16. Partan, S.R., Otovic, P., Price, V.L., Brown, S.E.: Assessing display variability in wild brown Anoles Anolis sagrei using a mechanical lizard model. Curr. Zool. **57**, 140–152 (2011)

17. Smith, C.B., Martins, E.P.: Display plasticity in response to a robotic lizard: signal matching or song sharing in lizards? Ethology **112**, 955–962 (2006)
18. Ord, T.J., Stamps, J.A.: Alert signals enhance animal communication in "noisy" environments. Proc. Natl. Acad. Sci. USA **105**(48), 18830–18835 (2008)
19. Bels, V.L.: Analysis of the display-action-pattern of Anolis clorocyanus (Sauria: Iguanidae). Copeia **1986**(4), 963–970 (1986)
20. Sellers, W.I., Hirasaki, E.: Markerless 3D motion capture for animal locomotion studies. Biol. Open. **3**, 656–668 (2014)

An Architecture for Pattern Recognition and Decision-Making

Amy de Buitléir[✉], Ronan Flynn, Michael Russell, and Mark Daly

Faculty of Engineering and Informatics,
Athlone Institute of Technology, Athlone, Ireland
amy@nualeargais.ie, {rflynn,mrussell,mdaly}@ait.ie

Abstract. We present a simple brain architecture that allows agents to recognise patterns and make decisions based on those patterns. It takes into account not only the type of situation the agent thinks it is facing, but also how confident the agent is in its assessment, and possible alternatives. An agent using this brain was applied to two classification tasks: handwritten numeral recognition and spoken numeral recognition. In both cases, its accuracy was comparable to more traditional classifiers. This suggests that the new architecture could be useful as a general-purpose brain, for agents in a variety of domains.

Keywords: Artificial life · Decision-making · Handwriting recognition · Automatic speech recognition

1 Introduction

Decision-making is the ability of an animal to choose an action from a set of possible actions. In *goal-directed* decision-making, the animal weighs the anticipated reward (e.g., food) against the cost (e.g., energy expenditure) [14]. Thus, a good decision-making process, and the ability to learn from previous decisions, improve the animal's chance of survival. The same logic can be used by artificial (software) agents as well as animals.

Wains are an artificial life species created for data mining. For wains, data mining is a survival problem. In order to stay alive, they must discover patterns in the data, build a model of the data, classify new data based on the model, decide how to respond to data, and adapt to changes in the patternicity of the data [6].

De Buitléir et al. [6] demonstrated that a population of wains can indeed discover patterns, make survival decisions based on those patterns, and adapt to changes in the patternicity. Individual wains learned to make better decisions during their lifetimes, and evolution optimised the (genetic) operating parameters of their brains over a few generations. Several directions for future research were identified, including improving the wain's decision-making process, and implementing cultural transmission (allowing children to learn by observing the actions of their parents, and adults to learn by observing their peers).

© Springer International Publishing Switzerland 2016
E. Tuci et al. (Eds.): SAB 2016, LNAI 9825, pp. 22–33, 2016.
DOI: 10.1007/978-3-319-43488-9_3

The original brain design used a self-organising map (SOM) as a classifier, with a neural network to make decisions [6]. A SOM is a technique for representing high-dimensional data in fewer dimensions (typically two), while preserving the topology of the input data [9]. As part of the work to improve the wain's decision-making process, the SOM algorithm was modified for artificial life; we call the modified version a *self-generating model* (SGM). The SGM has been presented previously [5]. In this paper, we build on that work by redesigning the brain to use one SGM to classify inputs, and a second to predict the outcome of possible actions. The process is explained in Sect. 2.2.

It has already been demonstrated that wains can *learn* through trial and error [6]; we now wish to show that they can be *taught*. The focus of this paper is on the individual wain rather than a population, but the wain will trained using the same mechanism that allows wains to learn from one another. In addition to demonstrating the decision-making ability of the wain, we hope to show that a wain can be a useful general-purpose classifier (one that might be used when specialised classifiers are not available).

To demonstrate how the new design could be used as a general-purpose brain, for agents in a variety of domains, we will demonstrate that it can classify two very different types of data: images and audio. Common classification tasks such as handwriting recognition and Automatic Speech Recognition (ASR) have benefitted from years of research, resulting in classifiers that are designed and fine-tuned for specific types of data. Since the wain is intended as a general-purpose data miner, we do not expect it to outperform a domain-specific classifier. Instead, we hope to demonstrate that wains can provide comparable accuracy.

The image data consists of handwritten numerals; the wain will attempt to identify the numeral. To evaluate the performance of the brain at handwriting recognition, we compare it with a traditional classifier. Other classification techniques can achieve better accuracy at handwriting recognition than the SOM, for example, support vector machines [8] and traditional neural networks [7]. However, the wain's new brain design is partly based on modified SOMs (see Sect. 2.2). For this reason, we chose the SOM as the benchmark.

The audio data consists of spoken numerals; again the wain will attempt to identify the numeral. One widely used ASR technique is hidden Markov models (HMM) [13]. The hidden Markov model toolkit (HTK) provides the ability to construct and manipulate HMMs [15]. HTK is widely used for speech recognition research, making an HMM-based classifier implemented using HTK a suitable benchmark.

As will be explained in Sect. 2.2, a wain maintains a set of internal models for the range of objects that it has encountered. These internal models need not (and usually do not) map directly to human categories. Based on the resemblance between a stimulus and its internal models, the wain chooses, from a predefined set, the response that it predicts will lead to the greatest happiness. Then how can we get a wain to perform classification? By making the set of available responses be classifications! By using the wain as a classifier, we are also demonstrating its ability to make good decisions.

2   Implementation

This project uses a computational ecosystem called Créatúr[1]. Créatúr is both a software framework for automating experiments with artificial life, and a library of modules that can be used (with or without the framework) to implement agents. The system architecture is illustrated in Fig. 1. The package `creatur` provides the ecosystem. The package `creatur-wains` provides a general-purpose implementation of a wain, `creatur-image-wains` contains tools for working with images, and `creatur-audio-wains` contains tools for working with audio feature files.

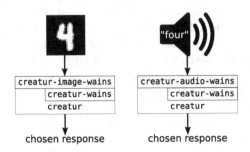

Fig. 1. System architecture for working with MNIST images (left) and TIDIGITS feature files (right). The rectangles represent software packages. A horizontal boundary between two packages indicates that the upper package calls functions provided by the lower package. For example, `creatur-wains` calls functions provided by `creatur`, and `creatur-image-wains` calls functions provided by `creatur-wains`, but also makes calls directly to functions provided by `creatur`.

The wain implementation has been described in detail elsewhere [6]; a summary is provided below, which focuses on the features used in the experiments presented in this paper and highlights changes that have been made to the implementation.

2.1   Condition

Wains have an *energy level* from 0 to 1. They gain or lose energy as a result of the reward system, which is unique to the type of experiment. For example, a wain might be rewarded for accurately identifying a pattern. If a wain's energy falls below 0, it dies. Wains also have a *boredom level* and a *passion level*, each from 0 to 1. Depending on the reward system, boredom might be decreased as a result of novelty-seeking behaviour. The wain's passion level is set to 0 at birth or as a result of mating, and increases at a genetically determined rate until the next mating. (A "genetically determined" value is one that is specified by an

---

[1] *Créatúr* (pronounced kray-toor) is an Irish word meaning animal, creature, or unfortunate person.

agent's genes, can be different for each agent, is inherited by offspring, and is subject to evolutionary pressures.) Collectively, the wain's energy level, passion level, boredom level, and whether or not it is currently rearing a child, are called its *condition*.

Wains seek to maximise their *happiness*, which is given by

$$happiness = w_e e + w_p(1 - p) + w_b(1 - b) + w_l l, \tag{1}$$

where e is the wain's energy level; p its passion level; b its boredom level; l is 1 if the wain is currently rearing a child, 0 otherwise; and w_e, w_p, w_b, w_l are genetically-determined weights. The weights are normalised so that the happiness is from 0 to 1.

2.2 The Brain

The brain has three components: a *classifier*, a *muser*, and a *predictor*. This structure is fixed; however, evolution can fine-tune operating parameters such as the learning rate. The classifier maintains a model of the space of patterns encountered, the muser generates possible responses to situations, and the predictor maintains a model of the space of responses selected.

Both the classifier and predictor use a modified SOM called a *self-generating model* (SGM) [5]. In a SOM, the models are arranged on a two-dimensional grid; in an SGM the models form an unconnected set. Unlike a SOM, the SGM does not preserve the topology of the input space. Another difference is that the SOM has a fixed number of models, but the number of models in the SGM is variable. When the difference (according to a chosen metric) between the input pattern and the closest matching model exceeds a predefined threshold, and the SGM is not at capacity, the SGM creates a new model based on the input pattern. Therefore, while the SOM must be initialised with a set of models (possibly random data), the SGM can begin empty, adding new models as needed to reflect the diversity of the input data.

The process by which the brain makes decisions is illustrated in Fig. 2. When one or more patterns are presented to the agent, the classifier produces a *signature*, a vector whose elements indicate how similar each input pattern is to each classifier model, and reports this to the brain.

For each object and model, the brain estimates the probability that the object actually belongs to the category represented by the model. This is a simple calculation,

$$\mathbf{p_i} = \frac{1 - \mathbf{d_i}}{|1 - \mathbf{d_i}|},$$

where $\mathbf{p_i}$ is a vector where each element p_{ij} is the estimated probability that object i belongs to the category represented by model j, and $\mathbf{d}$ is a vector where each element d_{ij} is the difference between object i's pattern and model j.

The brain generates *hypotheses* by considering each possible combination of object and model. The estimated probability for each hypothesis is the product of the individual object-model probabilities. Next, the muser chooses one or more

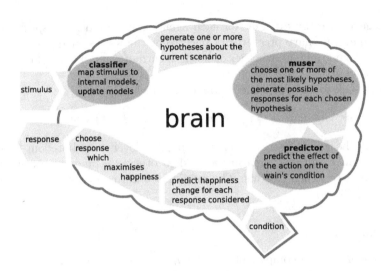

Fig. 2. The decision-making process

of the most likely hypotheses (the number of hypotheses chosen is genetically determined), and generates a set of responses to evaluate.

The predictor then estimates how each proposed response will affect each aspect of the agent's condition (energy, passion, boredom, litter size). It does this by selecting the response model that best matches the proposed response, and returning the condition changes predicted by that model, adjusted according to the probability that the hypothesis is true. If no response model is sufficiently similar, a new model may be created.

The brain combines the agent's current condition with the predicted changes, and calculates the resulting happiness change, according to Eq. 1. The brain chooses the action that is predicted to have the most favourable (most positive or least negative) effect on happiness. After the agent has received any rewards or penalties as a result of that action, the predictor adjusts its models according to the actual change in happiness.

By considering more than one hypothesis, the agent can employ more subtle reasoning. It can base its actions not only on what scenario it thinks it is facing, but also on how confident it is, and what is likely to happen if the agent is wrong. For example, suppose the agent considers two hypotheses, where the estimated payoff (happiness increase) is given by Table 1. If the agent is reasonably confident that the more likely hypothesis is actually true, the best response is action #1. Otherwise, it may be worth the gamble to go for action #2, in hope of the large payoff.

The brain can also learn as a result of *imprinting*, which is a shortcut where the agent is shown one or more patterns and an action, and concludes that taking the action in a similar situation would optimise its condition, maximising its happiness. This can be used to allow children to learn by observing their

Table 1. Sample payoff matrix

	Payoff if more likely hypothesis is true	Payoff if less likely hypothesis is true
Action #1	medium	small
Action #2	small	large

parents, or for adults to learn by observing other adults. Although this feature was originally intended to allow wains to learn from each other, it can also be used by the operator to train wains.

3 Experimental Setup

The methods used for the experiments presented in this paper are described below. These experiments use an individual wain rather than a population, but the wain is trained using the same mechanism that allows wains to learn from one another.

3.1 Images

The MNIST database is a collection of images of hand-written numerals that is a useful benchmark for comparing classification methods [11]. The training set contains 60,000 images, while the test set contains 10,000 images. All images are 28×28 pixels, and are grey-scale. The numerals are centred within the image. The centre of pixel mass of the numeral has been placed in the centre of the image. A sample image is shown in Fig. 3.

Fig. 3. Sample MNIST image of a handwritten "2" [11].

Images from the MNIST database were used without modification. We presented the images to the agent as a sequence of integers. Each element of the sequence was a number from 0 to 255, indicating the intensity of the pixel. The agent was not given any information about the geometry of the image. For example, it did not know that in a 28×28 image, the 29th pixel is immediately below the first pixel.

The brain was configured to use the mean of absolute differences (MAD) as a measure of difference between an input image and the classifier models.

This is calculated by taking the absolute difference between each pair of corresponding pixels, and taking the mean to obtain a number from 0 (identical) to 1 (maximally dissimilar). All the images in the MNIST database have the same size, viewing direction (normal to the plane of the image, from above), and comparable intensity, so the MAD is an appropriate difference metric.

The learning function of the SOM is given by Eq. 2,

$$f(d,t) = re^{-\frac{d^2}{2w^2}},\tag{2}$$

where

$$r \equiv r_0 \left(\frac{r_f}{r_0}\right)^a, \quad w \equiv w_0 \left(\frac{w_f}{w_0}\right)^a, \quad \text{and} \ a \equiv \frac{t}{t_f}.$$

The function input d is the distance between the node being updated and the winning node; t is the "time", a counter of the number of patterns learned so far. The parameter r_0 is the initial learning rate, r_f is the learning rate at time t_f, w_0 is the radius of the initial neighbourhood, w_f is the radius of the neighbourhood at time t_f, and a indicates the brain's "age".

For the winning node, $d = 0$, and Eq. 2 reduces to Eq. 3, which is the learning function for the SGM.

$$f(t) = r = r_0 \left(\frac{r_f}{r_0}\right)^a.\tag{3}$$

Note that at all times the learning rate of the SGM matches the learning rate of the winning node in the SOM. This permits a fairer comparison of the SOM and the SGM.

Table 2 shows the configuration of the two classifiers. The values r_0 and r_f were chosen so that the learning rate would start at maximum and be near

Table 2. Configuration for working with MNIST images

Variable	SOM	Brain
Final node count	1024	956
Grid type	rectangular	unconnected nodes
Classifier r_0	1	1
Classifier r_f	1×10^{-15}	1×10^{-15}
Classifier w_0	3	not applicable
Classifier w_f	1×10^{-7}	not applicable
Classifier t_f	60000	60000
Classifier threshold	not applicable	0.12
Predictor r_0	not applicable	1×10^{-9}
Predictor r_f	not applicable	1×10^{-10}
Predictor t_f	60000	60000
Predictor threshold	not applicable	0.1

zero by the end of training. The values w_0 and w_f were determined empirically. The value of t_f is the number of training images. To determine the difference threshold, we tried a range of values near the mean difference between images of the same numeral, and chose the one that resulted in the best accuracy.

3.2   Audio Samples

The TI46 speech database is a corpus of 46 isolated spoken words recorded for both male and female speakers. The corpus is intended for the evaluation of ASR products [12]. The words in the corpus include the numerals "zero" through "nine". In the experiments presented in this paper, only numerals are used. The training set contains 1,594 samples of spoken numerals; the test set contains 2,541 samples.

We extracted the MFCC feature vectors from the samples in the TI46 corpus using the HCopy tool provided as part of HTK [15]. Each frame had 13 static coefficients (cepstral coefficients C1-C12 and energy). The corresponding velocity and acceleration coefficients were also calculated to give 39 coefficients per frame. First order pre-emphasis was applied using a coefficient of 0.97. There were 23 filterbank channels and 22 cepstral liftering coefficients. The frame rate used was 10 ms with a 25 ms Hamming window. The feature vectors for each audio sample were concatenated, in time order, and presented to the brain as a sequence of double-precision floats.

The HMM-based classifier is implemented using the HTK Speech Recognition Toolkit [15]. There are ten whole word HMMs, one for each numeral, each of which has three states, with each state having three Gaussian mixtures. For working with non-endpointed samples, two additional models are defined to represent pauses in speech, "sil" and "sp". The "sil" model has three states and each state has six mixtures. The "sp" model has a single state.

End-pointing is the process of removing silence from the beginning and end of an audio sample, in order to simplify the classification task. The short-term energy for each frame is calculated as the sum of the absolute values of the sample amplitudes in the frame. End-pointing is performed by determining whether or not the short-term energy of successive frames is above a defined threshold (to determine the start of the utterance) or below a defined threshold (to determine the end of the utterance). For example, to get the start point, look for three consecutive frames with energy exceeding the threshold; the first frame of the three is assumed to be the start of the utterance.

The brain was configured to use the square of the Euclidean distance as a measure of difference between an input sample and the classifier models. The length of samples differs, so the resulting number of vectors in each sample differs as well. However, brains require that all input patterns have the same length. Therefore, the agent was configured to "stretch" or "compress" the samples as needed so they all have the same number of vectors. Stretching is achieved by duplicating vectors; the duplications were distributed as evenly throughout the pattern as possible.

Table 3. Configuration of brain for working with audio samples

Variable	As-is samples	End-pointed samples
Classifier r_0	0.1	0.1
Classifier r_f	0.001	0.001
Classifier t_f	1594	1594
Difference threshold	0.00018	0.00018
Predictor r_0	0.1	0.1
Predictor r_f	0.001	0.001
Predictor t_f	1594	1594
Num. vectors	159	154

The algorithm for compressing samples is straightforward. First, calculate the differences between each consecutive pair of vectors. Second, find the vector with the smallest change from the previous one, and drop it. These two steps are repeated until the sample is of the desired length.

Table 3 shows the configuration of the brain. The values r_0 and r_f were chosen so that the learning rate would start at maximum and be near zero by the end of training. The values w_0 and w_f, and the number of vectors, were determined empirically. The value of t_f is the number of training images. To determine the difference threshold, we tried a range of values near the mean difference between samples of the same numeral, and chose the one that resulted in the best HMM accuracy.

3.3   Training and Testing

The general procedure for working with either images or audio samples is the same. In both cases, the training data set and the test data set are distinct; we used the standard training and test sets for both the MNIST and TI46 data. First, we presented the training patterns in random order to the agent, along with the correct identification. This was done using imprinting, as described at the end of Sect. 2.2.

Next, we presented the test patterns to the agent, again in random order. As each pattern was presented, the agent responded with an identification. For a fair comparison with the SOM or HMM, we needed to prevent learning during the testing phase. To achieve this, each time the wain responded, we restored it to the state it had at the end of the training (imprinting) phase. Although the wain's condition never actually changes, it continues to expect an increase in happiness, and to take that into account when making decisions.

4   Results and Interpretation

Table 4 compares the image classification performance of the brain with that of the SOM. The accuracy of both methods is comparable. Training and testing the

Table 4. Comparison of image classification results

Classifier	SOM	Brain
No. models	1024	941
numeral	accuracy	
0	0.952	0.9408
1	0.970	0.9736
2	0.837	0.9109
3	0.835	0.8634
4	0.725	0.6609
5	0.739	0.8341
6	0.967	0.9415
7	0.873	0.7772
8	0.753	0.7956
9	0.834	0.7929
All	0.853	0.8508
Time	6273 s	2514 s

Table 5. Comparison of audio classification results

Data type Classifier	As-is		End-pointed	
	HMM	Brain	HMM	Brain
word	accuracy			
"zero"	1.0000	1.0000	1.0000	0.9840
"one"	1.0000	0.9882	1.0000	0.9922
"two"	1.0000	1.0000	1.0000	1.0000
"three"	1.0000	0.9881	1.0000	0.9961
"four"	1.0000	1.0000	1.0000	0.9961
"five"	1.0000	1.0000	1.0000	0.9961
"six"	0.9961	0.9961	1.0000	1.0000
"seven"	1.0000	0.9922	1.0000	0.9961
"eight"	1.0000	1.0000	1.0000	0.9883
"nine"	0.9881	0.9763	1.0000	0.9802
all	**0.9984**	**0.9941**	**1.0000**	**0.9929**
Time	<1 m	14 m	<1 m	12 m

brain required less than half the time of the SOM. The reduction in processing time occurs primarily because the SGM only updates one model during training, while the SOM updates the models in the neighbourhood of the winning node.

Table 5 compares the audio classification performance of the brain with that of the HMM. The accuracy of both methods is comparable, however, the brain is significantly slower. The brain was slightly more accurate when working with the as-is data than with the end-pointed data. The compression algorithm has the side-effect of removing some of the silence from the beginning and end of the sample, thus an extra end-pointing step is not required.

The code and results for the experiments presented in this paper are open access [2–4]. A tutorial for Créatúr is available [1].

5   Conclusion

The wain was applied to two classification tasks: handwritten numeral recognition and spoken numeral recognition. In both cases, its accuracy was comparable to more traditional classifiers. This suggests that wains could be useful as a general-purpose classifier, applied to a variety of domains.

Why should anyone be interested in a new classifier that is no more accurate than traditional classifiers, and for audio, is significantly slower? One advantage is that the new brain design is not just a classifier; it also *makes decisions* by choosing the action that leads to the best predicted outcome. In the experiments described in this paper, the only available actions were to choose a classification; however, other types of actions could also be performed. Another advantage to the new design is its generality; it could be used in domains where custom classifiers have not yet been developed.

As this is a new approach to pattern recognition and decision-making, there is scope for improvement. Accuracy could be improved by choosing more sophisticated distance metrics. For images, the MAD could be replaced with a metric that takes into account a pixel's neighbours. This might allow it to cope better with writing that is heavily slanted, or is thinner or thicker than typical writing. For audio samples, a variable frame rate analysis such as that suggested by Le Cerf and Van Compernolle [10] could be used. The run-time of the software is dominated by the comparisons between models, so performance could also be improved by choosing a different distance metric.

Although a single wain was used in these experiments, wains were designed to be used in a population. The configuration parameters are genetic, so it is possible to have a population of wains with varying configurations. Awarding energy for accurate classifications would encourage evolution to find a range of suitable configurations. Wains have the ability to teach their young, as well as other adults, so each generation can augment the species' knowledge. A population of wains with slightly different configurations, and different life experiences, could give independent opinions on a classification.

References

1. de Buitléir, A.: Créatúr tutorial (2014). https://github.com/mhwombat/creatur-examples/raw/master/Tutorial.pdf
2. de Buitléir, A.: Software release: exp-audio-id-wains v2.17, March 2016. http://dx.doi.org/10.5281/zenodo.46980

3. de Buitléir, A.: Software release: exp-image-id-wains v2.18, March 2016. http://dx.doi.org/10.5281/zenodo.46981

4. de Buitléir, A.: Software release: som v9.0, January 2016. http://dx.doi.org/10.5281/zenodo.45039

5. de Buitléir, A., Daly, M., Russell, M.: The self-generating model: an adaptation of the self-organizing map for intelligent agents and data mining. Accepted for Proceedings of the Artificial Life and Intelligent Agents Symposium, Birmingham (2016)

6. de Buitléir, A., Russell, M., Daly, M.: Wains: a pattern-seeking artificial life species. Artif. Life **18**(4), 399–423 (2012)

7. Cireşan, D.C., Meier, U., Gambardella, L.M., Schmidhuber, J.: Deep, big, simple neural nets for handwritten digit recognition. Neural Comput. **22**(12), 3207–3220 (2010). doi:10.1162/NECO_a_00052

8. Decoste, D., Schölkopf, B.: Training invariant support vector machines. Mach. Learn. **46**(1–3), 161–190 (2002)

9. Kohonen, T.: Self-Organizing Maps. Springer Series in Information Sciences, vol. 30, 3rd edn. Springer, Berlin (2001). http://www.worldcat.org/isbn/3540679219

10. Le Cerf, P., Van Compernolle, D.: A new variable frame analysis method for speech recognition. IEEE Sig. Process. Lett. **1**(12), 185–187 (1994)

11. LeCun, Y., Cortes, C.: MNIST handwritten digit database, January 2010. http://yann.lecun.com/exdb/mnist/

12. Liberman, M., Amsler, R., Church, K., Fox, E., Hafner, C., Klavans, J., Marcus, M., Mercer, B., Pedersen, J., Roossin, P., Walker, D., Warwick, S., Zampolli, A.: Ti 46-word ldc93s9 (1991). https://catalog.ldc.upenn.edu/docs/LDC93S9/ti46.readme.html

13. Rabiner, L.R.; A tutorial on hidden markov models and selected applications in speech recognition. Proc. IEEE **77**(2), 257–286 (1989)

14. Rangel, A., Hare, T.: Neural computations associated with goal-directed choice. Curr. Opin. Neurobiol. **20**(2), 262–270 (2010)

15. Young, S., Evermann, G., Gales, M., Hain, T., Kershaw, D., Liu, X.A., Moore, G., Odell, J., Ollason, D., Povey, D., Valtchev, V., Woodland, P.: The HTK Book, htk version 3.4 edn. Cambridge University Engineering Department, Cambridge (2006)

Follow Flee: A Contingent Mobility Strategy for the Spatial Prisoner's Dilemma

Maud D. Gibbons, Colm O'Riordan$^{(\boxtimes)}$, and Josephine Griffith

National University of Ireland, Galway, Ireland
{m.gibbons11,colm.oriordan,josephine.griffith}@nuigalway.ie

Abstract. This paper presents results from a series of experimental simulations comparing the performances of mobile strategies of agents participating in the Spatial Prisoner's Dilemma game. The contingent movement strategies *Walk Away* and *Follow Flee* are evaluated and compared in terms of (1) their ability to promote the evolution of cooperation, and (2) their susceptibility to changes in the environmental and evolutionary settings. Results show that the *Follow Flee* strategy outperforms the *Walk Away* strategy across a broad range of environment parameter values, and exhibits the ability to invade the rival strategy. We propose that the *Follow Flee* movement strategy is successful due to its ability to pro-actively generate and maintain mutually cooperative relationships.

Keywords: Artificial life · Evolutionary game theory · Contingent mobility

1 Introduction

Mobility is a key factor in solving the puzzle of the evolution of cooperation. Intuitively, this is due to the fact that the individuals of a population prefer to interact with, and indeed benefit from interacting with, cooperative players rather than interacting with those who would try to exploit them. Mobility is a form of network reciprocity [14] that allows agents to respond to their current neighbourhood by moving within their environment; this movement can be random or reactive. These movements may also be classified as local or global. The inclusion of movement creates a more realistic framework than those adopted in some of the traditional, static, spatial models [15]. Models where agents are allowed to move are typically more intuitive, and create better analogies to human and animal behaviour. The role of mobility in the evolution of cooperation has grown in importance and recognition in recent decades, from researchers in the domains of evolutionary game theory, theoretical biology, physics, sociology, and political science. It has gone from being perceived as a hindrance to the emergence of cooperation to one of its primary supporters. While unrestrained movement can, and does, lead to the 'free rider' effect [5], allowing highly mobile defectors to go unpunished, simple strategy rules or mobility rates significantly curb this phenomenon allowing self-preserving cooperator clusters to form,

© Springer International Publishing Switzerland 2016
E. Tuci et al. (Eds.): SAB 2016, LNAI 9825, pp. 34–45, 2016.
DOI: 10.1007/978-3-319-43488-9_4

and cooperation to proliferate. Mobile strategies play a vital part as mechanisms for the emergence, promotion, and sustainability of cooperation.

Several mechanisms for the emergence of cooperation exist, but all essentially express a need for cooperators to either avoid interactions with defectors or increase and sustain those with other cooperators. Research in this domain is largely divided into two categories based on their categorisations of mobility; all movement should be random [12,18], or that movement is purposeful or strategically driven, but may indeed contain random elements [1,8]. The *Follow Flee* strategy [6] enables agents to increase their percentage of mutually cooperative interactions by pursuing other cooperators and avoiding defectors. Specifically, as the name suggests, it allows players to form and sustain clusters by following nearby cooperators, and by fleeing from invading defectors.

In this paper, we investigate a form of contingent mobility for agents participating in a Spatial Prisoner's Dilemma – the *Follow Flee* strategy – and present a comparison to the *Walk Away* strategy proposed by Aktipis and others [1,10]. We adopt an evolutionary model whereby agents obtaining higher payoffs in the Prisoner's Dilemma replace those with lower payoffs. Both strategies first compete on their own against a *Naïve* (or random) strategy and are then evaluated together. We discuss the relative performance of both strategies, and highlight the limitations of *Walk Away* as a movement strategy. This strategy is studied in a range of environments while varying a number of parameters including population density, and some evolutionary settings. We will demonstrate that *Follow Flee* outperforms *Walk Away* at every level of comparison, and does so with quite a large margin. We hypothesise that this is due to *Follow Flee*'s ability to maintain mutually cooperative, spatial relationships despite the pressure from defectors, and its ability to effectively maximise an agent's potential payoff.

The paper is laid out as follows: we review related work of mobility in the Spatial Prisoner's Dilemma in the next section. Section 3 outlines our methodology, including a description of the environment, agent representation, and the evolutionary mechanism. In Sect. 4, we present and discuss a number of experiments and results regarding the performance of agent strategies. Finally, we present our conclusions and suggest future avenues for this research.

2   Related Work

Evolutionary game theory has been studied since the 1980s when John Maynard Smith incorporated ideas from evolutionary theory into game theory [11]. Traditionally, spatial evolutionary game theory involved the study of evolutionary games where a participant's interactions were constrained by a particular static topology, such as a lattice [15]. The Prisoner's Dilemma [3], and its extensions in the iterated form, is the game most often studied in this domain. It has attained such popularity due to its succinct representation of the conflict between individually rational choices and those made for the common good. In this context, mobility was seen as a hindrance to the emergence of cooperation, leading to the creation of 'free riders'. These individuals always defected and could move quickly between, and exploit, cooperative clusters without repercussion. The work of Enquist and Leimar [5] only considers agent mobility at an individual or micro level without considering the macro effect of how a cluster of cooperators may become robust from invasion by the 'free riders'. Subsequent research into the effects of mobility on the evolution of cooperation is divided into two broad categories: contingent movement [1,7,8,19], and non-contingent or random movement [2,12,18].

Aktipis in her seminal paper [1] presents a contingent movement strategy for playing the spatial iterated prisoner's dilemma. Here, agents employ the simple movement rule *Walk Away* to disconnect from defecting partners by relocating to a local random cell, and to continue cooperative partnerships by staying still. Agents form pairs and repeatedly interact together when they meet in the environment, which is quite discordant with contemporary and subsequent environments. The strategy allows cooperators to take advantage of mobility rather than it being only beneficial to defectors. The main appeal of this strategy is its simplicity; agents are memoryless but *Walk Away* is still sufficient for cooperation to spread and dominate. In this paper the strategy is tested and shown to be effective against itself, *Tit-for-Tat* [3], and a spatial version of the *Win-Stay-Lose-Shift* [13] strategy. The key behind its success is that this form of mobility allows agents to avoid repeated interactions with defectors and maintain links with other cooperators without employing complex strategies. *My Way or the Highway (MOTH)*, the work of Joyce et al. [10], follows and extends Aktipis' *Walk Away* idea. The authors present a model that replicates Axelrod's tournament with the addition that players may conditionally refuse to participate in playing the game. One criticism that can be made of these models is that they do not attempt to maintain those crucial mutually cooperative pairings under pressure from defector invasion.

Contingent mobility also has the capacity to be proactive where individuals deliberately seek better neighbourhoods, rather than simply reacting to stimuli and randomly relocating. The works by Helbing and Yu [8,9] describe a form of contingent movement called *Success Driven Migration (SDM)*, which forms one of the most influential and important ideas within the scope of mobility. In this model, individuals can test potential sites for migration, both local and global, in order to discover neighbourhoods with the highest expected payoff. The authors demonstrate that cooperation can become dominant in a migratory population as it allows individuals to find other cooperators creating clusters, and to avoid defectors. The main appeals of *SDM* lie in its ability to establish cooperation, and its realism; it has a better narrative for real-world migration than diffusion or random models. *SDM* has been shown to generate spatial correlations between cooperators, even under noisy conditions, giving cooperative clusters the ability to regroup following invasion or dispersal. Buesser et al. [4] offer an extension to the *SDM* model that investigates systematically both the interaction and migration radii. The authors reveal that widespread cooperation is best obtained when agents interact locally in a relatively small neighbourhood. However, both these models are limited in that they incur high memory and complexity costs.

Random mobility can be used to describe the minimal conditions for the evolution of cooperation, and is the preferred template of many researchers. Vainstein et al. [18] wrote perhaps one of the most influential papers in this domain. It explores the minimal conditions for sustainable cooperation using a spatially structured population on a diluted lattice using unconditional, memoryless strategies with non-contingent movements in the context of the prisoners's dilemma. The authors have shown, for the first time, that cooperation is possible in the presence of mobility when the available space is somewhat reduced and that "intermediate mobilities enhance cooperation!" [18]. The authors deduce that at higher densities, and with moderate mobility, clusters of cooperators invade defectors. This work is further expanded upon to include the Stag Hunt game [16], and later a complete phase diagram of the temptation to defect, with transition lines, is constructed [17]. Meloni et al. [12], another prominent study, introduce an alternate random movement model in which prisoner's dilemma players are allowed to move in a two-dimensional plane.

There has been much success in this field to date with evidence even suggesting that migration mechanisms are more influential on the prevalence of cooperation than on the strategy update model used by individuals [4]. The area of non-contingent movement has been well studied, and the area of contingent mobility has also received a lot of attention. However, in our opinion, there is scope for a simple movement strategy that is guided by the rule "Cooperators attract-Defectors repel" [18], but also employs only minimal complexity. Additionally, there has been little success in establishing the outbreak of cooperation in the presence of high mobility levels; a more proactive migration strategy could be the key to unlocking this final puzzle.

3 Methodology

In the following sections we will describe the environmental settings, agent representation, game parameters, and evolutionary dynamics used to build the model for simulation.

3.1 Environment and Agent Representation

We use the standard parameters of the Prisoner's Dilemma game (see Table 1) for agent interaction as endorsed by Sicardi et al. [16]. The strategy with which agents play will be fixed; either always cooperate or always defect. We choose to implement pure strategies in order to emphasise the relevance of mobility in this context. The population of N agents inhabit a toroidal shaped diluted lattice with $L \times L$ cells, each of which can be occupied by up to one agent. We use the same values for N and L as used in the work of Aktipis [1] (see Table 2). However, we do deviate from the Aktipis setup in that we enforce the restriction of one agent per cell, and expand the interaction radius of agents. We did not adopt these particular rules because they deviate so far from the traditional spatial

Table 1. The Prisoner's Dilemma

	C	D
C	3,3	0,5
D	5,0	1,1

setup and in our opinion, are not properly justified as they confer a large advantage to any two cooperators who are placed in the same cell. The interaction and movement radii of agents is determined using the Moore neighbourhood of radius one. This comprises the eight cells surrounding an individual in a cell on the lattice. The agents can only perceive and play with those within this limited radius. At each time step, agents participate in a single round of the Prisoner's Dilemma with each of their neighbours, if any. Agents are aware of the actions taken by their partners in a single round, but these memories do not persist. Following this interaction phase, agents have the opportunity to take one step into an adjacent free cell according to their movement policy. Movement will not occur if there is no adjacent free space, or if their strategy dictates that they remain in their current location. Isolated agents will take one step in a random direction.

3.2 Movement Strategies

Three movement policies are employed for this study: *Follow Flee*, *Walk Away*, and *Naïve*.

Follow Flee has two rules that are applicable to any neighbourhood combination. These are (1) move to a cell adjacent to a neighbouring cooperator, and (2) move to a cell non-adjacent to a nearby defector. These rules combine when both agent types are present. This strategy emerged as a result of a study that used a genetic algorithm to co-evolve mobility and cooperation [6].

Walk Away instructs agents to (1) move to a cell non-adjacent to nearby defectors, or (2) stay still to continue to interact with neighbouring cooperators. The first rule takes precedent when both agent types are present. This strategy was first proposed by Aktipis [1], and later by Joyce et al. [10].

Naïve agents employing this strategy move to an empty adjacent cell without regard to the actions of its neighbours.

3.3 Evolutionary Dynamics

The reproduction and death mechanisms of this study will be determined by two variables: r and s. The number of time-steps per generation is determined

Table 2. Experimental parameters

Symbol	Description	Value
L	Length of lattice	25
N	Size of population	100
s	Time steps per generation	15
r	Reproduction rate	25

by s; the sampling rate; and the number of agents replicated after each generation is determined by r; the reproduction rate. In a single generation, agents will accumulate their payoffs received from playing the Prisoner's Dilemma with their neighbours. This will be used as a measure of fitness. At the end of each generation, the agents are ranked according to their fitness score. The bottom $r\%$ will die and the top $r\%$ will replicate themselves, passing on both their movement and C/D strategies. In this way, the population size will remain constant. These offspring will be placed randomly on the grid. The older agents remain in the same place, thus maintaining any spatial clustering between generations. Following reproduction, the fitness score of the whole population will be reset and a new generation will begin.

4 Experimental Results

In this section we will describe the experimental set up and results of the four experiments developed to compare and contrast the performances of the strategies *Follow Flee* and *Walk Away*. In the first instance, we perform a baseline experiment in which both strategies compete separately against the *Naïve* strategy. In the second experiment, we expand upon the baseline by varying both the number of time steps per generation (s), and the reproduction rate (r), over a wide range of values. Next, we continue the comparison by varying the grid size to investigate the effect, if any, of density on the outcome of a simulation. Finally, both the *Follow Flee* and *Walk Away* strategies are directly compared, competing in the same simulation without the influence of the *Naïve* strategy. To obtain a sufficient sample each simulation is run 100 times.

4.1 Experiment 1: Follow Flee and Walk Away vs. Naïve

In this experiment we run two sets of similar simulations, one with *Walk Away* the other with *Follow Flee*, comparing their respective performances against the random strategy *Naïve*. The population of agents is placed randomly on the $L \times L$ torus, and the strategies are assigned in equal proportion. A single simulation will last 1000 time-steps, in which the population of 100 agents will take 15 steps each generation. The distribution of spatial strategies, level of cooperation, the time taken for the simulation to converge on cooperation (or defection), and the

Table 3. Exp. 1 average results vs. naïve

Strategy	% Cooperator wins	Convergence	# Cooperative interactions
Walk Away	28 %	202 timesteps	328,000
Follow Flee	97 %	380 timesteps	382,000

total number of interactions will all be recorded. As is shown in Table 3, *Follow Flee* vastly outperforms the *Walk Away* movement strategy in terms of enabling cooperation to emerge and dominate the population. Against the *Naïve* strategy, the *Walk Away* strategy only induces cooperation in 28 % of simulations, whereas in this environment, the *Follow Flee* strategy leads to cooperative outcomes in 97 % of the simulations. This is surprising because in the original work Aktipis' strategy achieved dominance in 100 % of simulations against a similar naïve strategy. The simulations testing *Walk Away* typically converge on a solution more quickly than *Follow Flee*. This huge difference is probably due to the change in environmental conditions; we do not allow two cooperators to co-exist in the one cell and remain removed from any potential interaction with defectors. This modification perhaps ilustrates how important this constraint was in Aktipis' original paper in inducing cooperation. Our strategy generates on average 15 % more mutually cooperative interactions than Aktipis' and this is most significant in the early generations when defectors are more prevalent.

4.2   Experiment 2: Varying the Evolutionary Dynamics

In this experiment, we vary the parameters r, the reproduction rate (number of individuals replaced), and s, the number of time-steps per generation, of the model while testing the success of both *Follow Flee* and *Walk Away* as in the previous set up. Success is measured in terms of the strategy's ability to induce cooperation among the population. The length of a simulation is increased to 5000 time-steps to ensure that the population converges on a solution. The values $s = \{5, 10, 15, 20, 25\}$ and $r = \{3, 6, 9, 12, 15, 18, 21\}$ are investigated, with a separate set of simulations, as per Experiment 1, carried out for each pair of values. In each simulation agents will either take an increased number of steps per generation or a larger proportion will participate in the evolutionary process.

In Fig. 1a and b, we see the percentage of simulations that result in cooperator dominance as we vary r and s. Across the majority of the parameter space, *Follow Flee* outperforms *Walk Away* in terms of promoting the evolution of cooperation. *Walk Away* has more success in spreading cooperation at lowest values of r and s, as across the remainder of the space it performs relatively poorly. *Walk Away* at best only achieves wide-spread cooperation in 50 % of simulations for a very limited range of parameter values. On the other hand, *Follow Flee* dramatically improves upon its poor performance in very low parameter setting for r and s, and manages to almost completely counteract the influence of defectors. Additionally, we can identify that increasing the reproduction rate has a bigger

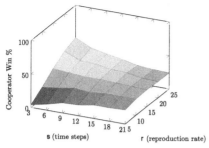
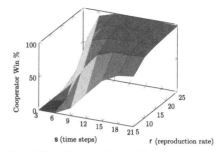

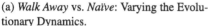

(a) *Walk Away* vs. *Naïve*: Varying the Evolutionary Dynamics.

(b) *Follow Flee* vs. *Naïve*: Varying the Evolutionary Dynamics.

Fig. 1. (a) *Walk Away* vs. *Naïve*: varying the evolutionary dynamics. (b) *Follow Flee* vs. *Naïve*: varying the evolutionary dynamics.

impact on the outcome of a simulation than increasing the number of time steps per generation; both need to be considered in order to produce the best results for the evolution of cooperation.

4.3   Experiment 3: Varying the Density

In this experiment we investigate the influence of density on the outcome of a simulation separately with both the *Walk Away* and *Follow Flee* strategies. The parameters from the baseline experiment will be restored, except for the grid size which is varied. The values $L = \{15, 20, 25, 30, 35, 40, 45\}$ are investigated, while the population size N remains constant. In this way, we first consider the performance of both strategies in very high densities, and then consider environments with lower densities. A new set of simulations is run for each value of N with each strategy competing against the *Naïve* strategy.

Figure 2 illustrates the relationship between grid size and the percentage of simulations in which cooperation dominates for both the *Walk Away* and *Follow Flee* strategies. At high densities neither strategy is able to induce cooperation. At low densities both strategies can induce a practically complete adoption of cooperation. However, as the grid size grows we can see that *Follow Flee* capitalizes on the dilution of the grid much earlier, and more swiftly than *Walk Away*. *Follow Flee* is capable of promoting the dominance of cooperation in a greater percentage of simulations in harsher environments. While *Walk Away* does achieve similar results in low densities, it has already been shown [17] that cooperation is enhanced by highly mobile agents in these environments. Density has such a significant influence on the emergence of cooperation because it directly impacts the number of interactions cooperative agents have with defectors, and it determines the space with which agents can avoid unfavourable interactions.

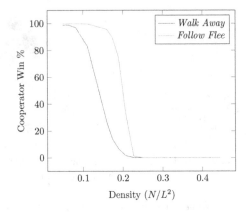

Fig. 2. *Walk Away* vs. *Naïve*: varying the density

4.4   Experiment 4: Walk Away vs. Follow Flee

In this experiment we attempt to directly compare both strategies. The *Naïve* strategy is removed as an option for players to keep the strategy proportions and population size constant, and to remove any additional complexities the presence of a third strategy may potentially introduce. As both *Walk Away* and *Follow Flee* are both mutually cooperative, we do not expect an evolutionary bias to favour either strategy once the defectors have died out. The population will be examined both at the end of the simulation and at the point at which defectors disappear. We record the percentage of simulations where the *Walk Away* strategy becomes dominant, where *Follow Flee* dominates, and the percentage of simulations where both strategies co-exist.

When *Walk Away* and *Follow Flee* compete in the same simulation, as one might expect, the defectors of both strategies are eliminated. In Table 4 we can see that in 90 % of simulations, at the point at which defectors die out, neither strategy is dominant and both coexist within the population. However, in these scenarios where both strategies co-exist, the *Follow Flee* strategy outnumbers the *Walk Away* strategy four to one. Additionally, *Follow Flee* is dominant in the remaining 10 % of simulations, and *Walk Away* is never fully dominant at the point defectors are eliminated. We also see that 73 % of simulations end with the population adopting *Follow Flee*, only 10 % of simulations result in the adoption of *Walk Away*, and the remaining 17 % of simulations ending in a draw. This is despite the fact that there should be no selective bias between two mutually

Table 4. Exp. 4 *Walk Away* vs. *Follow Flee* results

Simulation point	Walk Away	Follow Flee	Co-existence
Defector extinction	0 %	10 %	90 %
End	10 %	73 %	17 %

cooperative strategies. These results indicate a more substantial improvement of performance for *Follow Flee* than random fluctuation would permit.

5   Conclusion

In summary, we have presented *Follow Flee*, a contingent mobility strategy for playing the Spatial Prisoner's Dilemma, described the results of experiments designed to compare it to the noted *Walk Away* strategy, and in doing so demonstrated its superiority in promoting the evolution of cooperation. Both strategies were first independently tested and compared using a population of agents in a variety of evolutionary environments, including various density and reproductive settings, and then competed head-to-head in a single set of simulations. In every experiment conducted, *Walk Away* was outperformed by our *Follow Flee* strategy by significant margins; demonstrating that (1) *Follow Flee* is more resistant to the invasion of defectors, (2) it produces a greater percentage of cooperators victories in a wider range of evolutionary settings, (3) it is more successful in harsher density environments, and (4) can invade *Walk Away* agents despite the fact that both are mutually cooperative strategies.

We were unable to replicate the performance of *Walk Away* as demonstrated in Aktipis' paper [1]. Here, the traditional restriction of one agent per cell is relaxed, and the interaction radius of agents is reduced to those in the same cell. In addition, agents only participate in one 2-player game per turn, ignoring and oft-times excluding other agents from interactions. These incongruous environmental features, in combination with rules of the *Walk Away* strategy results in mutually cooperative pairings being unexpectedly difficult to break up or be exploited by defectors, giving cooperators a built-in advantage. We surmise that high levels of cooperation reported in this work may instead be credited to the environment implementation rather than the *Walk Away* strategy itself.

We attribute the success of *Follow Flee* to its highly mobile, proactive nature, and hypothesise that it is possible for it to make such significant gains due to its ability to generate and maintain cooperative clusters. As illustrated in Experiment 1, *Follow Flee* is capable of inducing the emergence of cooperation in a far greater percentage of simulations. The *Walk Away* cooperator pairs are immobile, which prevents them from actively seeking out new mutually cooperative interactions. The *Follow Flee* cooperators, on the other hand, are more likely to increase their number of mutually cooperative relationships, thus maintaining a higher average payoff, and so giving them an evolutionary edge. In contrast to the *Follow Flee* strategy, cooperators using *Walk Away* do not knowingly maintain these beneficial relationships when being pursued by defectors, and thus can more easily be broken up. Results indicate that the *Follow Flee* strategy can invade *Walk Away*, even though both strategies always cooperate.

The strengths of *Follow Flee* lie in its adaptability and simplicity. Previously, it has been stated that cooperation is enhanced in the presence of mobility [12,18,19], but only when those mobility rates were low or moderate. However, using *Follow Flee* we have managed to generate good levels of cooperation in this model's highly mobile and dynamic environment. We have constructed a promising contingent mobility strategy that is extremely successful at spreading cooperation throughout a mobile population without the need for complex computation, costly memories, or central control.

We have explored this contingent strategy in an abstract model. Future work will involve grounding these models in physically embodied agents using simple robots. We also wish to attempt to explore more realistic scenarios where simple contingent mobility strategies are witnessed in organisms that move towards fellow cooperators and move from defectors.

Acknowledgements. This work is funded by the Hardiman Research Scholarship, NUI Galway.

References

1. Aktipis, C.A.: Know when to walk away: contingent movement and the evolution of cooperation. J. Theor. Biol. **231**(2), 249–260 (2004)
2. Antonioni, A., Tomassini, M., Buesser, P.: Random diffusion and cooperation in continuous two-dimensional space. J. Theor. Biol. **344**, 40–48 (2014)
3. Axelrod, R.M.: The Evolution of Cooperation. Basic Books, New York (1984)
4. Buesser, P., Tomassini, M., Antonioni, A.: Opportunistic migration in spatial evolutionary games. Phys. Rev. E Stat. Nonlin. Soft Matter Phys. **88**(4), 042806 (2013)
5. Enquist, M., Leimar, O.: The evolution of cooperation in mobile organisms. Anim. Behav. **45**(4), 747–757 (1993)
6. Gibbons, M., O'Riordan, C.: Evolution of coordinated behaviour in artificial life simulations. In: Proceedings of the Theory and Practice in Modern Computing, TPMC (2014)
7. Hamilton, I.M., Taborsky, M.: Contingent movement and cooperation evolve under generalized reciprocity. Proc. Biol. Sci. R. Soc. **272**(1578), 2259–2267 (2005)
8. Helbing, D., Yu, W.: Migration as a mechanism to promote cooperation. Adv. Complex Syst. **11**(4), 641–652 (2008)
9. Helbing, D., Yu, W.: The outbreak of cooperation among success-driven individuals under noisy conditions. Proc. Nat. Acad. Sci. U.S.A. **106**(10), 3680–3685 (2009)
10. Joyce, D., Kennison, J., Densmore, O., Guerin, S., Barr, S., Charles, E., Thompson, N.S.: My way or the highway: a more naturalistic model of altruism tested in an iterative prisoners' dilemma. J. Artif. Soc. Soc. Simul. **9**(2), 4 (2006)
11. Maynard Smith, J.: Evolution and the Theory of Games. Cambridge University Press, Cambridge (1982)
12. Meloni, S., Buscarino, A., Fortuna, L., Frasca, M., Gómez-Gardeñes, J., Latora, V., Moreno, Y.: Effects of mobility in a population of prisoner's dilemma players. Phys. Rev. E Stat. Nonlin. Soft Matter Phys. **79**(6), 3–6 (2009)
13. Nowak, M., Sigmund, K., et al.: A strategy of win-stay, lose-shift that outperforms tit-for-tat in the prisoner's dilemma game. Nature **364**(6432), 56–58 (1993)
14. Nowak, M.A.: Five rules for the evolution of cooperation. Science **314**(5805), 1560–3 (2006)
15. Nowak, M.A., May, R.M.: Evolutionary games and spatial chaos. Nature **359**(6398), 826–829 (1992)

16. Sicardi, E.A., Fort, H., Vainstein, M.H., Arenzon, J.J.: Random mobility and spatial structure often enhance cooperation. J. Theor. Biol. **256**(2), 240–246 (2009)
17. Vainstein, M.H., Arenzon, J.J.: Spatial social dilemmas: dilution, mobility and grouping effects with imitation dynamics. Physica A Stat. Mech. Appl. **394**, 145–157 (2014)
18. Vainstein, M.H., Silva, A.T.C., Arenzon, J.J.: Does mobility decrease cooperation? J. Theor. Biol. **244**(4), 722–728 (2007)
19. Yang, H.X., Wu, Z.X., Wang, B.H.: Role of aspiration-induced migration in cooperation. Physic. Rev. E Stat. Nonlin. Soft Matter Phys. **81**(6), 1–4 (2010)

Local Interaction of Agents for Division of Labor in Multi-agent Systems

Wonki Lee[✉] and DaeEun Kim

Biological Cybernetics Lab, School of Electrical and Electronic Engineering,
Yonsei University, Seoul, Korea
{wonkilee,daeeun}@yonsei.ac.kr

Abstract. Task allocation problem has been an issue in multi-agent systems. Among many interesting tasks, we focus on an algorithm for the proportional regulation of population where the swarm is divided into groups depending on task demands. We take the response threshold model inspired by division of labor in several social insects. In our approach, the member proportion of each sub-group is regulated proportional to the external task demands and local social interactions among agents. Here, the interactions control the response thresholds for given tasks. The proposed algorithm was applied to simulation experiments of robots, and the experimental results show that the proposed method has adaptive and robust responses under dynamically changing environments.

Keywords: Task allocation · Multi-agent systems · Regulation of population · Response threshold model · Local interaction

1 Introduction

In this paper, we focus on the study of task allocation problem in the multi-agent system. Generally, in the multi-agent systems, the task allocation system efficiently manages labors which take lots of time and costs for completing tasks. An approach to this kind of problem is to set up an appropriate scheduling with an adaptive process under dynamically changing environments. In swarm intelligence, a task is assigned to each agent in a self-organized way with only limited capabilities and a few simple behaviors rules. There have been many related works and swarm intelligence algorithms inspired by many social insects.

In nature, we are able to observe many examples of adaptive behaviors in several insect societies. They exhibit a number of remarkable behaviors, such as formation motion control, division of labor based on age *polyethism*, and group foraging [1–3]. From many interesting phenomena observed in nature, it is remarkable that the performances of the overall colony may have synergy effect, compared to the independent runs of each member. Without any special leader controlling the behavior of the entire group, the collective behaviors are adaptable, flexible, and robust under environmental disturbances. The systems have

© Springer International Publishing Switzerland 2016
E. Tuci et al. (Eds.): SAB 2016, LNAI 9825, pp. 46–54, 2016.
DOI: 10.1007/978-3-319-43488-9_5

served as inspirations for many optimizations problems and control algorithms in many multi-agent systems. In robotics, many researchers have investigated multi-robot systems [4] and the methods inspired by biological systems were analyzed with their performance by real robot systems [5,6]. Homogeneous individuals show these collective behaviors by interacting each other through local communication or chemical materials, such as pheromones.

An interesting work is the division of labor in the insect colony such as ants and bees, which increases colony survival probability, They show proportion regulation phenomena that the proportion of each group is related to the external task demands adaptively without any centralized organization. Although the individual agents have the same ability, they are divided into certain sub-groups and the agents perform different tasks at other spots in a distributed way. Ultimately this phenomenon can improve the productivity. Forging foods or defense from predators are examples of such proportion regulation phenomena in the colonies. This regulation is also required under external disturbances, such as loss of some part of the colony or changing environment. Each individual is aware of changes of the surrounding situation and each agent selects its behavior accordingly if needed.

There were many works [7,8] that explain the division of labor in nature. Here, we apply the concept of the response threshold model [9–14] for solving the task allocation problem. This model is based on observations of many insect societies and explains the regulation of labor division by a simple mathematical model using the response threshold. Obtaining suitable thresholds is directly related to the performance of the overall system and there are generally two kinds of strategies that utilize fixed response thresholds [12–14] and variable thresholds [9–11].

In our study, we consider multi-agent systems as colonies of social insects and focus on the characteristics of division of labor. The individual agent needs a strategy in which the labor is assigned proportional to the demand of tasks, and selects the proper task adaptively. Such autonomous process maintains the proportion of population in the overall colony level among groups. The suitable threshold is obtained via social interaction and some experimental results show the regulation for each group, which means that the number of members for each group tends to increase or decrease depending on the task demand. The rest of the paper is written as follows: The next section shows division of labor based on social interaction in details. Section 3 presents the proposed algorithm and Sect. 4 presents the experimental results. We conclude this paper in Sect. 5 with future work.

2   Social Interaction

Usually, in insect societies, genetic factors play a role in division of labor, such as age-dependent and different body shapes [15–17]. The distributed task allocation in ants based on genetic factors can efficiently arrange the ants in proportion to the amount of work in the changing environment. In honey bee colonies, there is a general correlation between the age of the workers and tasks they normally perform at current time. Task allocation is associated with their physiological development such that the physiological age of a bee. Younger individuals perform internal task such as brood care and nest maintenance inside the hive while older workers perform foraging food and defense task outside the hive.

However, this tendency is flexible to be changed by the distribution of age in colony members. If the proportion of young honey bees in a colony is high, the age in which a bee starts a foraging task is lower than in a normal colony and presence of older bees delays or inhibits the development of physiological age of other younger bees. Worker to worker interactions in bees drive mechanisms of hormonal regulation resulting in a social inhibition and explain an adaptability to different age distributions [17,18]. This concept is improved toward developing partitioning of reproduction among workers based on social interaction [19,20].

3   Proposed Task Allocation Algorithm

Social insect colonies needs to be adaptable to changes in the environment and the individual worker needs to switch tasks according to the task demands. The mechanisms to solve such an adaptive task allocation problem in the face of various internal and external states are thus of great interest. Inspired from the task allocation in the insect colonies we propose a new task allocation algorithm using two terms, demand of tasks and the response threshold.

Every individual agent i has a threshold value θ_i. This variable is restricted to a range of $(\theta_{min}, \theta_{max})$. There is also a number of tasks with their associated demand. The tasks are ordered in a sequence as shown in Fig. 1 and an appropriate level of response thresholds can be defined. If an agent has its response threshold suitable for a specific task, it is assigned to the task. The concept is the same with the task assignment in honey bee colonies. The threshold represents the physiological age and different tasks are performed during its life-time in a process of behavioural development.

In this model, a distribution of thresholds determines the accuracy of division of labor and we are interested in how the patterns of all the thresholds are spread over the thresholds of the whole swarm uniformly over the range of $(\theta_{min}, \theta_{max})$. For this, we design a simple algorithm via social interaction inspired by jamming avoidance response. The jamming avoidance response or JAR is a

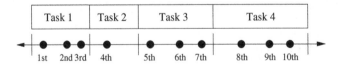

Fig. 1. Diagram of task allocation algorithm based on the response thresholds and task demands. Four tasks are ordered in a sequence proportional to demands and the threshold values of ten agents are spaced. Agents belonging to range that is split into segments relative th the task demands is assigned to the corresponding task.

behavior performed by some species of weakly electric fish [21]. It occurs when two electric fish with very similar discharge frequencies meet. Each fish shifts its discharge frequency to increase the difference between the two fish's discharge frequencies. By doing this, both fish prevent jamming of their sense.

The jamming avoidance behavior escapes jamming of close frequencies. Inspired by the idea, agents have evenly spaced intervals in their thresholds. Regulation of threshold values in the swarm occurs between a pair of individuals within a limited sensing range. If agent i meets agent j, the threshold value θ_i of agent i and θ_j of agent j are updated as follows:

If θ_i is larger than θ_j and $\theta_i - \theta_j < \alpha$, then $\theta_i = \theta_i + \delta$ and $\theta_j = \theta_j - \delta$.
If θ_i is smaller than θ_j and $\theta_j - \theta_i < \alpha$, then $\theta_i = \theta_i - \delta$ and $\theta_j = \theta_j + \delta$.
If θ_i is the same as θ_j, then $\theta_i = \theta_i + X$ and $\theta_j = \theta_j + X$.

where α is a limit difference of thresholds between individuals, δ is a constant parameter, and $X \in (-1, 1)$ is a random value. Each agent updates its threshold for every interaction with another agent. Many interactions among agent members can lead to an almost uniform distribution of thresholds over the range $(\theta_{min}, \theta_{max})$, regardless of initial thresholds.

In a decentralized approach, estimating the task demands is also important. For this, each agent stores the local information of sensed tasks in a history window of finite length. The agent performs sensing behavior periodically and the type of detected tasks within the sensing range are stored in sequence. New information is replaced with the oldest ones and the proportion of each task in a history is used as a measure of task demands without any centralized control methods.

4   Experiments

We simulate a swarm of robots that perform foraging tasks. The experiments are repeatedly run to see the averaged performance.

4.1   Task Scenario

Foraging task is performed in a circular arena as shown in Fig. 2. There are two types of 20 objects and 20 robots. Robots can forage both types of objects, but each robot can be simultaneously assigned to only one kind of task. Before starting, robots and objects are randomly located in a given arena. A robot has its own task state, foraging a red or green object, and it tries to find the closest red or green object to match its own task state. If a robot approaches a selected object, it is immediately removed from the environment. After an object is removed, a new object of the same type is placed in an arbitrary place to maintain a constant number of objects, that is, the same number of tasks to be processed.

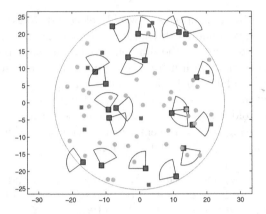

Fig. 2. Snapshot of simulation enviornment: Some robots and objects are distributed randomly in a circular arena. The large red-colored squares and green-colored circles are robots and small red-colored squares and green-colored circles are the objects to be collected by robots. The camera detecting range of robot is represented in fan-shaped. (Color figure online)

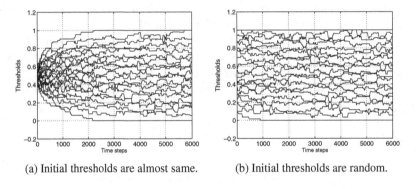

(a) Initial thresholds are almost same.   (b) Initial thresholds are random.

Fig. 3. Results of the spread thresholds with the different initial thresholds distribution with $\alpha = 0.1$ and $\delta = 0.001$.

The initial values of thresholds are uniformly randomized over the range of $(\theta_{min}, \theta_{max}) = (0, 1)$ to ensure that each robot task is not predetermined for tasks and the initial tasks of all the robots are assigned to foraging red-colored objects. A robot may switch its current task according to the individual control policy. Our goal is to regulate the proportion of red-colored robots and green-colored robots equally to the ratio of colored objects.

4.2   Simulation Results

Results of Distributed Thresholds. Figure 3 shows distributed thresholds when the initial thresholds of all agents are almost the same (a) or randomly given (b). From the results, we can see that the proposed method can distribute almost uniformly the response thresholds of the whole swarm agents.

Results with Changes in Task Demands. In the first experiment, we investigate the adaptability of the method responding to changes in task demands. There are two tasks, foraging a red object ('task 1') or a green object ('task 2'). At the begining, the proportion of each task is set to 20 % and 80 %, respectively. At the time step 2,000, it is changed to 70 % and 30 %, and at the time step 4,000, it is changed to 50 % and 50 % in sequence. Figure 4 represents the results of this experiment. Since all the robots start with the same task, they all start with task 1 and soon the swarm is split into two groups following the same proportion of task demands. By changing the task demands, the proper proportions of agents is re-assigned to the changes in task demands. The swarm perform tasks depending on the proportion of task demands. If the thresholds are assigned with a different distribution due to the effect of $alpha$ and δ, the accuracy of division of labor is a little changed, but the overall performance still convergenced to the desired state, according to the task demands.

Results with Changes in the Number of Agents. In the second experiment, we see the adaptability of the swarm when the number of agents is changed. During the first 1,000 simulation time steps, about 50 % agents are assigned to task 1 because the task demand of that task is set to 50 % and after that time, all agents assigned to task 1 are removed from the arena. Then the proportion of agents performing that task is dropped to 0 %, but about 50 % agents of the remaining agents are again assigned to task 1. Figure 5 (a) represents the behavior of the swarm in response to the changes and it shows that the swarm reacts properly, regardless of the number of agents. The threshold values are re-balanced among remaining agents after 1,000 simulation time step and the threshold difference between agents are larger than the previous period as shown in Fig. 5 (b) due to the decreasing number of swarm. This adaptive task allocation ability is possible in the variable threshold model. In the fixed threshold model, the thresholds are constant and in contrast, the thresholds are continuously updated by the self-organizing process in the variable threshold model. If we apply the fixed threshold model using randomly allocated thresholds, similar results with some error could be obtained in the first experiment. However, in the dynamically changing environment, it can have the limited performance.

Results with a Variety of Tasks. In the last experiment, we consider a distribution of a population of agents for more tasks, four tasks rather than two tasks. The proportion of each task is set to 30 %, 30 %, 20 %, and 20 % and the proportion of robots assigned to each task is shown in Fig. 6. The swarm reacts properly and the proportion of agents assigned to each task reaches stably the desired level regardless of the increasing number of tasks.

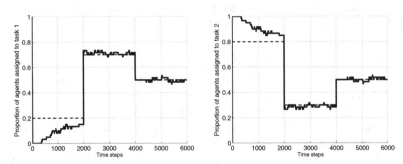

(a) Proportion of agents performing task 1 with $\delta = 0.01$.
(b) Proportion of agents performing task 2 with $\delta = 0.01$.

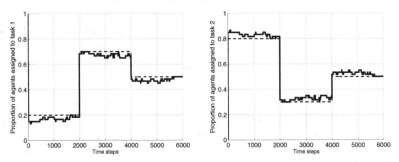

(c) Proportion of agents performing task 1 with $\delta = 0.001$.
(d) Proportion of agents performing task 2 with $\delta = 0.001$.

Fig. 4. Proportion of agents assigned to each task with changes in task demand. Demand of task 1 and 2 are set to 20 % and 80 % at the beginning. At time step 3,000, it is changed to 70 % and 20 %, and at time step 200, it is changed again to 50 % and 50 % in sequence.

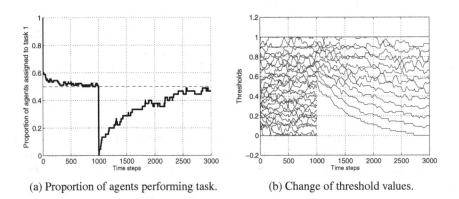

(a) Proportion of agents performing task.
(b) Change of threshold values.

Fig. 5. Proportion of agents assigned to task 1 when some agents are removed from the arena during task.

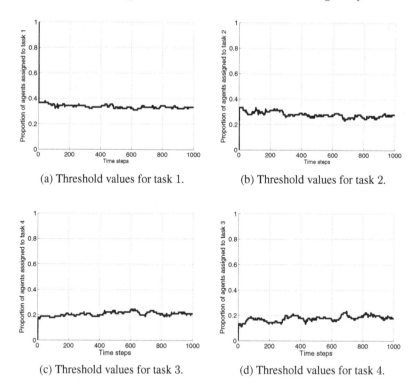

(a) Threshold values for task 1.

(b) Threshold values for task 2.

(c) Threshold values for task 3.

(d) Threshold values for task 4.

Fig. 6. Proportion of agents assigned to four tasks.

5   Conclusion and Future Work

In this paper, we introduce a novel decentralized, self-organized and self-regulated division of labor in multi-agent systems. The proposed algorithm is based on local interaction among agents and from various simulation results, we see that our proposed algorithm can regulate the proportion of agents for given task demands. In the future work, we plan to apply the propose algorithm to a swarm of robots in the real environment and analyze the performance of the proposed algorithm.

Acknowledgements. This work was supported by the National Research Foundation of Korea(NRF) grant funded by the Korea government(MEST) (No. 2014R1A2A1A11053839).

References

1. Gordon, D.: Ants at Work: How an Insect Society is Organized. Simon and Schuster, New York (1999)
2. Holldobler, B.: Journey to the Ants. A Story of Scientific Exploration, p. 228. Harvard University Press, Cambridge (1994)
3. Seeley, T.: The Wisdom of the Hive: The Social Physiology of Honey Bee Colonies. Harvard University Press, Cambridge (2009)
4. Cao, Y.: Cooperative mobile robotics: antecedents and directions. Auton. Robots **4**(1), 7–27 (1997)
5. Beckers, R.: From local actions to global tasks: stigmergy and collective robotics. Artif. life IV **11**, 189 (1994)
6. Kube, C.: Collective robotics: from social insects to robots. Adapt. Behav. **2**(2), 189–218 (1993)
7. Tofts, C.: Algorithms for task allocation in ants. (a study of temporal polyethism: theory). Bull. Math. Biol. **55**(5), 891–918 (1993)
8. Dorigo, M.: Ant algorithms for discrete optimization. Artif. Life **5**(2), 137–172 (1999)
9. Bonabeau, E.: Quantitative study of the fixed threshold model for the regulation of division of labour in insect societies. In: Proceedings of the Royal Society of London. Series B: Biological Sciences, vol. 263, No. 1376, pp. 1565–1569 (1996)
10. Bonabeau, E.: Adaptive task allocation inspired by a model of division of labor in social insects. In: Proceedings of BCEC, pp. 36–45 (1997)
11. Theraulaz, G.: Response threshold reinforcements and division of labour in insect societies. In: Proceedings of the Royal Society of London. Series B: Biological Sciences, vol. 265, No. 1393, pp. 327–332 (1998)
12. Bonabeau, E.: Fixed response thresholds and the regulation of division of labor in insect societies. Bull. Math. Biol. **60**(4), 753–807 (1998)
13. Jung, B.: Tracking targets using multiple robots: the effect of environment occlusion. Auton. Robots **13**(3), 191–205 (2002)
14. Krieger, M.: Ant-like task allocation and recruitment in cooperative robots. Nature **406**(6799), 992–995 (2000)
15. Sundstrom, L.: Sex allocation and colony maintenance in monogyne and polygyne colonies of formica truncorum (hymenoptera: formicidae): the impact of kinship and mating structure. Am. Nat. **146**, 182–201 (1994)
16. Winston, M.: The Biology of the Honey Bee. Harvard University Press, Cambridge (1991)
17. Huang, Z.: Regulation of honey bee division of labor by colony age demography. Behav. Ecol. Sociobiol. **39**(3), 147–158 (1996)
18. Beshers, S.: Social inhibition and the regulation of temporal polyethism in honey bees. J. Theor. Biol. **213**(3), 461–479 (2001)
19. Gordon, D.: Dynamics of task switching in harvester ants. Anim. Behav. **38**(2), 194–204 (1989)
20. Beshers, S.: Models of division of labor in social insects. Ann. Rev. Entomol. **46**(1), 413–440 (2001)
21. Watanabe, A.: The change of discharge frequency by AC stimulus in a weak electric fish. J. Exp. Biol. **40**(1), 57–66 (1963)

Rational Imitation for Robots

Dieter Vanderelst[(✉)] and Alan F.T. Winfield

Bristol Robotics Lab, University of the West of England, Bristol, UK
dieter.vanderelst@brl.ac.uk, Alan.Winfield@uwe.ac.uk

Abstract. Infants imitate behaviour flexibly. Depending on the circumstances, they copy both actions and their effects or only reproduce the demonstrator's intended goals. In view of this selective imitation, infants have been called rational imitators. The ability to selectively and adaptively imitate behaviour would be a beneficial capacity for robots. Indeed, selecting what to imitate is one of the outstanding unsolved problems in the field of robotic imitation. In this paper, we first present a formalized model of rational imitation suited for robotic applications. Next, we test and demonstrate it using two humanoid robots.

1 Introduction

Imitation is a very important form of social learning in humans and has been suggested to underlie human cumulative culture [15,21]. Given its importance in human development, the ability to imitate emerges early in human infants. From their second year on, infants can imitate actions and their intended goals from demonstrators [8,11]. Critically, infants imitate the demonstrated actions and their effects in a flexible way. Depending on the circumstances, they copy both actions and effects or only reproduce intended goals. In view of this selective imitation, infants have been called rational imitators [10].

In a landmark paper, Meltzoff [17] showed that 14-month-old children switch on a light by bending over and touching it with their head if they have seen an experimenter do so. However, later studies showed that if the experimenter's hands are occupied children tend to switch on the light using their hands [10]. The percentage of copied head-touch actions also declines when the demonstrator's hands are physically restrained [24]. These results have been replicated by [3,19], albeit with a different interpretation.

Initially, authors explained these results by assuming that infants reason teleologically about the goals and actions demonstrated [23]. Children are assumed to infer that (1) the demonstrator uses his or her head to switch on the lamp because his or her hands are constrained and (2), as such, the head touch is not necessary to successfully switch on the lamp. Therefore, when asked to switch on the lamp, the infant uses his or her hands. In contrast, when the demonstrator's hands are free, the infants are assumed to reason that the head touch is instrumental in obtaining the goal.

More recently, competing accounts have been advanced. In particular, it has been proposed that many experimental results can be explained by differences in

© Springer International Publishing Switzerland 2016
E. Tuci et al. (Eds.): SAB 2016, LNAI 9825, pp. 55–66, 2016.
DOI: 10.1007/978-3-319-43488-9_6

the difficulty for the infants to copy the demonstrator's actions [23]. According to this account, bending forward to touch a lamp with restrained hands is more difficult than doing so with free hands available to support the body. As such, an increased difficulty in exactly copying the demonstrated motion – termed a lack of 'motor resonance' [19] – is assumed to reduce the extent to which infants copy a demonstrated action. [3] advanced yet another account of rational imitation in infants. These authors have claimed that attentional processes can fully explain selective imitation.

While it is undoubtedly (and unsurprisingly) true that both the feasibility of the demonstrated actions and attentional processes determine the fidelity of action copying, neither account fully accommodates the experimental findings [23]. For example, even in the absence of obvious differences in action difficulty, 12-month old infants copy a model with constrained hands less often [24]. In addition, 12-month old – but not 9-month old – infants ignored the head touch action of a model with hands fixed to the table [24]. It is difficult to see how infants would be susceptible to 'a lack of motor resonance' at 12 months but not at 9 months. Likewise, attentional mechanisms cannot explain effects across conditions that do not seem to recruit different levels of attention [13,18].

While the motor resonance and attention theories fall short in accommodating for some data, the reasoning hypothesis suffers mainly from being under-specified – although it can be noted that the idea of 'motor resonance' is less than fully specified either [23]. As a result, the reasoning account can be made to accommodate most findings *post facto*. For example, [19] conducted an experiment to distinguish between the reasoning account and the motor resonance model. They concluded that findings were more in line with the predictions of the motor resonance model. However, it is unclear whether the predictions these authors derive for the teleological reasoning account are the only interpretation possible (See [23] for a similar remark).

In the absence of a complete and computationally explicit model, we propose a novel model for rational imitation, i.c. the CDM. In particular, we aim for a model that supports rational imitation in robots. In contrast to the accounts discussed above – and in accord with our goal to exploit rational imitation to optimize the imitation behaviour in robots – we depart from a normative analysis of imitation learning. That is, we postulate the desirable properties of rational imitation and build a model satisfying these requirements.

2   The Cost Difference Model

2.1   Rationale

In agreement with current views on its adaptive value [1,14], we propose that imitation is a method for acquiring better action policies [2]. Action policies can be thought of as a series of subgoals that lead towards attaining the final goal. For example, an action policy for making spaghetti (final goal) are the steps (subgoals) as set out in the recipe.

Assuming that imitation is a learning strategy for adopting better action policies for satisfying goals, imitation has the possible advantage of being a cheaper (less risky) route to policy learning than individual, asocial learning. Nevertheless, indiscriminately copying behaviour is unlikely to results in better policies [14]. Ideally, agents should only copy behaviour when an observed policy is better than the current existing action policy. Initially, we can assume better policies to be those requiring less energy. However, other optimization criteria could be imagined, including risk and time. In biological agents, better action policies are those ultimately resulting in increased fitness.

In this light, experimental findings on imitation in infants are somewhat puzzling. Infants copy demonstrated head touches in spite of clearly being able to switch on the light using their hands (which seems to be a better policy). Indeed, in control conditions, children spontaneously switch on the light using their hands. Moreover, even when infants eventually copy the head touch, most often they switch on the light using their hands first [9,18,19]. So why do children copy the ineffective head touch policy given they have an alternative policy that seems more efficient?

In our view, this discrepancy can be explained by assuming that an agent observing a demonstrated action policy has only limited knowledge of its energetic cost. The agent might be able to estimate the energy requirement of the demonstrated policy, for example, using its own action planner. However, this will yield an approximate estimate at best – especially when the demonstrated policy includes unfamiliar actions. In addition, the agent can estimate or retrieve the cost of its existing action policy and compare this to the estimated value of the demonstrated action policy. Theoretically, the agent should reject the demonstrated policy whenever its cost is higher than that of the existing policy. However, the cost of the demonstrated policy is not directly accessible and is only an estimate. As such, seeing some other agent executing a costly action policy might indicate that the estimated cost is inaccurate. If so, it would be reasonable to actually execute the demonstrated policy and obtain a corrected estimate of its cost. Indeed, the potential long-term gain of chancing on an innovative policy would generally outweigh the cost of testing out the action at least once. In summary, under our formalization, the rational imitation observed in infants is the overt outcome of uncertainty about the cost of the observed action policy. Thus, when copying an action policy they are exploring its cost by physically executing it. This will result in a better estimate of its real cost.

2.2   Formalization

In order to model imitation based on the assumptions introduced above, we need to propose a mechanism that allows agents to infer the demonstrated action policy from the observed sequence of states o_t. This is, the imitator needs to infer from o_t which intermediate goals the demonstrator satisfies en route to the final goal. To the best of our knowledge, no account of the method used by infants to select relevant subgoals from observed actions is available. Hence, in what follows, we present an approach that is suitable for the current robotic experiments.

It should be understood that this method is a first approach and could be refined in further work to suit other contexts.

In more formal terms, inferring the demonstrator's action policy can be thought of as selecting the *minimal* number of intermediate states from o_t required to explain the observed behaviour o_t. This set of minimal required states, denoted as s, are assumed to be the subgoals of the demonstrator. Below, we explain our current approach to selecting this minimal set of states s.

We suggest the robot should select an iteratively expanding set of states $s = \{o_0 \ldots o_n \ldots o_T\}$ from the observed states o_t. For each set s, the robot uses its own action planner to compute an action sequence a_t leading from o_0 to o_T through the intermediate states o_n. In planning the action sequence a_t, the robot should take into account the physical constraints C experienced by the demonstrator[1] Hence, the action sequence a_t is the action plan the robot would come up with itself (1) *if it were in the same situation as the demonstrator* and (2) *wanted to attain the selected subgoals s*.

For each set of selected states s and resulting action sequence a_t, the imitator estimates the cost of a_t. We tentatively suggest the cost is expressed in terms of energy expenditure. The estimated energetic cost $\hat{E}(a_t)$ is compared with the estimated cost of the demonstrated action sequence $\hat{E}(o_t)$ calculating the cost difference ΔE as,

$$\Delta E = |\hat{E}(o_t) - \hat{E}(a_t)| \text{ with } a_t = f(s, C) \tag{1}$$

At first, the set of selected states s only contains the initial and final observed states, i.e., $s = \{o_0, o_T\}$. However, the set is iteratively expanded by adding more intermediate states. Therefore, the set of selected states s will eventually approach the observed action sequence o_t. In consequence, ΔE approaches zero as the set s is expanded. When the value of ΔE is below a certain threshold τ_E, expanding s is terminated and the current set s (with the exception of the initial state o_0) is taken to contain the subgoals in the observed behaviour. The set s contains the minimum number of subgoals that are required to explain the (cost of the) observed behaviour o_t Also, notice that the iterative process implies that when $\Delta E(s = \{o_0, o_T\}) < \tau_E$, the imitator will simply plan an action sequence to attain the final state demonstrated – hence, no imitation of any intermediate goal will take place. The observed behaviour o_t can be inadequately explained by assuming the demonstrator is only attempting to reach the final goal. No subgoals need to be assumed.

Obviously, expanding the set s can be done in many ways. Here, we propose that on each iteration additional states are selected at time instances intermediate between the currently selected states. At first, only two states will be selected,

$$o_s = \{o_0, o_T\}. \tag{2}$$

---

[1] Therefore, the notation for the planned action sequence, a_t, could be considered as shorthand for $a_t = f(s, C)$ indicating that the planned action sequence is a function of (1) the currently selected action states (or subgoals) s and (2) the physical constraints C experienced by the demonstrator.

On the next iteration, an additional state in between these two will be added: $o_s = \{o_0, o_{\frac{T}{2}}, o_T\}$. Next, the set will be expanded to $o_s = \{o_0, o_{\frac{T}{4}}, o_{\frac{T}{2}}, o_{\frac{3T}{4}}, o_T\}$. In other words, at the nth iteration the length of o_s is given by $|o_s| = 1 + 2^{n-1}$.

Figure 1 illustrates the process outlined above. Figure 1b depicts a hypothetical path followed by a demonstrator (depicted as a black robot) from start to goal. Observing this path, an imitator (purple robot) iteratively selects an increasing number of states (here: n = 2, 3 and 4, respectively) from the demonstrated path. Selecting only the start and goal position (Fig. 1c) leads to a large cost difference ΔE (Fig. 1f). The reason is that the planned action a_t does not include the deviation present in the demonstrator's path. However, by including an additional third state (Fig. 1d), the imitator's planned action sequence a_t better matches the demonstrated path (and energetic cost). Adding more states does not improve the match (Fig. 1e). Hence, the imitator will copy the three states (depicted in Fig. 1d). The imitated path is shown in Fig. 1g.

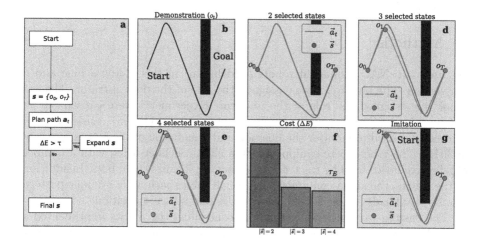

Fig. 1. Illustration of the process of selecting states s of the demonstrated action sequence o_t. (a) flow chart depicting the process of selecting s (b) The path taken by a demonstrator (black robot) from start to goal. An imitator (purple robot) is observing the path. Notice the demonstrated path consists of both an unnecessary curve (first) and necessary curve (to negotiate the black obstacle). (c) This panel illustrates the planned path a_t for s containing only the initial state and final states. Notice that this results in a discrepancy between the paths a_t and o_t. In particular, the first curve is not included in a_t. This will result in a value for ΔE that is larger than τ_E. Hence, additional states will be added to o_s. This is illustrated in panels d-e where s contains 3 and 4 selected states respectively. By selecting a single additional state in panel d, the match between paths a_t and o_t increases (and $\Delta E < \tau_E$, panel f). At this point, the iterative expansion of o_s is terminated and adding further states does not markedly decrease ΔE (panels e and f). Finally, panel g depicts the path the imitator would follow. Omitting state o_0 from o_s, it goes to o_T via o_1, thereby imitating the unnecessary (and energetically demanding) detour shown by the demonstrator. (Color figure online)

Finally, we briefly discuss how the CDM accommodates the experimental results obtained using popular head touch paradigm [17]. The CDM assumes that whenever a demonstrator with free hands performs a head touch, ΔE (Eq. 1) will be large. Indeed, the energetic demand of the head touch will be compared with that of a simple hand touch. In contrast, when the demonstrator's hands are occupied, the infant is assumed to plan an action taking into account these constraints (modelled using the parameter C in Eq. 1). We assume that this will result in infants planning a head touch themselves. As such, this will result in lower a value for ΔE and, therefore, a lower degree of action copying. One could object that is unlikely that children come up with a head touch as a way of dealing with the constraints C. However, a small percentage of infants who have not been shown the head touch still choose to touch the lamp with their heads [18], especially younger infants [24] (60 % of the 9-month old infants tested). Hence, it is not beyond plausibility that the context of these experiments spontaneously elicits head pushing as a solution to deal with the constraint of occupied hands.

3   Methods

We used two NAO humanoid robots (Aldebaran) in this study, a blue and a red version. The blue robot was assigned the role of the demonstrator. The red robot was assigned the role of the imitator. Experiments were carried out in a 3 by 2.5 m arena. An overhead 3D tracking system (Vicon) consisting of 4 cameras was used to monitor the position and orientation of the robots at a rate of 30 Hz. The robots were equipped with a clip-on helmet fitted with a number of reflective beads used by the tracking system to localize the robots. In addition to the robots, the arena contained three small tables each with a unique pattern of reflective beads. These served as obstacles and a target position.

The custom-written Python software controlling the robots implemented a path planning algorithm. This algorithm overlaid the arena with a rectangular graph with nodes spaced 10 cm apart [20]. Nodes closer than 0.5 m to an obstacle were removed from the graph. A path between the current position of a robot and the desired goal location was planned by finding the shortest path of connected nodes between the node closest to the robot's current position and the node closest to the goal position. By removing the nodes closer than 0.5 m to an obstacle, the path planning algorithm ensured the robots steered well clear of obstacles. In the current paper, the estimated energetic costs $\hat{E}(o_t)$ and $\hat{E}(a_t)$ are approximated by the length of the planned and observed paths, respectively. For robots moving at a constant speed, this is a fair approximation.

4   Experiment 1: Modelling Experimental Findings

Figure 2 illustrates the three conditions of experiment 1. In the first condition, the demonstrator is not hampered by obstacles. Hence, it moves towards the goal position using a direct path (Fig. 2a). In the second condition (Fig. 2b),

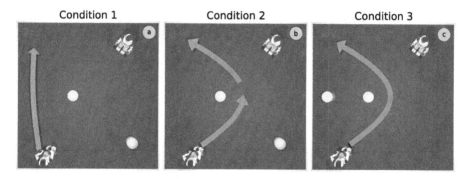

Fig. 2. Illustration of the three conditions in experiment 1. The blue robot is the demonstrator. The red robot is the imitator. The green arrows depict the path taken by the demonstrator. Note that in panel c the demonstrator cannot pass between the two round obstacles. Details in text. (Color figure online)

the demonstrator could approach the goal using a direct path. However, the demonstrator approaches the goal by a detour. In the third condition, obstacles between the demonstrator and the goal prevent a direct path. The path planning algorithm yields a path circumventing the obstacles (Fig. 2c).

The critical conditions, in modelling the experimental results regarding rational imitation in infants [10,17], are conditions 2 and 3. In both conditions, the demonstrator does not take the direct path to the goal. The difference between these conditions, however, is the presence of an obstacle in condition 3. In this condition, the obstacle forces the demonstrator to take the longer path. This is analogous to a demonstrator switching on the lamp with her head when her hands are occupied in the sense that the constraints of the situation necessitate the less direct (and energetically inefficient) mode of operation. Critically, the CDM assumes that the robot (infant) plans an indirect path (head touch) to cope with the constraints introduced by the obstacle (occupied hands). Hence, the robot (infant) is predicted not to imitate the indirect path (head touch). In contrast, in condition 2, given no obstacle (analogous to the free hands condition in behavioural experiments) the imitator will plan a direct path (a hand touch). The planned direct path (head touch) is assumed to differ sufficiently (in terms of energy expenditure) from the demonstrated indirect path (head touch) to incur imitation.

Figure 3 depicts the results of experiment 1. In condition 1, the demonstrator takes a direct route to the goal position (Fig. 3a). Calculating ΔE for a planned path a_t based on two selected states, $s = \{o_0, o_T\}$, results in a value lower than τ_E (Fig. 3j). Thus, the green path for $|s| = 2$ in Fig. 3d matches the demonstrated path o_t well. Hence, the imitator only retains the final goal o_T as policy. In consequence, the imitator proceeds to the goal, using a direct path (Fig. 3g).

In condition 2, the demonstrator takes a detour to the goal, in spite of a direct path being possible (Fig. 3b). Calculating ΔE for a planned path a_t based on $s = \{o_0, o_T\}$ results in a value higher than τ_E (Fig. 3j). As can be seen in Fig. 3e,

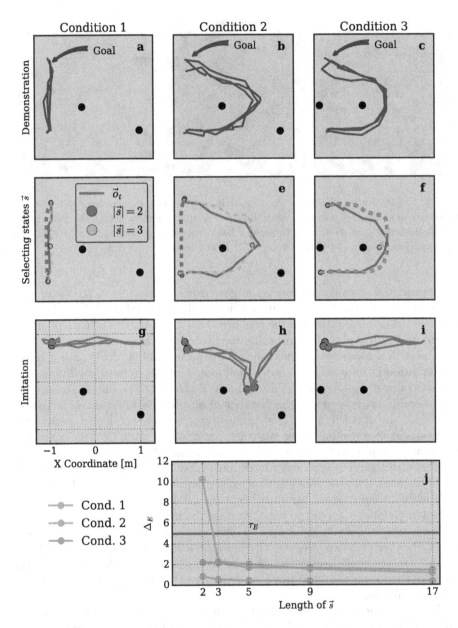

Fig. 3. Results of experiment 1. Panels a-c: paths taken by the demonstrator in conditions 1–3, respectively. Panels d–f depict the process of iteratively expanding s. In green, the planned path a_t is shown for s with two states, i.e., $s = \{o_0, o_T\}$. In yellow, the planned path a_t is shown for s with three states, i.e., $s = \{o_0, o_{T/2}, o_T\}$. Panels g-i depict the imitated behaviour for each condition. Notice that the imitator does not start from the same position as the demonstrator. Panel j: Values of ΔE as a function of the number of selected states in s for each of the three conditions. The value τ_E is indicated by a horizontal line. (Color figure online)

the green path for $|s| = 2$ does not match the demonstrated path o_t (grey) well. In contrast, calculating ΔE for $|s| = 3$ results in a value lower than τ_E (Fig. 3j). The yellow path a_t, based on s with three states, in Fig. 3e satisfies the requirement $\Delta E < \tau_E$. Hence, the policy copied will include an additional subgoal en route to the goal. The imitator proceeds to this intermediate goal before going to the final goal (Fig. 3h).

In condition 3, the demonstrator reaches the goal via a detour Fig. 3c). However, the presence of an obstacle makes this necessary. Indeed, the path a_t planned by the imitator from o_0 to o_T (i.e. $|s| = 2$) will also contain this detour. As such, the value of ΔE will be small, even for $|s| = 2$ (Fig. 3f and j). The green path a_t for $|s| = 2$ (Fig. 3f) matches the demonstrated path o_t sufficiently. As a result, the imitator proceeds directly to the final goal (Fig. 3i), as it did in condition 1.

Experiment 1 was aimed at modelling the basic findings of the behavioural experiments regarding rational imitation in infants [3,10,17,19,24]. As mentioned above, these authors showed that children copy the head-touch demonstrated by adults only if the adult's hands were unrestricted. In our robot experiments, the imitator only copied the demonstrated detour if the demonstrator was not forced to take this detour by the obstacles (Condition 2, Fig. 3b, e and h). In contrast, when the demonstrator took the same path – but was forced to do so on account of an obstacle – the imitator disregarded the detour (Condition 3, Fig. 3c, f and i). As such, conditions 2 and 3 reveal our robots modelling the behaviour of infants in the behavioural experiments discussed above.

5   Experiment 2: Learning Better Policies

In our view, the behavioural experiments concerning rational imitation cited above can be considered as cases of pathological imitation [22]. That is, the behavioural experiments are set up to induce imitation in spite of the behaviour being inefficient, i.e., the head touch is a less efficient way of switching on the light than a hand touch. The experiments in [12,16] illustrate how easily children can be tricked into imitating inefficient behaviour. In these experiments, the demonstrating adult exhibited a range of action irrelevant to attain a given goal. Nevertheless, the infants tended to copy these actions – even when explicitly instructed not to copy any 'silly' behaviour. However, when not experimentally controlled, adults' behaviour can generally be assumed to be more efficient or more adaptive than that of infants. Under these conditions, as will be shown below, the mechanism proposed above for selecting policies for imitation is adaptive.

In this section of the paper, we present a robotic experiment showing that the CDM can also select more efficient policies if these are observed in a demonstrator. Indeed, by virtue of Eq. 1, the CDM can select policies for explorative imitation that are *less* costly than the current policy. The current policy of the robot amounts to the planned route a_t for s with only two states (o_0 and o_T). For $|o_s| = 2$, the robot will generate a plan reaching the end goal without taking into account the demonstrated behaviour. If the observed policy o_t is significantly *less* costly than the currently held policy, ΔE will be larger than τ_E (by virtue of the absolute value operator in Eq. 1). This will trigger the expansion of the set of intermediate goals s until ΔE is smaller than τ_E.

In experiment 2, the imitator starts with a policy that is clearly not optimal. When going from the start position to the goal, the imitator takes an unnecessary detour (Fig. 4a). This detour is caused by the imitator's path planning algorithm not considering the locations in the hatched area (Fig. 4a). In effect, the hatched area is not part of the search space considered by the path planning algorithm. In contrast, panel b of Fig. 4 shows the demonstrator moving in a straight line from start to goal – as depicted in this panel, the whole arena is part of the demonstrator's search space. As such, the demonstrator can find a shorter path to the goal. Considering the observed behaviour o_t, the imitator iteratively expands a set of selected states s from the demonstrated states o_t. Each state o_s in s corresponds to a position of the demonstrator in the arena. By adding states o_s to s the imitator effectively expands its path planning search space. Iteratively expanding the set of selected states s will eventually lead to filling in the part of the search space that was initially not available to the imitator (in panel a). Indeed, in effect, a corridor between start and goal position is built (Fig. 4c). When this corridor is established the value $\Delta E < \tau_E$ (at $|s| = 5$, panel d) and expansion of s is stopped. Eventually, the imitator imitates the shorter path, as shown in Fig. 4c.

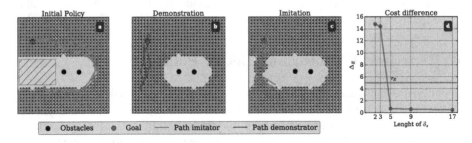

Fig. 4. Results of experiment 2. The paths of both the imitator (red paths) and demonstrator (blue paths) for three trials are plotted. The grids in the background of panels a-c represent the graph used in path planning by the imitator (panels a & c) and the demonstrator (panel b). Panel a: the initial policy of the imitator in reaching the goal position involves a detour. Part of the graph used by the imitator for path planning has been taken out (the hatched region). Panel b: the demonstrator approaches the goal in a straight line (its path planning graph has not been lesioned). Panel c: the imitator, based on observing the demonstrator's policy, adopts a more efficient policy. Panel d: cost difference ΔE as a function of the number of states in o_s averaged over the three trials. (Color figure online)

6   Discussion

Since the advent of robotics [4], imitation been suggested as a method for learning in robots. However, robotic imitation faces a number of challenges [7]. One of the most fundamental issues is determining what to imitate [5,6]. Among other aspects, this involves determining the relevant parts of a demonstrated action and only copying those. Hence, the selective and rational imitation shown by children would be a beneficial capacity for robots [9]. Unfortunately, in spite of the considerable body of experimental data, the cognitive mechanisms underlying rational imitation remain elusive. In particular, no satisfactory and computationally explicit model of rational imitation in infants is available. In this paper, we have presented a formalization that captures the most relevant aspects of the behaviour of infants in experiments. The CDM can be considered as a formalized version of the teleological reasoning hypothesis, which is underspecified [23]. As such, the CDM is explicit enough to be implemented on robots, as demonstrated above.

Acknowledgements. This work was supported by grant EP/L024861/1 ('Verifiable Autonomy') from the Engineering and Physical Sciences Research Council (EPSRC). All data are available at http://dx.doi.org/10.5281/zenodo.56272

References

1. Erbas, M.D., Winfield, A.F.T., Bull, L.: Embodied imitation-enhanced reinforcement learning in multi-agent systems. Adapt. Behav. **22**, 31–50 (2014)
2. Argall, B.D., Chernova, S., Veloso, M., Browning, B.: A survey of robot learning from demonstration. Robot Auton. Syst. **57**(5), 469–483 (2009)
3. Beisert, M., Zmyj, N., Liepelt, R., Jung, F., Prinz, W., Daum, M.M.: Rethinking 'rational imitation' in 14-month-old infants: a perceptual distraction approach. Plos One **7**(3), 1–5 (2012)
4. Billard, A., Calinon, S., Dillmann, R., Schaal, S.: Robot programming by demonstration. In: Siciliano, B., Khatib, O. (eds.) Handbook of Robotics, pp. 1371–1394. Springer, New York (2008)
5. Breazeal, C., Scassellati, B.: Robots that imitate humans. Trends Cogn. Sci. **6**(11), 481–487 (2002)
6. Carpenter, M., Call, J.: The question of 'what to imitate': inferring goals and intentions. In: Nehaniv, C.L., Kirstin, D. (eds.) Imitation and Social Learning in Robots, Humans and Animals Behavioural, Social and Communicative Dimensions, pp. 135–152. Cambridge University Press, Cambridge (2006)
7. Dautenhahn, K., Nehaniv, C.: Challenges in Building Robots That Imitate People, pp. 363–390. MIT Press, Cambridge (2002)
8. Gariépy, J.F., Watson, K.K., Du, E., Xie, D.L., Erb, J., Amasino, D., Platt, M.L.: Social learning in humans and other animals. Front Neurosci. **8**, 58 (2014)
9. Gergely, G.: What should a robot learn from an infant? Mechanisms of action interpretation and observational learning in infancy. Connect Sci. **15**(4), 191–209 (2003)
10. Gergely, G., Bekkering, H., Kiraly, I.: Rational imitation in preverbal infants. Nature **415**(6873), 755 (2002)
11. Jones, S.S.: The development of imitation in infancy. Philos. Trans. R. Soc. B-biol. Sci. **364**(1528), 2325–2335 (2009)
12. Keupp, S., Behne, T., Rakoczy, H.: Why do children overimitate? Normativity is crucial. J. Exp. Child Psychol. **116**(2), 392–406 (2013)

13. Kolling, T., Óturai, G., Knopf, M.: Is selective attention the basis for selective imitation in infants? An eye-tracking study of deferred imitation with 12-month-olds. J. Exp. Child Psychol. **124**, 18–35 (2014)
14. Laland, K.N.: Social learning strategies. Anim. Learn. Behav. **32**(1), 4–14 (2004)
15. Legare, C.H., Nielsen, M.: Imitation and innovation: the dual engines of cultural learning. Trends Cogn. Sci. **19**(11), 688–699 (2015)
16. Lyons, D.E., Young, A.G., Keil, F.C.: The hidden structure of overimitation. Proc. Nat. Acad. Sci. **104**(50), 19751–19756 (2007)
17. Meltzoff, A.N.: Infant imitation after a 1-week delay: long-term memory for novel acts and multiple stimuli. Dev. Psychol. **24**(4), 470–476 (1988)
18. Paulus, M., Hunnius, S., Bekkering, H.: Examining functional mechanisms of imitative learning in infancy: does teleological reasoning affect infants' imitation beyond motor resonance? J. Exp. Child Psychol. **116**(2), 487–498 (2013)
19. Paulus, M., Hunnius, S., Vissers, M., Bekkering, H.: Imitation in infancy: rational or motor resonance? Child Dev. **82**(4), 1047–1057 (2011)
20. Schult, D.A., Swart, P.: Exploring network structure, dynamics, and function using networkx. In: Proceedings of the 7th Python in Science Conferences (SciPy 2008), vol. 2008, pp. 11–16 (2008)
21. Tomasello, M.: The Cultural Origins of Human Cognition. Harvard University Press, Cambridge (2009)
22. Winfield, A.F., Erbas, M.D.: On embodied memetic evolution and the emergence of behavioural traditions in robots. Memetic Comput. **3**(4), 261–270 (2011)
23. Zmyj, N., Buttelmann, D.: An integrative model of rational imitation in infancy. Infant. Behav. Dev. **37**(1), 21–28 (2014)
24. Zmyj, N., Daum, M.M., Aschersleben, G.: The development of rational imitation in 9- and 12-month-old infants. Infancy **14**(1), 131–141 (2009)

Modular Neural Control for Object Transportation of a Bio-inspired Hexapod Robot

Chris Tryk Lund Sørensen and Poramate Manoonpong[✉]

Embodied AI and Neurorobotics Lab, Centre for BioRobotics,
Mærsk Mc-Kinney Møller Institute, University of Southern Denmark,
Odense M, Denmark
`chsoe14@student.sdu.dk`, `poma@mmmi.sdu.dk`

Abstract. Insects, like dung beetles, can perform versatile motor behaviors including walking, climbing an object (i.e., dung ball), as well as manipulating and transporting it. To achieve such complex behaviors for artificial legged systems, we present here modular neural control of a bio-inspired hexapod robot. The controller utilizes discrete-time neurodynamics and consists of seven modules based on three generic neural networks. One is a neural oscillator network serving as a central pattern generator (CPG) which generates basic rhythmic patterns. The other two networks are so-called velocity regulating and phase switching networks. They are used for regulating the rhythmic patterns and changing their phase. As a result, the modular neural control enables the hexapod robot to walk and climb a large cylinder object with a diameter of 18 cm (i.e., ≈ 2.8 times the robot's body height). Additionally, it can also generate different hind leg movements for different object manipulation modes, like soft and hard pushing. Combining these pushing modes, the robot can quickly transport the object across an obstacle with a height up to 10 cm (i.e., ≈ 1.5 times the robot's body height). The controller was developed and evaluated using a physical simulation environment.

Keywords: Object manipulation · Locomotion · Modular neural network · Central pattern generator · Walking machines · Autonomous robots

1 Introduction

Over the last few decades, a number of animal-like walking robots have been developed. Most of them can perform only locomotion, like walking [1], climbing [2], and swimming [3]. Typically, if object manipulation or transportation tasks are required, additional manipulators/grippers need to be installed [4–6] instead of using existing legs. This becomes energy inefficient due to added load and the requirement of additional energy to power the manipulator or gripper system. Only a few works have shown walking robots which can locomote and transport an object using existing legs [7–9]. However, these robots require precise kinematic and force control; thereby they can only move or hold an object with the

© Springer International Publishing Switzerland 2016
E. Tuci et al. (Eds.): SAB 2016, LNAI 9825, pp. 67–78, 2016.
DOI: 10.1007/978-3-319-43488-9_7

stop-and-go motion. In other words, they cannot perform continuous movements for transporting an object, especially a large one.

In contrast, dung beetles with little neural computing can use their legs to continuously walk and at the same time move large objects - dung balls that can be larger than their body size [10]. In order to do so, the beetle walks backwards, climbs onto it, and uses its hind legs sometimes together with its middle legs to push the ball while its front legs are for walking. Inspired by the strategy of the beetle, we present here a modular neural control approach which allows a bio-inspired hexapod robot to walk backwards with a tripod gait, autonomously climb a large cylinder object, and use its hind legs to manipulate (i.e., push) the object while its front and middle legs are for walking. This results in continuous locomotion as well as object manipulation and transportation. With this technique, the robot can even perform different object manipulation modes including soft push, hard push, and boxing-like motion. A combination of soft and hard pushing strategies enables the robot to effectively transport a large cylinder object (larger than its body height) across an obstacle. We believe that the study in this direction will expand the usability of robots towards domains, like transportation and agriculture, in which (autonomous) mobile robots with multi functions are in high demand.

However, the rationale behind this study is not only to demonstrate the hexapod robot with multi functions (i.e., locomotion with object manipulation and transportation) but also to show that such complex functions can be achieved by a combination of neural modules. This pure neural network control has a layered, modular architecture which is inspired by the biological neural systems of insects [11]. Such a structure is also considered as a major advantage [12], compared to many other controllers [1], since it is able to deal with transferring and scaling issues; i.e., applying to different robots [13–15]. Thus, this modular neural control approach can be a powerful technique to solve sensorimotor coordination problems of many degrees-of-freedom systems (like walking robots) and to effectively provide complex multi functions to the systems.

2   Modular Neural Control for Object Transportation

To control the locomotion and object manipulation of a bio-inspired hexapod robot for continuous transporting an object, we employ neural mechanisms as the key ingredient of our controller. Although different methods [1] can be employed for the task, this neural control with a layered, modular architecture is selected in order to provide a basic control structure to the hexapod robot system. This way, neural learning mechanisms with synaptic plasticity for control parameter adaptation [16] could be later applied to obtain adaptive behavior.

The modular neural control is manually designed in a hierarchical way with seven neural modules (CPG, PSN1-4, and VRN1-2, Fig. 1(a)). There are four inputs $I_{1,2,3,4}$ (Fig. 1(a)) which are used to activate different motor patterns for forward/backward walking and different object manipulation modes. The complete structure of this modular neural control and the location of the

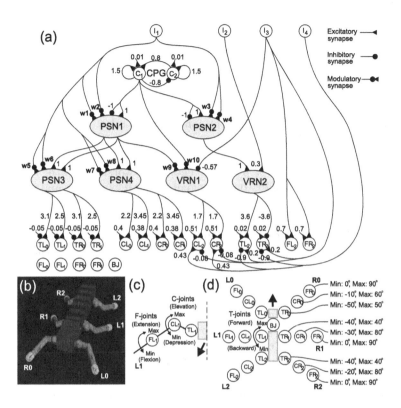

Fig. 1. (a) Modular neural control for locomotion and object manipulation. It is manually designed where its connection weights and inputs $I_{1,2,3,4}$ are tuned to obtain desired behavior (e.g., locomotion, object manipulation, etc.). Switching from one behavior to the other is achieved by manually setting the input values. By activating locomotion using the front and middle legs and object manipulation using the hind legs of a bio-inspired hexapod robot, the robot can perform object transportation (i.e., continuously transporting a cylinder object). Abbreviations are: BJ = a backbone joint, TL(R) = thoraco-coxal joints of left (right) legs, CL(R) = coxa-trochanteral joints of left (right) legs, FL(R) = femur-tibia joints of left (right) legs. (b) The simulated bio-inspired hexapod robot using the LPZRobots simulation environment (see http://robot.informatik. uni-leipzig.de/software). The robot consists of 19 joints: three joints for each leg and one backbone joint. The robot model is qualitatively consistent with our real hexapod robot AMOSII [16] in the aspect of size, mass distribution, motor torque/speed, and sensors. Its joint orientations follow the ones of the dung beetle *Geotrupes stercorarius*; i.e., the front legs are oriented slightly to the front while the middle and hind legs are oriented to the back. (c) The movements of the C- and F-joints. (d) The location of the motor neurons on the simulated robot and the movements of the T-joints. Minimum and maximum angles can be seen for all joints of the right legs where the same values are also set to the left ones.

corresponding motor neurons on the hexapod robot are shown in Fig. 1. The structural design of the control is based on our previous developed neural loco-motion control [15,16].

The seven neural modules of the controller are derived from three generic neural networks[1]: A neural oscillator network (abbreviated CPG), a velocity regulating network (VRN), and a phase switching network (PSN). The neural oscillator network serves as a central pattern generator (CPG) module. It gen-erates basic rhythmic signals. Here, the output signal C_1 of the CPG mod-ule (see Fig. 1(a)) is used to drive the joints of the robot for locomotion and object manipulation. To obtain proper motor patterns for locomotion and object manipulation, the CPG output signal is post-processed at the PSN and VRN modules. These modules act as premotor neuron networks. Here, the PSN1 and PSN2 modules receive the CPG output signal through excitatory and inhibitory synapses; i.e., they obtain the original CPG signal and its inversion. The out-puts of these PSN modules are projected to the thoraco-coxal (T-) and coxa-trochanteral (C-) joints through the other PSN modules (PSN3 and PSN4) and the VRN modules (VRN1 and VRN2). These PSN modules are basically used to switch the phase of the T- and C-joint signals of the front and middle legs for forward/backward walking while the VRN modules are to regulate the ampli-tude of the hind legs to obtain different object manipulation modes (e.g., soft and hard pushing and boxing-like motion) as well as to maintain stability dur-ing object transportation. Note that the femur-tibia (F-) joints of the front and middle legs are kept fixed to a certain position while the F-joints of the hind legs are controlled by I_3 for object manipulation.

All these CPG, PSN, and VRN networks are described in details in the fol-lowing sections. Their neurons are modelled as discrete-time non-spiking neurons with an update frequency of approx. 10 Hz. The activity of each neuron develops according to $a_i(t+1) = \sum_{j=1}^{n} w_{ij} o_j(t) + b_i$; $i = 1, \ldots, n$ where n denotes the number of units, b_i represents a fixed internal bias term of neuron i, w_{ij} the synaptic strength of the connection from neuron j to neuron i. The neuron out-put o_i is given by a hyperbolic tangent (tanh) transfer function. Input neurons ($I_{1,2,3,4}$) are here configured as linear buffers ($a_i = o_i$). All connection strengths together with bias terms are indicated by the small numbers (Fig. 1(a)) except w_{1-10} which are modulatory synapses (see section below for details). These fixed bias and synaptic connection values are here empirically set to obtain the desired locomotion and object manipulation patterns. However, they can be changed depending on robot configuration, e.g., the position of actuators.

2.1 Neural Oscillator Network (CPG)

The concept of central pattern generators (CPGs) for legged locomotion [11] has been studied and used in several robotic systems in particular walking robots.

---

[1] These networks have been successfully applied for locomotion control of various robot systems [14–16]. They are, for the first time here, employed for locomotion and object manipulation and transportation of a bio-inspired hexapod robot.

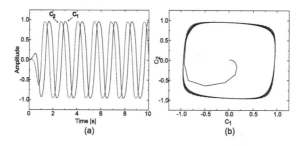

Fig. 2. (a) The periodic output signals from the CPG with the defined parameters shown in Fig. 1(a). Here we use the output signal C_1 for generating locomotion and object manipulation. (b) The phase space with the quasi-periodic attractor of the oscillator network [17].

Here, the model of a CPG is realized by using the discrete-time dynamics of a simple 2-neuron oscillator network with full connectivity (see Fig. 1(a)). Such a CPG model has been successfully used for locomotion control [15]. We empirically adjust the synaptic weights of this network to achieve a proper frequency of leg movements for stable locomotion and object manipulation. Figure 2 shows the outputs from the CPG network.

2.2   Phase Switching Network (PSN)

To obtain different modes (i.e., forward/backward locomotion and object manipulation), one possibility is to reverse the phase of the periodic signals driving the T- and C-joints (Fig. 1). That is, these periodic signals can be switched to lead or lag behind each other depending on the given input I_1. To do so, we use four phase switching network (PSN) modules (PSN1-4). The PSN was developed in our previous study [15]. It is a hand-designed feedforward network consisting of four hierarchical layers with 14 neurons P_{1-14} (Fig. 3). The synaptic weights and bias terms of the network were determined in a way that they do not change the periodic form of its input signals and keep the amplitude of the signals as high as possible (i.e., between -0.5 and $+0.5$). The detail of the network development is referred to [15]. For our implementation here (Fig. 1(a)), $P_{1,2}$ of the PSN1 and PSN2 modules receive the CPG signal C_1 through an excitatory synapse $(+1)$ and its inversion through an inhibitory synapse (-1) while their $P_{3,4}$ receive the input I_1 through the modulatory synapses $w_{1,2}$ for the PSN1 module and $w_{3,4}$ for the PSN2 module (Fig. 1(a)). $P_{1,2}$ of the PSN3 and PSN4 modules in a lower layer receive the outputs $P_{13,14}$ of the PSN1 module through an excitatory synapse $(+1)$ while their $P_{3,4}$ receive the input I_1 through the modulatory synapses $w_{5,6}$ for the PSN3 module and $w_{7,8}$ for the PSN4 module (Fig. 1(a)). The final outputs $P_{13,14}$ of the PSN3 and PSN4 modules are directly connected to the motor neurons of the T- and C- joints of the front and middle legs. The modulatory synapses of all PSN modules (Fig. 1(a)) are modelled as $w_{1,4,6,7} = I_1$ and $w_{2,3,5,8} = -I_1$. In this study, the bias terms $b_{1,2}$ (Fig. 3(a)) of the PNS1

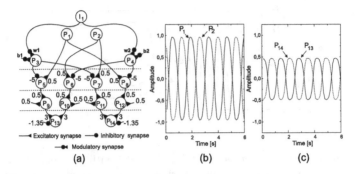

Fig. 3. (a) The phase switching network of the PSN1 module. The other PSN modules have the same structure. (b) The inputs of the PSN1 module which come from the CPG module. (c) The outputs of the PSN1 module where $I_{1,2}$ are set to (1,1) or (0,1). The outputs are inverted if $I_{1,2}$ are set to (1,–1), (–1,–1), or (1,0). Note that the inputs and outputs of the other PSN modules behave in a similar way.

and PSN4 modules are modelled as input-driven functions and described as $b_1 = \frac{-(I_1^2 I_2(I_2+1))}{2}$, $b_2 = -b_1$, while the ones of the PNS2 and PSN3 modules are set to $b_1 = -1$ and $b_2 = 0$. Note that the input-driven functions used here will basically activate or deactivate the neurons $P_{3,4}$ with respect to the inputs $I_{1,2}$.

2.3   Velocity Regulating Network (VRN)

To obtain different object manipulation modes (e.g., soft and hard pushing and boxing-like motion) and to maintain stability during object transportation, we need to regulate the signals controlling the T- and C-joints (TL_2, TR_2, CL_2, CR_2, see Fig. 1(a)) of the hind legs. According to this, we use two velocity regulating network (VRN) modules (VRN1,2) where one is for controlling the T-joints (TL_2, TR_2) and the other is for the C-joints (CL_2, CR_2). The VRN taken from [15] is a simple feed-forward neural network with two input $V_{1,2}$, four hidden V_{3-6}, and one output V_7 neurons (Fig. 4). It was trained by using the backprop-agation algorithm to act as a multiplication operator on two input values on the neurons $V_{1,2} \in [-1, +1]$ (see [15] for details). For our purpose here, the neuron V_1 of the VRN1 module receives the input I_3 through an inhibitory synapse (e.g., –0.57, Fig. 1(a)) while the one of the VRN2 module receives the input I_2 through an excitatory synapse (e.g., 0.3, Fig. 1(a)). The bias term of the neu-ron V_1 of the VRN1 module is set to 1 while the one of the VRN2 module is set to 0.7 (Fig. 4(a)). The neuron V_2 of the VRN1 module receives two inputs (x, y) from the CPG output C_1 and the output P_{13} of the PSN1 module, respec-tively, through the modulatory synapses $w_{9,10}$ while the one of the VRN2 module receives only one input (x) from the output P_{13} of the PSN2 module through an excitatory synapse (+1, Fig. 1(a)). Additionally, the neuron V_2 of the VRN1 module has the bias term b_3 which is modelled as an input-driven function and described as $b_3 = 0.02((I_1^2 - I_2^2)^2 + \frac{I_1 I_2(I_2+I_1)}{2})^2)$ while there is no bias term for

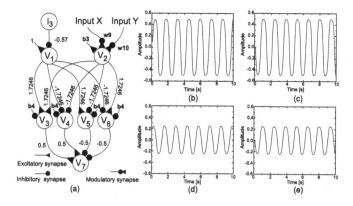

Fig. 4. (a) The velocity regulating network of the VRN1 module. The bias b_4 is equal to -2.48285. The VRN2 module has the same structure. (b–e) Different output signals of the VRN1 module for forward/backward walking (b), hard pushing (c), soft pushing (d), boxing-like motion (e). The VRN2 output behaves in a similar way.

the neuron V_2 of the VRN2 module (Fig. 4(a)). According to this input-driven function, b_3 will be 0.02 for all cases except soft pushing where it will be zero. Here, the synaptic weights $w_{9,10}$ are driven by the inputs $I_{1,2}$ and described as $w_9 = 2((I_1^2 - I_2^2)^2 + \frac{I_1 I_2(I_2 + I_1)}{2})^2)$ and $w_{10} = 1 - \frac{w_9}{2}$. According to these equations, w_9 will be equal to 2 for all actions except the soft pushing action for which it will be zero and the weight w_{10} will be zero for all actions except the soft pushing action for which it will be one. Finally, the outputs V_7 of the VRN1 and VRN2 modules are set to control the C-joints (CL_2, CR_2) and the T-joints (TL_2, TR_2), respectively. Note that all these functions of $b_3, w_{9,10}$ are used to scale the input signals (x, y) into proper ranges for different behavioral modes.

2.4   Neural Control Parameters for Different Behavior Modes

The integration of the different functional neural modules described above gives the complete modular neural controller. It can generate different behavioral modes[2] (locomotion, object manipulation, and their combination (i.e., object transportation)) through the four input parameters $I_{1,2,3,4}$. Appropriate input parameter sets for the different modes are presented in Table 1. $I_{1,2}$ are basically for generating different motor modes through the PSN and VRN modules while $I_{3,4}$, which can vary between -1.0 and 1.0, are for shifting the offsets of the leg joints upward/downward for object manipulation. Additionally, I_3 is used to scale the CPG and PSN signals through the VRN1 module to obtain proper movements for soft pushing and boxing-like motion. Note that the input values shown in Table 1 can be changed with respect to, e.g., robot configuration.

---

[2] See http://manoonpong.com/SAB2016/V1.mp4.

Table 1. Input parameters for different behavior modes.

Actions	I_1	I_2	I_3	I_4
Locomotion: Forward walking	1	1	0	0
Locomotion: Backward walking	0	1	0	0
Object manipulation: Soft pushing	1	−1	1	1
Object manipulation: Boxing-like motion	−1	−1	1	0
Object manipulation: Hard pushing	1	0	0	−0.3

3 Experiments and Results

To evaluate the performance of the developed controller, we used the simulated bio-inspired hexapod robot (see Fig. 1(b)) with a body height of 6.5 cm and
a weight of ≈ 5 kg and a cylinder object (see Fig. 5(b)) with a length of 60 cm,
a diameter of 18 cm (i.e., ≈ 2.8 times the robot's body height), and a weight
of 2 kg. The friction coefficient of robot feet was set based on a rubber material
used for the feet of the real robot while the friction coefficients of the object
and ground were empirically set to obtain high friction and to avoid slipping
during locomotion and object transportation. With the controller, the robot can
walk forward with a tripod gait and can walk backward by changing the phase
of the T-joints through the PSN2 and PSN3 modules. Note that the C-joint
signals are clipped to ensure that the legs touch the ground during the stance
phase; resulting in a stable walking behavior. Here, the F-joints stay in a certain
position.

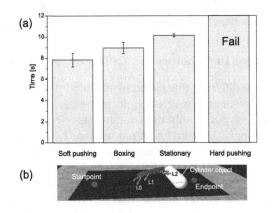

Fig. 5. Result of the speed test for object transportation using different object manipulation modes. (a) The bars show the average object transportation time with the
standard deviation. The time was measured from the starting point to the end point
where the distance is 1.46 m. We performed in total ten tests for each mode. (b) The
startpoint and endpoint locations from which the robot has to transport the object.
Note that in this experiment the robot was activated to walk backward without any
additional steering command.

To let the robot transport the object, we drive the robot to walk backward. While walking backward and approaching an object, the robot will automatically climb the object since we set the backbone joint (BJ) in a slightly bending position. With this BJ setup, the body of the robot bends slightly upwards; thereby allowing the robot to swing its hind legs slightly more upwards during a swing phase and place its leg tips above the center line of the object during a stance phase. This way, the robot can climb the object. Once the robot has been stayed on the object partly, which is detected by a body inclination sensor, specific hind leg movements for different object manipulation modes will be activated while the front and middle legs remain unchanged. For soft pushing, the hind legs will slowly roll a cylinder object while the robot walks backward. For the boxing-like motion, as the word describes, the robot uses the hind legs to hit or punch the object and in this way move it. For hard pushing, the robot uses the hind legs to dig under the object in order to make it across an obstacle.

Two main experiments were carried out for our evaluation. The first experiment evaluates an object transportation speed of the robot without an obstacle when different object manipulation modes were used. The soft pushing, hard pushing, and boxing modes, where the hind legs actively move in specific patterns (see Footnote 2), were tested. Additionally, we also compare them with a situation where the hind legs were kept fixed in a certain position (not moving) and stayed on top of the object to avoid it run away (i.e., stationary mode[3]). Figure 5 shows the result of this experiment. It can be seen that the robot can transport or move the object with the fastest speed (i.e., less time) in a straight backward direction when the soft pushing mode was used while other modes required more time to reach the target location. The robot failed to do the task when the hard pushing mode was used because with this mode it pushed the object away in an arbitrary direction (see Footnote 2).

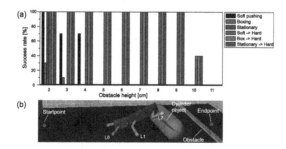

Fig. 6. Result of the obstacle test for the different object manipulation techniques. (a) Success rate in a total of ten experiments for each strategy. (b) The startpoint and endpoint locations from which the robot has to transport the object. In this experiment the robot was activated to walk backward without any additional steering command.

---

[3] See http://manoonpong.com/SAB2016/V2.mp4.

The second experiment evaluates the performance of the robot with different manipulation strategies to transport the object across an obstacle at different heights. The obstacle width was set to 1 mm while the obstacle height was varied from 2 cm to 11 cm. In total, we tested six strategies including soft pushing, boxing, stationary, and their combination with hard pushing. For the combination modes (i.e., soft pushing (Mode1) → hard pushing (Mode2), boxing (Mode1) → hard pushing (Mode2), and soft pushing (Mode1) → hard pushing (Mode2)), we switch from one pushing mode (Mode1) to another pushing mode (Mode2) when the object has reached or hit the obstacle. This is detected by the joint angle sensors of the F-joints of the front legs. If the angle sensors decrease below a threshold, then the switching occurs. Figure 6 presents the success rate of object transportation; i.e., the percentage of success from ten experiments each. A success is considered if the object gets across the obstacle within one minute. It can be seen that the combination modes outperform individual modes and allow the robot transport the object across the obstacle at the maximum height of 10 cm. However, when we take the transportation time into account the combination of soft pushing (Mode1) → hard pushing (Mode2) is the best since, with this mode, the robot uses first the soft pushing mode to roll the object leading to

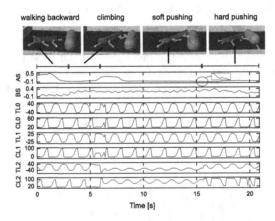

Fig. 7. Example of sensor and motor signals of the hexapod robot for object transportation. The robot first walked backward and then autonomously climbed the object due to the interaction between the leg movements and the object. Afterwards it performed soft pushing and finally hard pushing to move the object across the obstacle with a height of 5 cm. The soft pushing behavior was activated by the body inclination sensor signal (BS). It will be activated if the sensor value is higher than a threshold after a certain time step. The hard pushing behavior was activated by the joint angle sensor signals of the F-joints of the front legs. We used the average value of the angle signals (AS) for this activation. Basically, the hard pushing behavior will be activated if the value is smaller than a threshold. $TL_{0,1,2}$ are the thoraco-coxal (T-) joints of the left front, middle, and hind legs. $CL_{0,1,2}$ are the coxa-trochanteral (C-) joints of the left front, middle, and hind legs (see Fig. 1). The F-joints are not shown since they have constant values. The joint angle signals of the right legs are shown in degree. The left angle signals are similar to the right ones.

fast transportation speed compared to the others (see Fig. 5) and then the hard pushing mode to strongly push the object across the obstacle. Figure 7 shows the sensors and motor signals of the robot during object transportation using the combination of the soft pushing and hard pushing modes[4].

4   Conclusion

We present the modular neural controller of a bio-inspired hexapod robot. The controller is derived from three neural networks (CPG, PSN, and VRN). Each network has its functional origin in biological neural systems (see [14] for details). The controller can generate various motor patterns for locomotion, object manipulation, and their combination (resulting in object transportation). Different object manipulation strategies can be obtained from the controller. Among them, the strategy that combines soft pushing and hard pushing allows the robot to quickly roll a large cylinder object (i.e., ≈ 2.8 times the robot's body height) and to strongly push it across an obstacle with a height up to ≈ 1.5 times the robot's body height. Although the resulting object transportation behavior is inspired by the strategy of a dung beetle, the object used in this study is still smaller than and different from the one that the beetle can transport (i.e., dung ball). Furthermore, the beetle can also transport the ball on rough terrain using its middle and hind legs while walking with its front legs. Thus, in the future work, we will investigate another object transportation mode using the middle and hind legs to transport a large ball on rough terrain. We will also apply this approach to a real hexapod robot and test it in a real environment.

Acknowledgments. We would like to thank Georg Martius for technical advise about the LpzRobots simulation software.

References

1. Cully, A., Clune, J., Tarapore, D., Mouret, J.B.: Robots that can adapt like animals. Nature **521**, 503–507 (2015)
2. Inoue, K., Fujii, S., Takubo, T., Mae, Y., Arai, T.: Ladder climbing method for the limb mechanism robot asterisk. Adv. Robot. **24**, 1557–1576 (2010)
3. Crespi, A., Karakasiliotis, K., Guignard, A., Ijspeert, A.J.: Salamandra robotica II: an amphibious robot to study salamander-like swimming and walking gaits. IEEE Trans. Robot. **29**, 308–320 (2013)
4. Bartsch, S., Planthaber, S.: Scarabaeus: a walking robot applicable to sample return missions. In: Gottscheber, A., Enderle, S., Obdrzalek, D. (eds.) EUROBOT 2008. CCIS, vol. 33, pp. 128–133. Springer, Heidelberg (2009)
5. Rehman, B.U., Focchi, M., Frigerio, M., Goldsmith, J., Caldwell, D.G., Semini, C.: Design of a hydraulically actuated arm for a quadruped robot. In: Proceedings of the International Conference on Climbing and Walking Robots, pp. 283–290 (2015)

---

[4] see http://manoonpong.com/SAB2016/V3.mp4.

6. Heppner, G., Buettner, T., Roennau, A., Dillmann, R.: Versatile - high power gripper for a six legged walking robot. In: Proceedings of the International Conference on Climbing and Walking Robots, pp. 461–468 (2014)
7. Koyachi, N., Adachi, H., Arai, T., Izumi, M., Hirose, T., Senjo, N., Murata, R.: Walk and manipulation by a hexapod with integrated limb mechanism of leg and arm. J. Robot. Soc. Jpn. **22**, 411–421 (2004)
8. Inoue, K., Ooe, K., Lee, S.: Pushing methods for working six-legged robots capable of locomotion and manipulation in three modes. In: Proceedings of the IEEE International Conference on Robotics and Automation, pp. 4742–4748 (2010)
9. Takeo, G., Takubo, T., Ohara, K., Mae, Y., Arai, T.: Internal force control for rolling operation of polygonal prism. In: Proceedings of the IEEE International Conference on Robotics and Biomimetics, pp. 586–591 (2009)
10. Philips, T.K., Pretorius, E., Scholtz, C.H.: A phylogenetic analysis of dung beetles (Scarabaeinae): unrolling an evolutionary history. Invertebr. Syst. **18**, 53–88 (2004)
11. Bässler, U., Büschges, A.: Pattern generation for stick insect walking movements-multisensory control of a locomotor program. Brain Res. Rev. **27**, 65–88 (1998)
12. Valsalam, V., Miikkulainen, R.: Modular neuroevolution for multilegged locomotion. In: Proceedings of the Genetic and Evolutionary Computation Conference, pp. 265–272 (2008)
13. Hornby, G., Takamura, S., Yamamoto, T., Fujita, M.: Autonomous evolution of dynamic gaits with two quadruped robots. IEEE Trans. Robot. Autom. **21**, 402–410 (2005)
14. Manoonpong, P., Wörgötter, F., Laksanacharoen, P.: Biologically inspired modular neural control for a leg-wheel hybrid robot. Adv. Robot. Res. **1**, 101–126 (2014)
15. Manoonpong, P., Pasemann, F., Wörgötter, F.: Sensor-driven neural control for omnidirectional locomotion and versatile reactive behaviors of walking machines. Robot. Auton. Syst. **56**, 265–288 (2008)
16. Grinke, E., Tetzlaff, C., Wörgötter, F., Manoonpong, P.: Synaptic plasticity in a recurrent neural network for versatile and adaptive behaviors of a walking robot. Front. Neurorobot. **9**, 1–15 (2015). doi:10.3389/fnbot.2015.00011
17. Pasemann, F., Hild, M., Zahedi, K.: So(2)-networks as neural oscillators. In: Proceedings of 7th International Work-Conference on Artificial and Natural Neural Networks (IWANN 2003), pp. 1042–1042 (2003)

An Adaptive Neural Mechanism with a Lizard Ear Model for Binaural Acoustic Tracking

Danish Shaikh[✉] and Poramate Manoonpong

Embodied AI and Neurorobotics Lab, Centre for BioRobotics,
Maersk Mc-Kinney Moeller Institute, University of Southern Denmark,
Odense M, Denmark
{danish,poma}@mmmi.sdu.dk

Abstract. Acoustic tracking of a moving sound source is relevant in many domains including robotic phonotaxis and human-robot interaction. Typical approaches rely on processing time-difference-of-arrival cues obtained via multi-microphone arrays with Kalman or particle filters, or other computationally expensive algorithms. We present a novel bio-inspired solution to acoustic tracking that uses only two microphones. The system is based on a neural mechanism coupled with a model of the peripheral auditory system of lizards. The peripheral auditory model provides sound direction information which the neural mechanism uses to learn the target's velocity via fast correlation-based unsupervised learning. Simulation results for tracking a pure tone acoustic target moving along a semi-circular trajectory validate our approach. Three different angular velocities in three separate trials were employed for the validation. A comparison with a Braitenberg vehicle-like steering strategy shows the improved performance of our learning-based approach.

Keywords: Binaural acoustic tracking · Correlation learning · Lizard peripheral auditory system

1 Introduction

There are several applications where acoustic target tracking can be useful. Human-robot interaction in social robots is deemed to be richer if the robot's acoustomotor response maintains its auditory focus on the subject of interest [16,19]. During phonotaxis a robot can localise acoustic sources and navigate towards them [22].

Acoustically tracking a sound source moving with fixed but unknown speed along a fixed but unknown trajectory requires that the sound source must first be successfully localised in space and this localisation must then be repeated sufficiently quickly to minimise the static tracking error. Localising a sound can be done using both interaural intensity difference (IID) and interaural time difference (ITD) cues, requiring a multi-microphone setup with at least two microphones. Generating IID cues requires a sufficiently large solid obstruction between the individual microphones to create sound shadows, while ITD cues

© Springer International Publishing Switzerland 2016
E. Tuci et al. (Eds.): SAB 2016, LNAI 9825, pp. 79–90, 2016.
DOI: 10.1007/978-3-319-43488-9_8

can be generated without the need of such obstructions. We focus on acoustic tracking of a moving sound source using only ITD cues. A sound source moving with a given velocity in a given direction with respect to the microphones generates dynamic ITD cues. The instantaneous values of these cues vary with the relative position of the sound source and the speed with which they vary depends on the relative speed of the sound source. Tracking a moving sound source thus requires transforming these relative position- and velocity-dependent cues into a desired behaviour such as robotic orientation or phonotaxis.

Acoustic target tracking has been approached via a number of techniques [7,8,11–13,17,18,24,25]. All techniques use multi-microphone arrays in various geometric configurations such as linear, square, circular or distributed arrays to extract ITD cues for localisation. Computationally intensive algorithms are also a common feature among these techniques.

We present a acoustic tracking system using two microphones that implements a neural learning mechanism. The mechanism is adapted from Input Correlation (ICO) learning [21] which is derived from a class of differential Hebbian learning rules [10]. The ICO learning architecture is characterised by its stability, fast convergence and adaptability via synaptic plasticity all of which are desirable qualities in an acoustic tracking system. The proposed learning mechanism is coupled with a model of the lizard peripheral auditory system [26] which provides sound direction information. The peripheral auditory model has been extensively studied via various robotic implementations as reviewed in [23]. The proposed mechanism is a first step towards developing a biologically-plausible neural predictive mechanism for binaural acoustic tracking, rather than an alternative to existing well-engineered approaches to acoustic tracking.

The paper is organised in the following manner. Section 2 describes the lizard ear model, its directional response and its role in sound localisation. It also briefly describes ICO learning, which is the basis for the learning mechanism presented in Sect. 3. The experimental setup is also described in Sect. 3. Section 4 presents the results of the proposed approach in tracking a moving sound source. Section 5 summarises the research and discusses future directions.

2   Background

2.1   Lizard Peripheral Auditory System Model

Lizards such as the bronze grass skink or *Mabuya macularia*, and the tokay gecko or *Gekko gecko* as depicted in Fig. 1(a), are known for their remarkably directional peripheral auditory system [3,4]. Thanks to an internal acoustical coupling of the two eardrums of the animal, formed by efficient transmission of sound through internal pathways in the head as shown in Fig. 1(b), the lizard ear achieves a directionality higher than that of any known vertebrate [3].

The lizard peripheral auditory system is small in size (the distance between the eardrums for most lizard species is 10–20 mm) with respect to the sound wavelengths (340–85 mm, corresponding to 1–4 kHz) for which it exhibits strong directionality [4]. For these wavelengths the sound pressure difference between

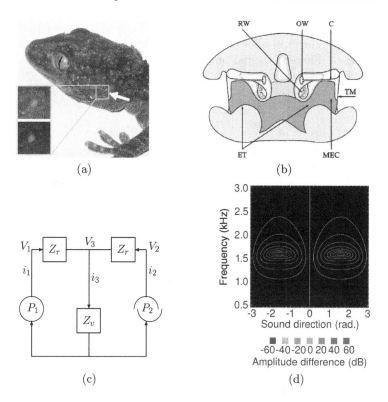

Fig. 1. (a) An eardrum visible on the side of the gecko head (redrawn from [4]). (b) early cross-sectional diagram of the lizard (*Sceloporus*) auditory system (taken from [3]). (c) ideal lumped-parameter circuit model (based on [5,6] and taken from [28]). (d) contour plot modelling binaural subtraction (refer to Eq. (2)) of the ipsilateral and contralateral responses (redrawn from [28]).

the ears is negligible due to acoustic diffraction around the animals head, thus generating negligible (1–2 dB) IID cues. The system thus converts μs-scale interaural phase differences (corresponding to ITDs) between incoming sound waves at the two ears due to the physical separation, into relatively larger (up to 40 dB) interaural vibrational amplitude differences [3] which encode information about sound direction relative to the animal. Each eardrum's vibrations are the result of the superposition of two components – an external sound pressure acting on its outer side and the equivalent internal sound pressure acting on its inner side, generated due to sound interference in the internal pathways. This process leads to contralateral (away from the sound source) cancellation and ipsilateral (towards the sound source) amplification of eardrum vibrations. In other words, the ear closer to the sound source vibrates more strongly than the ear further away from the sound source. The strengths of the vibrations depend on the relative phase difference between the incoming sound waves at the two ears.

An equivalent electrical circuit model as shown in Fig. 1(c) of the peripheral auditory system [5,6] allows one to visualise the directionality as shown in Fig. 1(d) as a difference signal obtained by subtracting the two vibrational amplitudes. The difference signal can be formulated as

$$\left|\frac{i_1}{i_2}\right| = \left|\frac{G_\mathrm{I} \cdot V_1 + G_\mathrm{C} \cdot V_2}{G_\mathrm{C} \cdot V_1 + G_\mathrm{I} \cdot V_2}\right|, \tag{1}$$

where frequency-dependent gains G_I and G_C model the effect of sound pressure on the motion of the ipsilateral and contralateral eardrum respectively. These gains are analogue filters in signal processing terminology with coefficients determined experimentally by measuring the eardrum vibrations of individual lizards via laser vibrometry [3]. Expressing i_1 and i_2 in decibels,

$$i_\mathrm{ratio} = 20 \left(\log |i_1| - \log |i_2|\right) \text{ dB}. \tag{2}$$

The model responds well for frequencies between 1–2.2 kHz, with a peak response at approximately 1.6 kHz. i_ratio is positive for $|i_1| > |i_2|$ and negative for $|i_2| > |i_1|$. The model's symmetry implies that $|i_\mathrm{ratio}|$ is the same on either side of the centre point $\theta = 0°$ and is locally symmetrical within the range $[-90°, +90°]$ (considered henceforth as the relevant range of sound direction). The difference signal given by Eq. (2) provides sound direction information in that its sign indicates whether the sound is coming from the left (positive sign) or from the right (negative sign), while its magnitude corresponds to the relative angular displacement of the sound source with respect to the median.

2.2   Input Correlation (ICO) Learning

ICO learning [21] is online unsupervised learning in which synaptic weight update is driven by cross-correlation of two types of input signals – "predictive" signal(s) which are earlier occurring stimuli and a "reflex" signal which is a later occurring stimulus arriving after a finite delay and drives a reflex (Fig. 2). The output of the ICO learning mechanism is a linear combination of the reflex input and the predictive input(s). The synaptic weight of the reflex input is set to a constant positive value such as 1, representing an unchanging reflex signal. The learning goal of ICO learning is to predict the occurrence of the reflex signal by using the predictive signal, thereby allowing an agent to react earlier. Essentially, the agent learns to execute an anticipatory action to avoid the reflex. During learning, the synaptic weight(s) of the predictive signal(s) are updated through differential Hebbian learning [9,10] using the cross-correlation between the predictive and reflex inputs. The synaptic weights tend to stabilise when the reflex signal is nullified [21], which implies that the reflex signal has been successfully avoided. ICO learning is characterised by its speed and stability and has been successfully applied to generate adaptive behaviour in real robots [14,15,20].

3   Materials and Methods

The task of acoustic tracking is defined as follows – a robotic agent must learn the correct angular turning velocity which allows it to rotate sufficiently quickly along a fixed axis so as to point in the direction of the instantaneous position of a sound source moving with an unknown velocity in a given direction along a pre-defined semi-circular arc-shaped trajectory. To solve this task we employ an adaptive neural architecture that combines the auditory preprocessing of the lizard peripheral auditory model and the neural ICO learning mechanism as described next.

3.1   The Adaptive Neural Architecture

Figure 2 shows the neural mechanism embedded as a closed-loop circuit in the task environment. The central idea is for the robotic agent to learn the temporal relationship between the perceived sound direction *before* turning and *after* turning. The temporal relationship is encoded in the synaptic weights of the neural mechanism, which are used to calculate the correct angular turning velocity. Since the temporal relationship depends on the angular velocity, a given set of learned synaptic weights can only represent a given angular velocity. To learn a new angular velocity, the synaptic weights must therefore be re-learned.

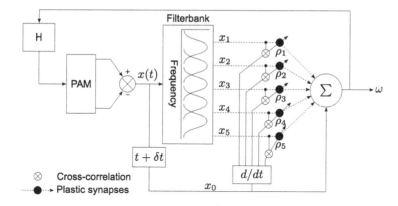

Fig. 2. Neural mechanism for acoustic tracking as a closed-loop system.

The output of the neural mechanism ω is the angular velocity, defined as the angular deviation per time step, required to turn the robot fast enough to point at the appropriate loudspeaker in one time step. ω is transformed into corresponding ITD cues via the environmental transfer function H. The peripheral auditory model (PAM) translates these cues to a difference signal $x(t)$ (given by Eq. (2)) which encodes information regarding sound direction. A filter bank decomposes $x(t)$ into frequency components $x_k(t)$, where $k = 1, \ldots, N$, to extract frequency information. The filter bank comprises 5 bandpass filters, each with a 3 dB cut-off frequency of 200 Hz and center frequencies at 1.2 kHz, 1.4 kHz, 1.6 kHz, 1.8 kHz and 2.0 kHz. This results in $N = 5$ filtered signals outputs of the filter bank. This step is necessary because in the absence of sound frequency information the peripheral auditory model provides ambiguous information regarding the sound direction. This is because the output of the peripheral auditory model is non-linearly dependent on the sound frequency. The magnitude responses of the filters in the filter bank represent the receptive fields of individual auditory neurons. These receptive fields, better known as spectro-temporal receptive fields [1], are the range of sound frequencies that most optimally stimulate the neuron. The filtered signals $x_k(t)$ are used as inputs which are then correlated with the derivative of the unfiltered difference signal $x_0(t)$. The input signals $x_k(t)$ can be viewed as the predictive signals used to predict the instantaneous sound direction before turning, while the unfiltered difference signal $x_0(t)$ can be viewed as the "reflex" or the retrospective signal generated after turning.

In ICO learning, once the reflex signal is nullified, the synaptic weights are stabilised; thereby generating a behavioural response that prevents future occurrences of the reflex signal. Here, as soon as the sound moves to a new position along its trajectory, a new and finite retrospective signal x_0 is generated. This signal is then nullified after turning, before the sound moves to a new position along its trajectory. Our approach can therefore be viewed as one successful iteration of ICO learning being repeated for each new position of the sound source as it moves along its trajectory. This implies that the synaptic weights can grow uncontrollably if the learning continues indefinitely. To avoid this condition, we introduce a stopping criterion for the learning – the learning stops when the tracking error θ_e becomes less than $0.5°$. θ_e is defined as the difference between the angular deviation of the robot and the angular deviation of the sound source in *one* time step. In other words, the learning stops when the robot is able to point to within $0.5°$ from the position of the sound source within *one* time step.

3.2   The Experimental Setup

The experimental setup in simulation, as illustrated in Fig. 3, comprises a virtual loudspeaker array which generates relevant tones. The array comprises 37 loudspeakers arranged in a semi-circle in the azimuth plane. The angular displacement between consecutive loudspeakers is $5°$. To simulate motion of a single sound source, the loudspeakers are turned on sequentially starting from the loudspeaker at one of the ends of the array. To maintain sound continuity and simulate a continuously moving sound source (albeit in discrete steps), the next loudspeaker plays immediately after the previous loudspeaker has stopped. A given tone can thus be moved across the array along a semi-circular trajectory from either the left or the right with a given angular velocity. The angular velocity is defined as the angular displacement in radians every 10 time steps. When a given loudspeaker is turned on, it plays a tone for 10 time steps before it is turned off and the next consecutive loudspeaker is turned on immediately afterwards. This process is repeated until the last loudspeaker in the array is reached.

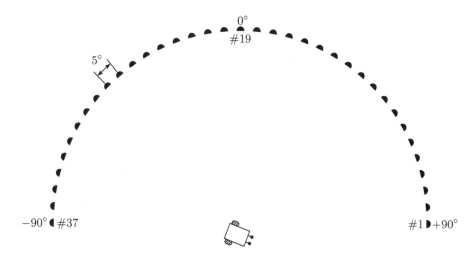

Fig. 3. The simulation setup.

In the current setup, the direction of movement of sound is chosen to be from the left to the right of the array. The movement of sound from loudspeaker #1 to loudspeaker #37 is defined as one complete iteration. Since one iteration may be insufficient to learn the correct angular velocity, the process is repeated from the first to the last loudspeaker until the synaptic weights converge.

The robot that must track the moving sound source is located at the midpoint of the diameter of the semi-circle and is only allowed to rotate on a fixed axis. To track the sound source by rotational movements, the robot must turn with a sufficiently large angular velocity in order to point towards the instantaneous position of sound source before the sound moves to a different position along its trajectory. The angular velocity of the robot is defined as the angular rotation per time step. The goal of the learning algorithm is to learn the correct angular velocity that would allow the robot to turn and point towards the current loudspeaker in *one* time step, starting from the time step at which the given loudspeaker started playing the tone.

The learning takes place as follows. The robot initially points in a random direction (chosen as 97°). Loudspeaker #1 emits a 2.2 kHz tone, chosen because sufficient directional information from the peripheral auditory model is available at this frequency. The robot uses the extracted sound direction information to turn towards the current loudspeaker with an angular velocity given by

$$\omega = \rho_0 x_0 + \sum_{k=1}^{N} \rho_k x_k, \text{ where } N = 5. \tag{3}$$

After the turn is complete, the robot again extracts sound direction information via the peripheral auditory model and determines $x_0(t+\delta t)$. Finally, the synaptic weights ρ_k are updated according to the learning rule

$$\frac{d\rho_k(t)}{dt} = \mu x_k(t)\frac{dx_0(t)}{dt}, \text{ where } k = 1,\ldots,N. \tag{4}$$

After this step, loudspeaker #1 is turned off and the next loudspeaker in the array (loudspeaker #2) emits a tone of the same frequency as earlier and the learning procedure described above is repeated.

The acoustic tracking performance is individually evaluated for three different angular velocities of the sound source – $0.5°$/time step, $1.0°$/time step and $1.5°$/time step. For all trials, the neural parameters are set to the following values – the learning rate $\mu = 0.0001$ and synaptic weight $\rho_0 = 0.00001$. All plastic synaptic weights ρ_k are initially set to zero and updated according to Eq. (4). The neural mechanism's performance is also compared with a Braitenberg vehicle-like [2] sensorimotor mechanism that generates rotational motion. The Braitenberg mechanism is simulated by turning off the learning and setting the weights ρ_k to constant values. Two sets of randomly-chosen weights are used – one ($\rho_k = [0.0114, 0.0303, 0.0301, 0.0152, 0.0227]$) resulting in a relatively small angular turning velocity and another ($\rho_k = [0.0652, 0.0725, 0.0102, 0.0731, 0.0506]$) resulting in a relatively large angular turning velocity.

4   Results and Discussion

Figure 4 shows the tracking error θ_e which reduces exponentially over time for the three trials. The insets reveal the evolution of θ_e for the last iteration of the movement of the sound source.

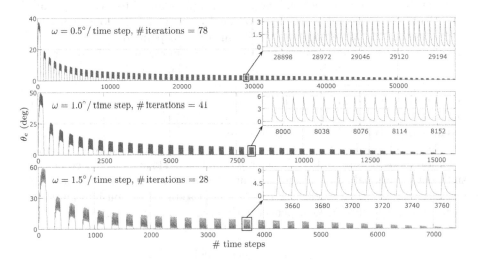

Fig. 4. Evolution of tracking error θ_e over time for the three separate trials in which the sound source is moving with three separate angular velocities – $0.5°$/time step (top panel), $1.0°$/time step (middle panel) and $1.5°$/time step (bottom panel). The insets show θ_e for a single iteration as an example.

The spikes in θ_e represent a mismatch between the position at which the robot was pointing last and the new position of the sound source. This creates finite ITD cues from which the robot extracts sound direction information via the peripheral auditory model. The robot then turns towards the sound source with the last learned angular turning velocity, reducing the tracking error. This process repeats over each subsequent time step, exponentially reducing the tracking error, until the stopping criterion is met. The number of iterations required to reach the stopping criterion, where the weights stabilise, decreases for increasing angular velocity of the sound source. This is because the mismatch between the direction at which the robot was pointing last and the current position of the sound source is relatively greater for greater angular velocity of the sound source. This results in relatively larger predictive signals, and consequently a relatively larger correlation term $x_k(t)\frac{dx_0(t)}{dt}$ per time step in Eq. (4). This consequently results in relatively faster weight updates, reducing the overall time taken to learn the correct angular velocity.

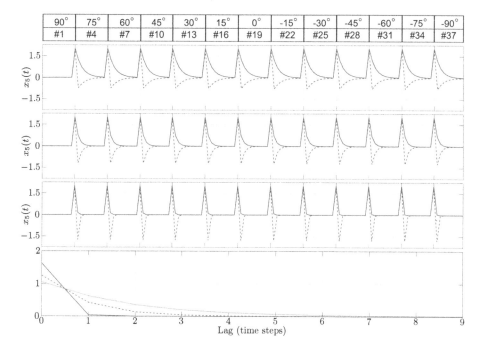

Fig. 5. Snapshots of the evolution of the predictive signal $x_5(t)$ (solid line) and the derivative of retrospective signal $\frac{dx_0(t)}{dt}$ (dashed line) for a sound source moving with angular velocity of $1.5°/$ time step. **Top panel**. The instantaneous position of the sound and the corresponding loudspeaker designation. **Second − fourth panels**. Example snapshots for iteration #14 (second panel), #21 (third panel) and the last iteration (#28, fourth panel). **Bottom panel**. The positive-lag cross-correlation of $x_5(t)$ and $\frac{dx_0(t)}{dt}$ for iteration #14 (dotted line), #21 (dashed line) and #28 (solid line).

An example of the predictive signal x_5 and the derivative $\frac{dx_0(t)}{dt}$ of the retrospective signal x_0, for three separate iterations for the sound source moving with an angular velocity of 1.5°/ time step, is shown in Fig. 5. The learning results in faster turns by the robot as indicated by the decreasing slope of $x_5(t)$ as shown.

The maximum correlation as shown in the bottom panel in Fig. 5 between the predictive and retrospective signals increases as the number of iterations increases. This confirms that as the synaptic weights increase, consequently increasing the learned angular turning velocity as learning progresses, the correlation between the predictive and retrospective signals also increases, resulting in an increasing correlation term in Eq. (4).

Figure 6 shows a comparison of the correlation learning mechanism to the Braitenberg vehicle-like sensorimotor mechanism for rotational turning. Depending on the synaptic weights chosen, the angular turning velocity of the robot may be either less or greater than the angular velocity of the sound source. Thus the robot either takes a relatively long time to reach the target's position or overshoots the target's position, resulting in a relatively greater tracking error in both cases. On the other hand, the learning mechanism allows the robot to learn a relatively accurate angular turning velocity that closely matches that of the sound source, resulting in a relatively smaller tracking error.

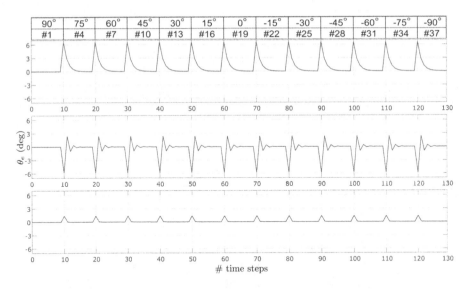

Fig. 6. Braitenberg vehicle-like mechanism for rotational turning versus the correlation learning mechanism. The panels show the evolution of tracking error θ_e over time in the last iteration for the sound source moving with an angular velocity of 1.5°/ time step. **Top panel**. The instantaneous position of the sound and the corresponding loudspeaker designation. **Second and third panels**. θ_e for the Braitenberg approach where the angular turning velocity is less (second panel) and greater (third panel) than 1.5°/ time step. **Bottom panel**. θ_e with correlation learning where the learned angular turning velocity closely matches with 1.5°/ time step.

5   Conclusions and Future Directions

A neural mechanism for acoustic tracking is presented which allows a simulated robotic agent to learn the correct angular velocity necessary to turn and align itself towards the instantaneous position of a virtual sound source moving along a semi-circular arc-shaped trajectory. The learning rule correlates the perceived sound direction information, obtained via a peripheral auditory model of lizard hearing, before and after turning to update the synaptic weights. The learned synaptic weights thus correspond to the angular velocity of the sound source. The mechanism successfully learned three different angular velocities. We aim to validate the approach as a next step in an identical experimental setup by implementing the neural mechanism on a real mobile robot.

In the presented approach the robot only turns after the sound source has moved to a new location along its trajectory. There is a finite and unavoidable delay between the sound source moving to a new location and the robot completing its turn. The same mechanism may be used to predict this time delay, so that after learning the robot would turn fast enough to point at the next position of the sound source at the same instant as the sound source itself. Such a system could be viewed as an internal forward model [27] for acoustic tracking.

References

1. Aertsen, A., Johannesma, P., Hermes, D.: Spectro-temporal receptive fields of auditory neurons in the grassfrog. Biol. Cybern. **38**(4), 235–248 (1980)
2. Braitenberg, V.: Vehicles: Experiments in Synthetic Psychology. MIT Press, Bradford Books, Cambridge (1984)
3. Christensen-Dalsgaard, J., Manley, G.: Directionality of the lizard ear. J. Exp. Biol. **208**(6), 1209–1217 (2005)
4. Christensen-Dalsgaard, J., Tang, Y., Carr, C.: Binaural processing by the gecko auditory periphery. J. Neurophysiol. **105**(5), 1992–2004 (2011)
5. Fletcher, N.: Acoustic Systems in Biology. Oxford University Press, New York (1992)
6. Fletcher, N., Thwaites, S.: Physical models for the analysis of acoustical systems in biology. Q. Rev. Biophys. **12**(1), 25–65 (1979)
7. Ju, T., Shao, H., Peng, Q.: Tracking the moving sound target based on distributed microphone pairs. In: 2013 10th International Computer Conference on Wavelet Active Media Technology and Information Processing (ICCWAMTIP), pp. 330–334, December 2013
8. Ju, T., Shao, H., Peng, Q., Zhang, M.: Tracking the moving sound target based on double arrays. In: 2012 International Conference on Computational Problem-Solving (ICCP), pp. 315–319, October 2012
9. Klopf, A.: A neuronal model of classical conditioning. Psychobiology **16**(2), 85–125 (1988)
10. Kosko, B.: Differential Hebbian learning. AIP Conf. Proc. **151**(1), 277–282 (1986)
11. Kwak, K.: Sound source tracking of moving speaker using multi-channel microphones in robot environments. In: 2011 IEEE International Conference on Robotics and Biomimetics (ROBIO), pp. 3017–3020, December 2011

12. Liang, Z., Ma, X., Dai, X.: Robust tracking of moving sound source using multiple model Kalman filter. Appl. Acoust. **69**(12), 1350–1355 (2008)
13. Liang, Z., Ma, X., Dai, X.: Robust tracking of moving sound source using scaled unscented particle filter. Appl. Acoust. **69**(8), 673–680 (2008)
14. Manoonpong, P., Geng, T., Kulvicius, T., Porr, B., Wörgötter, F.: Adaptive, fast walking in a biped robot under neuronal control and learning. PLoS Comput. Biol. **3**(7), 1–16 (2007)
15. Manoonpong, P., Wörgötter, F.: Adaptive sensor-driven neural control for learning in walking machines. In: Leung, C.S., Lee, M., Chan, J.H. (eds.) ICONIP 2009, Part II. LNCS, vol. 5864, pp. 47–55. Springer, Heidelberg (2009)
16. Nakadai, K., Lourens, T., Okuno, H., Kitano, H.: Active audition for humanoid. In: Proceedings of 17th National Conference on Artificial Intelligence (AAAI-2000), pp. 832–839. AAAI (2000)
17. Ning, F., Gao, D., Niu, J., Wei, J.: Combining compressive sensing with particle filter for tracking moving wideband sound sources. In: 2015 IEEE International Conference on Signal Processing, Communications and Computing (ICSPCC), pp. 1–6, September 2015
18. Nishie, S., Akagi, M.: Acoustic sound source tracking for a moving object using precise Doppler-shift measurement. In: 2013 Proceedings of the 21st European Signal Processing Conference (EUSIPCO), pp. 1–5, September 2013
19. Okuno, H., Nakadai, K., Hidai, K.I., Mizoguchi, H., Kitano, H.: Human robot non-verbal interaction empowered by real-time auditory and visual multiple-talker tracking. Adv. Robot. **17**(2), 115–130 (2003)
20. Poor, B., Wörgötter, F.: Fast heterosynaptic learning in a robot food retrieval task inspired by the limbic system. Biosystems **89**(1–3), 294–299 (2007). Papers Presented at the 6th International Workshop on Neural Coding
21. Porr, B., Wörgötter, F.: Strongly improved stability and faster convergence of temporal sequence learning by utilising input correlations only. Neural Comput. **18**(6), 1380–1412 (2006)
22. Reeve, R., Webb, B.: New neural circuits for robot phonotaxis. Philos. Trans. R. Soc. Lond. A Math. Phys. Eng. Sci. **361**(1811), 2245–2266 (2003)
23. Shaikh, D., Hallam, J., Christensen-Dalsgaard, J.: From "Ear" to there: a review of biorobotic models of auditory processing in lizards. Biol. Cybern. (2016, in press)
24. Tsuji, D., Suyama, K.: A moving sound source tracking based on two successive algorithms. In: 2009 IEEE International Symposium on Circuits and Systems, ISCAS 2009, pp. 2577–2580, May 2009
25. Valin, J.M., Michaud, F., Rouat, J.: Robust localization and tracking of simultaneous moving sound sources using beamforming and particle filtering. Robot. Auton. Syst. **55**(3), 216–228 (2007)
26. Wever, E.: The Reptile Ear: Its Structure and Function. Princeton University Press, Princeton (1978)
27. Wolpert, D., Ghahramani, Z., Jordan, M.: An internal model for sensorimotor integration. Science **269**(5232), 1880–1882 (1995)
28. Zhang, L.: Modelling directional hearing in lizards. Ph.D. thesis, Maersk McKinney Moller Institute, Faculty of Engineering, University of Southern Denmark (2009)

Artificial Neural Network Based Compliant Control for Robot Arms

Vince Jankovics[1], Stefan Mátéfi-Tempfli[1], and Poramate Manoonpong[2(✉)]

[1] The Mads Clausen Institute,
University of Southern Denmark, Sonderborg, Denmark
`vincejankovics@gmail.com`
[2] Embodied AI and Neurorobotics Lab, Center for BioRobotics, The Maersk
Mc-Kinney Moeller Institute, University of Southern Denmark, Odense M, Denmark
`poma@mmmi.sdu.dk`

Abstract. The aim of this paper is to present an artificial neural network (ANN) based adaptive nonlinear control approach of a robot arm, with highlight on its capability as a compliant control scheme. The approach is based on a computed torque law and consists of two main components: a feedforward controller (approximated by the ANN) and a proportional-derivative (PD) feedback loop. Here, the feedforward controller is used to approximate the nonlinear system dynamics and can also adapt to the long-term dynamics of the arm while the PD feedback loop can be tuned to obtain proper compliant behaviour to deal with instantaneous disturbances (e.g., collisions). The employed controller structure makes it possible to decouple these two components for individual parameter adjustments. The performance of the control approach is evaluated and demonstrated in physical simulation which shows promising results.

Keywords: Nonlinear control · Artificial neural network · Compliance · Robot arm

1 Introduction

Although robot arms have been developed in the past decades, there are still several concerns about their development. In many cases linear control strategies are sufficient by suppressing the nonlinear characteristics of the robot arm system, or using gain scheduled techniques [21]. However, in some cases nonlinear behaviour due to dry friction and backlash can be observed. Therefore, further investigation has to be made in order to achieve a high performance control system that can compensate the nonlinearity [4,6]. Control techniques to deal with nonlinear systems usually require precise knowledge of the system (e.g. dynamic inversion). Thus, they are difficult to implement in many cases.

From this point of view, model-free control techniques can be used to provide a solution for the system where the equations governing the system are unknown [17]. Artificial neural networks (ANNs) are universal approximators [2], i.e., they

E. Tuci et al. (Eds.): SAB 2016, LNAI 9825, pp. 91–100, 2016.
DOI: 10.1007/978-3-319-43488-9_9

are able to approximate any unknown function after a sufficient learning phase. This makes them a good solution for model-free control of nonlinear systems [3,9,12,13,17].

In addition to the nonlinear control aspect, safety is a key concern for robot arms, since they might have to interact with humans. In order to avoid injuries and achieve safe human-robot interaction different approaches have been developed, such as variable stiffness actuators [14,18], which requires special hardware development, or safe planning [16], which requires complete perception of the environment. Other approaches include collision detection and reaction [1,10] that can deal with more dynamic collisions but can complicate the control system design process.

Compared to all these approaches, we present here an alternative control technique that combines the adaptive nature of ANN based control and the virtual compliance control provided by an additional proportional-derivative (PD) control law. This control technique, inspired by [8,15], can decouple between short-term (collisions) and long-term (changes in the environment and the system) disturbance compensation.

This provides a simple and intuitive controller design without any hardware modification for a robot arm. Additionally, in this study, we aim to also investigate whether the tracking error of the arm can be kept low via the ANN based control and proper compliant tuning such that the arm can react to collisions with flexibility.

The article is organized as follows. First we describe the robot arm model used in this study. Second, we present the artificial neural network based compliant control approach together with its subcomponents for generating movement and compliant behaviour of the arm. Third, we illustrate the performance of the controller as an adaptive compliant control solution, followed by conclusion.

2   Robot Arm Model

The dynamics of an n-link rigid robotic manipulator can be expressed in the Lagrange form as:

$$\mathbf{M}(\mathbf{q})\ddot{\mathbf{q}} + \mathbf{C}(\mathbf{q},\dot{\mathbf{q}})\dot{\mathbf{q}} + \mathbf{G}(\mathbf{q}) + \mathbf{F}(\dot{\mathbf{q}}) + \boldsymbol{\tau}_d = \boldsymbol{\tau}(t), \tag{1}$$

where $\mathbf{q}(t) \in \mathbb{R}^n$ the joint variable vector, $\mathbf{M}(\mathbf{q})$ the inertia matrix, $\mathbf{C}(\mathbf{q},\dot{\mathbf{q}})$ the Coriolis and centripetal matrix, $\mathbf{G}(\mathbf{q})$ the gravity vector, and $\mathbf{F}(\dot{\mathbf{q}})$ the friction. Bounded unknown disturbances (including modelling errors) are denoted by $\boldsymbol{\tau}_d$, and the applied torque is $\boldsymbol{\tau}(t)$ [7]. The structure of the 2DOF robot arm used in this study is shown in Fig. 1a and its physically 3D model simulated in the realistic robot simulator LpzRobots [11] is shown in Fig. 1b.

The computed torque control law can cancel all nonlinearity of the system by adding a linear error correction term to the feedforward part, which can be described as:

$$\boldsymbol{\tau}(t) = \underbrace{\mathbf{M}(\mathbf{q})\ddot{\mathbf{q}} + \mathbf{C}(\mathbf{q},\dot{\mathbf{q}})\dot{\mathbf{q}} + \mathbf{G}(\mathbf{q}) + \mathbf{F}(\dot{\mathbf{q}})}_{\text{feedforward}} - \underbrace{\mathbf{M}(\mathbf{q})(\mathbf{K}_v\dot{\mathbf{e}} + \mathbf{K}_p\mathbf{e})}_{\text{feedback}}, \tag{2}$$

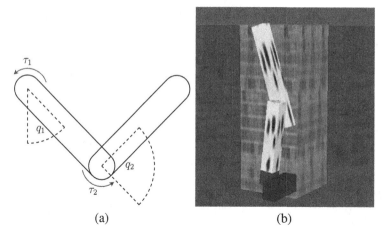

(a)   (b)

Fig. 1. (a) 2-link planar robot arm. (b) The simulated robot arm using the LPZRobots simulation environment [11].

where $\mathbf{e} = \mathbf{q}_d - \mathbf{q}$ (subtracting desired joint position vector from the actual one), and $\mathbf{K}_v$, $\mathbf{K}_p$ are constant gain matrices.

With this strategy, the computed torque consists of two components, which are feedforward and feedback. This separability makes it possible to generate compliant behaviour, and still keep the tracking error low. The feedforward part, acting as trajectory control, takes care of the desired movement generation of the system (i.e., carrying an object along a path) while the feedback part with its gains ($\mathbf{K}_v$, $\mathbf{K}_p$) allows for compliance and flexibility of the robot joints when instantaneous disturbances (such as collisions) occur.

3   Artificial Neural Network Based Compliant Control

Based on (2), the control of the 2-link robot arm (Fig. 1) consists of two parts, where an ANN can approximate the feedforward component (Fig. 2).

Function Representation: A multilayer ANN is proven to be able to approximate any function with finitely many discontinuities to arbitrary precision [5]. This makes it an excellent tool for nonlinear control systems [8], i.e. a properly trained network can represent any function, so:

$$\mathbf{f}(\mathbf{x}) = \mathbf{W}^T \mathscr{F}(\mathbf{V}^T \mathbf{x}) + \varepsilon(\mathbf{x}), \tag{3}$$

where $\mathbf{f}(x)$ is an unknown function, and $\varepsilon(\mathbf{x})$ is the reconstruction error. It is proven in [2] that there exists ideal weights $\mathbf{W}$ and $\mathbf{V}$ with finite number of neurons such that the reconstruction error is 0 ($\varepsilon = 0$). In practice it is sufficient if $\|\varepsilon\| < \varepsilon_n$, i.e., the function approximation is good enough for the application.

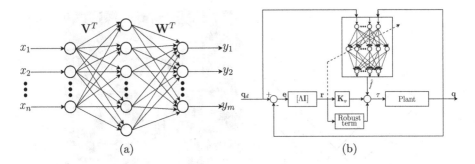

Fig. 2. The ANN's and the control system's structure. (a) A 3 layer ANN with $\mathbf{x}$ as input (e.g. [$\mathbf{q}_d$, $\mathbf{q}$]) and $\mathbf{y}$ as output ($\mathbf{f}$, the torques required), which is described by (3), (b) The whole system with the control and tuning signals.

The choice of activation function can change the approximation capabilities of the network significantly [5]. Even though it is possible in theory to reconstruct an arbitrary function, a prior knowledge of the system can reduce the adaptation time and increase the overall performance.

Since the system in question is mechanical, it can be mostly approximated with smooth functions but there are also nonlinear friction effects (static friction) which can be approximated by piecewise continuous functions. Taking this into account an augmented network structure was considered as it is suggested in [15], which consist of a hidden layer with 2 different neurons, with $\mathscr{F}_1$ and $\mathscr{F}_2$ activation functions (smooth and nonsmooth, respectively).

The network's output is then:

$$\mathbf{f}(\mathbf{x}) = \hat{\mathbf{W}}_1^T \mathscr{F}_1(\hat{\mathbf{V}}_1^T \mathbf{x}) + \hat{\mathbf{W}}_2^T \mathscr{F}_2(\hat{\mathbf{V}}_2^T \mathbf{x}) + \varepsilon(\mathbf{x}), \tag{4}$$

where the weights $\mathbf{W}_1$, $\mathbf{V}_1$ connect the neurons with smooth, and the weights $\mathbf{W}_2$, $\mathbf{V}_2$ connect the neurons with the nonsmooth activation function to the input and output layers.

Here, a sigmoid transfer function is used as our smooth activation function while a nonsmooth activation function for friction compensation can be modelled as [15]:

$$\mathscr{F}_2(x) = \begin{cases} 0 & \text{if } x \leq 0 \\ 1 - \exp(-x) & \text{if } x > 0 \end{cases} \tag{5}$$

The computed torque law as shown in (2) combined with (4) becomes:

$$\boldsymbol{\tau}(t) = \underbrace{\hat{\mathbf{W}}_1^T \mathscr{F}_1(\hat{\mathbf{V}}_1^T \mathbf{x}) + \hat{\mathbf{W}}_2^T \mathscr{F}_2(\hat{\mathbf{V}}_2^T \mathbf{x})}_{\text{feedforward}} + \underbrace{\mathbf{K}_v \mathbf{r}}_{\text{feedback}} + \underbrace{\mathbf{K}_z (\|\hat{\mathbf{Z}}\| + Z_M)\mathbf{r}}_{\text{robustifying term}}, \tag{6}$$

where the signals:

$$\mathbf{e} = \mathbf{q}_d - \mathbf{q} \qquad \text{tracking error,}$$

$$\mathbf{r} = \dot{\mathbf{e}} + \Lambda \mathbf{e} \qquad \text{filtered tracking error,}$$

$$\mathbf{x} = \left[\mathbf{e}^T \dot{\mathbf{e}}^T \mathbf{q}_d^T \dot{\mathbf{q}}_d^T \ddot{\mathbf{q}}_d^T\right]^T \qquad \text{ANN input vector,}$$

and $\hat{\mathbf{Z}}$ is a block diagonal matrix containing $\hat{\mathbf{V}}$ and $\hat{\mathbf{W}}$.

The *robustifying term* is added to guarantee stability with higher weights, proposed by [8], and the design parameters Λ, $\mathbf{K}_v$, $\mathbf{K}_z$ are symmetric, positive definite gain matrices, and Z_M is a bound on the unknown target weight norms.

Weight Tuning: We use a standard error backpropagation learning algorithm with an additional so-called forgetting term to train the network. The forgetting term is used to introduce saturation of the weights, which guarantees bounded weights, i.e. stable behaviour [9]. The weights are adjusted during the learning process, which is described by the differential equations:

$$\dot{\hat{\mathbf{W}}}_1 = \mathbf{F}\left[\left(\hat{\mathscr{F}}_1 - \hat{\mathscr{F}}_1' \hat{\mathbf{V}}_1 \mathbf{x}\right) \mathbf{r}^T - \kappa \|\mathbf{r}\| \hat{\mathbf{W}}_1\right], \tag{7a}$$

$$\dot{\hat{\mathbf{W}}}_2 = \mathbf{G}\left[\hat{\mathscr{F}}_2 \mathbf{r}^T - \kappa \|\mathbf{r}\| \hat{\mathbf{W}}_2\right], \tag{7b}$$

$$\dot{\hat{\mathbf{V}}}_1 = \mathbf{H}\left[\mathbf{x}\left(\hat{\mathscr{F}}_1'^T \hat{\mathbf{W}}_1 \mathbf{r}\right)^T - \kappa \|\mathbf{r}\| \hat{\mathbf{V}}_1\right], \tag{7c}$$

$$\dot{\hat{\mathbf{V}}}_2 = 0. \tag{7d}$$

$\mathbf{F}$, $\mathbf{G}$, and $\mathbf{H}$ are the learning rates, and $\hat{\mathscr{F}} \equiv \mathscr{F}(\hat{\mathbf{V}}^T x)$ and in case of sigmoid activation function, the derivative is $\hat{\mathscr{F}}' \equiv \hat{\mathscr{F}}(1 - \hat{\mathscr{F}})$. Choosing higher rates makes the leaning process faster, but increasing them too much can produce oscillatory and unstable behaviour. $\hat{\mathbf{V}}_2$ is here kept constant.

Note that this learning rule is described in continuous time, but in a discrete time controller the forward Euler method is sufficient with small enough dt, so the weights are updated at each time step as:

$$\hat{\mathbf{W}}_{1,k+1} = \hat{\mathbf{W}}_{1,k} + \mathrm{d}t\dot{\hat{\mathbf{W}}}_{1,k}, \tag{8a}$$

$$\hat{\mathbf{W}}_{2,k+1} = \hat{\mathbf{W}}_{2,k} + \mathrm{d}t\dot{\hat{\mathbf{W}}}_{2,k}, \tag{8b}$$

$$\hat{\mathbf{V}}_{1,k+1} = \hat{\mathbf{V}}_{1,k} + \mathrm{d}t\dot{\hat{\mathbf{V}}}_{1,k}. \tag{8c}$$

Compliant Control: As mentioned above, the feedforward part is responsible for providing the necessary input to the system based on the modelled dynamics, and on top of that the feedback part (PD loop) eliminates the unmodelled or instantaneous disturbances, which are not present in the system long enough for the adaptation, so the behaviour can be described by:

$$\mathbf{f}(\mathbf{q}, \dot{\mathbf{q}}) + \boldsymbol{\tau}_d = \hat{\mathbf{f}} + \boldsymbol{\tau}_{PD}, \tag{9}$$

where $\mathbf{f}$ describes the dynamics of the system, as it is described by (1), $\hat{\mathbf{f}}$ is the approximation of this by the ANN, and $\boldsymbol{\tau}_{PD}$ is the PD compensation. If it is assumed that $\mathbf{f} \approx \hat{\mathbf{f}}$, then the disturbance is eliminated by the feedback control. The PD law is described as:

$$\boldsymbol{\tau}_{PD} = \mathbf{K}_p \mathbf{e} + \mathbf{K}_d \dot{\mathbf{e}}. \tag{10}$$

This law results in a virtual spring-damper system, with $\mathbf{e} = 0$ equilibrium point. Choosing higher or lower $\mathbf{K}_p$ and $\mathbf{K}_d$ can make the system's response stiffer or softer.

This can be analogously applied with the control law described by (6) for robot arm control. It is important to note that the robustifying term, which has the same effect as the PD part, needs to be taken into account when choosing $\mathbf{K}_v$ and $\boldsymbol{\Lambda}$. It will make the arm stiffer with the increasing weight norms, so the compliant performance requirements can be violated in the initial learning phase and in extreme approximation errors (i.e., when the network is not trained properly).

4   Simulation Results

The control algorithm was tested in simulations. The performance was compared to a conventional PID controller.

Here, the parameters of our developed controller, described by (6) and (7) were set to: $K_v = 1$, $\Lambda = 5$, $K_z = 20$, $Z_m = 1$, $\kappa = 0.0001$, $F = 100$, $G = 100$, $H = 100$. The network's input was the vector $\mathbf{x} = \begin{bmatrix} \mathbf{e}^T \dot{\mathbf{e}}^T \mathbf{q}_d^T \dot{\mathbf{q}}_d^T \ddot{\mathbf{q}}_d^T \end{bmatrix}^T$ and the output was the approximated torques τ required to follow the desired trajectories. Therefore, the number of input, output, and hidden neurons was set to 10, 2, and 16, respectively.

Figure 3 shows the performance of the PID and the ANN controller for a sinusoidal reference signal. The PD gains for the developed algorithm is kept low so the response mainly represents the ANN's performance. The learning curve is shown in Fig. 4. It can be seen that the network successfully learned after $t = 0.5$ s where the weights converge.

Figure 5 shows the response to disturbances, an instantaneous push force at $t = 2.5$ s, and a change of the weight of the carried mass at $t = 5.0$ s. The learning curve shown in Fig. 6, which shows that the weights are not changed significantly at $t = 2.5$ s, so the disturbance is compensated by the PD loop, however at $t = 5.0$ s the ANN learns the new dynamics of the system eliminating the tracking error, that the PID controller cannot do with low feedback gains.

Changing the learning rates (F, G, H) can increase the speed of learning, but it also means that the network reacts to collisions which is undesirable (and can also lead to oscillatory response), so the rates were empirically set to the values described above to achieve the desired performance.

The arm in motion can be seen at youtu.be/ZHHx3eUzBc4.

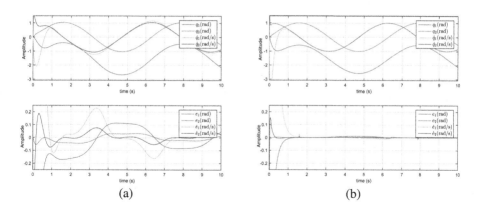

Fig. 3. The system's performance for sinusoidal reference signal, showing the joint positions and velocities, and the tracking errors. (a) PID with $K_p = 100$, $K_d = 30$, $K_i = 20$. (b) ANN with $K_v = 1$, $L = 5$, $K_z = 20$, $Z_m = 1$, $\kappa = 0.0001$, $F = 100$, $G = 100$, $H = 100$.

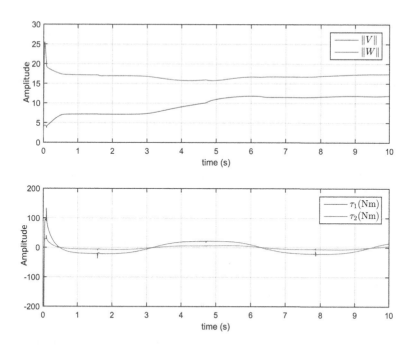

Fig. 4. ANN learning curve and actuator torques with $K_v = 1$, $L = 5$, $K_z = 20$, $Z_m = 1$, $\kappa = 0.0001$, $F = 100$, $G = 100$, $H = 100$, without disturbances.

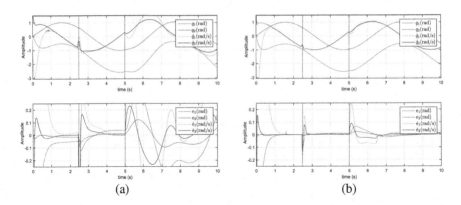

Fig. 5. The system's performance for sinusoidal reference signal with disturbances at $t = 2.5\,$s and $t = 5\,$s (dotted lines), showing the joint positions and velocities, and the tracking errors. (a) PID with $K_p = 300$, $K_d = 90$, $K_i = 60$. (b) ANN with $K_v = 1$, $L = 5$, $K_z = 20$, $Z_m = 1$, $\kappa = 0.0001$, $F = 100$, $G = 100$, $H = 100$.

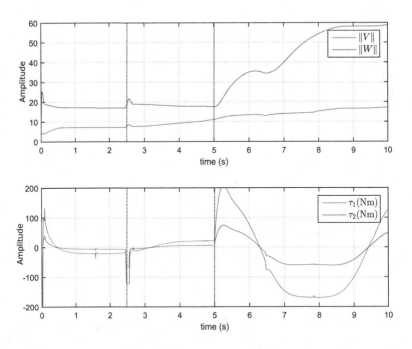

Fig. 6. ANN learning curve and actuator torques with $K_v = 1$, $L = 5$, $K_z = 20$, $Z_m = 1$, $\kappa = 0.0001$, $F = 100$, $G = 100$, $H = 100$, with disturbances at $t = 2.5\,$s and $t = 5\,$s (dotted lines).

5 Conclusions

In this work we developed an ANN based adaptive compliant control algorithm and investigated its performance. The main benefit of using this algorithm is the simple and intuitive way of decoupling the adaptive ANN based control and compliant behaviour making the controller design more intuitive. The algorithm was successfully applied to a simulated 2DOF robot arm for robust, adaptive, compliant behaviour generation of the arm.

A similar approach is described by [19, 20], using a modular neural network together with a virtual agonist-antagonist muscle mechanism to generate energy-efficient walking pattern on different surfaces. That solution requires force sensors at the end-effectors (i.e., the tip of the legs) to achieve the compliant behaviour; while, in our solution and implementation, extra force sensors are not required. We only use joint position feedback embedded in the motors. Furthermore, our control approach is torque control which is different from the position control approach of [19, 20]. In principle, torque control allows for better compliant adaptation and regulation (e.g., when the robot is in contact with objects or receives disturbances) compared to position control; thereby, our developed approach here is suitable for robot arm control and object manipulation.

In the future work, we will implement the controller on a real robot arm and test its performance to evaluate in pick and place tasks involving disturbances.

References

1. Haddadin, S., Albu-Schäffer, A., Luca, A.D., Hirzinger, G.: Collision detection and reaction: a contribution to safe physical human-robot interaction. In: 2008 IEEE/RSJ International Conference on Intelligent Robots and Systems, IROS 2008, pp. 3356–3363. IEEE (2008)
2. Hornik, K., Stinchcombe, M., White, H.: Multilayer feedforward networks are universal approximators. Neural Netw. **2**, 359–366 (1989)
3. Hunt, K.J., Sbarbaro, D., Zbikowski, R., Gawthrop, P.J.: Neural networks for control systems - a survey. Automatica **28**(6), 1083–1112 (1992)
4. Isidori, A.: Nonlinear Control Systems. Springer Science & Business Media, New York (2013)
5. Kröse, B., van der Smagt, P.: An Introduction to Neural Networks, 8th edn. The University of Amsterdam, The Netherlands (1996)
6. Krstic, M., Kokotovic, P.V., Kanellakopoulos, I.: Nonlinear and Adaptive Control Design. Wiley, New York (1995)
7. Lewis, F.L., Dawson, D.M., Abdallah, C.T.: Robot Manipulator Control. Marcel Dekker Inc., New York (2004)
8. Lewis, F.L., Yegildirek, A., Liu, K., Member, S.: Multilayer neural-net robot controller with guaranteed tracking performance. IEEE Trans. Neural Netw. **7**(2), 388–399 (1996)
9. Lewis, F., Jagannathan, S., Yesildirak, A.: Neural Network Control of Robot Manipulators and Non-linear Systems. CRC Press, Boca Raton (1998)
10. Luca, A., Albu-Schaffer, A., Haddadin, S., Hirzinger, G.: Collision detection and safe reaction with the DLR-III lightweight manipulator arm. In: IEEE/RSJ International Conference on Intelligent Robots and Systems, pp. 1623–1630. IEEE, October 2006

11. Martius, G., Hesse, F., Güttler, F., Der, R.: LPZROBOTS: a free and powerful robot simulator (2010). http://robot.informatik.uni-leipzig.de/software
12. Miller, W.T., Werbos, P.J., Sutton, R.S.: Neural Networks for Control. MIT Press, Cambridge (1995)
13. Omidvar, O., Elliott, D.L.: Neural Systems for Control. Elsevier, Amsterdam (1997)
14. Schiavi, R., Grioli, G., Sen, S., Bicchi, A.: VSA-II: a novel prototype of variable stiffness actuator for safe and performing robots interacting with humans. In: 2008 IEEE International Conference on Robotics and Automation, ICRA 2008, pp. 2171–2176. IEEE (2008)
15. Selmic, R.R., Lewis, F.L.: Neural-network approximation of piecewise continuous functions: application to friction compensation. IEEE Trans. Neural Netw. 13(3), 745–751 (2002)
16. Sisbot, E.A., Marin-Urias, L.F., Alami, R., Simeon, T.: A human aware mobile robot motion planner. IEEE Trans. Robot. 23(5), 874–883 (2007)
17. Spall, J.C., Cristion, J.A.: Model-free control of nonlinear stochastic systems with discrete-time measurements. IEEE Trans. Autom. Control 43(9), 1198–1210 (1998)
18. Tonietti, G., Schiavi, R., Bicchi, A.: Design and control of a variable stiffness actuator for safe and fast physical human/robot interaction. In: 2005 Proceedings of the 2005 IEEE International Conference on Robotics and Automation, ICRA 2005, pp. 526–531. IEEE (2005)
19. Xiong, X., Wörgötter, F., Manoonpong, P.: Neuromechanical control for hexapedal robot walking on challenging surfaces and surface classification. Robot. Auton. Syst. 62(12), 1777–1789 (2014)
20. Xiong, X., Wörgötter, F., Manoonpong, P.: Virtual agonist-antagonist mechanisms produce biological muscle-like functions: an application for robot joint control. Ind. Robot Int. J. 41(4), 340–346 (2014)
21. Yang, W., Hammoudi, N., Herrmann, G., Lowenberg, M., Chen, X.: Dynamic gain-scheduled control and extended linearisation: extensions, explicit formulae and stability. Int. J. Control 88(1), 163–179 (2015)

UESMANN: A Feed-Forward Network Capable of Learning Multiple Functions

James C. Finnis$^{(\boxtimes)}$ and Mark Neal

Computer Science, Aberystwyth University, Aberystwyth, UK
{jcf1,mjn}@aber.ac.uk

Abstract. A number of types of neural network have been shown to be useful for a wide range of tasks, and can be "trained" in a large number of ways. This paper considers how it might be possible to train and run neural networks to respond in different ways under different prevailing circumstances, achieving smooth transitions between multiple learned behaviours in a single network. This type of behaviour has been shown to be useful in a range of applications, such as maintenance of homeostasis. We introduce a novel technique for training multilayer perceptrons which improves on the transitional behaviour of many existing methods, and permits explicit training of multiple behaviours in a single network using gradient descent.

Keywords: Neuromodulation · Neural network · Backpropagation · Endocrine

This work introduces UESMANN, a neural network which can smoothly switch between different behaviours using a very simple neuromodulatory paradigm. The network is currently trained using UESMANN-BP, a simple modification to the standard backpropagation algorithm [9,13]. It is likely that heuristic search techniques will also prove successful, but these have yet to be explored. UESMANN's major advantages over naïve linear interpolation between outputs are a wider and more consistent "transition region" between behaviours, and the ability for intermediate points along the transition to also be trained.

We will not deal with applications in this paper, concentrating instead on simple functions to explore the system. However, smooth switching between learned functions is useful in situations where an embodied system's behaviour needs to be synchronised with changes in its environment, or where the behaviour needs to change over time. In such systems, a small change in the controlling parameter should result in a small change in the behaviour, along a continuum between the two trained behaviours: i.e. behaviour blending, not behaviour selection. One example is the maintenance of homeostasis, such as husbanding battery charge in a solar-powered robot. Another is striking a balance between exploration and exploitation of resources [10].

© Springer International Publishing Switzerland 2016
E. Tuci et al. (Eds.): SAB 2016, LNAI 9825, pp. 101–112, 2016.
DOI: 10.1007/978-3-319-43488-9_10

1   Background

Most artificial neural networks model electrical communications between neurons, but this is not the only communication neurons have. Neuronal behaviour is also modified by chemicals which diffuse through the intercellular space: this is termed *neuromodulation* [5]. Our technique uses a simple model – perhaps the simplest possible – of neuromodulation in the weights of a multilayer perceptron.

Two other techniques which model neuromodulation are GasNets and Artificial Endocrine Systems (AES). In GasNets, the modulation is of the activation function in a recurrent network [4]. Topology, weights, modulator emission and sensitivity are trained using genetic algorithms. They are useful in solving problems with temporal elements [3,11], and prove more evolvable than the CTRNN [1,7], perhaps the most common recurrent network used in robotics. This may be due to the loosely-coupled co-evolution of two communications channels [12].

AESs are inspired by the endocrine system, modelling glands releasing hormones in response to environmental or internal changes. In an AES, the modelled substances modulate multilayer perceptron weights [8]. The network is typically trained with backpropagation to perform a task, and the modulation implemented "by hand", uniformly across the entire network [8] or on a single layer [10]. Engineering the hormone in this way, rather than allowing the hormone to be evolved (as in a GasNet), provides deterministic behaviour and allows the designer to focus the time-dependent aspect of the behaviour on a particular part of the problem. AESs have applications in stress response [8] and homeostasis [10].

Both GasNets and AESs provide a modulator release, saturation and decay model. UESMANN currently does not, concentrating only on the modulation itself. However, the AES hormone model could be used.

2   Motivation

The core of the GasNet and AES models is the modulation of a neural network by a global parameter decoupled from the network proper, allowing the network to respond to its environment. This response typically takes the form of a smooth transition between modes of operation. However, it is difficult to design systems which can move smoothly between qualitatively different learned behaviours. GasNets, NSGasNets and CTRNNs rely on evolutionary search to find an overarching behaviour which provides the required sub-behaviours (and which may contain undesired emergent behaviours). Current AES implementations simply generate less or more behaviour dependent on the hormone level: although the system is capable of considerably more, it is difficult to design.

For many applications it is useful to construct a system which is explicitly trained for two behaviours, with the modulator providing a smooth switch between them. It would also be useful if the network could be trained to behave a certain way at intermediate modulator levels – that is, if some control over the transitional behaviour were available.

The present work demonstrates a neuromodulatory technique which can be so trained (currently using a supervised learning technique), and which can sensibly interpolate between trained behaviours for intermediate values of the modulator.

The technique effectively creates a single feed-forward network whose weights are modulated. As such, each of the functions it performs cannot be temporal in nature, although the entire system may be if the modulator has a temporal element. This is essentially true of GasNets and AES: the networks themselves and their function at any given time are atemporal, but the modulation adds the temporality.

3   The UESMANN-BP Algorithm

The UESMANN algorithm is based on the AES given in [10], but all weights have equal sensitivity to the modulator. This "simplest possible" form of neuromodulation consists of a network in which each node has the function

$$a_i^l = \sigma \left(b_i^l + \sum_j (h+1) w_{ij}^l a_j^{l-1} \right) \tag{1}$$

where a_i^l is the activation of node i in layer l, b_i^l is the bias of node i in layer l, and w_{ij}^l is the weight of the connection between node j in layer $l-1$ and node i in layer l. The activation function σ is a sigmoid (we use the logistic function).

Each weight is modulated by a "hormone" parameter h such that $h < 0$ inhibits the connection, and $h > 0$ excites it. In the current work $0 \leq h \leq 1$, so the hormone is always excitatory.

Given that we train the network for different functions $h = 0$ and $h = 1$, the initial $h = 0$ function will have the weights take their nominal values, while the $h = 1$ function will have the weights effectively doubled. Thus, our algorithm should find a set of weights and biases $(\mathbf{b}, \mathbf{w})$ which performs one function, while $(\mathbf{b}, 2\mathbf{w})$ performs the second. The training algorithm we shall use is dubbed UESMANN-BP, and is a supervised learning algorithm based on alternating backpropagation for each modulator level. We train the weights and biases $(\mathbf{b}, \mathbf{w})$ for the first function, and alternate this with training the weights and biases $(\mathbf{b}, 2\mathbf{w})$ for the second function. Thus, in each training iteration the weights will move towards a solution for the first function, then towards a solution for the second. This is shown in Algorithm 1.

Algorithm 1. Training UESMANN for two functions using backpropagation. Each example is (in, out_1, out_2) where in is the input vector, out_1 and out_2 are the output vectors for the two functions, and a^L is the network output.

---

   repeat
      for all examples (in, out_1, out_2) **do**
         present input in and run the network
         update $(\mathbf{b}, \mathbf{w})$ using UESMANN-BP with $a^L = out_1, h = 0$
         present input in and run the network
         update $(\mathbf{b}, \mathbf{w})$ using UESMANN-BP with $a^L = out_2, h = 1$
      end for
   until converged for both functions or training limit reached

---

Because backpropagation is done by calculating the cost gradient with respect to the weight, which is effectively $(h+1)w$, we must adjust the algorithm accordingly. This gives the following equations:

$$\frac{\partial C}{\partial w_{ij}^l} = (h+1)a_j^{l-1}\delta_i^l \qquad \text{error surface gradient wrt. weight} \quad (2)$$

$$\frac{\partial C}{\partial b_i^l} = \delta_i^l \qquad \text{error surface gradient wrt. bias} \quad (3)$$

$$\delta_j^L = (a_j^L - y_j) \cdot a_j^L \cdot (1 - a_j^L) \qquad \text{error in output layer} \quad (4)$$

$$\delta_j^l = a_j^l(1 - a_j^l)\sum_i (h+1)w_{ij}^{l+1}\delta_i^{l+1}. \qquad \text{error in hidden layer} \quad (5)$$

where C is the quadratic cost function of the output layer and y_j is the required value of output j. These are the standard backpropagation functions modified so that the cost gradients are now with respect to $w(h+1)$. As in standard backpropagation, we repeatedly run the network forwards, calculate the error, and add (given an learning rate η) $\eta\frac{\partial C}{\partial w_{ij}^l}$ to each weight and $\eta\frac{\partial C}{\partial b_i^l}$ to each bias.

4   Methodology

What UESMANN attempts to do is novel: generate a multilayer perceptron with two (or more) functions, such that the functions are smoothly switched between as the modulator varies. Therefore it does not directly compare with any of the existing neuromodulatory systems, or with CTRNNs. However, we can compare it with other ways of "morphing" between two feed-forward multilayer perceptrons. The two other methods we shall evaluate are linear interpolation between the outputs of two networks (which we term "output blending"), and linear interpolation of the weights and biases of two networks ("network blending"). These are selected because they are the most obvious and straightforward techniques for generating the required behaviour.

We will not be concerned with how the modulator is released, nor how it decays, simply how it affects the network. We wish to find out how well our system behaves in transition: how wide the transition region is, how useful it is, and how consistent the behaviour is across multiple training runs on the same data. Therefore we shall run the three techniques multiple times, and qualitatively examine the results. We have chosen classification problems as examples of typical problems for which perceptrons are used, in which a "transition region" might seem meaningless. However, the assigned classifications should shift gradually between the two behaviours over a large hormone range. In all cases, parameters such as learning rate and initial weights were determined after informal experimentation.

Our first experiments show the behaviour of UESMANN-BP attempting to learn pairings of the logical boolean connectives, chosen as the simplest possible binary functions. We shall then investigate the transition region widths for a particular pairing (XOR and AND). We will then attempt to transfer UESMANN-BP to a real problem: smooth switching between two classifications of handwritten digits. The transition widths will be compared against output and network blending for different hidden node counts.

Finally, an attempt will be made to train a single network at three levels of modulator. Two different intermediate functions (for modulator 0.5) will be compared to see how the choice of intermediate function affects the convergence behaviour. For this test, a new problem will be used: detecting horizontal or vertical lines which may or may not appear in a noisy image. This is chosen both to demonstrate a new domain, and because it is easier to evaluate and classify intermediate functions.

5   Experimental Results

5.1   Logical Connectives

Our first experiment is designed to show whether UESMANN-BP is able to learn pairings of a wide range of functions. 400 runs of the algorithm were performed in networks with 2 and 3 hidden nodes. Weights and biases were initialised to uniform random numbers in the range $[-0.5, 0.5]$. The system was given up to 100000 iterations to converge to an output layer error of < 0.05 for both functions, with a learning rate $\eta = 1$. The results, showing how many of the runs converged for both functions, are shown in Fig. 1.

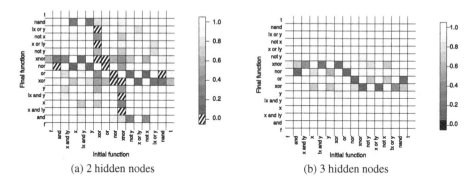

(a) 2 hidden nodes   (b) 3 hidden nodes

Fig. 1. Proportion of 400 runs which converged to a network able to perform both functions in all possible pairings of logical connectives. Two different hidden node counts were used. Cross-hatched squares mark pairings where no solution was found.

The results for the simplest 2-2-1 network are good, but certain pairs of functions will not converge to a network which produces both functions. Intuitively, these functions seem to be those for which it is hard to conceive of a useful intermediate stage (a large Hamming distance between the truth tables is a factor), although the exact relationship needs to be determined. It is interesting that a network with 2 hidden nodes – the minimum number for linearly inseparable functions such as XOR – is able to learn two functions in a single network.

These difficulties remain but are surmountable when the hidden layer is increased to 3 nodes, although for some pairings the number of convergent runs is low. No analysis of the transition regions – either their size or functions – was performed.

Using the same η and initialisation range parameters, the transition behaviour of 2-2-1 UESMANN-BP networks was compared with output blended and network blended (see Sect. 4) networks for the pairing XOR→AND (i.e. with a zero modulator perform XOR, then transition to AND when the modulator is 1). 12 randomly initialised converging runs were performed of each, and the function performed by the network when the output is thresholded at 0.5 was plotted at each modulation value. The results are shown in Fig. 2.

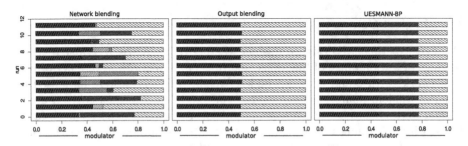

Fig. 2. Examples of different transition behaviours in output blended, network blended, and UESMANN-BP networks. The shading represents the actual function being performed by the generated network at the given modulator value, when the output is thresholded at 0.5.

Output blending produces almost no transition, with the network behaviour switching at 0.5. Network blending produces wider transitions, which appear random. This is probably because two unrelated networks are being blended, leading to a "competing conventions" problem. UESMANN-BP produces a wide, predictable transition consisting of the false function: a compromise between XOR and AND.

6   The MNIST Database

Having established that UESMANN-BP can generate networks which perform two different functions with a wide and predictable transition in simple cases, we now move on to a more difficult problem: the MNIST handwriting recognition database. This database has become a *de-facto* test problem for image classifiers, and consists of 70000 handwritten digits, divided into a training set of 60000 and a test set of 10000 examples. Each example consists of a 28 × 28 8-bit monochrome image of a digit, size normalised and centered, with its associated label (the numerical value of the digit) [6].

Our experiment aims to learn two different labellings of MNIST examples at different network node counts. We wish to establish firstly that UESMANN-BP can learn such a complex pair of functions, secondly examine the transition behaviour of such a network, and thirdly explore the effect of node count in comparison with a control (i.e. a plain backpropagation network learning only one labelling).

In our networks there are 784 inputs, one for each pixel normalised to the range [0,1], and 10 outputs. In each example, the output corresponding to the correct label is set to 1, while the others are set to 0. During testing, the index of the highest output is considered to be the result.

The basic training algorithm is the same as for the previous experiments: each example is presented first for the function with $h = 0$, then for the function with $h = 1$, with different outputs for each function being learned. The examples are iterated over in the order they appear in the training set. In these tests, the initial weights and biases were set by Bishop's rule of thumb [2]: each value is in the range $\left(\frac{-1}{\sqrt{d}}, \frac{1}{\sqrt{d}}\right)$, where d is the number of inputs to the node. It is likely that more tests should be done to determine an optimal value.

Convergence was measured by holding a validation set of 10000 examples out from the training set, and using a small slice from that set every 300 iterations. The resulting network, after 300000 iterations, is the one which performed best in all validations throughout training. Once trained, the test set is used to evaluate this best network.

The two mappings to be learned are the nominal mapping, where each image is assigned the label it has in the database; and a mapping in which adjacent labels are swapped – i.e. a image showing "0" will set output 1 high, while a "1" will set output 0 high and so on. The Hamming distance between the functions is maximal: for no input do the two functions give the same result.

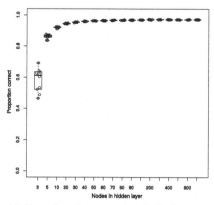

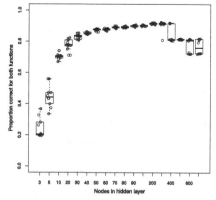

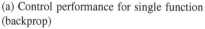

(a) Control performance for single function (backprop)

(b) Performance for learning two functions in one network (UESMANN-BP)

Fig. 3. The means of the success rate at both functions by validation for all runs at each node count for both control and UESMANN-BP.

Table 1. Most common output given the first 1000 MNIST examples passed to the best 300-node network generated using UESMANN-BP, at each value of h. The transition region is marked with vertical lines. For clarity, repeated values are shown with dots.

h	0.00	.05	.10	.15	.20	.25	.30	.35	.40	.45	.50	.55	.60	.65	.70	.75	.80	.85	.90	.95	1.00
Label 0	0	·	·	·	·	·	·	·	0	1	·	·	·	·	·	·	·	·	·	·	1
Label 1	1	·	·	·	·	·	·	·	1	0	·	·	·	·	·	·	·	·	·	·	0
Label 2	2	·	·	·	·	·	·	·	·	2	3	·	·	·	·	·	·	·	·	·	3
Label 3	3	·	·	·	·	·	3	2	·	·	·	·	·	·	·	·	·	·	·	·	2
Label 4	4	·	·	·	·	·	4	5	·	·	·	·	·	·	·	·	·	·	·	·	5
Label 5	5	·	·	·	·	5	4	·	·	·	·	·	·	·	·	·	·	·	·	·	4
Label 6	6	·	·	·	·	·	·	6	7	·	·	·	·	·	·	·	·	·	·	·	7
Label 7	7	·	·	·	·	·	7	6	·	·	·	·	·	·	·	·	·	·	·	·	6
Label 8	8	·	·	·	·	·	8	9	·	·	·	·	·	·	·	·	·	·	·	·	9
Label 9	9	·	·	·	·	9	8	·	·	·	·	·	·	·	·	·	·	·	·	·	8
Behaviour	Function 1						Transition				Function 2										

The results are shown in Fig. 3. In the control, peak performance is achieved at 400 nodes with a 2.6 % error rate, but all node counts over 30 give at worst a 5 % error rate. This roughly agrees with the performance reported by LeCun et al. in [6].

For UESMANN-BP, which learns two functions in one network, the best performance is achieved at 300 nodes, with a 7.6 % error rate — i.e. the best network for the best run at 300 nodes correctly performed both functions for all but 7.6 % of the examples. After this, the ability of the network to find a solution rapidly falls, suggesting poor local minima.

The transition behaviour of the best network was reconstructed in Table 1. We can see that the transition starts at around 0.25 and ends at 0.5, with values generally changing separately, giving a smooth transition.

To compare the transition regions, 10 training runs were performed with all three methods. These were then run at 100 different modulator values on the test set. The sizes of the transition regions obtained are shown in Fig. 4.

Output blending clearly produces an abrupt transition, while network blending produces transitions whose width depends on the hidden node count. However, as has already been discussed, the transitional networks produced in the latter are likely to be of little use, because of competing conventions. For UESMANN-BP runs where both functions converge, the transition width is consistent, at about a third of the modulator range.

Thus, UESMANN-BP is capable of producing a consistent and potentially useful smooth switching behaviour between two classifications in a real-world problem. Although output blending will converge to better solutions, it produces much more abrupt transition regions and cannot be trained at intermediate values (which is possible with UESMANN, as we shall see).

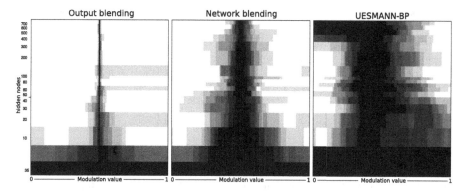

Fig. 4. The transition zones for networks learning two different MNIST mappings using output blending, network blending and UESMANN-BP. 100 examples were run for each network at 100 different morph points, and the networks were generated by 10 different attempts at learning at each node count. Brightness shows how many of the attempts are performing one of the two learned functions, rather than some intermediate.

7   Training at Intermediate Modulation Values

While the behaviour demonstrated thus far is useful, it gives no control over the transitional region. It may be possible to train a different function for a third, intermediate modulator value to provide this control. It seems likely that it will be considerably more difficult to find a solution when the intermediate function is not a "natural" intermediate between the two end functions.

The MNIST handwriting recognition set is not ideally suited for experiments here, because it is hard to identify a clear intermediate between two functions at all 10 outputs. A simpler case is needed, with a single output. Therefore a new experiment was devised: recognising horizontal or vertical lines in an image.

This experiment uses data in the same format as the MNIST data. Each image contains either a horizontal line, a vertical line or no line, labelled 0, 1 and 2 respectively. Each image was overlaid with Gaussian noise ($\mu = 0.4, \sigma = 0.15$) and blurred with a 3×3 Gaussian kernel. The data set sizes were the same as for the MNIST database, with equal proportions of each image type provided. The networks trained had a single output, indicating whether a line of the appropriate orientation was detected or not. A representative sample of the images is shown in Fig. 5. In all experiments, the initialisation values were determined using Bishop's rule, and $\eta = 0.05$: a lower η was required for convergence when intermediate values were used.

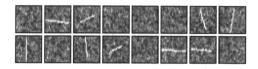

Fig. 5. Examples of images used for line detection experiments.

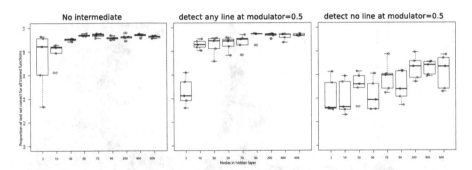

Fig. 6. Performance of line detection, with $h = 0$ detecting horizontal and $h = 1$ detecting vertical lines. Experiments show no intermediate function being trained, $h = 0.5$ detecting any line and $h = 0.5$ detecting no line.

Three experiments were performed: in the first, no intermediate training point was given. In the others, two different intermediate functions were trained at modulator $h = 0.5$: the first detects any line (i.e. output is 1 when either a vertical or horizontal line is present), the second detects no lines (i.e. output is 1 for blank images). 5 runs were performed for a limited subset of the hidden node counts used in previous experiments, and each network analysed against the test set. The results are in Fig. 6.

Without an intermediate function peak performance is at 200 nodes with a 4.28 % error, but even modest node counts can perform well: one 50 node network achieves 4.6 % error, and even a 3 node network achieves 7.18 % error. It is possible that more runs would produce significantly better results.

For additionally detecting either line when $h = 0.5$, best performance is 4.89 % error at 90 nodes – i.e. for all but 4.89 % of the examples, the network gives the correct output for all three learned functions. This clearly shows that it is possible to train at least this intermediate function to a high level of performance.

For detecting no line as the intermediate function, best performance is much worse at 20.88 % error at 200 nodes, and convergence is slower by about an order of magnitude. This is to be expected, because we are moving from three functions which detect lines to two functions which detect lines and a third which detects no lines — there is now an implicit negation in the intermediate function. It seems harder to learn intermediate functions which are not some "natural" intermediate of the two end points.

To determine the "default" intermediate behaviour, the best 200-node network from the first experiment was run with each example from the test set, at three different modulator values (0, 0.5, 1). The number of images detected with each of the three labels is shown in Table 2. Without a trained intermediate function, the network appeared to detect some (about a two thirds) of either vertical and horizontal lines when $h = 0.5$. Looking at the images, it is hard to establish why certain lines are detected while others are not. However, the fact that the default intermediate behaviour is detection of both kinds of lines shows that this is a natural intermediate.

Table 2. Number of lines of each type detected by a network set to detect horizontal lines when $h = 0$, vertical lines with $h = 1$ with no intermediate function trained, at different modulator values.

Modulator	H-lines detected	V-lines detected	Blanks detected
0	3258	83	67
0.5	2122	2283	4
1	29	3221	77

8   Conclusions and Further Work

The UESMANN network is a simple modulated network which achieves smooth switching between qualitatively different functions in a consistent way, with a wide transition region. When compared with naïve linear interpolation between outputs of different networks, the transition region is much wider. Wide transition regions are desirable because they provide a smooth transition between the different functions, permitting adaptive behaviour where the modulator value (often from the environment) is between the two extremes.

Naïve blending of network weights and biases produces wider regions, but they are unpredictable and likely to contain "nonsensical" functions because of the competing conventions of the two parent networks. UESMANN transition behaviour tends to have functional "compromises" between the end-point functions, although this behaviour needs to be explored and analysed further. Providing the modulator as an additional input, rather than a global modulator, should also be tested: we predict that while this may converge well, it will result in narrower transition regions than UESMANN due to the shape of the sigmoid activation function.

A UESMANN network can be successfully trained using backpropagation as a supervised learning technique if suitable examples of both functions are available. The backpropagation parameters need to be investigated, such as initialisation range: preliminary work suggests that larger initial values often have more success. To provide consistent convergence it is likely that more hidden nodes should be used than are required for the "parent" functions. However, some runs do succeed without significantly more nodes.

While a typical UESMANN application may feature only two functions, the network can be trained to perform other functions at intermediate values of the modulator parameter. How successful this training is depends on the nature of these intermediate functions compared with the two end-point functions.

UESMANN and UESMANN-BP may prove useful in any application which requires smooth switching between qualitatively different learned behaviours. These include the maintenance of homeostasis in autonomous systems, power management and so on.

As well as deeper analysis of the parameters of the algorithm itself, further work includes building a UESMANN network into a robot for field tests of homeostatic behaviour, and using genetic algorithms for reinforcement learning of UESMANN networks (UESMANN-GA), with a suitable modulator release/saturation/decay scheme. These experiments will use continuous inputs and outputs, which should show the benefit of smooth, wide transition regions by avoiding the oscillation around the switching transition often exhibited by such systems.

References

1. Beer, R.D., Gallagher, J.C.: Evolving dynamical neural networks for adaptive behavior. Adapt. Behav. **1**(1), 91–122 (1992)
2. Bishop, C.M.: Neural Networks for Pattern Recognition. Oxford University Press, New York (1995)
3. Husbands, P., McHale, G.: Quadrupedal locomotion: GasNets, CTRNNs and Hybrid CTRNN/PNNs compared. In: Proceedings of the 9th International Conference on the Simulation and Synthesis of Living Systems (ALIFE IX), pp. 106–112 (2004). http://sro.sussex.ac.uk/16037/
4. Husbands, P., Smith, T., Shea, M.O., Jakobi, N., Anderson, J., Philippides, A.: Brains, gases and robots. In: ICANN 1998: Proceedings of the 8th International Conference on Artificial Neural Networks, Skövde, Sweden, 2–4 September 1998 (Perspectives in Neural Computing), pp. 51–63 (1998)
5. Kaczmarek, L.K., Levitan, I.B.: Neuromodulation: the biochemical control of neuronal excitability. Oxford University Press, New York (1987)
6. Lecun, Y., Cortes, C.: The MNIST database of handwritten digits. http://yann.lecun.com/exdb/mnist/
7. Magg, S., Philippides, A.: GasNets and CTRNNs – a comparison in terms of evolvability. In: Nolfi, S., et al. (eds.) SAB 2006. LNCS (LNAI), vol. 4095, pp. 461–472. Springer, Heidelberg (2006)
8. Neal, M., Timmis, J.: Timidity: a useful emotional mechanism for robot control? Informatica (Slovenia) **27**(2), 197–204 (2003)
9. Rumelhart, D.E., Hinton, G.E., Williams, R.J.: Learning representations by back-propagating errors. Nature **323**(6088), 533–536 (1986)
10. Sauze, C., Neal, M.: Artificial endocrine controller for power management in robotic systems. IEEE Trans. Neural Netw. Learn. Syst. **24**(12), 1973–1985 (2013). doi:10.1109/TNNLS.2013.2271094
11. Smith, T., Husbands, P., Philippides, A., O'Shea, M.: Neuronal plasticity and temporal adaptivity: GasNet robot control networks. Adapt. Behav. **10**(3–4), 161–183 (2002)
12. Vargas, P.A., Di Paolo, E.A., Husbands, P.: A study of GasNet spatial embedding in a delayed-response task. In: Artificial Life XI, Proceedings of the Eleventh International Conference on the Simulation and Synthesis of Living Systems, pp. 640–647 (2008)
13. Werbos, P.: Beyond regression: new tools for prediction and analysis in the behavioral sciences. Ph.D. thesis, Harvard (1974)

Adaptation of Virtual Creatures to Different Environments Through Morphological Plasticity

Peter Krcah[(✉)]

Faculty of Mathematics and Physics, Charles University, Prague, Czech Republic
peter.krcah@ruk.cuni.cz

Abstract. Many animals are able to modify their morphology during their lifetime in response to changes in the environment. Such modifications are often adaptive—they can improve individual's chances of survival and reproduction. In this paper we explore the effects of such morphological plasticity on body-brain coevolution of virtual creatures. We propose a method where morphological plasticity is achieved through learning during individual's lifetime allowing each individual to quickly adapt its morphology to the current environment. We show that the resulting plasticity allows evolution of creatures better adapted to different simulated environments. We also show that evolution combined with the new learning rule reduces the total computational cost required to evolve an individual with a given target fitness compared to evolution without learning.

Keywords: Bio-inspired algorithms · Virtual creatures · Body-brain coevolution · Adaptation · Learning

1 Introduction

Phenotypic plasticity, defined as the capacity of a single genotype to exhibit a range of phenotypes in response to changes in the environment [15], is a well studied phenomenon in biology. Some of the most striking examples of such plasticity occur in animals that are capable of modifying their morphology during their lifetime. Water flea (see Fig. 1a) has been shown to grow protective spines when exposed to chemicals released into water by its predators. Wasps and ants adjust size and shape of their bodies depending on which caste they are born into [10] (see Fig. 1b). Morphological changes in these cases do not arise through mutation, but purely in response to some property of the environment experienced by the individual. Such morphological plasticity can allow individuals to adapt to different environments quickly, without having to wait for slow mutations to discover the necessary changes [1,10,15].

Previous works in evolutionary robotics have traditionally focused on optimizing morphology of robots during evolution [4,6,7,12] while investigations of phenotypic plasticity have been limited to the control system of robots with fixed

This research was supported by SVV project number 260 333.

E. Tuci et al. (Eds.): SAB 2016, LNAI 9825, pp. 113–125, 2016.
DOI: 10.1007/978-3-319-43488-9_11

(a)   (b)

Fig. 1. Morphological changes exhibited by (a) *Daphnia Lumholtzi* when exposed to chemicals produced by a predatory fish (long spines in the individual on the left reduce predation compared to individual on the right that has not been exposed to the chemicals) [1] and (b) minor vs. major worker ant of *Acanthomyrmex* species [10] (drawn by Turid Hölldobler).

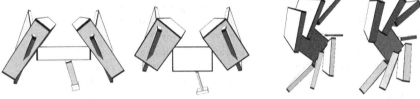

(a) Presence of the sea floor induces increased body mass allowing creature to gain more traction against the ground (right) compared to morphology used for swimming in open water (left).

(b) Decreased viscosity of the surrounding fluid (left) induces reduction in the body mass of a swimming creature.

Fig. 2. Examples of morphological plasticity in creatures adapted for swimming in different environments. Video available at https://youtu.be/d9Rc3gKRwTk

morphology [9]. One recent exception is the work by Bongard [2] which demonstrates that modifying morphology during the lifetime of the creature according to a predetermined plan can lead to evolution of creatures with higher fitness. However, morphological changes in this work are not made in response to the environment and the purpose was not to study learning of morphology during individual's lifetime but to improve control system of the robot.

In this paper we propose a method of evolving virtual creatures that can adapt their morphology to the current environment during their lifetime. In contrast to nature, where the rules governing morphological plasticity are optimized by evolution and encoded in the genotype [15], virtual creatures in our experiments improve their morphology during their lifetime using a hill-climbing learning rule (interaction of evolution and learning has previously been studied outside of evolutionary robotics, e.g. by Hinton and Nowlan [3] or by Mayley [8]). Bodies of creatures are composed of blocks connected by joints (see Fig. 2). Morphological changes during the learning phase are limited to adjustments to the size of each block while the overall structure of the creature remains unmodified. While such changes may not be sufficient to adapt the creature to a

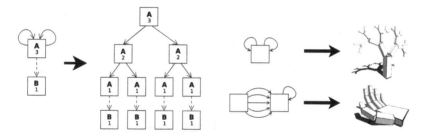

Fig. 3. Manually designed examples of genotype-to-phenotype mapping. Dashed line represents a terminal connection. Recursive limit is shown inside each node.

completely new task (which might require learning new behaviors or making more radical changes to the morphology), we show that even such relatively minor adjustments allow the creature to adapt to significantly different environments and perform the given task more efficiently than creatures not capable of such adaptation. At the same time, limiting morphological plasticity makes future construction of such robots more feasible—constructing a robot that can adjust sizes of its parts is likely to be more practical than building a robot that can restructure its morphology more dramatically (a simple physical robot consisting of a resizable box has been demonstrated by Roper et al. [11] in Voxbot system).

The rest of this paper is organized as follows. Section 2 provides background information: overview of the virtual creatures and the evolutionary algorithm. Section 3 then describes the learning algorithm used to optimize morphology of a creature. Section 4 describes experiments demonstrating the learning capability in different environments and Sect. 5 provides further analysis of the computational cost and explanation of the performance increase.

2   Background

2.1   Virtual Creatures

Design of virtual creatures used in this paper is based on Sims [12]. Each creature is composed of a set of blocks connected by joints. An indirect encoding scheme is used to construct the phenotype of the creature from its genotype. The genotype is a directed graph where each vertex represents a body part of the creature (a block) and each edge represents a joint connecting two blocks. Transcription of a genotype into a phenotype is performed by starting from a designated *root* vertex and recursively traversing the graph in depth-first order, copying all encountered vertices and edges to an acyclic phenotype graph. Each vertex has a defined *recursive limit* which limits the number of times a given vertex can be visited. Edges with *terminal flag* enabled are expressed only when recursive limit is reached. Each edge also defines three reflection flags (one for each axis) each of which results in a mirrored copy of the sub-tree starting at the target vertex to be added to the phenotype. Indirect encoding provides a compact way of encoding features such as symmetry and repeated segments (see Fig. 3).

Control system is distributed along the body of the creature: each body part contains a local feed-forward neural network, a single local effector used for controlling the joint connecting the body part to its parent and a local joint angle sensor. Local neural networks in any two body parts that are connected by a joint can communicate using inter-block neural connections. In each simulation step, values of all sensors are first updated, all neural networks are then evaluated (one block a time) and the resulting effector value in each block is applied as torque to the joint connecting the block to its parent.

2.2   Fitness Evaluation

Fitness of a creature is evaluated by placing the creature in a water environment with rigid body dynamics provided by OpenDynamicsEngine [13]. Additional forces are applied to each block to simulate water friction (with strength controlled by the *viscosity* parameter), gravity and buoyancy. Performance of each creature is defined as the displacement of the center of mass of the creature divided by the duration of the test (creatures are evolved for fast swimming). To evaluate performance of a creature in two different environments, each creature is tested in both environments independently and the smaller of the two values is used as the final fitness. Creature therefore needs to perform well in both environments to receive a high fitness value.

2.3   Evolutionary Algorithm

HierarchicalNEAT [5] algorithm has been chosen due to its previously demonstrated performance in virtual creature evolution, although main results of this paper do not rely on the choice of the specific evolutionary algorithm.

HierarchicalNEAT is based on the concept of *historical markings* (introduced first in NEAT algorithm by Stanley [14]), inheritable unique identifiers assigned to each body part, joint, neuron and neural connection when they are first created. Since historical markings are inheritable, they provide mapping between structural elements of any two creatures based on their shared evolutionary history (previously, expensive topology matching algorithms had to be used instead). Furthermore, the mapping is hierarchical: corresponding body parts of two creatures are aligned first, and then correspondences between individual neurons within matching body parts are found. Historical markings are used to define (1) an efficient recombination operator (where only compatible parts of parent creatures take part in recombination) and (2) similarity measure for any two creatures (proportional to the number of corresponding structural elements).

HierarchicalNEAT uses speciation to maintain diversity in the population and to protect new mutations from direct competition with existing well-adapted creatures. The algorithm starts with an initial population of small randomly generated creatures. Creatures in each new generation are assigned to species based

Algorithm 1. Lifetime Learning of Morphology.

Require: N (the number of learning steps), t_{learn} (duration of each learning step), t_{test} (duration of the final fitness evaluation), L_{geno} (array of block sizes encoded in the genotype of a virtual creature)

1: Initialize $L_{best} = L_{geno}$, $f_{best} = 0$
2: **for all** $i \in \{1, ..., N\}$ **do**   ▷ Hill-climbing learning phase
3:     $L_{current} \leftarrow$ RANDOMLYADJUST(L_{best})
4:     $f_{current} \leftarrow$ TESTMORPHOLOGY$(L_{current}, t_{learn})$
5:     **if** $f_{current} > f_{best}$ **then**
6:         $f_{best} \leftarrow f_{current}$
7:         $L_{best} \leftarrow L_{current}$
8:     **end if**
9: **end for**
10: **return** TESTMORPHOLOGY(L_{best}, t_{test}) ▷ Final fitness evaluation

2s|2s|2s|2s|2s|2s|2s|2s| 48s

Learning   Evaluation

Fig. 4. Creature life starts with a learning phase that tests different morphologies.

on their similarity to representatives of the same species from the previous generation, or by creating a new species if no sufficiently similar species exists already. New generation is created by first allocating a number of slots to each species proportional to the average fitness value of all creatures in the same species in the previous generation (a fitness sharing scheme designed to protect innovation). Each slot is then populated with a creature created by recombination and mutation of creatures selected from the same species in the previous generation.

3   Method

To evolve virtual creatures capable of adapting to different environments we run the evolutionary algorithm as described above with a modified fitness evaluation: evaluation in each environment starts with a *learning phase* (lines 2–9 in Algorithm 1) consisting of a fixed number of short experiments designed to test if a selected morphology adjustment has the potential to improve fitness of the individual. After the learning phase, full fitness test is performed to verify if the creature can sustain discovered improvements for a longer time period (line 10). Result of the full test is used as the fitness score for a given environment (see Fig. 4).

Morphology changes during the learning phase are limited to the size of blocks while the structure of the creature remains unchanged. In the first learning step, sizes of all blocks are set to the values encoded in the individual's genotype (line 1). In each subsequent step, the best block sizes found so far are modified by a small random amount (i.e. the size of each block is adjusted along each

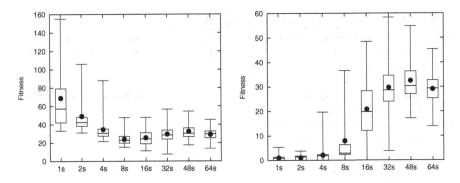

Fig. 5. Fitness of the best creatures evolved for swimming using different fitness evaluation durations (left) compared to the fitness of the same creatures after a long (64 s) fitness evaluation (right). Short evaluations result in creatures that achieve high speed initially but fail to maintain it for a longer period.

dimension, line 3). Sizes of blocks generated using reflection are adjusted by the same amount in each step to preserve symmetry. Performance of each creature is measured as average speed achieved during a given learning step (line 4). Relative positions of all blocks are reset to their initial positions after each learning step to ensure that early learning steps do not interfere with later learning steps.

Since dimensions of all body parts are optimized by learning, learning occurs in $3n$-dimensional space (where n is the number of blocks forming creature's body, excluding any mirrored or repeated blocks). For example, creature in Fig. 6 contains 3 blocks resulting in 9-dimensional learning space. Figure 6a–c show a cross-section of this space for different environments. The learning landscape is smooth with a single global optimum suggesting that the swimming task is well-suited for an incremental hill-climbing search through the morphology space.

3.1 Parameter Selection

The learning rule described in the previous section has three parameters: (1) the duration of the final fitness evaluation, (2) the duration of each learning step and (3) the number of learning steps. This section discusses how the value for each of these parameters was selected.

The first parameter significantly impacts the behavior of evolved creatures. With short fitness evaluations, evolution favours creatures which simply perform a strong initial push but fail to continue moving afterwards. Longer evaluations are needed to prevent such behaviors, however long durations also incur extra computational cost. A set of preliminary experiments was performed to find the minimum duration of the fitness evaluation that results in creatures that maintain their speed for a long time period. Each evaluation duration was tested using 50 runs each ending after 200 generations. Average speeds of the best creatures evolved for each duration are shown in Fig. 5 (left). The fastest creature evolved in each run has been re-evaluated using a long (64 s) fitness evaluation to see if the average speed was maintained. Results (shown in Fig. 5, right) show that very short durations of fitness evaluation result in creatures that fail to maintain their speed in the longer simulation[1]. Based on these preliminary experiments, 48 s duration of the fitness evaluation was chosen for all experiments in this paper—the smallest value that reliably results in creatures that perform at least as well as creatures evolved using the longest duration.

The second parameter (duration of the learning step) was set to 2 s—a time in which most evolved creatures complete their first swimming stroke. On its own, learning based on such short tests is not guaranteed to produce creatures good at swimming for long periods of time (in fact, short learning steps can fail to correctly predict the outcome of the full test), but as results of our experiments show, even such short tests provides enough information to guide evolution towards more promising areas of the fitness landscape if each creature is also evaluated in a long-duration test after learning.

The third parameter controls the number of learning steps performed for each individual. Larger values allow hill-climbing to explore neighborhood more extensively, while also increasing the learning cost. To keep the computational cost low, 8 learning steps have been used in all experiments in this paper[2].

4   Experiments

Three different environments were used to test the ability of virtual creatures to adapt their morphology to the environment through learning:

Open Water. Creature is placed in water without any obstacles. No gravity or buoyancy forces are added so the creature is suspended in water unless it actively performs movement. Forces simulating viscosity of water are enabled.

Sea Floor. A single plane is added to the environment simulating the sea floor. At the start of the simulation, creature is positioned such that its lowest point is in contact with the plane. Reduced gravity of $2 \, m/s^2$ is enabled to simulate density of blocks higher than the surrounding water. The environment is otherwise identical to the open water environment.

Low Viscosity Fluid. Viscosity forces applied to the creature are reduced by 50 % to simulate low viscosity fluid surrounding the creature (such as water at moderately higher temperatures). The environment is otherwise identical to the open water environment.

Two different experimental setups are tested, each using a different pair of environments. In the first setup creatures are evolved in open water and on the sea floor. In the second setup open water and low viscosity fluid are used.

---

[1] All boxplots use whisker bars for minimum and maximum value, box boundaries for 1st and 3rd quartile, horizontal line for the median and black dot for the mean.

[2] Preliminary experiments have shown that while longer learning phase further decreases the number of generations required to reach a given fitness value, it decreases the performance when the extra computational cost is also taken into account.

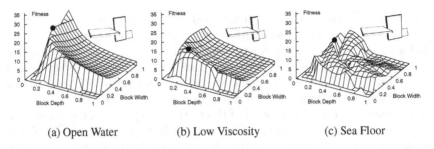

(a) Open Water   (b) Low Viscosity   (c) Sea Floor

Fig. 6. Two-dimensional cross-sections of nine-dimensional learning space for a simple evolved swimming creature (each dimension of each block contributes one dimension). Each plot shows swimming speeds achieved in a given environment for varying widths (horizontal across the page) and depths (into the page) of the central block of the creature. Creature displayed next to each plot shows the best size of the central block (also marked using black dot in the plot).

While creatures can generally use the same movements to propel themselves forward in all three environments with some degree of success, the differences between environments can be exploited to achieve higher fitness. For example, since the sea floor is immovable, creatures can push against it more effectively than against the water to achieve movement. Since the floor is perfectly smooth such push must rely on the surface friction forces to be effective, which in turn depend on the weight of the creature. Heavier creatures thus might be able to push against the floor more effectively and achieve higher speeds. Figure 6 illustrates the differences between the three environments in more detail. The shape and ruggedness of the learning space are different in each environment, as is the position of the optimum.

The following configurations have been tested for each pair of environments:

Evolution with learning. Learning was performed during evolution as part of each fitness evaluation as described in Sect. 3. This configuration allows creatures to learn morphology specific to each environment.

Evolution without learning. No learning was performed as part of fitness evaluation. In this configuration, creatures were forced to use the same morphology in both environments.

Evolution in one environment only (baseline). Creatures were evolved using only one of the environments and without learning. The best creature from each generation was evaluated in both environments, using the same method as in configurations above (smaller of the environment-specific fitness values was used as the final fitness value). This configuration serves as a baseline to see how do the creatures evolved in one of the environments perform in the other environment without any previous exposure to it.

4.1   Parameter Settings

Population size was set to 300 in all experiments. All evolutionary runs were stopped after 200 generations. Each configuration was tested 50 times. All other settings of HierarchicalNEAT algorithm were set to the same values as in [5]. Significance levels were calculated using Student's t-test (normality of the data has been verified visually using Q-Q plots). Maximum size of each block along each dimension was set to 1. Volume of any block was not permitted to decrease below 0.008 during learning or mutation. Random changes to each side of each block were selected uniformly from range $[-0.05, 0.05]$ in each learning step.

5   Results and Discussion

In both experiments, evolution combined with learning achieved higher average fitness values in the last generation compared to evolution without learning (an improvement of 15 % in both cases, $p < 0.01$, see Fig. 7). Moreover, evolution with learning outperforms evolution without learning (by 9 % and 7 %, $p < 0.05$) even when accounting for the extra computational cost that learning incurs[3]. These results show that allowing creatures to specialize for each environment allows them to reach higher fitness values compared to creatures that are constrained to use the same morphology in both environments.

Large diversity of creatures has been evolved in all experiments. The most common type was a snake-like creature swimming in a sinusoidal pattern. Snake-like creatures were more common in evolution with learning (14 % of all runs) than in evolution without learning (6 % of all runs), suggesting that this type of creature benefits from being able to adapt to different environments. In general, evolved creatures made significant use of features provided by the encoding, such as symmetry and repetition (see examples in Fig. 2).

Morphological adaptations learned through creature's lifetime strongly reflect the environment. Learning in low viscosity environment on average lead to reduction of the total volume (and therefore mass) of creature's body by 30.1 % compared to environment with higher viscosity (0.51 vs 0.73, $p < 0.02$). Conversely, in the open-water/sea-floor experiment the volume of phenotypes expressed in the sea floor environment was on average 44 % larger than for phenotypes swimming in open water (1.13 vs. 0.78, $p < 0.05$). As discussed in Sect. 3, the difference likely comes from the fact that larger blocks provide more weight, and thus more friction against the sea floor allowing the creatures to make better use of the floor for locomotion.

Results of baseline experiments confirm that evolution of creatures exposed to only one of the environments results in creatures that perform significantly worse in the other environment compared to creatures exposed to both environments. For instance, creatures evolved for swimming near the sea floor without

---

[3] Since learning increases the cost of each fitness evaluation by one third (from 48 s to 64 s, see Fig. 4), the extra computational cost was accounted for by comparing results from generation 150 of evolution with learning with results from generation 200 of evolution without learning.

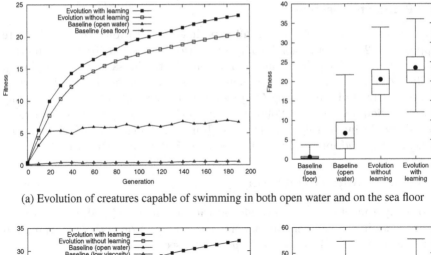

(a) Evolution of creatures capable of swimming in both open water and on the sea floor

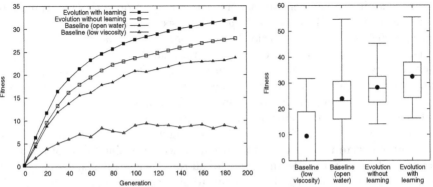

(b) Evolution of creatures capable of swimming in fluids with different viscosities

Fig. 7. Results of experiments with creatures adapting to a pair of environments. The main result is that allowing creatures to adapt their morphology to each environment improves performance compared to evolution without learning.

being exposed to open-water environment often rely on sea floor friction to such an extent that they are not able to move forward at all without the sea floor (see "Baseline (sea floor)" in Fig. 7a). On the other hand creatures evolved for swimming in higher-viscosity fluid (see "Baseline (open water)" in Fig. 7b) without being exposed to lower-viscosity fluid performed quite well in low-viscosity fluid without any further adaptation (although still significantly worse than creatures exposed to both environments). Results also show that performance of creatures evolved only in open water is better retained in lower viscosity environment ("Baseline (open water)" in Fig. 7b, final fitness of 6.7) than in the sea floor environment ("Baseline (open water)" in Fig. 7a, best fitness 23.9), suggesting that lower viscosity environment is more similar to the open water environment than the sea floor environment.

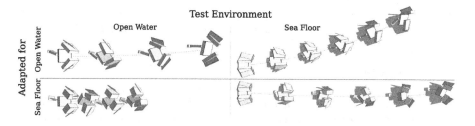

Fig. 8. Comparison on the left shows that phenotype adapted for open water (top) performs better in open water than phenotype adapted for swimming near the sea floor (bottom). Performance is reversed in the sea floor environment (right).

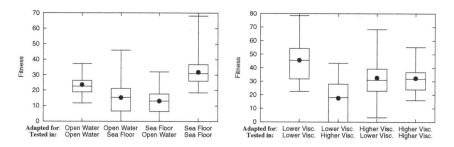

Fig. 9. Performance of creatures when tested in a different environment than the one used for learning. The main result is that improvements discovered through learning in one environment are detrimental in the other environment.

To see the effect of learning more clearly, the best creature discovered in each run of evolution with learning was subjected to learning in one of the environments and then placed in the other environment with no further learning. Results (shown in Fig. 9) show that morphological adaptations discovered through learning are specific to one environment and cause degradation of performance in the other environment. Morphological plasticity thus allows creatures to increase their fitness in each environment independently (see Fig. 8 for an example of an evolved creature adapted to two different environments through learning).

Results presented so far do not make it clear whether learning improves evolution by altering the paths evolution takes through the fitness landscape, or whether learning is *orthogonal* to evolution, i.e. final result of evolution with learning would be the same if learning was performed only at the end of evolution. To answer this question, the best creature from each run without learning was subjected to a learning phase consisting of 100 steps each 48 s long (in each environment separately) and its fitness was measured afterwards. The average improvement from this extended learning was only 0.8 % in the sea floor experiment and 0.9 % in the low viscosity experiment and large proportion of creatures failed to improve at all (42 % and 47 % respectively). This suggests that when learning is performed during evolution as opposed to after evolution, it helps evolution guide the search to more promising areas in the fitness landscape and it cannot be replaced by performing learning only after evolution.

6   Conclusion

We have shown that morphological plasticity achieved through lifetime learning can be used to evolve virtual creatures capable of adapting to different environments. Even when changes to morphology are relatively minor (i.e. body parts of the creature are resized, but overall structure of the creature remains unchanged) and when the number of such changes tested during learning is small, resulting morphological plasticity allows creatures to adapt to modified environments and perform a given task significantly better than without such adaptation. Moreover, the performance improvements from learning outweigh the computational cost of learning, showing that combining learning with evolution can be a valuable tool in the evolution of virtual creatures.

References

1. Agrawal, A.A.: Phenotypic plasticity in the interactions and evolution of species. Science **294**(5541), 321–326 (2001)
2. Bongard, J.: Morphological change in machines accelerates the evolution of robust behavior. Proc. Nat. Acad. Sci. **108**(4), 1234–1239 (2011)
3. Hinton, G.E., Nowlan, S.J.: How learning can guide evolution. Complex Syst. **1**(3), 495–502 (1987)
4. Hornby, G.S., Pollack, J.B., et al.: Body-brain co-evolution using l-systems as a generative encoding. In: Proceedings of the Genetic and Evolutionary Computation Conference (GECCO-2001), pp. 868–875 (2001)
5. Krčah, P.: Towards efficient evolutionary design of autonomous robots. In: Hornby, G.S., Sekanina, L., Haddow, P.C. (eds.) ICES 2008. LNCS, vol. 5216, pp. 153–164. Springer, Heidelberg (2008)
6. Lessin, D., Fussell, D., Miikkulainen, R.: Adapting morphology to multiple tasks in evolved virtual creatures. In: Proceedings of the Fourteenth International Conference on the Synthesis and Simulation of Living Systems (ALIFE 2014) (2014)
7. Lipson, H., Pollack, J.B.: Automatic design and manufacture of robotic lifeforms. Nature **406**(6799), 974–978 (2000)
8. Mayley, G.: Guiding or hiding: explorations into the effects of learning on the rate of evolution. In: Proceedings of the Fourth European Conference on Artificial Life, vol. 97, pp. 135–144 (1997)
9. Nolfi, S., Floreano, D.: Learning and evolution. Auton. Robots **7**(1), 89–113 (1999)
10. Oster, G.F., Wilson, E.O.: Caste and Ecology in the Social Insects. Princeton University Press, Princeton (1978)
11. Roper, M., Katsaros, N., Fernando, C.: Voxel robot: a pneumatic robot with deformable morphology. In: del Pobil, A.P., Chinellato, E., Martinez-Martin, E., Hallam, J., Cervera, E., Morales, A. (eds.) SAB 2014. LNCS, vol. 8575, pp. 230–239. Springer, Heidelberg (2014)

12. Sims, K.: Evolving virtual creatures. In: Proceedings of the 21st Annual Conference on Computer Graphics and Interactive Techniques, pp. 15–22. ACM (1994)
13. Smith, R.: ODE manual. http://www.ode.org
14. Stanley, K.O., Miikkulainen, R.: Evolving neural networks through augmenting topologies. Evol. Comput. **10**(2), 99–127 (2002)
15. Whitman, D.W., Agrawal, A.A.: What is phenotypic plasticity and why is it important? Phenotypic Plast. Insects **10**, 1–63 (2009)

A Moment Measure Model of Landmarks for Local Homing Navigation

Changmin Lee[✉] and DaeEun Kim

Biological Cybernetics Lab, School of Electrical and Electronic Engineering,
Yonsei University, Shinchon, Seoul 120-749, South Korea
{lcmin,daeeun}@yonsei.ac.kr
http://cog.yonsei.ac.kr

Abstract. Visual navigation in robotics is one of the challenging issues, and many navigation approaches are based on localization of a mobile robot in the environment. The snapshot model is a biologically inspired model of insect behaviour to return home and it shows a simple algorithm to compare the snapshot images at the current position and the destination, instead of complex localization process. Here, we propose a new homing navigation method based on a moment measure to characterize the snapshot image efficiently. The method uses range values or pixel values of surrounding landmarks. Then it defines a moment measure to evaluate the environmental features, or landmark distributions, and the measure forms a convex shape of landscape with respect to robot positions in the environment. Based on the landscape, the mobile robot can return home successfully. Range sensors or image sensors can sufficiently provide the landscape information. Our experimental results demonstrate that the method is effective even in real environments.

Keywords: Visual navigation · Moment model · Convergence point · Landmark vector · Range data · Triangulation method · Localization · Fast alignment without compass

1 Introduction

Many animals in nature show interesting navigation behaviors, following their various senses including vision, olfactory, auditory, odometry, and magnetic information [2,9,14–16,24,25,27]. Especially, honeybees [10,23], dessert ants [2], jellyfish [7], gerbils [4], rodents [3], and fiddler crabs [28] have high homing navigation capability. Many researchers have observed their astonishing performances of the creatures with small brains and built a biologically inspired navigation model.

The snapshot model [1] is one of popular navigation models and numerous variations of this approach, 'bio-inspired homing navigation', have been constantly studied. In this part, the term 'home' is the destination of an agent and homing navigation is a technique for returning home. According to the snapshot method, if the agent can move along the homing direction, the difference

© Springer International Publishing Switzerland 2016
E. Tuci et al. (Eds.): SAB 2016, LNAI 9825, pp. 126–137, 2016.
DOI: 10.1007/978-3-319-43488-9_12

between images at the current position and at the nest can be reduced. Thus, it can reversely calculate the homing direction by finding the way to make the difference reduced using only a pair of images at the current spot and at the home site. In this process, we need a metric to evaluate the similarity between two images. There have been many methods depending on features appearing in the snapshot images or how to extract those features.

The Average Landmark Vector (ALV) method [13] models landmark features in the image. An image itself does not include the distance information to landmarks. We only estimate the angular position of each object called 'landmark. The method draws a unit vector (landmark vector) for each landmark and calculates the sum of landmark vectors to reflect the environmental features, which is then divided by the number of landmarks. It is called the ALV. We can estimate the ALV at the nest and at the current position, and then the difference vector of the two ALVs can guide an agent to return home successfully. The algorithm is quite simple and its convergence to the home position is verified. It is also tested in robotic experiments [21]. However, it needs a process to identify each object or landmark in the snapshot image and it does not handle the distance or size of landmarks.

Another landmark vector model, called 'Average Correctional Vector, the ACV method [22, 26] has been suggested. It calculates the amount of differences between angular locations of landmarks in the snapshot images. However, a feature extraction step to identify landmarks and further the angular position of the landmarks is still a necessary step for this method. Both the ALV and the ACV methods require angular position information of landmarks in the image.

As an alternative to the above landmark vector models, the warping methods [5, 6, 8, 12, 19, 20] have been suggested. It has an image matching process using all pixels in the images instead of extracting landmark features from the snapshot images. The snapshot images at the current position and at the home position are compared. There have been many variations with the method, considering pixel values in one-dimenstional line or two-dimenstional space of images. The methods show successful results without any object feature extraction.

The Descent in Image Distance (DID) method [17, 18, 29] uses image changes in the vicinity. It finds the homing direction by comparing the whole image pixels of two snapshots at the home site and at the current position. The snapshot images at neighbor positions can determine the homing direction. If the image discrepancy is smaller, it indicates that the position is closer to the home position. This method needs additional movements of robots and has a considerable amount of computing time.

Previously, a SLAM model with an elevation moment of inertia has been tested [11]. The measure can be the representative value at each position, and it covers the surrounding range values and height information with a single scalar value. However, the approach only focused on the scalar characteristics of the moment function.

In this paper, we introduce a new homing navigation method in an local area based on moment metric information. Here, we define a new style of moment measure. The moment measure is designed for a general form of features with range values of surrounding landmarks. The moment measure uses the distance of surrounding landmarks for landmark features and characteristics of landmarks in the environment. Here, instead of the feature extraction, we use each pixel value as visual information and range value for a landmark near the horizontal line. As the height value is difficult to collect and 3D range sensors are costly, we use both visual and range information. It can find the convergence point (minimal potenial point) of the moment measure and this point can be a reference in homing navigation, which is unchanged in local area. With a mobile robot with both range sensor and omni-directional camera, we test the homing navigation for a designated home place.

2   Methods and Materials

2.1   Sensors and Test Environment

Experiments were tested with MALTAB software and the arena consists of 6 m by 6 m space with various objects including drawers, trash cans, large vases, windows, and partition boards (Fig. 2(a)). We use i-Robot ROOMBA with two wheel motors for experiments, and a lap-top computer is mounted on the Roomba robot. We use two types of sensors to read the environmental information as shown in Fig. 1(c), an omnidirectional camera to sense color images and a laser sensor to read the distance of landmarks. The omnidirectional camera has Logitech Webcam E3500 vision sensor and a metal ball used as a reflection mirror. The robot also has HOKUYO Laser sensor URG-04 LX model as a range sensor. This laser sensor has about 240° measuring area with 0.36° resolution, and two shots were taken at a given robot position to cover the omnidirectional view. The above sensors provide both omni-directional color information and depth information. In Fig. 2(c), we can see a reconstructed sketch of the environment with the laser sensor. The red marker x's are the landmark positions for the surrounding environment.

Fig. 1. Mobile robot (a) i-Robot ROOMBA mobile (b) omnidirectional camera (640 × 480 pixels) (c) HOKUYO laser sensor measurement part (240° measuring area with 0.36° resolution) (d) mobile robot nounted with sensors

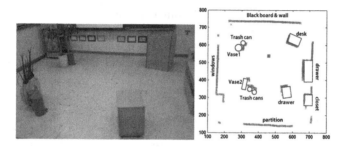

Fig. 2. Experimental environment (a) top-view of entire space, (b) reconstructed reference map by range data from laser sensor

For navigation experiments, a mobile robot takes the snapshot image at a given home position in the office environment. The robot keeps the snapshot image or landmark information at the home position as a reference image. Then a new image at an arbitrary position is taken and the homing direction is estimated.

2.2 Data Processing

The omni-directional images in Fig. 2(b) have 640×480 RGB pixels. Then we can change them into a panoramic form of image with $0.5°$ resolution as shown in Fig. 3(a). To get higher time efficiency for the processing time, our algorithms will take a series of pixel values along the horizontal line. Most of our experiments show that a single line of pixel values near the horizon are sufficient to provide the environmental characteristics. The readings of laser sensor were sampled appropriately to fit the panoramic image. Thus, the two types of sensor readings together include the distance and color information of surrounding landmarks roughly.

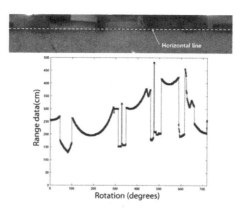

Fig. 3. Data from sensors (a) reduced panorama image 720×120 pixels (with 0.5 angle resolution) and (b) reduced laser data

We assume a reference compass in our experiments. In some experiments, no reference compass is available. In that case, we apply Zeil's visual compass method to estimate the current head direction in the environment. It uses the entire image matching between the home image and the image at the current position.

2.3   Navigation Algorithm: Moment Measure

We define a moment measure as a measure to evaluate a distribution of surrounding landmarks. This moment depends on robot positions, but it is equal at the same position in the environment. The moment measure is a characteristic function of localization in the navigation. We analyse a landmark distribution with the moment measure which considers the positions and features of landmarks. The color intensity of RGB or height of each object can be the features of landmarks. We design the first moment model as a potential function in Eq. (1). We suppose that there are N landmarks. r_n is the range value of the n-th landmark and C_n is the designated feature of the n-th landmark. In the equation, a_n is the x-axis position and b_n is the y-axis position for the n-th landmark. Each landmark is regarded as a point measured with a laser sensor.

The potential function of the first moment measure is given by

$$M = \sum_{n=1}^{N} r_n{}^2 C_n = \sum_{n=1}^{N} ((x - a_n)^2 + (y - b_n)^2) C_n \tag{1}$$

Then, we can find the gradient (2) as the first derivative of potential function. This gradient vector means the change of the potential in position (x, y) for a unit movement.

The gradient of potential function :

$$\nabla M = (\frac{dM}{dx}, \frac{dM}{dy}) = \sum_{n=1}^{N} (2(x - a_n)C_n, 2(y - b_n)C_n) \tag{2}$$

The convergence point can be estimated with Eqs. (3) and (4). The convergence point indicates the point with the minimal potential value of the moment measure.

$$\nabla M(X, Y) = \sum_{n=1}^{N} (2(X - a_n)C_n, 2(Y - b_n)C_n) = 0 \tag{3}$$

$$X = \frac{\sum_{n=1}^{N} a_n C_n}{\sum_{n=1}^{N} C_n}, \quad Y = \frac{\sum_{n=1}^{N} b_n C_n}{\sum_{n=1}^{N} C_n} \tag{4}$$

The first moment model of potential function has convergence to (X, Y), using the landmark features. Estimation of (X, Y) does not rely on the robot

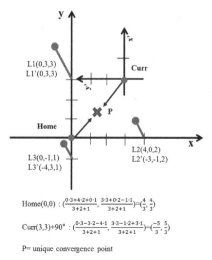

Home(0,0) : $(\frac{0\cdot3+4\cdot2+0\cdot1}{3+2+1}, \frac{3\cdot3+0\cdot2-1\cdot1}{3+2+1})=(\frac{4}{3},\frac{4}{3})$

Curr(3,3)+90° : $(\frac{0\cdot3-3\cdot2-4\cdot1}{3+2+1}, \frac{3\cdot3-1\cdot2+3\cdot1}{3+2+1})=(\frac{-5}{3},\frac{5}{3})$

P= unique convergence point

Fig. 4. Convergence point P in the potential landscape of landmarks. The potential function consists of landmark features, for example, landmark colors or landmark heights. Finally the convergence points are equal at the home position and the current position

position (x, y). If there is no change in the environment and there is no occlusion, then we can estimate the same convergence point, regardless of any robot position or any orientation. Figure 4 shows an example of convergence point in the convex landscape of the landmark potential function.

We apply the moment measure to the environmental situations. The detailed process is described as below.

Landmark Vectors with Features with Range Information. First of all, we extract landmark vectors from the features with range information, that is, a distance vector in the omnidirection. Then each landmark has its own position in the reference map at the home position with its feature value. This is similar to the reference map in 2(b).

Finding Convergence Point of Moment Model Using Features. Then we can calculate the convergence point of the moment measure at each position. Then we obtain both direction and distance to the convergence point from the current position. Then we can plot this convergence point in the reference map. The convergence point is different from the home position, and it is determined by the landmark distribution.

At home position:

$$X = \frac{\sum\limits_{n=1}^{N} a_n C_n}{\sum\limits_{n=1}^{N} C_n}, \quad Y = \frac{\sum\limits_{n=1}^{N} b_n C_n}{\sum\limits_{n=1}^{N} C_n}$$

$$\text{direction\_}\theta_{Home} = \tan^{-1}(Y/X)$$
$$\text{distance\_}d_{\text{hom}\,e} = \sqrt{X^2 + Y^2}$$

At the current position, we can find the convergence point by taking the minimal potential value in the convex landscape. The observation landmark features change depending on the robot position, but the convergence point is equal at any position, if we plot it in the reference map.

At the current position:

$$X' = \frac{\sum\limits_{n=1}^{N} a'_n C'_n}{\sum\limits_{n=1}^{N} C'_n}, \quad Y' = \frac{\sum\limits_{n=1}^{N} b'_n C'_n}{\sum\limits_{n=1}^{N} C'_n}$$

$$\text{direction\_}\theta_{curr} = \tan^{-1}(Y'/X')$$
$$\text{distance\_}d_{curr} = \sqrt{X'^2 + Y'^2}$$

Localization. We can calculate the convergence point, and from that, we can determine the distance and direction to the point. Reversely, we can estimate the current position from the convergence point. In the experiments, the reference map for the home position is given, and the convergence point can be marked in the reference map. Additionally, the current position of a mobile robot in the map can be inferred. It implies that we can successfully localize the mobile robot in the reference map.

$$Home = (X_{\text{hom}\,e}, Y_{\text{hom}\,e})$$

$$Current = Home + \overrightarrow{C_{\text{hom}\,e}} - \overrightarrow{C_{curr}}$$

3   Result

In this part, we show our results using new methods.

Homing Navigation. By the prior information, we can find the current location and the home position in the reference map using convergence point as a reference and thus the homing vector can be calculated. Here, the minimal point in the convex landscape of landmark potential is a reference point and it plays an important role on localization. Figure 5 shows the convex landscape and homing navigation process.

Homing vector:

$$\overrightarrow{H} = (\overrightarrow{C_{curr}} - \overrightarrow{C_{\text{hom}\,e}}) = ((X',Y') - (X,Y))$$
$$= (\frac{\sum a'_n C'_n}{\sum C'_n} - \frac{\sum a_n C_n}{\sum C_n}, \frac{\sum b'_n C'_n}{\sum C'_n} - \frac{\sum b_n C_n}{\sum C_n})$$

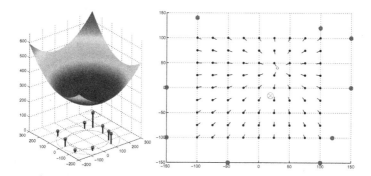

Fig. 5. Simulation (a) a distribution of metric potential as surface and contour lines on the floor, (b) calculated homing direction at each point. In (b), the large red dots are landmarks and thin red circle at (30, 40) is the home position. The black circle is the current location and the black dot is estimated as the current position. Green circle with x-shape in second figure is minimum moment location using equal distance assumption (Color figure online)

Then we can find the homing direction and a sequence of the operation can lead to the nest. We have tested the method. In Fig. 5(a), we can check the unique convergence using some landmarks in simulation. There is only one convergence point in the field, which has the lowest position of moment distribution. We can use a variety of features each of which can lead to a convergence point. A collection of convergence points include more information about the environment. In Fig. 5(b), there are color circles and x-shapes (pink, green, blue, red). They are the convergence points for different features.

3.1 Simulation

We built a virtual simulation environment using MATLAB. There are a set of landmarks with heights for landmark features. Then we can find the convergence point using our model. In Fig. 5, (a) shows a potential curve with the moment model, and (b) shows the output of localization and homing navigation using (a). In the simulation, the agent perfectly finds the homing direction without errors.

3.2 Using Only Vision Sensor

We tested real robots with our proposed method. First, we performed experiments with a vision sensor and the compass information was given. In this step, it is impossible to get the range data and only the visual input is given. Then we use equal distance assumption and put all the pixels in horizontal line at equal distances. The color values affect the landscape of moment potential function. Here, we simply used the gray intensity, which is the mean of RGB values. In Fig. 6, it can find the homing direction at each current position. The homing

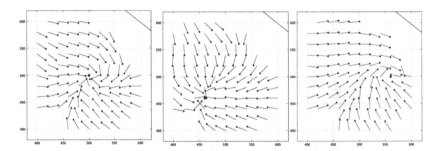

Fig. 6. Robot experiment results using only vision sensor with compass information. Range values are same by the equal distance assumption like ALV method. The black rectangle at (500, 500) in (a), (460, 460) in (b) and (560, 500) in (c) are home positions and the arrows show the homing direction at each point. The black lines at outer side of the vector map show the outline of object in the field.

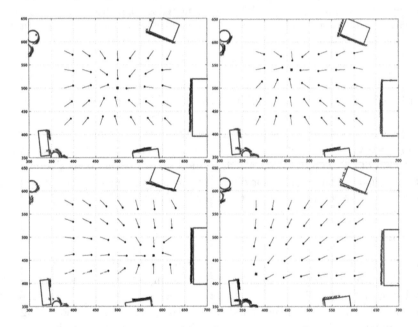

Fig. 7. Robot experiment results using both range data from laser sensor and gray intensities with aligned images. Black x-shapes are the observed information about surrounding objects at each home position. Following red boxes (a: (500, 500), b: (460, 540), c: (580, 460) and d: (380, 420)) are home and the arrows show the homing direction at each point. The blue lines on the vector map show the outline of object in the field. (Color figure online)

direction output is not perfect, since the landscape follows an equal distance assumption. However, it shows reasonable results for homing directions. As a result, the robot can return home at the end of travel, following the flow of moment function.

3.3   Using Both Vision Sensor and Laser Sensor

We also tested experiment using both vision sensor and range sensor. Compass information is also given. We use the laser sensor to get range data and the vision sensor to fetch colour information. Then the moment function can be complete with distance information. In Fig. 7, we can see the homing performance. The robot almost perfectly finds the homing direction at each current position.

4   Conclusion

In this paper, we suggest a new homing navigation method using a moment measure. The moment measure evaluates a distribution of landmarks in the environment, and it forms a landmark potential function. We have a theoretical foundation on the convergence of the minimal potential with the moment measure. Using the minimal convergence point as a reference point, we can estimate the current position in a reference map of landmarks drawn at home position, and ultimately determine the homing direction.

Our moment metric allows various characteristics such as RGB color, gray intensity and height, which are not largely dependent on the measurement positions. In addition to, if the uniqueness of the feature is preserved, many variations of the landmark feature extraction are also possible. For instance, each RGB value of landmarks can be a feature and the ratio of RGB, for example, blue intensity over the green intensity, can be another variation to be used with the moment metric. Actually, we have tested many types of features in real experiments and if invariant features are available, then our algorithm is highly effective for homing navigation. Furthermore, the information about the range sensor readings and the image pixel values can be combined effectively in our moment metric method. Home navigation is possible even when the equal distance assumption is applied without the range sensor. However, we do not deny that with our moment metric, the distance information with a laser sensor is critical for localization of a mobile robot.

Our proposed method can reduce the computing time for homing navigation with the snapshot model. We treated the pixel values as landmark information. In this way, more abstact form of the feature can be available for each snapshot.

We need further study to find more suitable features or more robust features for homing navigation. Possibly we can test if more variety of features are helpful for navigation. Next, we will compare our method with other conventional methods to check the robustness of our algorithm. We used Zeil's visual compass method in the experiments without reference compass. We need to find more efficient approach which is helpful to estimate the current head direction. Our method is limited in a static environment, and it needs further work to find valid landmarks in a dynamic environment and process occluded landmarks.

Acknowledgement. This work was supported by the National Research Foundation of Korea (NRF) grant funded by the Korea government (MEST) (No. 2014R1A2A1A11053839).

References

1. Cartwright, B., Collett, T.: Landmark learning in bees. J. Comp. Physiol. A **151**(4), 521–543 (1983)
2. Collett, M., Collett, T.: How do insects use path integration for their navigation? Biol. Cybern. **83**(3), 245–259 (2000)
3. Etienne, A., Jeffery, K.: Path integration in mammals. Hippocampus **14**(2), 180–192 (2004)
4. Etienne, A., Maurer, R., Seguinot, V.: Path integration in mammals and its interaction with visual landmarks. J. Exp. Biol. **199**, 201–209 (1996)
5. Franz, M., Scholkopf, B., Mallot, H., Bulthoff, H.: Where did I take that snapshot? Scene-based homing by image matching. Biol. Cybern. **79**(3), 191–202 (1998)
6. Franz, M.: Minimalistic visual navigation = Minimalistische visuelle navigation. Ph.D. thesis, Universitat Tubingen (1999)
7. Garm, A., Oskarsson, M., Nilsson, D.: Box jellyfish use terrestrial visual cues for navigation. Curr. Biol. (2011)
8. Hong, J., Tan, X., Pinette, B., Weiss, R., Riseman, E.: Image-based homing. IEEE Control Syst. Mag. **12**(1), 38–45 (1992)
9. Kimchi, T., Etienne, A., Terkel, J.: A subterranean mammal uses the magnetic compass for path integration. Proc. Natl. Acad. Sci. U.S.A. **101**(4), 1105 (2004)
10. Kirchner, W., Braun, U.: Dancing honey bees indicate the location of food sources using path integration rather than cognitive maps. Anim. Behav. **48**(6), 1437–1441 (1994)
11. Kwon, T., Song, J.: A new feature commonly observed from air and ground for outdoor localization with elevation map built by aerial mapping system. J. Field Robot. **28**(2), 227–240 (2011)
12. Labrosse, F.: Short and long-range visual navigation using warped panoramic images. Robot. Auton. Syst. **55**(9), 675–684 (2007)
13. Lambrinos, D., Moller, R., Labhart, T., Pfeifer, R., Wehner, R.: A mobile robot employing insect strategies for navigation. Robot. Auton. Syst. **30**(1–2), 39–64 (2000)
14. Lent, D., Graham, P., Collett, T.: Image-matching during ant navigation occurs through saccade-like body turns controlled by learned visual features. Proc. Natl. Acad. Sci. **107**(37), 16348–16353 (2010)
15. Luschi, P., Papi, F., Liew, H., Chan, E., Bonadonna, F.: Long-distance migration and homing after displacement in the green turtle (Chelonia mydas): a satellite tracking study. J. Comp. Physiol. A **178**(4), 447–452 (1996)
16. Mather, J.: Navigation by spatial memory and use of visual landmarks in octopuses. J. Comp. Physiol. A: Neuroethology Sens. Neural Behav. Physiol. **168**(4), 491–497 (1991)
17. Moller, R., Vardy, A.: Local visual homing by matched-filter descent in image distances. Biol. Cybern. **95**(5), 413–430 (2006)
18. Moller, R., Vardy, A., Kreft, S., Ruwisch, S.: Visual homing in environments with anisotropic landmark distribution. Auton. Robots **23**(3), 231–245 (2007)
19. Moller, R.: Local visual homing by warping of two-dimensional images. Robot. Auton. Syst. **57**(1), 87–101 (2009)
20. Moller, R., Krzykawski, M., Gerstmayr, L.: Three 2D-warping schemes for visual robot navigation. Auton. Robots **29**(3), 253–291 (2010)
21. Ramisa, A., Goldhoorn, A., Aldavert, D., Toledo, R., de Mantaras, R.: Combining invariant features and the ALV homing method for autonomous robot navigation based on panoramas. J. Intell. Robot. Syst. 1–25 (2011)

22. Smith, L., Philippides, A., Graham, P., Baddeley, B., Husbands, P.: Linked local navigation for visual route guidance. Adapt. Behav. **15**(3), 257–271 (2007)
23. Srinivasan, M.: Honey bees as a model for vision, perception, and cognition. Ann. Rev. Entomol. **55**, 267–284 (2010)
24. Steck, K., Knaden, M., Hansson, B.: Do desert ants smell the scenery in stereo? Anim. Behav. **79**(4), 939–945 (2010)
25. Ugolini, A., Borgioli, G., Galanti, G., Mercatelli, L., Hariyama, T.: Photoresponses of the compound eye of the sandhopper talitrus saltator (Crustacea, Amphipoda) in the ultraviolet-blue range. Biol. Bull. **219**(1), 72–79 (2010)
26. Weber, K., Venkatesh, S., Srinivasan, M.: Insect-inspired robotic homing. Adapt. Behav. **7**(1), 65–97 (1999)
27. Zeil, J.: Visual homing: an insect perspective. Curr. Opin. Neurobiol
28. Zeil, J., Hemmi, J.: The visual ecology of fiddler crabs. J. Comp. Physiol. A **192**(1), 1–25 (2006)
29. Zeil, J., Hofmann, M., Chahl, J.: Catchment areas of panoramic snapshots in outdoor scenes. J. Opt. Soc. Am. A **20**(3), 450–469 (2003)

A Landmark Vector Approach Using Gray-Colored Information

Changmin Lee[✉] and DaeEun Kim

Biological Cybernetics Lab, School of Electrical and Electronic Engineering,
Yonsei University, Shinchon, Seoul 120-749, South Korea
{lcmin,daeeun}@yonsei.ac.kr
http://cog.yonsei.ac.kr

Abstract. Homing navigation is an important aspect in navigation behaviours of animals. There has been many types of navigation but we focus on the vision-based landmark navigation to return home. Visual navigation is involved with image matching process over snapshot images. Landmark vector methods simplify the environmental information into a set of landmark vectors, and then compare the landmark vectors obtained from each snapshot. In this paper, we encode landmark vectors using the gray-colored values as the length of vectors. Then we apply the landmark arrangement method to those landmark vectors. Using the gray-colored information, we can estimate the homing direction at a given position. We show that the suggested method is effective in homing navigation.

Keywords: Vision-based homing navigation · Landmark vector · Localization · Landmark arrangement matching

1 Introduction

Navigation is the process or activity of accurately ascertaining one's position and planning and following a route, according to the Oxford dictionary. That is, it is the work that makes one go to the goal following a proper direction. If the accurate homing direction is estimated at an arbitrary position, then it can complete the homing navigation. There have been many sensor solutions to handle the navigation. Some animals including ants, bees, and rats show a prominent feature of homing navigation. They explore the environment for foraging food, even at a considerable distance from the nest, they come back successfully to their nest. The navigation performance directly influences their survival.

There have been many studies about the insect's homing navigation using their various sensory information like vision, auditory sense, magnetic sense, olfactory information and odometry [2,9]. The insects use landmark information from visual information [3]. The role of landmarks is critical in the navigation [1].

Path integration is a well-known navigation subject used by desert ants [2], honeybees [7], fiddler crabs [14] and rodents [4]. The agent accumulates the

© Springer International Publishing Switzerland 2016
E. Tuci et al. (Eds.): SAB 2016, LNAI 9825, pp. 138–144, 2016.
DOI: 10.1007/978-3-319-43488-9_13

amount of changes in location from the starting point, and at the final position, the agent can estimate the relative location to the starting point. It is useful for homing navigation. Another interesting work is about he route following [6]. The agent moves around, but remembers the route. The agent can follow the same path using the memory. The snapshot model [11] is a simple navigation method with two snapshots at the current site and the home position, which is inspired by insect navigation. The agent compares the two snapshots to estimate the homing direction. In this paper, we use this snapshot model for homing navigation of a mobile robot.

There have been many visual navigation methods using the snapshot model. The Average Landmark Vector method [8], image matching algorithm [5], the ACV method [10], Distance Estimated Landmark Vector method [12] are examples based on the snapshot model. They need to identify landmarks with accurate location information. Such an process is a time-consuming job and more efficient approach is desirable.

In this paper, we propose a new bio-inspired visual navigation algorithm using gray-color information. We take pixels in the gray-scale image as landmarks or background information. The continuous gray intensities for each direction can be treated as landmark vectors. From that, we can apply the landmark arrangement matching method [13] for localization. We will investigate the performance of our method in robotic experiments.

2   Methods and Materials

Our experimental environment is about 260 cm by 260 cm arena. There are objects including desks, chairs, trash cans, and flowerpots. Initially we take snapshots at intervals of 20 cm. We transform the omnidirectional image into a panoramic view and a sequence of RGB color values are used as a series of landmarks, since we only use vision sensor for the surrounding environment. Figure 1 shows experimental environment and a mobile robot Roomba with the omnidirectional camera. The camera is equipped with Logitech Webcam E3500 and a reflector.

(a)   (b)   (c)

Fig. 1. (a) Environment for Robotic Experiments (b) Mobile robot Roomba loaded with an omnidirectional camera (c) omnidirectional image from the cam

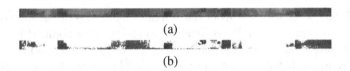

(a)

(b)

Fig. 2. Image Processing (a) gray-colored panoramic image (b) gray-colored image after filtering

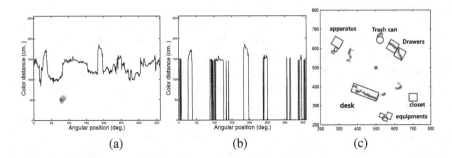

(a)   (b)   (c)

Fig. 3. Image filtering (a) spectrum of color values, (b) spectrum with brightness compensation and filter operations, (c) gray-colored intensity map (intensity distance map) with real landmarks

Here, a new navigation algorithm is introduced, which is called Gray Landmark vector (GLV) method. The snapshot image at a given position has the surrounding environmental information, which includes the landmarks and background component. In many cases, landmarks and the background are not easily distinguishable. The panoramic image has an angular position information along the horizontal axis and the distance-like information in the vertical axis. Figure 2(a) shows a strip of panoramic image. Then the gray intensities are compared with a threshold and we obtain a picture in Fig. 2(b). Then we have a line of gray pixel values from each snapshot. Figure 3(a) is an example of gray spectrum from the original color image and Fig. 3(b) is the result after a fixed threshold is applied to the image. Thus, the background component has zero intensity.

For landmark navigation, we need to extract landmarks from the snapshot image. We assume that the above gray-colored image after thresholding process has a rough distribution of landmarks. That is, the landmark distance information is replaced byh the gray-color intensity. The panoramic image includes the angular position and the gray distance of landmarks. As shown in Fig. 3(c), the gray distance is different from the actual distance of landmarks, but it has a rough sketch of landmark distribution.

In our method, we apply the landmark arrangement matching method [13]. The method encodes the environmental information with a set of landmark vectors. Each landmark vector includes the angular position and the distance of a landmark. It the distance information is a unit value, then the method is equivalent to the Averaged Landmark Vector method. A set of landmark vectors at the current position and at the home position are compared and then we can estimate the current position in a reference map by projecting the landmark vectors at the current position in the map reversely. As a result, we can determine the homing direction.

The above gray distance vectors from the snapshot image are extracted and then applied to the landmark arrangement matching method. We suppose that a mobile robot has no compass sensor and needs to estimate the head direction by itself. All possible angles of head direction are checked to find the best match of two sets of landmark vectors with the landmark arrangement matching process.

3 Experiments

We take robotic experiments in a given arena and show the performance of the landmark vector method based on gray-colored information. We investigated the performance of estimating the homing directions when two snapshots are given at the home site and at an arbitrary position. Also, we checked if the mobile robot can return home ultimately when it follow a sequence of homing directions. In Fig. 4, the x shapes represent the location of extracted landmarks from a snapshot image at the home site. The square at $(500, 500)$ indicates the home position. The arrow shows the homing direction for each location. Estimation of homing directions is reasonably good as shown in Fig. 4(a)–(c). They show some angular errors, but the homing pattern of the field is still observed. Through a consecutive operation of homing vector, Fig. 4(e) and (f) show successful route to the home position. The lines show the route of the homing robot.

In Fig. 5, we numerically show the angular errors and homing rate of robotic experiments with some variation in the experimental condition (I–V). We tested variable thresholds to extract landmarks from the gray-colored image. Smaller thresholds indicates more landmarks, more pixel values extracted. The angular errors and homing rates depend on the number of landmarks as shown in Fig. 6, and especially for successful homing rate (100%), an appropriate range of landmarks should be used. That is, a proper threshold should be selected to have a considerable effect of removing the background.

Here, we introduced a new visual navigation method purely based on a gray-colored image. The Gray Landmark Vector method handles a set of landmark vectors instead of the whole image colors, and thus it reduces the overall computing time. The gray intensities greatly depend on the lumious light source. The light source direction or intensity influences the gray landmark vectors. We need an image pre-processing like histogram equalization to handle the brightness of a snapshot image. Multiple light sources or the change of the light condition will degrade the navigation performance.

In our experiments, we choose only a part of pixel values in the panoramic image. The information may not be sufficient to estimate the current location of a robot with the image arrangement matching method. We need a further work to find what parts of the snapshot image is effective for localization. Also, we

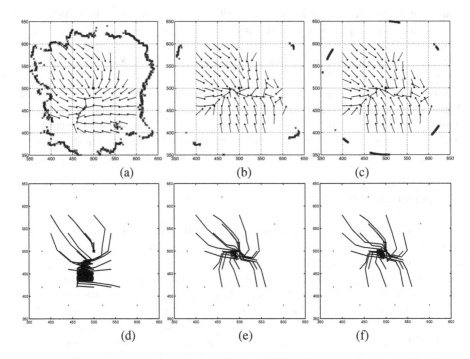

Fig. 4. Vector map (a, b, c) and routes of homing navigation (d, e, f) using gray distance landmark vector method with a fixed threshold. (a) and (d) using the original information without compass, (b) and (e) using the threshold and bright compensation without compass, (c) and (f) using the threshold and a fixed distance information without compass.

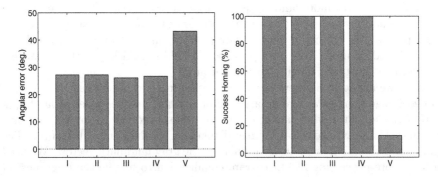

Fig. 5. Angular errors (left) and homing rates (right) of the algorithm for each five fitting method. 'I' uses both brightness compensation and threshold with compass, 'II' is without compass, 'III' uses the threshold and make a unit vector without compass, 'IV' uses the threshold and gray distance vectors without compass and 'V' use no threshold filter and no compass.

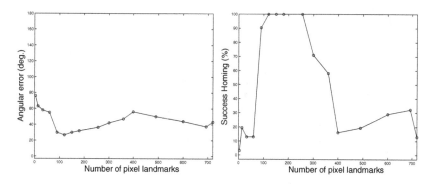

Fig. 6. Angular errors (left) and homing rates (right) of the algorithm (each threshold value changes the number of extracted pixels in an image)

need a more delicate choice of threshold for landmarks in a gray-colored image. A bad choice of the threshold may lose the landmark information or add an unnecessary background image.

4   Conclusion

We propose a new navigation method based on gray-colored images. The landmark vectors are built with gray-colored intensities in the omnidirectional view. To remove the background image, a theshold-filter operation is applied to snapshot images. Interestingly, without distance information of landmarks, the intensity-differentiation can define a landmark property and it plays a role of localizing the agent. The landmark arrangement matching process [12] automatically pinpoints the location of the agent and thus determines the homing direction appropriately. The method follows the idea of snapshot model [11]. Only two snapshots at the home site and the current location are sufficient to determine the homing direction, if the environment is isotropic.

There have been manu visual navigation methods. We need further work to compare our method with other conventional methods. Better filter operations over the gray-colored image are required for a robust navigation system. The filter threshold greatly affected the navigation performance in our experiments. More sophisticated search for the color intensity landmark vectors will strongly support the proposed method.

Acknowledgement. This work was supported by the National Research Foundation of Korea (NRF) grant funded by the Korea government (MEST) (No. 2014R1A2A1A11053839).

References

1. Collet, T.S., Land, M.F.: Visual spatial memory in a hoverfly. J. Comput. Physiol. **100**, 59–84 (1975)
2. Collett, M., Collett, T.S.: How do insects use path integration for their navigation? Biol. Cybern. **83**(3), 245–259 (2000)
3. Collett, T.: Insect navigation en route to the goal: multiple strategies for the use of landmarks. J. Exp. Biol. **199**(1), 227–235 (1996)
4. Etienne, A.S., Jeffery, K.J.: Path integration in mammals. Hippocampus **14**(2), 180–192 (2004)
5. Franz, M.O., Schölkopf, B., Mallot, H.A., Bülthoff, H.H.: Where did I take that snapshot? Scene-based homing by image matching. Biol. Cybern. **79**(3), 191–202 (1998)
6. Goedemé, T., Tuytelaars, T., Van Gool, L., Vanacker, G., Nuttin, M.: Feature based omnidirectional sparse visual path following. In: 2005 IEEE/RSJ International Conference on Intelligent Robots and Systems, (IROS 2005), pp. 1806–1811 (2005)
7. Kirchner, W.H., Braun, U.: Dancing honey bees indicate the location of food sources using path integration rather than cognitive maps. Anim. Behav. **48**(6), 1437–1441 (1994)
8. Lambrinos, D., Moller, R., Labhart, T., Pfeifer, R., Wehner, R.: A mobile robot employing insect strategies for navigation. Robot. Auton. Syst. **30**(1–2), 39–64 (2000)
9. Mather, J.A.: Navigation by spatial memory and use of visual landmarks in octopuses. J. Comp. Physiol. A: Neuroethology Sens. Neural Behav. Physiol. **168**(4), 491–497 (1991)
10. Weber, K., Venkatesh, S., Srinivasan, M.: Insect-inspired robotic homing. Adapt. Behav. **7**(1), 65–97 (1999)
11. Wehner, R., Michel, B., Antonsen, P.: Visual navigation in insects: coupling of egocentric and geocentric information. J. Exp. Biol. **199**, 129–140 (1996)
12. Yu, S.-E., Kim, D.: Distance estimation method with snapshot landmark images in the robotic homing navigation. In: 2010 IEEE/RSJ International Conference on Intelligent Robots and Systems (IROS), pp. 275–280. IEEE (2010)
13. Yu, S.-E., Kim, D.: Image-based homing navigation with landmark arrangement matching. Inform. Sci. **181**(16), 3427–3442 (2011)
14. Zeil, J., Hemmi, J.M.: The visual ecology of fiddler crabs. J. Comp. Physiol. A **192**(1), 1–25 (2006)

Simulation of an Optional Strategy in the Prisoner's Dilemma in Spatial and Non-spatial Environments

Marcos Cardinot[(⊠)], Maud Gibbons, Colm O'Riordan, and Josephine Griffith

Department of Information Technology,
National University of Ireland, Galway, Ireland
marcos.cardinot@nuigalway.ie

Abstract. This paper presents research comparing the effects of different environments on the outcome of an extended Prisoner's Dilemma, in which agents have the option to abstain from playing the game. We consider three different pure strategies: cooperation, defection and abstinence. We adopt an evolutionary game theoretic approach and consider two different environments: the first which imposes no spatial constraints and the second in which agents are placed on a lattice grid. We analyse the performance of the three strategies as we vary the loner's payoff in both structured and unstructured environments. Furthermore we also present the results of simulations which identify scenarios in which cooperative clusters of agents emerge and persist in both environments.

Keywords: Artificial life · Game theory · Evolutionary computation

1 Introduction

Within the areas of artificial life and agent-based simulations, evolutionary games such as the classical Prisoner's Dilemma [2,15], and its extensions in the iterated form, have garnered much attention and have provided many useful insights with respect to adaptive behaviours. The Prisoner's Dilemma game has attained this attention due to its succinct representation of the conflict between individually rational choices and choices that are for the better good. However, in many social scenarios that we may wish to model, agents are often afforded a third option — that of abstaining from the interaction. Incorporating this concept of abstinence extends the Prisoner's Dilemma to a three-strategy game where agents can not only cooperate or defect but can also choose to abstain from a game interaction. There have been a number of recent studies exploring this type of game [5,7–9,16].

In addition to analysing the evolution of different strategies and different outcomes, previous work has also explored the effect of imposing spatial constraints on agent interactions. Traditionally, these studies assume no such constraints and agents are free to interact with all other agents in well-mixed populations [2]. However, many models consider restricting interactions to neighbourhoods

© Springer International Publishing Switzerland 2016
E. Tuci et al. (Eds.): SAB 2016, LNAI 9825, pp. 145–156, 2016.
DOI: 10.1007/978-3-319-43488-9_14

of agents on some pre-defined topology. These more expressive models include lattices [6,13], cycles and complete graphs [9], scale-free graphs [16] and graphs exhibiting certain properties, such as clustering coefficients [11].

In this paper we adopt an evolutionary approach to evolve populations of agents participating in the extended Prisoner's Dilemma [12]. We consider two different environmental settings: one with no enforced structure where agents may interact with all other agents; and another in which agents are placed on a lattice grid with spatial constraints enforced, where agents can play with their immediate eight neighbours (Moore neighbourhood). In both environmental settings, an agent's fitness is calculated as the sum of the payoffs obtained through the extended Prisoner's Dilemma game interactions. We investigate the evolution of different strategies (cooperate, defect and abstain) in both spatial and non-spatial environments. We are particularly interested in the effect of different starting conditions (number of different strategies and placement of different strategies) and the different values for the loner's payoff (L) on the emergence of cooperation. We identify situations where the simulations converge to an equilibrium, where no further changes occur. These equilibria can be fully stable (no change) or quasi-stable (with a small cycle length).

The paper outline is as follows: In Sect. 2 an overview of work in the extended game and of spatial evolutionary game theory is presented. Section 3 gives an overview of the methodology employed. In Sect. 4, we discuss the non-spatial environment. We firstly present an analysis of pairwise interactions between the three pure strategies. Secondly, evolutionary experiments using all three strategies are presented. Thirdly, we explore the robustness of a population of cooperative and abstaining strategies when a defecting strategy is added to the population. In Sect. 5, we discuss the environment where agents are placed on a lattice grid, in which their interactions are constrained by their local neighbourhood. Again an analysis of pairwise interactions is first undertaken followed by an exploration of the outcomes when all three strategies are randomly placed on the grid. Based on these findings, we explore different starting groupings of the three strategies, i.e. placed in a non-random manner on the grid. This will allow identification of starting configurations that lead to stable cooperation.

2   Related Work

Abstinence has been studied in the context of the Prisoner's Dilemma (PD) since Batali and Kitcher, in their seminal work [3], first introduced the optional variant of the game. They proposed the opt-out or "loner's" strategy, in which agents could choose to abstain from playing the game, as a third option, in order to avoid cooperating with known defectors. Using a combination of mathematical analysis and simulations, they found that populations who played the optional games could find routes from states of low cooperation to high states of cooperation. Subsequently, as this extension has grown in popularity and renown, optional participation has been successfully incorporated into models alongside other cooperation enhancing mechanisms such as punishment [7] and reputation [5,14], and has been applied to probabilistic models [16].

The study of optional participation can be broadly separated into approaches: one that directly incorporates abstinence into the traditional PD game (the loner's strategy), and another known as conditional cooperation. Models that incorporate the loner's strategy treat the option to abstain as an alternative strategy for agents to employ [3,9], separate to the option to cooperate or defect. These models tend to be more grounded in mathematical models with less of an emphasis on experimental simulations, which often-times have been shown to produce unexpected results [6]. On the other hand, conditional cooperation models [1,8,10], also known as conditional disassociation, incorporate abstinence into cooperation strategies. These models lend themselves more easily to Axelrod-style tournaments [2]. They tend to focus on exit options or partner-leaving mechanisms, and often lack a spatial aspect, which has since been shown to increase the number of abstainer strategies thus increasing the chances of cooperation evolving [9].

The work that most closely resembles our own is that of Hauert and Szabó [6]. They consider a spatially extended PD and public goods game (PGG), where a population of N agents are arranged and interact on a variety of different geometries, including a regular lattice. Three pure strategies (cooperate, defect and abstain) are investigated using an evolutionary approach. Results showed that the spatial organisation of strategies affected the evolution of cooperation, and in addition, they found that the existence of abstainers was advantageous to cooperators, because they were protected against exploitation. However, there exists some major differences between their model and the one proposed here. Hauert and Szabó focus on a simplified PGG as their primary model for group interactions, and separately use the PD only for pairwise interactions. In our model, agents interact by playing a single round of the PD with each of their neighbours. Additionally, Hauert and Szabó focused on one set of initial conditions for their simulations, using a fixed ratio of strategies. Our work explores a wider range of initialization settings from which we gleam more significant insights, and identify favourable configurations for the emergence of cooperation.

3   Methodology

In order to explore these strategies and, in particular, the effect of introducing abstinence, we propose a set of experiments in which each agent randomly plays a number of one-shot, two-person extended Prisoner's Dilemma game. An evolutionary approach is adopted with a fixed-size population where each agent in the population is initially assigned a fixed strategy. Fitness is calculated and assigned based on the payoffs obtained by the agents from playing the game. Simulations are run until the population converges on a single strategy, or configuration of strategies.

In the traditional Prisoner's Dilemma game there are four payoffs corresponding to the pairwise interaction between two agents. The payoffs are: reward for mutual cooperation (R), punishment for mutual defection (P), sucker's payoff (S) and temptation to defect (T). The dilemma arises due to the following

Table 1. Prisoner's Dilemma game matrix.

	C	D	A
C	R,R	S,T	L
D	T,S	P,P	L
A	L	L	L

(a) Extended game matrix.

Payoff	Value
T	5
R	3
P	1
S	0
L	$]0, 3[$

(b) Payoff values.

ordering of payoff values: $S < P < R < T$. When extending the game to include abstinence, a fifth payoff is introduced, the loner's payoff (L) is awarded to both participants if one or both abstain from the interaction.

The value of L should be set such that: (1) it is not greater than R, otherwise the advantage of not playing will be sufficiently large to ensure that players will always abstain and (2) it is greater than S, otherwise there are no benefits to abstaining. This enables us to investigate the values of L in the range $[S, R]$, which in turn contrasts with the definition used by Hauert and Szabó [6] who define abstainers as strategies who perform better than groups of defectors but worse than groups of mutually cooperating strategies. In their model, abstainers receive a payoff less than R and greater than P. We choose to explore a more exhaustive range of values. The payoffs for the extended Prisoner's Dilemma game are illustrated in Tab. 1 and are based on the standard values used by Axelrod [2].

As we aim to study the behaviour of agents in different scenarios, our first model allows all agents to potentially interact (Sect. 4). Our second model places topological constraints on the agent population which restricts the potential interactions that can take place (Sect. 5). This allows for the comparison between spatial and non-spatial environments and allows us to identify similarities and differences in conditions that promote cooperation. For both environments, two common sets of experiments are considered:

1. Pairwise comparisons: The abstainer strategies compete with one of the other strategies; firstly, an equal number of cooperators (C) and abstainers (A); and secondly, an equal number of defectors (D) and abstainers (A).
2. All three strategies present: We adopt an unbiased environment in which initially each agent is designated as a cooperators (C), defector (D) or abstainers (A) with equal probability.

Moreover, to further explore the effect of adding the option of abstinence, a third experiment is undertaken in the non-spatial environment, where we seed the population with a majority of one type of strategy (abstainers) and explore if the population is robust to invasion from (1) a cooperator and (2) a cooperator and a defector (Sect. 4.3). In order to explore the effect of different initial spatial configurations, we also undertake a third set of experiments in the spatial environment, which provide an insight in to the necessary spatial conditions that may lead to robust cooperation (Sect. 5.3).

4 Non-spatial Environment

In this section, we present results of the experiments in the non-spatial environment and settings as described previously in Sect. 3. We use a tournament selection with size 2.

4.1 Pairwise Comparisons

The simulations involving cooperators, C and abstainers A, verified the expected outcomes where the cooperators quickly spread throughout the population resulting in complete cooperation. This can be shown to be correct by calculating the difference in the payoffs each strategy receives:

$$P_C - P_A = (|C - 1|R + |A|L) - (|C|L + |A - 1|L)$$
$$= |C - 1|(R - L)$$

As $R > L$, $P_C - P_A > 0$ and thus the cooperators always dominate. Our simulations confirm this result.

When comparing D and A strategies and their payoffs, we see:

$$P_D - P_A = |D - 1|P + |A|L - |A + D - 1|L$$
$$= |D - 1|P - |D - 1|L$$
$$= |D - 1|(P - L)$$

If $L = P$, then either defectors or abstainers may dominate at any stage. If $L > P$, then abstainers dominate. If $L < P$ then defectors dominate. Figure 1a illustrates this behaviour in simulations for different values of L with an initial equal population of defectors and abstainers. For each simulation, 100 separate runs are undertaken and the average of the numbers of each strategy present per run are averaged per generation and plotted. It can be seen that when $L < P$, the defectors have a selective advantage and dominate. At $L = P$, neither the defectors nor the abstainers have a clear advantage. When $L > P$, the abstainers have the selective advantage and they now dominate in the majority of cases. The above calculations assume all players play all other players; our simulations approximate this result.

4.2 All Three Strategies

In this experiment, an unbiased environment, with an initial population consisting of the same number of cooperators (C), defectors (D) and abstainers (A), is created. Figure 1b illustrates the behaviour at generation 50 across 100 individual runs. For $L < P$ defectors have already dominated the population. For $L = P$, defectors still dominate but on a minority of runs abstainers dominate. For $L > P$ this dominance of the abstainers becomes more pronounced as the payoff for abstainers increases. In fact, in some runs given the selective advantage of abstainers over defectors, some cooperators outperform the defectors resulting in a fully cooperative run.

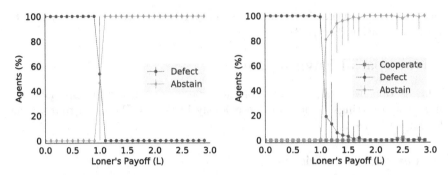

(a) Generation 50 given an initial equal popula-(b) Generation 50 given an initial equal population of defectors and abstainers.   tion of defectors, cooperators and abstainers.

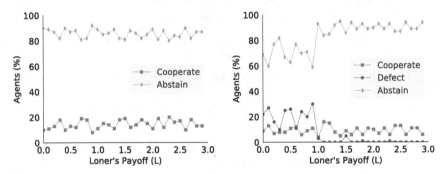

(c) Robustness: initial non-spatial population of(d) Robustness: initial non-spatial population of
1 cooperator and 99 abstainers.   1 cooperator, 1 defector and 98 abstainers.

Fig. 1. Experiments with a non-spatial population.

4.3   Robustness

The previous experiments show the outcome for a range of starting conditions.
In this section, we explore the robustness of states to the introduction of a
defector. Initially, a population is created comprising one cooperator strategy
and the remainder of the strategies are all abstainers. In this situation, in the first
generation all strategies receive the same payoffs, L. Via tournament selection,
subsequent generations may comprise more than one cooperative strategy. If
this is the case, and these cooperative strategies are chosen to play against each
other, they receive a higher payoff than abstainers, and cooperation will flourish.
On the other hand, if the cooperative strategy is not selected for subsequent
generations, then the population will consist only of abstainer strategies. This is
illustrated in Fig. 1c, which shows the average of 100 runs. In any of these runs,
the evolutionary outcome is either a population comprising fully of cooperators
or a population comprising fully of abstainers. The value of L does not affect
this outcome as $L < R$ is always true.

In the second robustness experiment, the initial population consists of 98 abstainers, 1 cooperator and 1 defector. Figure 1d shows the outcomes after 50 generations. When $L < P$, as seen previously, the defectors will have an advantage over abstainers. However, due to tournament selection, there is a possibility that a defector will not be chosen for subsequent generations. When $L > P$, the abstainers have the advantage over the defectors given the possibility of mutual defection among defectors. The defectors may continue to survive in the population given the presence of cooperators whom they can exploit. We witness that the cooperators can still do well given the benefits of mutual cooperation. However, the number of runs in which cooperation flourishes is reduced due to the presence of defectors. When $L = P$, defectors and abstainers achieve the same payoff in their pairwise interactions. However, defectors may do better in that they will exploit any cooperators. As the cooperators die out, there is no selective advantage for defectors but a level of robustness to invasion is observed.

In summary, these results show, when introducing one cooperator, abstainers and cooperators can co-exist; but when adding one cooperator and one defector more complex outcomes are possible.

5   Spatial Environments

In this section, we are interested in exploring the larger range of outcomes that result from the introduction of the spatial constraints. For the following experiments, we replace the tournament selection used in the non-spatial experiments with a mechanism whereby an agent adopts the strategy of the best performing neighbour strategy. This is in line with standard approaches in spatial simulations [6,13].

5.1   Pairwise Comparison Between Agents

When placing cooperator and defector agents randomly on the lattice grid, the defecting agents will spread amongst the cooperators echoing previous findings. When cooperator and abstainer agents are randomly placed on the grid, we find that if there are at least two cooperators beside each other, cooperation will spread, irrespective of the value of L as cooperative agents playing with each other will obtain a higher payoff than any adjacent abstainer agents. Thus, neighbours will copy the cooperating strategy. Finally, when defector and abstainer agents are randomly placed on the grid, we see from Fig. 2 that different outcomes occur depending on the value of L. This is similar to the results observed in the non-spatial pairwise comparison.

5.2   All Three Strategies

In this experiment, equal numbers of the three strategies are placed randomly on the grid. The outcome for $L < P$ is as expected with defectors quickly

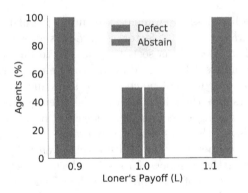

Fig. 2. Percentage of defectors and abstainers at L = 0.9, 1.0 and 1.1.

dominating the population. However, in 65 % of simulations small clusters of cooperators survive thanks to the presence of the abstainers. The abstainers give the cooperators a foothold, allowing them to ward off invasion from the defectors.

For $L = P$, defectors once again dominate, despite the tie, as they are able to exploit cooperators in the population. Once again, some small groups of cooperators survive with the same probability.

A number of simulations are run varying L from 1.1 to 2.0 where results show similar emergent evolutionary stable patterns across all values of L in this range. There are two distinct outcomes; abstainers dominate; and abstainers dominate with some sustained cooperation. Some level of cooperation is achieved on average in 51.5 % of simulations for values of L in the range [1.1, 2.0]. In these runs, a cooperative cluster (of minimum size 9), surrounded by defectors, forms in the early generations and remains a stable feature in subsequent generations. The presence of defectors, surrounding the cooperative cluster, prevents the abstainers from being invaded by the cooperators. Similarly the defector strategies remain robust to the spread of abstainers given their ability to exploit the cooperators. In essence, a symbiotic relationship is formed between cooperators and defectors. Figure 3b shows a screenshot of a cooperator and defector cluster in a simulation where abstainers have dominated. This configuration, once reached, is stable in these settings.

As the value of L increases we also witness newer phenomena. For $L = 1.5$ and $L = 2.0$, we see cycles between two states where some of the surrounding defectors fluctuate from defector to abstainer and back again. We also see an increase in the size and amount of clusters when they are formed. For $L = [1.7, 1.9]$, we see "gliders" [4] where a group of defectors flanked by a row of cooperators seemingly move across the grid, as shown in Fig. 3a. In reality, the cooperators invade the abstainers, the defectors invade the cooperators, and the abstainers in turn invade the defectors.

5.3   Exploration of the Effect of Different Initial Spatial Configurations

The aim of this experiment is to investigate different initial spatial settings of cooperators, defectors and abstainers to further explain the results witnessed in the previous experiment (Sect. 5.2). One interesting outcome from the previous simulations involved a stable situation where one strategy (inner) could survive in a cluster of the same strategies due to being surrounded fully by another strategy (middle) which, in turn, is itself surrounded fully by the third (outer) strategy (see Fig. 3b). In this case, it appeared that the inner strategy needs the protection of the middle strategy to avoid invasion by the outer strategy and that the middle strategy in turn needs the inner strategy to avoid invasion by the outer strategy. It was noted that for cooperators surrounded by defectors, a minimum inner cluster size of 9 was needed in order for this outcome to emerge.

Given three strategies, we consider all six permutations with respect to the placement of strategies in the three different positions of inner, middle and outer with an inner cluster of size 9, a middle cluster comprising 3 layers around the inner cluster, and the remaining outer portion of the grid containing only the third strategy. We label these six spatial configurations according to the first letter of the strategy (C, D, A) and their initial position (inner, middle, outer). Figure 3c is an illustration of the initial conditions for the "C-A-D" spatial configuration. We note that given any initial configuration the outcome will not vary. This means that there is no reason, other than for verification, to run a configuration multiple times. Two values of L are explored: $L < P$ and $L > P$ for each configuration. For $L = P$, simulations reveal no selective pressure for interactions between defectors and abstainers. These results involve a level of stochasticity which do not give any meaningful insights, and thus are not further discussed in this paper.

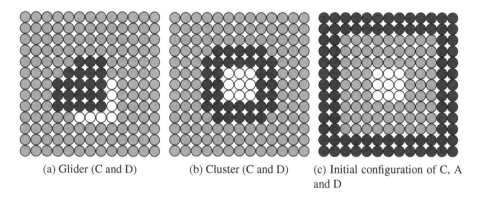

(a) Glider (C and D)   (b) Cluster (C and D)   (c) Initial configuration of C, A and D

Fig. 3. Experiments with a spatially organised population in a 100×100 lattice grid full populated with agents. The white dots represent cooperators (C), the black dots indicate defectors (D), and the grey dots are the abstainers (A).

In every permutation of A, C, and D when $L < P$ the defectors dominate. Both defectors and cooperators invade the abstainers and then the defectors begin to invade the cooperators. We again observe that many clusters of cooperators, of different sizes but of minimum size 9, remain robust to this invasion, as a result to the presence of the abstainers. The initial placement of the strategies dictates how many cooperative clusters are likely to remain robust to invasion by defection. Table 2 provides an overview of the results from each scenario when $L > P$. The existence of the abstainer strategies, in addition to the initial placement of the strategies, ensures that defection will not dominate in all of the scenarios. In fact, in one scenario (CAD), it results in a fully cooperative population.

We have seen in comparison in the non-spatial experiments that all strategies may influence each other's payoffs and we observe a smaller set of outcomes. When all the strategies are placed together, either defectors or abstainers dominate. In the spatial scenarios, there are outcomes with robust clusters of cooperators. In the robustness experiments, in the non-spatial scenarios, a largely cooperative population is easily invaded by defectors; this is not the case in the spatial scenario where we have shown that cooperators can be robust to invasion for specific initial settings. In the non-spatial scenarios, with the existence of abstainers, the population is largely robust and results in a mixed equilibrium.

Table 2. Results of seeded initial settings.

Shape	Outcome	Description
DCA	Defection spreads	Abstainers are invaded. Clusters of cooperators survive amongst dominant defectors
DAC	Defection spreads	Similar outcome as above
CDA	Structurally stable	A symbiotic cluster of cooperators and defectors persist among the abstainers
CAD	Cooperation spreads	Abstainers buffer cooperators against defectors, allowing them to dominate
ACD	Abstainers invaded	Cooperators invade the inner abstainers to create a cluster resistant to defector invasion
ADC	Abstinence spreads	Clusters of cooperators, surrounded by defectors survive within the abstainer majority (see Fig. 3b)

6   Conclusions and Future Work

In this paper, two different environments in which populations of agents played an extended version of the Prisoner's Dilemma were considered: non-spatial where all N agents were potential partners for each other, and a population organised on a lattice grid where agents can only play with their 8 immediate neighbours. For both scenarios, three sets of experiments were performed: a pairwise comparison of two strategies; experiments involving all three strategies and an exploration of the conditions leading to cooperative outcomes.

In the non-spatial environment, for the pairwise comparison, with agents initially having equal number of cooperators and abstainers, cooperation spreads throughout the population. The outcome when agents initially have an equal number of defectors and abstainers is dependent on the loner's payoff (L). When all three strategies are initially equally present in the population the value of the loner's payoff is again crucial. When the value of L is less than or equal to the punishment for mutual defection, the dominant strategy is defection; in other cases abstinence spreads as a strategy and this in turn can lead to cooperation spreading. In the robustness experiments, we consider populations comprising of agents with abstainer strategies and explore the effects of perturbing the population by the addition of firstly, a cooperative agent and secondly agents with strategies of cooperation and defection. Results show that only in the second scenario does the value of L influence the outcome.

In the spatial experiments, similar outcomes arise for the pairwise comparisons. When considering equal numbers of agents with all three strategies some similarities between the spatial and non-spatial results are noticed, but the spatial organisation allows for the clustering of cooperative agents. For all values of the loner's payoff, defection dominates in addition to the presence of some clusters of cooperators where these clusters are protected by abstainers. As the loner's payoff increases above 1.5, the size of these clusters of cooperative agents increases. In the experiments considering different initial spatial configurations interesting behaviour was noted for the six different possible starting initialisations. In all cases, irrespective of the position of the cooperative strategies initially, and the value of L, cooperative clusters persisted.

In previous work in the spatial Prisoner's Dilemma, it has been shown that cooperation can be robust to invasion if a sufficiently large cluster of cooperators form. However, given a random initialisation, this rarely happens and defectors can dominate in most scenarios. With the introduction of abstainers, we see new phenomena and a larger range of scenarios where cooperators can be robust to invasion by defectors and can dominate.

Future work will involve extending our abstract model to more realistic scenarios. There are many documented scenarios of symbiosis between entities (individuals, species, plants, companies, etc.). In our simulations, we model symbiosis between three distinct entities. We are interested in identifying scenarios where insights obtained in out spatial configurations may apply; for example, the planting of specific plants (abstainers) to prevent the invasion one plant species (defector) into another native species (cooperator).

Future work will also involve performing a more detailed investigation into emergent evolutionary stable patterns witnessed at different values of L and the exploration of other topologies with the goal of identifying structures that allow robust cooperation.

Acknowledgments. Funded by CNPq–Brazil and the Hardiman Scholarship, NUI Galway.

References

1. Arend, R.J., Seale, D.A.: Modeling alliance activity: an iterated Prisoner's Dilemma with exit option. Strateg. Manag. J. **26**(11), 1057–1074 (2005)
2. Axelrod, R.M.: The Evolution of Cooperation. Basic Books, New York (1984)
3. Batali, J., Kitcher, P.: Evolution of altruism in optional and compulsory games. J. Theor. Biol. **175**(2), 161–171 (1995)
4. Gardner, M.: Mathematical games: the fantastic combinations of John Conway's new solitaire game life. Sci. Am. **223**(4), 120–123 (1970)
5. Ghang, W., Nowak, M.A.: Indirect reciprocity with optional interactions. J. Theor. Biol. **365**, 1–11 (2015)
6. Hauert, C., Szabö, G.: Prisoner's Dilemma and public goods games in different geometries: compulsory versus voluntary interactions. Complexity **8**(4), 31–38 (2003)
7. Hauert, C., Traulsen, A., Brandt, H., Nowak, M.A.: Public goods with punishment and abstaining in finite and infinite populations. Biol. Theor. **3**(2), 114–122 (2008)
8. Izquierdo, S.S., Izquierdo, L.R., Vega-Redondo, F.: The option to leave: conditional dissociation in the evolution of cooperation. J. Theor. Biol. **267**(1), 76–84 (2010)
9. Jeong, H.C., Oh, S.Y., Allen, B., Nowak, M.A.: Optional games on cycles and complete graphs. J. Theor. Biol. **356**, 98–112 (2014)
10. Joyce, D., Kennison, J., Densmore, O., Guerin, S., Barr, S., Charles, E., Thompson, N.S.: My way or the highway: a more naturalistic model of altruism tested in an iterative Prisoners' Dilemma. J. Artif. Soc. Soc. Simulat. **9**(2), 4 (2006)
11. Li, M., O'Riordan, C.: The effect of clustering coefficient and node degree on the robustness of cooperation. In: 2013 IEEE Congress on Evolutionary Computation (CEC), pp. 2833–2839. IEEE (2013)
12. Nowak, M.A.: Evolutionary Dynamics: Exploring the Equations of Life. Harvard University Press, Cambridge (2006)
13. Nowak, M.A., May, R.M.: Evolutionary games and spatial chaos. Nature **359**(6398), 826–829 (1992)
14. Olejarz, J., Ghang, W., Nowak, M.A.: Indirect reciprocity with optional interactions and private information. Games **6**(4), 438–457 (2015)
15. Smith, J.M.: Evolution and the Theory of Games. Cambridge University Press, Cambridge (1982)
16. Xia, C.Y., Meloni, S., Perc, M., Moreno, Y.: Dynamic instability of cooperation due to diverse activity patterns in evolutionary social dilemmas. EPL **109**(5), 58002 (2015)

A Comparison of Multiobjective Algorithms in Evolving Quadrupedal Gaits

Jared M. Moore and Philip K. McKinley$^{(\boxtimes)}$

Department of Computer Science and Engineering, Michigan State University,
East Lansing, MI, USA
`moore112@msu.edu, mckinley@cse.msu.edu`

Abstract. Robotic systems, whether physical or virtual, must balance multiple objectives to operate effectively. Beyond performance metrics such as speed and turning radius, efficiency of movement, stability, and other objectives contribute to the overall functionality of a system. Optimizing multiple objectives requires algorithms that explore and balance improvements in each. In this paper, we evaluate and compare two multiobjective algorithms, NSGA-II and the recently proposed Lexicase selection, investigating distance traveled, efficiency, and vertical torso movement for evolving gaits in quadrupedal animats. We explore several variations of Lexicase selection, including different parameter configurations and weighting strategies. A control treatment evolving solely on distance traveled is also presented as a baseline. All three algorithms (NSGA-II, Lexicase, and Control) produce effective locomotion in the quadrupedal animat, but differences arise in performance and efficiency of movement. The NSGA-II algorithm significantly outperforms Lexicase selection in all three objectives, while Lexicase selection significantly outperforms the control in two of the three objectives.

Keywords: Evolutionary robotics · Multiobjective algorithms · Genetic algorithms · Computational evolution · Lexicase selection · NSGA-II

1 Introduction

Many animals demonstrate a remarkable combination of speed, agility, and efficiency in locomotion. To produce such behaviors in artificial systems requires controllers capable of balancing objectives associated with performance, efficiency of movement, and stability. Multiobjective evolutionary algorithms, such as NSGA-II [7], address such problems by optimizing objectives concurrently. NSGA-II progresses along a Pareto optimal front, considering all objectives equally during the optimization process. In contrast, Lexicase selection, recently proposed by Spector [22], adopts a non-Pareto based approach to address multiple objectives. During a selection event, Lexicase evaluates a group of individuals based on one or multiple objectives, with the order of objectives randomized. After comparing performance in the first selected objective, additional objectives are considered only if two or more individuals are tied.

© Springer International Publishing Switzerland 2016
E. Tuci et al. (Eds.): SAB 2016, LNAI 9825, pp. 157–169, 2016.
DOI: 10.1007/978-3-319-43488-9_15

Lexicase selection has recently been shown to be effective in genetic programming problems. In this paper, we compare Lexicase selection to NSGA-II in the context of evolutionary robotics. Specifically, we evaluate the performance of the two algorithms in evolving gaits for quadrupedal animats. We also conduct a control experiment based on a single-objective genetic algorithm that selects only for distance traveled. Results indicate that the NSGA-II algorithm finds superior solutions in all three objectives when compared to Lexicase selection. However, we note that Lexicase solutions are significantly better than those of the control in two of the three objectives.

The contributions of this work are as follows: First, we compare the performance of NSGA-II, Lexicase, and the control in evolving quadrupedal gaits. Second, we examine alternative Lexicase parameter configurations and discuss differences that arise. Finally, we present our findings on a weighted objective approach with Lexicase selection. Although Lexicase does not outperform NSGA-II in this study, the experimental results show that it may still be an effective multiobjective algorithm. Evolved individuals from Lexicase exhibit gaits that are both effective and efficient. Moreover, Lexicase has been shown to perform well with large numbers of objectives. Further investigation, taking into account additional factors in movement through uncertain environments is warranted.

2   Background and Related Work

Evolutionary robotics (ER) [4,5,9,20] draws upon concepts observed in natural evolution and applies them to the design of robots. ER approaches have proven effective in areas such as gait evolution [6,8], agent-environment interaction [3,4], and rocket guidance systems [10]. In addition to control, optimizing morphology can exploit relationships between brain and body [17,18], as occurs in the evolution of biological organisms. In many problems, single objective evolutionary algorithms (e.g., distance traveled) produce effective systems. However, addressing a single objective does not satisfy the expectations placed on a typical robotic system. Additional metrics are needed to assess conditions related to battery life, robustness to uncertain conditions, navigation, and resilience, among others. Multiobjective algorithms are one approach to addressing these more complex problems.

Evolutionary multiobjective optimization (EMO) algorithms take multiple metrics into account when assessing the performance of individuals. NSGA-II, developed by Deb et al. [7], is a Pareto-based EMO that has proven effective in ER and other applications [12,16,23]. The first principle of the algorithm is non-domination. An individual *dominates* another individual if it is better in at least one objective and no worse in the other objectives. Non-dominated individuals form a Pareto-optimal front across the objective space. Second, the distribution along the Pareto front is balanced by a crowding distance metric. By analyzing the location of non-dominated individuals on the Pareto front, the selected solutions cover the objective space equally. These two principles result in a Pareto optimal front, wherein non-dominated individuals are distributed around the objective space, providing different solutions that balance multiple objectives. Over evolutionary time, NSGA-II evolves individuals toward the optimal values in each objective along the Pareto front. Schrum and Miikkulainen [19] have shown that NSGA-II produces effective controllers for agents with distinct behaviors for each task in a game environment. Mouret [15] used NSGA-II to solve a maze navigation task, demonstrating that a multiobjective approach was more effective than novelty search [13] alone. Auerbach and Bongard [2] employed NSGA-II to evolve both control and morphology, producing highly cohesive robotic systems.

NSGA-II and other Pareto-based algorithms consider all objectives equally at each generation. A recently proposed approach is to evaluate individuals on a subset of the total objective space. Lexicase selection was originally proposed by Spector [22] to address modal problems in GP. It was inspired by the lexicographic parsimony pressure technique proposed by Luke and Panait [14] to control growth in GP trees by considering objectives lexically. The key idea is that, in each selection event, the objectives are randomly ordered and considered one at a time. After the individuals are compared based on the first selected objective, additional objectives are used to evaluate the individuals only in the case of a tie in the previous objective. Depending upon the random ordering, an individual may undergo selective pressure on one objective for multiple generations, and is then evaluated on a second objective at a later time. In contrast to Pareto optimization algorithms, each selection event considers only a subset of the objective space, potentially discovering solutions different from those obtained with evolutionary search directed along a Pareto front. Lexicase selection has proven effective in solving challenging GP problems, where many objectives must be met simultaneously [11], but to our knowledge has not previously been explored in the context of evolutionary robotics. In this paper, we evaluate Lexicase selection and assess its performance against a known multi-objective evolutionary algorithm, NSGA-II.

3   Methods

Simulation Environment: Evolved behaviors are evaluated with the Open Dynamics Engine (ODE) [21], a 3D rigid body physics-based simulation environment. ODE handles collisions between rigid bodies, forces (friction and gravity), and joints between rigid components. Figure 1 shows an (evolved) instance of the quadrupedal animat used in this study. The four legs are connected to the main body by a hip joint and divided into upper, middle, and lower segments. Each joint is a hinge allowing for movement along the long-axis of the main body. Movement of a joint is determined by specifying the angular velocity per simulation timestep. An individual is simulated for 10 s at a timestep of 0.005 s. The environment is configured as a flat, high-friction surface resulting in minimal slippage between the animat and substrate.

Fig. 1. The quadrupedal animat used in this study features twelve hinge joints. Each leg has three segments. Limb lengths, joint range of motion, and the initial offset of each leg are evolvable morphological parameters.

Genome: As shown in Table 1, each genome comprises 42 separate parameters defining aspects of both control and morphology. The controller is a central pattern generator with joint behavior defined as follows. Joints are driven by a shared periodic oscillating signal with evolved oscillation frequency. A gene specifies maximum joint velocity, limiting the upper angular velocity of all joints in an animat. Two levels of phase offsets create a custom oscillation signal for each joint in the animat. Each leg has its own phase offset which applies to the three joints (hip, knee, ankle) comprising the leg. The front and rear legs are then paired with phase offsets for hip, knee, and ankle. This encoding allows for left/right symmetry to evolve, but does not require it as the legs in each pair (front and rear) can move out of phase. Six genes specify the maximum force each joint can exert during movement. Morphologies of the animats evolve in terms of the initial rotations of the leg segments, the lengths of the leg segments and the upper/lower limits of the joints.

Table 1. Genes comprising a quadrupedal animat.

Description	# Genes
Oscillation frequency	1
Max joint velocity	1
Phase offset (per leg)	4
Phase offset (per joint with left/right symmetry)	6
Max joint force (left/right symmetry)	6
Initial joint rotation (left/right symmetry)	6
Leg segment length (left/right symmetry)	6
Upper joint range limit (left/right symmetry)	6
Lower joint range limit (left/right symmetry)	6
Total	42

Fitness Metrics: We assess individuals with three fitness objectives. The first is the Euclidean distance traveled by an individual over the course of the simulation. Distance is not constrained to only forward movement in order to minimize the influence of direction on evolved gaits. The second objective is efficiency, defined as the distance traveled per unit of power exerted by an individual. Finally as the third objective, we evaluate the vertical movement of the center of mass over time and record the total displacement. Many biological organisms tend to exhibit low vertical movement of the center of mass during locomotion, and it has also been shown to be effective at producing efficient legged gaits in robotic systems [1]. Our goal is to maximize objectives one and two, while minimizing objective three.

Forces are recorded over the course of an evaluation to calculate efficiency. In situations where the maximum joint power is low, the joint is unable to actively move its connected bodies. An underpowered joint moves passively, regardless of the control signal being applied. Joint movement is thus a combination of desired angle, force output from the controller, and interaction of the morphology with the environment. This configuration allows for different degrees of efficiency to arise among evolved individuals as higher joint power increases force output.

Treatments: As described above, we conducted three separate treatments: Control, NSGA-II, and Lexicase. In all three treatments, populations comprise 120 individuals and evolve for 6000 generations. Each treatment consists of 20 replicate runs initialized with a unique random number seed. Two-point crossover is employed with a probability of 0.5. Genes are mutated with a probability of 0.04 and perturbed within a range of $\pm 10\%$ of the gene's range. For the Control treatment, tournament selection is used with a tournament size of 4 individuals and elitism with one elite individual.

NSGA-II Selection: NSGA-II evolves individuals along a Pareto-optimal front. For a given generation, the next population is selected from both the previous generation's population and the current set of child individuals produced from selection, crossover and mutation. Individuals are selected based on their non-domination ordering, with each non-dominated front added to the new population until the population size would be exceeded. The last front is then added to the population by sorting in descending order based on crowding distance. Individuals with the largest distance are selected until the population size is reached, ensuring that the most diverse solutions for the last front are included in the new population. For an in-depth discussion of NSGA-II, please refer to [7].

Lexicase Selection: Algorithm 1 is pseudocode for Lexicase selection as used in this study. Lexicase selection replaces the tournament selection mechanism in the Control treatment. Crossover and mutation are handled after selection and are identical to how they are treated in the Control. Rather than consider all metrics equally in a selection event, for each selection event, Lexicase considers subsets of the objectives in a random order. Thus, a set of individuals may be evaluated on one objective, or multiple, depending upon the selection process described below. A sample of n individuals from the population ($n = 4$ in this study) is obtained and the order in which objectives will be considered is randomized (lines 1–2). Individuals in the sample are then compared on the first objective (lines 3–19) and ranked from best to worst in terms of performance for that objective (line 4). All sampled individuals are then compared to the best individual from the sample in the objective and checked to see if they are within a specified threshold (10 %) of performance (lines 5–11). If there is a tie, we select the subset of individuals within the threshold, removing low performing individuals in the selected objective and proceed to the next objective (lines 12–13). Otherwise we select the best individual and exit the for loop (lines 14–17). If multiple individuals fall within the threshold across all objectives, we randomly select an individual from the tied set (line 21).

Algorithm 1. Lexicase selection pseudocode. Adapted from [22]

1: $sample \leftarrow SamplePopulation(population, 4)$
2: $obj\_order \leftarrow Shuffle(fitness\_objectives)$
3: **for** obj in obj_order **do**
4:      $r\_sam \leftarrow RankSample(sample, obj)$
5:      $tie\_index \leftarrow 0$
6:      **for** i in 1 to $length(r\_sam)$ **do**
7:          **if** $r\_sam[i][obj] \geq 0.9 * r\_sam[0][obj]$ **then**
8:              $tie \leftarrow True$
9:              $tie\_index \leftarrow i$
10:          **end if**
11:      **end for**
12:      **if** tie **is** $True$ **then**
13:          $sample \leftarrow r\_sam[0 : tie\_index]$
14:      **else**
15:          $tie \leftarrow False$
16:          $sample \leftarrow r\_sam[0]$
17:          **break**
18:      **end if**
19: **end for**
20: **if** tie **is** $True$ **then**
21:      **return** $RandomChoice(sample)$
22: **else**
23:      **return** $sample[0]$
24: **end if**

Our implementation is similar to that described in [22] except for the introduction of the threshold. The threshold allows us to customize performance comparison between individuals. For example, in gait evaluation, the performance of an individual that travels 30 units and that of one traveling 29 units can be considered almost identical. A separate treatment, not discussed in the results, was run with a threshold of 5 %. Evolutionary results were nearly identical to the Lexicase treatment presented here. We therefore opt to present the Lexicase results with only the 10 % threshold in Sect. 4.

4   Experiments and Results

For our purposes, we treat evolution as a tool for finding the most effective solutions as opposed to studying the evolutionary trajectories of populations. Therefore, the results presented here are for the farthest traveling individual per replicate, with performance analyzed in all three objectives. Figure 2 provides boxplots of the farthest traveling individual in each replicate when evaluated on each of the three objectives. Table 2 gives the pairwise comparisons (Wilcoxon Rank-Sum Test) between the distributions of the farthest traveling individual per treatment in the three objectives. NSGA-II significantly outperforms both Lexicase and Control in the distance traveled objective while Lexicase and the Control are not significantly different. Lexicase significantly outperforms the Control in both efficiency and vertical movement. This result suggests that Lexicase does in fact produce individuals with better performance across all three objectives. NSGA-II significantly outperforms the Control in efficiency and vertical movement. There is no significant difference between NSGA-II and Lexicase in efficiency, but the two are significantly different in vertical movement.

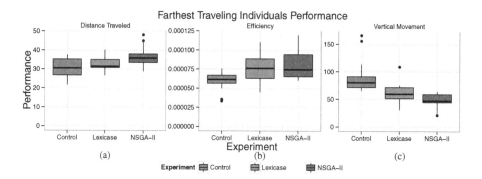

Fig. 2. Performance in the three metrics of the farthest traveling individual per replicate across the three treatments. Refer to Table 2 for significance comparisons between treatments. (Color figure online)

Figure 3(a) plots the distance traveled versus efficiency for the best individual per replicate. Although NSGA-II generally outperforms Lexicase, a few individual Lexicase replicates are competitive with the best NSGA-II replicates, and one replicate from the Lexicase treatment lies on a Pareto front of distance versus efficiency. However, five Lexicase replicates exhibit lower efficiency than many replicates from the Control treatment. Not considering these five replicates, Lexicase would actually be competitive with NSGA-II in terms of efficiency.

Figure 3(b) plots the distance traveled versus vertical movement of the best individual per replicate. NSGA-II again produces the majority of the best individuals although Lexicase does produce one of the best solutions, located near a Pareto front along the bottom-right of the figure. The Control treatment is not effective, as there is no selective pressure in the vertical movement metric.

Table 2. Pairwise Wilcoxon Rank-Sum Test between the farthest traveling individual per replicate.

Objective	Treatment	Treatment	P-Value
Distance	Control	Lexicase	0.080
Distance	Control	NSGA-II	<0.001
Distance	Lexicase	NSGA-II	0.010
Efficiency	Control	Lexicase	0.007
Efficiency	Control	NSGA-II	<0.001
Efficiency	Lexicase	NSGA-II	0.603
Vert. Move.	Control	Lexicase	<0.001
Vert. Move.	Control	NSGA-II	<0.001
Vert. Move.	Lexicase	NSGA-II	0.015

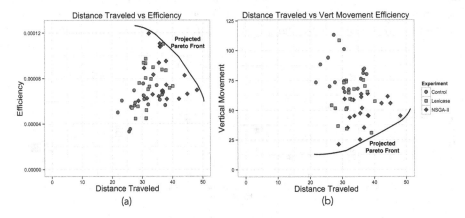

Fig. 3. (a) Distance traveled versus efficiency and (b) distance traveled versus vertical movement for the farthest traveling individual per replicate across the treatments.

Alternative Parameters: NSGA-II is a well studied algorithm, whereas, Lexicase selection was only recently proposed. In the initial experiment, parameters were chosen based on a review of the current literature, but other parameter values may be better suited to this specific problem. The Lexicase treatment described above evaluated 4 individuals and randomized the order of the objectives per selection event. We conducted two other treatments exploring different configurations. In the first, we increased the number of evaluated individuals to 8 per selection event. The increased sample size did not produce any significant difference between the farthest traveling individual per replicate in terms of distance traveled or efficiency compared to the original Lexicase treatment. However, there was a significant increase in vertical movement ($p < 0.001$) which is an objective to be minimized. It is unclear why vertical movement is higher, but we speculate that the increased sample size could lead to more ties when comparing individuals. If ties were to increase when considering vertical movement as the first objective, multiple objectives would then be used to evaluate individuals, producing less selective pressure acting on the vertical movement objective alone. NSGA-II would be less likely to face this risk, as the Pareto-front optimization, and specifically the crowding distance measure, consider individuals across the objective space that have both large and small vertical movements. Future work is planned to investigate this difference.

The second variation we investigated involved shuffling the objective ordering per generation instead of per selection event. That is to say, in each generation all child individuals are selected using the same ordering of objectives. Surprisingly, results for this experiment were not significantly different than the Lexicase treatment in any of the three objectives.

Weighted Lexicase: Another proposed variation of Lexicase selection suggested by Spector et al. [11] is to assign weights to the objectives, thereby affecting the frequency of orderings during selection. This weighting strategy is intended to bias the search. We conducted an additional three treatments to explore this strategy. The 75-15-10 strategy (WLex-75_15_10) assigns a weight of 0.75 to distance traveled, 0.15 to energy efficiency, and 0.10 to vertical movement. We also tested WLex-50_25_25 and WLex-15_75_10.

Table 3 presents the pairwise comparison among treatments of the farthest traveling individual from each replicate. It appears that the weighting strategies do not have a large impact on performance when compared to the regular Lexicase treatment, except in vertical movement. Lexicase significantly outperformed the weighted Lexicase variants (WLex-75_15_10 and WLex-15_75_10) in reducing vertical movement during locomotion. This result is likely due to the low weight (10 %) assigned to the vertical movement objective in the two weighted treatments.

Table 3. Pairwise Wilcoxon Rank-Sum Test between the farthest traveling individual per replicate.

Objective	Treatment	Treatment	P-Value
Distance	Lexicase	WLex-50_25_25	0.857
Distance	Lexicase	WLex-75_15_10	0.945
Distance	Lexicase	WLex-15_75_10	0.742
Efficiency	Lexicase	WLex-50_25_25	0.428
Efficiency	Lexicase	WLex-75_15_10	0.478
Efficiency	Lexicase	WLex-15_75_10	0.322
Vert. Move.	Lexicase	WLex-50_25_25	0.513
Vert. Move.	Lexicase	WLex-75_15_10	0.018
Vert. Move.	Lexicase	WLex-15_75_10	0.028

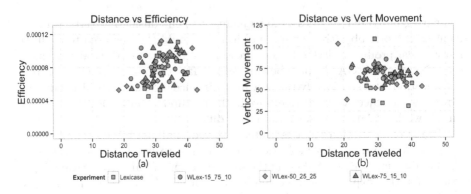

Fig. 4. (a) Distance traveled versus efficiency and (b) distance traveled versus vertical movement for the farthest traveling individual per replicate across the treatments.

Figure 4(a) plots the farthest distance traveled versus efficiency for all Lexicase treatments. Even when attempting to bias the ordering of the objectives, the distance traveled and efficiency remain quite similar among treatments. Perhaps surprisingly, the farthest traveling individuals do not arise in the WLex-75_15_10 treatment but instead in the WLex-50_25_25 treatment. In 2 of the 20 replicates, increasing weights for efficiency and vertical movement (25 % each) allow individuals to evolve higher distances traveled. We speculate that overweighting a single objective and therefore biasing the search process limits the space of solutions tested. However, further research is necessary to investigate this hypothesis.

Figure 4(b) plots the farthest traveling individual per replicate's distance traveled versus vertical movement. Here, vertical movement is significantly higher in the WLex-75_15_10 and WLex-15_75_10 versus the Lexicase treatment. A low weight, in this case 10 %, potentially degrades performance in vertical movement. Further investigation is required to determine if there is an appropriate distribution of weights to assign to each objective. There is also a possibility that the results here are only encountered in specific experimental configurations and under/overweighting is not generally an issue.

5   Discussion

This paper is intended to evaluate the recently proposed Lexicase selection in an evolutionary robotics task and to compare it to a well known EMO algorithm, NSGA-II. Lexicase has mainly been employed in many objective modal problems in GP. Here, the objectives are not necessarily modal, that is, the objectives are likely related to each other as they define specific characteristics of a quadrupedal gait. Efficiency, calculated as the distance traveled per unit of power, is intrinsically linked to the distance traveled metric. Furthermore, vertical oscillation (metric 3) is likely influenced by efficiency as efficient biological organisms tend to exhibit low degrees of vertical oscillation [1].

The low number of objectives may also favor NSGA-II, as Pareto-based algorithms are effective in these smaller spaces. As the number of objectives increases, Pareto algorithms begin to break down due to the reduction of dominating solutions [24]. A large objective set allows most solutions to be dominant in at least one objective. In these situations, Lexicase selection might optimize solutions across these many objectives better than Pareto-based approaches by evaluating subsets of the objectives per selection event. The challenge, however, is to identify those objectives and the specific goals for a problem. Here, we considered only efficiency in terms of energy consumption versus distance traveled and the vertical movement of the torso. Additional objectives might include minimizing touches with the surface, pitch changes in the torso, constraints on the morphology relating to mass distribution among components, and response to sudden changes in substrate or obstacles.

6   Conclusions

In this paper we have explored Lexicase selection in a quadrupedal gait evolution task. While capable of generating effective solutions, Lexicase selection does not significantly outperform a standard genetic algorithm in terms of distance traveled. However, it does produce more efficient solutions with less vertical movement. On the other hand, NSGA-II significantly outperforms Lexicase selection in both distance traveled and energy efficiency. NSGA-II thus appears to be the better algorithm for quadrupedal gait evolution involving three objectives. Still, the Lexicase selection mechanism shows that it can produce effective gaits. Additional objectives might lead to better relative performance.

We have investigated a few variations of the Lexicase selection algorithm, but many other configurations are yet to be explored. An alternative ER experiment could consider situations where the objectives are independent, for example, with each objective assigned to a unique behavior. This approach might more closely align an ER experiment with the original studies of Lexicase selection in GP. Another possible extension would be to change the objective ordering in a more principled manner. In our investigations, we randomly shuffled the objectives either per selection event or per generation. Alternative ordering strategies might improve the performance of the algorithm, but we leave those issues to future investigations.

Acknowledgments. The authors gratefully acknowledge the contributions and feedback provided by Anthony Clark, Xiaobo Tan, Craig McGowan, and members of the BEACON Center at Michigan State University. This work was supported in part by National Science Foundation grants CNS-1059373, CNS-0915855, and DBI-0939454, and by a grant from Michigan State University.

References

1. Ackerman, J., Seipel, J.: Energy efficiency of legged robot locomotion with elastically suspended loads. IEEE Trans. Robot. **29**(2), 321–330 (2013)
2. Auerbach, J.E., Bongard, J.C.: Environmental Influence on the Evolution of Morphological Complexity in Machines. PLoS Comput. Biol. **10**(1), e1003399 (2014)
3. Beer, R.D.: Toward the evolution of dynamical neural networks for minimally cognitive behavior. In: Proceedings of the Fourth International Conference on Simulation of Adaptive Behavior, vol. 1, pp. 421–429. MIT Press (1996)
4. Brooks, R.A.: A robot that walks; emergent behaviors from a carefully evolved network. Neural Comput. **1**(2), 253–262 (1989)
5. Cliff, D., Husbands, P., Harvey, I.: Explorations in evolutionary robotics. Adapt. Behav. **2**(1), 73–110 (1993)
6. Clune, J., Beckmann, B.E., Ofria, C., Pennock, R.T.: Evolving coordinated quadruped gaits with the HyperNEAT generative encoding. In: Proceedings of the IEEE Congress on Evolutionary Computation, Trondheim, Norway, pp. 2764–2771 (2009)
7. Deb, K., Pratap, A., Agarwal, S., Meyarivan, T.: A fast and elitist multiobjective genetic algorithm: NSGA-II. IEEE Trans. Evol. Comput. **6**(2), 182–197 (2002)
8. Doncieux, S., Mouret, J.B.: Behavioral diversity with multiple behavioral distances. In: Proceedings of the 2013 IEEE Congress on Evolutionary Computation, pp. 1427–1434. IEEE, Cancun (2013)
9. Floreano, D., Husbands, P., Nolfi, S.: Evolutionary robotics. In: Siciliano, B., Khatib, O. (eds.) Handbook of Robotics, pp. 1423–1451. Springer, Berlin (2008)
10. Gomez, F., Miikkulainen, R.: Active guidance for a finless rocket using neuroevolution. In: Proceedings of the 2003 Genetic and Evolutionary Computation Conference, Chicago, Illinois, USA, pp. 2084–2095 (2003)
11. Helmuth, T., Spector, L., Matheson, J.: Solving uncompromising problems with Lexicase selection. In: IEEE Transactions on Evolutionary Computation, vol. 99, p. 1 (2014)
12. Koos, S., Mouret, J.B., Doncieux, S.: Crossing the reality gap in evolutionary robotics by promoting transferable controllers. In: Proceedings of the 2010 ACM Genetic and Evolutionary Computation Conference, pp. 119–126. ACM, Portland (2010)
13. Lehman, J., Stanley, K.O.: Efficiently evolving programs through the search for novelty. In: Proceedings of the 12th Annual Conference on Genetic and Evolutionary Computation, pp. 837–844. ACM, Portland (2010)
14. Luke, S., Panait, L.: Lexicographic parsimony pressure. In: Proceedings of the Genetic and Evolutionary Computation Conference, pp. 829–836. Morgan Kaufmann Publishers, New York (2002)
15. Mouret, J.-B.: Novelty-based multiobjectivization. In: Doncieux, S., Bredèche, N., Mouret, J.-B. (eds.) New Horizons in Evolutionary Robotics. SCI, vol. 341, pp. 139–154. Springer, Heidelberg (2011)
16. Ollion, C., Doncieux, S.: Towards behavioral consistency in neuroevolution. In: Ziemke, T., Balkenius, C., Hallam, J. (eds.) SAB 2012. LNCS, vol. 7426, pp. 177–186. Springer, Heidelberg (2012)
17. Paul, C.: Morphological computation: a basis for the analysis of morphology and control requirements. Robot. Auton. Syst. **54**(8), 619–630 (2006). http://www.sciencedirect.com/science/article/pii/S0921889006000613

18. Paul, C., Bongard, J.C.: The road less travelled: morphology in the optimization of biped robot locomotion. In: Proceedings of the 2001 IEEE/RSJ International Conference on Intelligent Robots and Systems, Maui, Hawaii, USA, pp. 226–232 (2001)
19. Schrum, J., Miikkulainen, R.: Evolving multimodal networks for multitask games. IEEE Trans. Comput. Intell. AI Games **4**(2), 94–111 (2012)
20. Sims, K.: Evolving virtual creatures. In: Proceedings of the 21st Annual Conference on Computer Graphics and Interactive Techniques, pp. 15–22 (1994)
21. Smith, R.: Open Dynamics Engine (2013). http://www.ode.org/
22. Spector, L.: Assessment of problem modality by differential performance of Lexicase selection in genetic programming: a preliminary report. In: Proceedings of the 14th Annual Conference Companion on Genetic and Evolutionary Computation, pp. 401–408. ACM, Philadelphia (2012)
23. Szerlip, P., Stanley, K.O.: Indirectly encoded sodarace for artificial life. In: Proceedings of the 12th European Conference on Artificial Life, Taormina, Italy, pp. 218–225 (2013)
24. Zitzler, E., Laumanns, M., Thiele, L.: SPEA2: improving the strength Pareto evolutionary algorithm. Technical report, Swiss Federal Institute of Technology (ETH), Zurich (2001)

Learning to Switch Between Sensorimotor Primitives Using Multimodal Haptic Signals

Zhe Su[1(✉)], Oliver Kroemer[2], Gerald E. Loeb[1], Gaurav S. Sukhatme[2], and Stefan Schaal[2]

[1] Department of Biomedical Engineering,
University of Southern California, Los Angeles, CA, USA
zhesu@usc.edu
[2] Department of Computer Science,
University of Southern California, Los Angeles, CA, USA

Abstract. Most manipulation tasks can be decomposed into sequences of sensorimotor primitives. These primitives often end with characteristic sensory events, e.g., making or breaking contact, which indicate when the sensorimotor goal has been reached. In this manner, the robot can monitor the tactile signals to determine when to switch between primitives. In this paper, we present a framework for automatically segmenting contact-based manipulation tasks into sequences of sensorimotor primitives using multimodal haptic signals. These signals include both the robot's end-effector position as well as the low- and high-frequency components of its tactile sensors. The resulting segmentation is used to learn to detect when the robot has reached a sensorimotor goal and it should therefore switch to the next primitive. The proposed framework was evaluated on guided peg-in-hole tasks. The experiments show that the framework can extract the subtasks of the manipulations and the sensorimotor goals can be accurately detected.

Keywords: Multimodal tactile sensing · Sensorimotor primitives · Primitive segmentation · Learning from demonstration

1 Introduction

Manipulation tasks typically involve executing a series of discrete sensorimotor primitives. For example, humans pick and place objects by grasping, lifting, transporting, placing, and releasing the objects. These primitives are usually bound by mechanical events that represent sensorimotor subgoals of the task [6], e.g., making or breaking contact between either the hand and an object or a grasped object and another object.

These changes in the contact state result in discrete and distinct sensory events that are characterized by specific neural signatures in human tactile afferents [7]. For example, when fingers make contact with an object during grasping, signals from the slow- and fast-adapting type one afferents (SA-I, FA-I) provide

© Springer International Publishing Switzerland 2016
E. Tuci et al. (Eds.): SAB 2016, LNAI 9825, pp. 170–182, 2016.
DOI: 10.1007/978-3-319-43488-9_16

information about the outcome of the grasp. Similarly, the FA-II afferents detect the contact vibrations during tool use when contact between the grasped object and another object is made or broken, or when slip occurs. An example of a sensory event for a robot is shown in Fig. 1. The tactile signals indicate that the fingers made contact, and thus reached the goal, earlier than expected. If this sensory event was completely absent, then it would indicate that the goal was not achieved. These sensory events thus provide information about if and when a primitive's goal has been reached. Given this information, the robot can determine when to terminate the current primitive and start the next one.

In this paper, we present a framework for segmenting manipulation tasks into sensorimotor primitives and subsequently learning to switch between these primitives based on tactile events. The segmentation is performed using Bayesian on-line changepoint detection [1] with multimodal haptic signals. Each changepoint indicates a sensorimotor subgoal of the task. The haptic time series signals include the Cartesian position of the

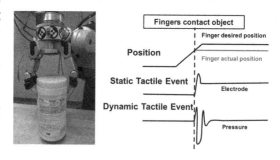

Fig. 1. An illustration of a sensorimotor event resulting from finger-object contact during grasping.

robot's hand and the low- and high-frequency signals of the tactile sensors [23].

The sensory signals before and after each changepoint are used to learn a classifier for detecting the sensory event when the primitive is executed. In this manner, the robot can monitor whether the subgoal has been reached and switch to the next sensorimotor primitive accordingly. Rather than manually designing features for representing the haptic signals, the robot uses Spatio-Temporal Hierarchical Matching Pursuit (ST-HMP) [12] to learn suitable features. The detection of the sensory events is then achieved using linear support vector machines.

The proposed framework was evaluated using guided peg-in-hole tasks. The experiments evaluated the segmentation using different sets of sensor modalities, and the accuracy of the classifiers for switching between sensorimotor primitives. In a validation experiment, the robot used the learned primitives and switching behaviours to autonomously perform guided peg-in-hole tasks.

2   Related Work

Learning from demonstration (LfD) methods have emerged as an effective approach to transfer human manipulation skills to robots. Many of these methods learn libraries of movement primitives that adapt to the context of the task [4,13,18]. These primitives are often trained on presegmented data, and they are usually run for a fixed duration or until they reach a predefined threshold from the goal state. Kappler et al. [8] also proposed a framework for switching between primitives based on multimodal signals. However, their approach is based on modeling the stereotypical sensor values at every time step of the primitives rather than detecting the characteristic sensory event of the primitive's sensorimotor goal.

Previous work has also proposed methods for automatically segmenting manipulation tasks into sequences of skills [15,17]. These approaches focus on using proprioceptive signals to segment the tasks. By including tactile data, our segmentation approach results in primitives that terminate in sensory events that can be monitored to determine if contact goals have been reached. Methods have also been proposed for segmenting tasks into phases based on changes in the dynamics [9,10]. Primitives can then be learned for transitioning between the segmented phases. Our approach learns primitives directly and does not require learning explicit models of the task.

A primitive that terminates early depending on sensory conditions is also known as a guarded motion. Guarded motions have been widely adopted for industrial robotic manipulators and prosthetic hands to avoid applying excessive force to the external objects [5,14]. The sensory conditions for switching between the primitives are usually hand-designed by human experts.

Tactile servoing has also been successfully integrated into direct robot control to continuously follow distinctive surface features of objects, such as edges [11,20]. Our work focuses on switching between primitives based on discrete sensory events and is thus a complimentary approach to including tactile feedback.

Approximate online Bayesian changepoint detection has been used in combination with articulation models to segment demonstrated manipulation tasks by detecting changes in the motions of objects [16]. In this work, authors relied only on the relative pose of two objects/parts to segment manipulation tasks, and not the force-torque or tactile signals. Given the importance of high frequency tactile signals in manipulation tasks [19,21], our approach incorporates these signals into the online Bayesian changepoint detection.

3   Approach

The goal of our work is to autonomously segment manipulations into sensorimotor primitives and to subsequently learn classifiers for determining when to switch between the primitives. We introduce the multimodal signals and the sensorimotor primitives used in this work in Sects. 3.1 and 3.2 respectively. We then explain the segmenting of the demonstrations into primitives in Sect. 3.3, and learning to detect sensory events for switching between primitives in Sect. 3.4.

3.1   Multimodal Haptic Signals

In our experiments, we use a robot consisting of a 7-DOF Barrett WAM arm and Barrett hand, whose three fingers are equipped with biomimetic tactile sensors (BioTacs). This system provides rich multimodal haptic signals, including proprioceptive signals, and both static and dynamic tactile signals. On our robot, the proprioceptive signals include the Cartesian position of the robot's end-effector $\mathbf{y}_{\text{pos}} \in \mathbb{R}^3$ derived from the forward kinematics of the robot manipulator, as well as the force-torque signals $\mathbf{y}_{\text{FT}} \in \mathbb{R}^6$ measured on the robot's wrist force-torque sensor.

Static tactile signals are mainly sensitive to constant contacts, such as static forces applied to an object being grasped. BioTacs [20] consist of a rigid core housing an array of 19 electrodes surrounded by an elastic skin. The skin is inflated with an incompressible and conductive liquid. When the skin is in contact with an object, the liquid is displaced, and the conductance of the electrodes changes. The electrode conductance changes $\mathbf{y}_{\text{E}} \in \mathbb{R}^{19}$ are used to measure the static contact forces at 100 Hz.

Dynamic tactile signals are sensitive to transient mechanical events, e.g., making and breaking contact between hand-held tools and other objects. Micro-vibrations in the skin can propagate through the fluid in the BioTac and are detected as high-frequency signals by the hydro-acoustic pressure sensor embedded in the sensor's core. These high-frequency 2200 Hz vibration signals, $\mathbf{y}_{\text{PAC}} \in \mathbb{R}^{22}$ at 100 Hz, are used to detect transient mechanical events.

3.2   Sensorimotor Primitives

A sensorimotor primitive is a parametrized synergy of motion and sensing that can be used to build task strategies. For example, the motion for inserting a peg into a hole and the sensory feedback from the peg hitting the hole bottom form a sensorimotor primitive. This sensorimotor primitive can be sequenced together with other sensorimotor primitives to perform insertion tasks.

The sensorimotor primitives used in this paper consist of a force-position controller and a sensory goal detector. The closed-loop controller defines the behaviour for reaching a desired state while the goal detector continuously monitors if the sensory goal has been reached. The primitives are segmented such that they each terminate with a sensory event, as shown in Fig. 2. These sensory events have a short duration, which is chosen to be 160ms long. This duration

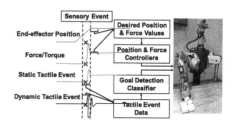

Fig. 2. Illustration of our framework of segmentation of sensorimotor primitives from demonstrated trajectories.

is chosen by comparing the goal detector's success rates under different durations of sensory events. The signals observed during the sensory event are used to train the goal detector, as detailed in Sect. 3.4. The position and force signals 100ms after the sensory event are used to compute the final desired state for the controller. The feedback gains for the controllers are predefined. The desired force is incrementally increased by 1N, if the primitive failed to reach the desired sensory event. The desired position is defined relative to the starting position of the skill. Thus, if a skill terminates early, the following primitives' desired positions are offset accordingly.

3.3   Sensorimotor Primitives Segmentation

Proprioceptive signals are often used to segment action primitives [15,17]. However, these signals do not capture task-specific tactile events during motions involving contact with the environment. As a result, it is often difficult to verify if the contact goal of a primitive was achieved in these cases.

In contrast to the relatively smooth proprioceptive signals, the dynamic tactile signals are sensitive to contact events. Some of these events will be relevant to the task and result in switching between primitives, but others may be irrelevant. For example, in a peg-in-hole task, the vibrations from the peg entering the hole and making contact with the bottom of the hole both relate to task-relevant contact events. However, the vibrations resulting from scratching the peg over a rough surface are not considered to be relevant to this task and are effectively noise.

We use unsupervised Bayesian online changepoint detection (BOCPD) [1] to segment trajectories into unknown numbers of primitives with discrete sensory events. We apply this method jointly on both the proprioceptive and the tactile signals. BOCPD sequentially calculates the posterior distribution over the current run length $r_t \in \mathbb{Z}$ at time t, i.e., r_t is the number of time steps since the last changepoint. The posterior distribution $p(r_t|y_{1:t})$, given the previously observed data $y_{1:t}$, is computed by normalizing the joint likelihood $P(r_t|y_{1:t}) = \frac{P(r_t, y_{1:t})}{P(y_{1:t})}$.

The joint likelihood over the run length and the observed data is computed online using a recursive message passing scheme [1]

$$P(r_t, y_{1:t}) = \sum_{r_{t-1}} P(r_t|r_{t-1}) P(y_t|r_{t-1}, y_t^{(r)}; \theta_m) P(r_{t-1}, y_{1:t-1}) , \qquad (1)$$

where $P(r_t|r_{t-1})$ is the conditional changepoint prior over r_t given r_{t-1}, which is nonzero in only two scenarios: $H(r_{t-1}+1|\theta_h)$ when a changepoint occurs $r_t = 0$ or $1 - H(r_{t-1}+1|\theta_h)$ when the run length continues to grow $r_t = r_{t-1}+1$. The function $H(\tau)$ is the hazard function $H(\tau) = \frac{P(g=\tau)}{\sum_{t=\tau}^{\infty} P(g=\tau)}$, where $P(g)$ is a geometric distribution with timescale θ_h. The hazard function is constant at $H(\tau) = 1/\theta_h$. The predictive distribution $P(y_t|r_{t-1}, y_{1:t}; \theta_m)$ only depends on the recent data $y_t^{(r)}$ and the model parameters θ_m. The parameters $\theta = \{\theta_h, \theta_m\}$ form the set of hyperparameters for the model.

Similar to Turner et al. [22], we use a joint BOCPD algorithm with multivariate time series sensory signals by modelling the signals as a joint Student's t-distribution $P(\mathbf{y_t}|r_{t-1}, \mathbf{Y_{1:t}}; \theta_m)$, where $\mathbf{y_t}$ could be any unimodal or multimodal sensory signals mentioned in Sect. 3.1. The joint model, with multimodal sensory signals, can extract more information from the data as simultaneous changes in multiple time series is a stronger indication of a changepoint.

3.4   Learning to Detect Sensory Events

After segmenting a demonstrated skill into a sequence of sensorimotor primitives, the robot should learn to autonomously determine when to switch from one primitive to the next. We treat this detection process as a classification problem. We train a classifier using the segmented sensorimotor primitives.

In order to detect different sensory events, we use Spatio-Temporal Hierarchical Matching Pursuit (ST-HMP) [12] to learn rich feature representations from the time series data of both static and dynamic tactile signals. The ST-HMP method was built upon the Hierarchical Matching Pursuit (HMP) [3] algorithm, which is a multilayer sparse coding network that creates feature hierarchies from raw data. It extends HMP by also extracting features across time series data. The ST-HMP method has achieved high accuracy in grasp stability assessment and object recognition using only low-frequency tactile sensory data on several synthetic and real tactile datasets [12]. In this paper, we incorporate signals from other sensor modalities, including high-frequency tactile data.

Including both spatial and temporal patterns of tactile information is important for achieving high classification accuracy. The ST-HMP extracts rich spatial structures from raw multimodal data without predefining discriminative data characteristics. Given a set of high-dimensional observations, it uses K-SVD [2] to learn a dictionary and the associated sparse code matrix in an unsupervised fashion over a large collection of spatial patches sampled from multimodal data. With the learned dictionary, the ST-HMP computes sparse code features for each high-dimensional observation in a small neighborhood using orthogonal matching pursuit. Then those sparse code features are max pooled over the spatial and temporal dimensions at several scales with an increasing size of a receptive field

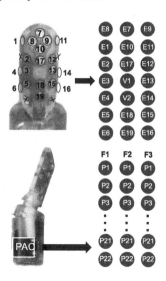

Fig. 3. Schematic of the electrode and pressure sensor arrangement on the BioTac (left). Tactile data array used for the ST-HMP features (right).

(cell) to generate robust feature vectors for both spatial and temporal variations. The final feature describing the whole sensor data sequence is the concatenation of aggregated sparse codes in each spatio-temporal cell. Algorithm details can be found in the paper of Madry et al. [12].

In order to represent the robot's haptic data using HMP features, we need to first arrange the tactile signals into 2D tactile data arrays. The layout of the BioTac sensor's electrodes is shown in Fig. 3. The Xs on the finger indicate the reference electrodes, and the 19 BioTac electrodes $E1...E19$ are measured relative to these 4 reference electrodes. $V1$ and $V2$ are two virtual electrodes computed by taking an average response of the neighboring electrodes $V1 = \mathbb{E}[E17, E18, E12, E2, E13, E3]$ and $V2 = \mathbb{E}[E17, E18, E15, E5, E13, E3]$. The high-frequency vibration signals (PAC) from one pressure sensor on each finger are separated into 22 virtual channels over time $P1...P22$, and the vibration signals from the three fingers ($F1, F2, F3$) are concatenated side by side. Thus, HMP is essentially extracting temporal features from these 22 virtual vibration channels within one finger as well as learning features to reflect the dependencies of sensors on multiple fingers.

In order to structure the data, the 19 electrodes and two virtual electrodes ($V1$ and $V2$) on each finger are laid out as a 7×3 2D data array. The vibration signals (PAC) on the three fingers are laid out as 22×3 2D tactile data array, as shown in Fig. 3. In this manner, three BioTacs create total four 2D tactile data arrays: three 7×3 tactile arrays for electrodes and one 22×3 tactile data array for vibration signals. We then apply the HMP to each tactile data array separately and then concatenate feature vectors. HMP learns a dictionary of size $M = 100$ with the sparsity level set to $K = 4$. The spatial pooling is performed with a 3 level pyramid: the data array is divided into 1×1, 2×2 and 3×3 cell grids, which results in $S = (1 + 2^2 + 3^2) = 14$ spatial cells. The temporal pyramid consists of 4 max-pooling levels: the sequence is divided into 1, 2, 4, and 8 parts, which results in $T = (1 + 2 + 4 + 8) = 15$ temporal cells. To prevent losing the signs of HMP features due to max-pooling on absolute values, we save the feature vector with both positive and negative signs. Therefore, the size of the feature descriptors is doubled. The total number of ST-HMP features is $4 \times S \times T \times M \times 2 = 4 \times 14 \times 15 \times 100 \times 2 = 168000$.

Given the ST-HMP tactile features, a Support Vector Machine (SVM) is then used to classify these features. For rich features provided by sparse coding, a linear kernel obtains satisfactory results and there is no need to apply more complex distance measures.

4   Evaluation and Discussion

In this section we describe the experiments and results obtained for evaluating the proposed sensorimotor primitive segmentation and goal detection framework.

4.1   Sensorimotor Primitives Segmentation for Peg-in-hole Tasks

Experimental Setup. We evaluated our method on our robot platform. For the guided peg-in-hole tasks, we use a 3D printed peg-in-hole set consisting of holes with 1 mm clearance and various geometric features, including a curved groove leading into a hole, a straight groove leading into a hole, and a squared groove with a hole at one of its corners. These geometric features of the board are shown in the inset of Fig. 4. These features are designed to create constraints that guide the robot while performing the peg-in-hole tasks. Interacting with these geometric features results in tactile events. The robot should therefore learn sequences of sensorimotor primitives that reach the individual geometric features, and switch between the primitives accordingly to perform the task. An adapter was 3D printed to hold the 5.7 mm diameter peg, such that it can be firmly grasped by two BioTacs using a pinch grasp, as shown in Fig. 4.

In the experiment, the robot was taught by a demonstrator to perform the guided peg-in-hole tasks using kinesthetic teaching. For example, to use the curved groove, the demonstrator moved the robot's hand down until the peg made contact with the surface of the board, slid the peg into the curved groove, traced the groove with the peg until reaching the opening of the hole, and finally inserted the peg into the hole. We collected 50 demonstrations with each geometric feature on the peg board.

We recorded the 3D Cartesian position of the robot's end-effector from the robot's motor encoders using its forward kinematics. We also tracked the 3D Cartesian position of the board with a Vicon motion capture system. Thus, we can calculate the relative position

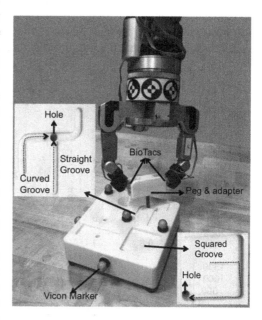

Fig. 4. Experiment setup of the peg-in-hole manipulation task.

of the end-effector and the board (pos). In order to compare the segmentation performance with different sensor modalities, we also recorded the signals from the signals from the force/torque sensor at the wrist (FT), the BioTacs' electrodes (E), and the BioTacs' high-frequency pressure sensor (vib).

The joint predictive distributions over the sensor values were modelled using Student's t-distributions with hyper-parameters θ_m: $\mu_{pos} = 0.02, \sigma_{pos} = 10^{2.5}$; $\mu_{FT} = 0$, $\sigma_{FT} = 1$; $\mu_E = 0, \sigma_E = 1$; and $\mu_{vib} = 1000, \sigma_{vib} = 10^{-2}$, respectively. The hazard function's hyper-parameter was set to $\theta_h = 250$.

Results. The results of using joint BOCPD with the proprioceptive and tactile data for the curved-groove task is shown in Fig. 5. The ground truth primitive switches were manually labeled, as indicated in Fig. 5 by double vertical dashed lines. In this example case, five significant sensorimotor events were labeled, including the peg impacting the surface of the board, entering the groove, reaching the corner of the groove, reaching the top of the hole, and making contact with the bottom of the hole, as shown in Fig. 4. The changepoints detected by the BOCPD algorithm are indicated by black crosses. If these changepoints are between the double vertical dashed lines, we consider the BOCPD algorithm as having successfully segmented the primitive. If there is no changepoint between these double vertical dotted lines (red), then BOCPD missed the event, e.g., the corner of the curved groove. If changepoints fall between two consecutive sensorimotor events, we consider these changepoints as false positives, such as the changepoint at 0.93 s and 2.76 s shown by circles (blue). The first of these false positive is caused by the bumpy surface of the peg board. The second false positive is caused by the peg jamming against the inner surface of the hole.

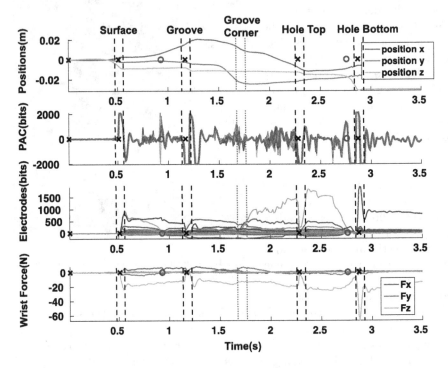

Fig. 5. An example of joint BOCPD to segment sensorimotor primitives in a peg-in-hole task with curved groove. (Color figure online)

The joint BOCPD on the multimodal signals performed better than the independent BOCPD on the unimodal signals. Figures 6, 7, 8 show the segmentation success rates and false positive rates for each sensorimotor event in the three guided peg-in-hole tasks, i.e., curved groove, straight groove, and square groove respectively. The proprioceptive and multimodal tactile signals, including the electrodes and pressure sensors, usually achieved the highest success rates and the lowest false positive rates. This result is due to the changepoints of the joint BOCPD using the effects of both the low- and high-frequency sensory information. Thus, the joint model can extract more information from the data as simultaneous changes in multiple time series is a stronger indication of a senso-rimotor changepoint.

4.2 Sensorimotor Primitives Goal Detection

Experimental Setup. We evaluated the sensorimotor primitive goal detec-tion method using the changepoints detected by the joint proprioceptive and tactile BOCPD. The goal is to have the robot autonomously detect whether it has reached the goal of the current sensorimotor primitive. For every change-point detected by the segmentation method, except the first one, we extracted 16 sensory data samples (160 ms) directly before and after the changepoint. These samples represent the tactile signals from the goal's sensory event. We also extracted 16 samples randomly selected between the last changepoint and the current changepoint. These samples correspond to the signal before the goal has been reached. In this manner, we collected 560 positive (goal detected) and 560 negative (goal not detected) samples from 35 trials for the evaluation.

In this experiment, we compared the goal detection accuracies using either HMP or ST-HMP features. The difference between ST-HMP and HMP is that ST-HMP combines the tactile information from multiple time steps t to create the features. In contrast, HMP creates features for each time step separately and then concatenates them. To evaluate the HMP and ST-HMP features for goal detection, we performed a 5-fold cross-validation on the data set by using 896 samples for training the classifier and the rest for testing.

Results. By using all tactile sensor modalities, as shown in Fig. 3, the average classification accuracies among the different sensorimotor primitives range from 77.5 % to 100 %. The classification accuracies and the standard deviations for the different sensorimotor primitives are shown in Fig. 9.

Overall, the ST-HMP achieves higher accuracies and lower standard devia-tions than the HMP. This is due to ST-HMP pooling over the time steps, which results in temporal invariances. The results thus show the importance of com-bining information from multiple time scales when detecting sensory events.

4.3 Robot Performing Peg-in-hole Task

In this experiment, the robot uses the segmented primitives and goal detectors from the previous experiments to autonomously perform the guided peg-in-hole task with the curved groove. The segmentation was performed using the pro-prioceptive and tactile signals, while the sensory event detection only uses the tactile data. The position and force signals 100ms after each segmentation are used to compute the final desired position and contact force for each controller. The desired positions generated by a minimum jerk trajectory generator are tracked by a velocity-based operational space controller together with an inverse dynamic law and PD feedback error compensation in joint space [18]. Track-ing of desired contact forces on the arm is achieved with a PI controller on the force/torque sensor located at the wrist [18].

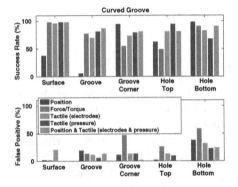

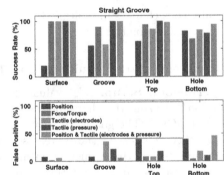

Fig. 6. Curved groove's segmentation success rate and false positive rate. (Color figure online)

Fig. 7. Straight groove's segmentation success rate and false positive rate (Color figure online)

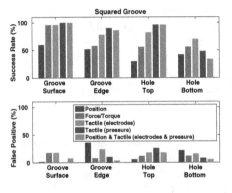

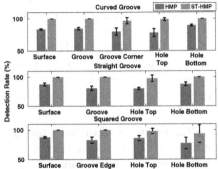

Fig. 8. Squared groove's segmentation success rate and false positive rate. (Color figure online)

Fig. 9. Peg-in-hole sensorimotor primitive detection results. (Color figure online)

An example sequence of sensorimotor primitives successfully executing the peg-in-hole task with a curved groove is shown in Fig. 10. Without the sensory event detection, we observed two common failure modes: (i) the robot misses the groove (failed transition from 2nd to 3rd picture), and (ii) the robot jams the peg around the groove corner (failed transition from 4th to 5th picture). The sensory event detection alleviates these issues by detecting when the goal state was not reached, i.e., the sensory event was not detected, and repeating the current primitive to reach the goal. The required correction is usually rather small, and the primitive terminates once the goal has been reached.

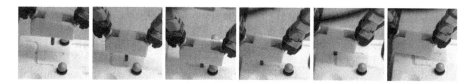

Fig. 10. Sensorimotor primitive sequence for the curved groove peg-in-hole task.

5   Conclusions

We presented a framework for segmenting contact-based manipulation tasks using both proprioceptive and tactile signals. We used the unsupervised online Bayesian changepoint detection algorithm to automatically segment manipulations into sensorimotor primitives. Classifiers using ST-HMP features, were trained to detect sensory events for switching between primitives. The proposed method was successfully evaluated on guided peg-in-hole tasks. The robot could accurately segment the tasks and detect the sensory events using the proposed approach.

In the future, we will extend the proposed framework to learn to detect failure events through autonomous exploration.

Acknowledgments. Research supported by the MPI for Intelligent Systems. BioTac sensors were provided by SynTouch LLC. Gerald E. Loeb is an equity partner in SynTouch LLC, manufacturer of the BioTac sensors used in this research. Special thanks to Felix Grimminger for helping design the 3D printed parts.

References

1. Adams, R.P., MacKay, D.J.: Bayesian online changepoint detection. arXiv preprint (2007). arxiv:0710.3742
2. Aharon, M., Elad, M., Bruckstein, A.: k -svd: An algorithm for designing overcomplete dictionaries for sparse representation. Trans. Sig. Proc. **54**(11), 4311–4322 (2006)
3. Bo, L., Ren, X., Fox, D.: Hierarchical matching pursuit for image classification: architecture and fast algorithms. In: NIPS, pp. 2115–2123 (2011)
4. Chebotar, Y., Kroemer, O., Peters, J.: Learning robot tactile sensing for object manipulation. In: IROS, pp. 3368–3375. IEEE (2014)
5. Deiterding, J., Henrich, D.: Automatic adaptation of sensor-based robots. In: IROS, pp. 1828–1833. IEEE (2007)
6. Flanagan, J.R., Bowman, M.C., Johansson, R.S.: Control strategies in object manipulation tasks. Curr. Opin. Neurobiol. **16**(6), 650–659 (2006)
7. Johansson, R.S., Flanagan, J.R.: Coding and use of tactile signals from the fingertips in object manipulation tasks. Nat. Rev. Neurosci. **10**(5), 345–359 (2009)
8. Kappler, D., Pastor, P., Kalakrishnan, M., Manue, W., Schaal, S.: Data-driven online decision making for autonomous manipulation. In: RSS (2015)
9. Kroemer, O., van Hoof, H., Neumann, G., Peters, J.: Learning to predict phases of manipulation tasks as hidden states. In: ICRA, pp. 4009–4014. IEEE (2014)

10. Kulick, J., Otte, S., Toussaint, M.: Active exploration of joint dependency structures. In: ICRA, pp. 2598–2604. IEEE (2015)
11. Li, Q., Schürmann, C., Haschke, R., Ritter, H.J.: A control framework for tactile servoing. In: Robotics: Science and systems (2013)
12. Madry, M., Bo, L., Kragic, D., Fox, D.: ST-HMP: Unsupervised spatio-temporal feature learning for tactile data. In: ICRA, pp. 2262–2269. IEEE (2014)
13. Manschitz, S., Kober, J., Gienger, M., Peters, J.: Learning movement primitive attractor goals and sequential skills from kinesthetic demonstrations. RAS **74**, 97–107 (2015)
14. Matulevich, B., Loeb, G.E., Fishel, J.A.: Utility of contact detection reflexes in prosthetic hand control. In: IROS, pp. 4741–4746. IEEE (2013)
15. Meier, F., Theodorou, E., Stulp, F., Schaal, S.: Movement segmentation using a primitive library. In: IROS, pp. 3407–3412. IEEE (2011)
16. Niekum, S., Osentoski, S., Atkeson, C.G., Barto, A.G.: Online bayesian changepoint detection for articulated motion models. In: ICRA, pp. 1468–1475. IEEE (2015)
17. Niekum, S., Osentoski, S., Konidaris, G.D., Chitta, S., Marthi, B., Barto, A.G.: Learning grounded finite-state representations from unstructured demonstrations. IJRR **34**(2), 131–157 (2015)
18. Pastor, P., Kalakrishnan, M., Righetti, L., Schaal, S.: Towards associative skill memories. In: Humanoids, pp. 309–315. IEEE (2012)
19. Romano, J.M., Hsiao, K., Niemeyer, G., Chitta, S., Kuchenbecker, K.J.: Human-inspired robotic grasp control with tactile sensing. Trans. Rob. **27**(6), 1067–1079 (2011)
20. Su, Z., Fishel, J., Yamamoto, T., Loeb, G.: Use of tactile feedback to control exploratory movements to characterize object compliance. Front. Neurorob. **6**(7), (2012)
21. Su, Z., Hausman, K., Chebotar, Y., Molchanov, A., Loeb, G.E., Sukhatme, G.S., Schaal, S.: Force estimation and slip detection/classification for grip control using a biomimetic tactile sensor. In: Humanoids, pp. 297–303. IEEE (2015)
22. Turner, R., Saatci, Y., Rasmussen, C.E.: Adaptive sequential bayesian change point detection. In: Temporal Segmentation Workshop at NIPS (2009)
23. Wettels, N., Santos, V., Johansson, R., Loeb, G.: Biomimetic tactile sensor array. Adv. Robot. **22**(8), 829–849 (2008)

A More Basic Version of Agency? As If!

Simon McGregor[(✉)]

University of Sussex, Brighton, England
s.mcgregor@sussex.ac.uk

Abstract. At present there is just one definition [2] that attempts to explicitly naturalise the concept of (general, embodied) agency, and it is unapologetically autopoietic-enactivist. This fact constitutes a public challenge to other traditions in cognitive science.

A 'bare' problem of defining agency remains, even after paring away hard phenomenological and normative problems by limiting the scope of the problem to describing 'as-if' agency (i.e. the external appearance of agency). Building on [2], I identify an extended list of criteria that a theory of agency (whether 'true' or 'as-if') should meet.

I argue that autopoiesis is the wrong foundation even for 'bare' agency, let alone phenomenological and volitional agency; instead, I recommend starting with an 'as-if' definition that relates agency to some theory of embodied rationality, effectively providing a generalised version of Dennett's intentional stance [9], and taking a step towards a rigorous formal definition.

Keywords: Agency · Autopoiesis · Cognition · Embodied · Enactivism · Dennett · Definition · Intentional stance

1 Introduction

The concept of agency plays a major role in how neurotypical humans understand the world. We draw a basic distinction between two different types of occurrence:

- An *act*, which is *done* by an *agent*; and
- A mere *happening*, which occurs as a result of *purely mechanical* causes.

Di Paolo [11] characterises this as a difference between *doings* and *undergoings*.

For instance, imagine a lever with a rickety bookshelf above it. We will consider two different scenarios: a person pulling a lever by contracting their muscles; and the shelf collapsing onto the lever, pressing it downwards. In one case, the pulling of the lever is an action done by the person; in the other, the pulling of the lever is not an action done by anyone, but happens for purely mechanical reasons.

The intuitive distinction between the two scenarios seems obvious, but it is surprisingly difficult to characterise in scientific terms what the difference between acts and mere happenings is. From a scientific point of view, all causes are mechanical: the person's pulling of the lever is also a mere happening that

© Springer International Publishing Switzerland 2016
E. Tuci et al. (Eds.): SAB 2016, LNAI 9825, pp. 183–194, 2016.
DOI: 10.1007/978-3-319-43488-9_17

occurs as the laws of physics unfold. How can we reconcile the intuitive qualitative disparity between acts and mere happenings, with the scientific qualitative parity between persons and metal weights?

Agency is, or at least should be, a central topic in cognitive science and Artificial Life. The objects of study of embodied cognitive science are agents - those systems that are capable of performing actions - rather than inanimate objects such as metal weights. The distinction between systems that can 'do' and systems that cannot seems to underpin our intuitive notions of animacy and inanimacy; for example, NASA's working definition of life is '[a] self-sustaining chemical system capable of Darwinian evolution' [3]. Stipulating that the system must not just be sustained, but be *self-sustaining*, implies that the sustenance must be an act and not a mere happening.

While certain authors take agency to entail conscious volition (for instance, Juarrero [16] defines agency as 'the difference between a wink and a blink'), we will make no such assumptions. In the sense that it achieves some goal or value for the agent, a blink - unlike, say, a Parkinson's tremor [2, p. 5] - is still an action, albeit an involuntary one.

This article will be concerned with the question of what makes an occurrence an action, regardless of whether it is consciously undertaken or an automatic reflex. If such a notion makes sense, let us call it a theory of 'bare agency' to distinguish it from a theory of what makes particular actions voluntary rather than automatic.

2   Background

Barandiaran, Di Paolo and Rohde (hence, BDR) provide an admirable discussion of agency in [2]. They point out that previous definitions of agency within cognitive science (e.g. [13]; see [2, p. 2] for other examples) have merely replaced the problem of defining agency with the problem of defining other cognitive concepts such as perception, action, or goals. Given this level of vagueness, it should be no surprise that we do not have a well-accepted operational definition of what distinguishes acts from mere happenings, let alone a formal mathematical theory of it.

This article will use [2] as a starting point: by virtue of being specific enough to allow detailed analysis, their treatment advances the agency debate significantly. BDR identify three main phenomena that a theory of agency must account for: *individuality*, *interactional assymetry*, and *normativity*. They also provide a definition of agency that purports to account for these phenomena. I summarise BDR's contributions[1] below:

2.1   Individuality

BDR observe that a naturalised theory of agency must describe how a holistic agent-environment system should be separated into an agent and an environment.

---

[1] Apart from their discussion of the nature of space and time from the agent's perspective, which is interesting, but not the focus of the current article.

They then argue that this must include an account of how "an agent defines itself as an individual". I explain in Sect. 4 why I do not find this argument, which appears to be motivated by phenomenological considerations, convincing.

2.2 Interactional Asymmetry

BDR point out that to understand something as an agent is to see it, rather than its environment, as the source of its actions. A theory of agency must explain what constitutes this asymmetry, given that (at a physical level) the actions are symmetric agent-environment interactions. In other words, it must justify why responsibility for the act is allocated to the agent rather than the environment.

They dismiss thermodynamic or statistical avenues, and propose the notion of *modulation* to account for asymmetry. I argue in Sect. 5.1 that modulation is not a well-defined concept. In Sect. 5.2 I explore our intuitive notion that agents alone are the cause of the events that constitute their actions, and see what meaning can be made of this within modern statistical models of causality.

2.3 Normativity

BDR's last point is that actions are purposive in nature: when an agent acts, there is something it is trying to do, and that attempt can be successful or unsuccessful. This consideration necessarily introduces a normative scheme of value, and a theory of agency must account for how actions are goal- or value-directed.

The BDR solution is autopoietic: the "source" of value is (roughly speaking) precarious self-maintenance. I discuss in Sect. 6 the need to take into account values that are not derived from survival, particularly in the context of deliberately self-destructive actions.

2.4 Definition

BDR propose a definition of agency that purports to meet their three criteria: effectively, an agent S is a network of interdependent processes that modulates its coupling with its environment E in a manner that contributes to the maintenance of some of the processes in S.

In terms of definitional precision, BDR have set the bar for future theories. While I believe their definition lacks mathematical rigour, and disagree in any case that autopoiesis is the correct foundation for a theory of agency, readers are urged to inspect the definition on [2, p. 8] as an example of what we should be aiming to surpass.

3 Agency and Phenomenology

The relation of subjective experience to agency deserves discussion: should a theory of agency account not just for what makes a system an agent, or an event an act, but also for there being something that it is *like to be* the agent? BDR clearly believe so; they clearly appeal to what [8] describes as a Jonasian (ontological) conception of phenomenology as opposed to a Kantian (epistemic) one (i.e. they want there to be a naturalisable, objective fact of the matter about the presence or absence of a first-person perspective). However, I believe this 'appeal to phenomenology' [5] is problematic.

Accounting for the subjective experience of bats [19] is extraordinarily ambitious, let alone the subjective experience of simpler biological agents such as single-celled organisms, and it hardly seems fair that a theory of agency should be required to solve the "hard problem" [6] of consciousness. See [4] for a discussion of the challenges in scientifically studying consciousness even in non-mammalian animals with brains.

It seems plausible that a theory could account (in some sense) for a basic distinction between acts and mere happenings, without needing to invoke the notion of phenomenal experience. Such a theory would still explain something of real relevance to cognitive science.

Even if we are prepared to attempt the hard problem, any claim that phenomenology is a prerequisite for action needs to be justified explicitly: we still draw a distinction between actions and mere happenings, including cases where the agent in question is consciously unaware of the action they are taking, or perhaps even entirely unconscious (for instance, breathing while asleep, versus being sustained by a ventilator); we also allow that 'locked-in' patients may possess phenomenal consciousness during a period of time in which they are unable to act, i.e. do not function as agents. These cases suggest that the relation between agency and phenomenology is not a simple one.

4   Individuality

BDR rightly point out that, at a bare minimum, to talk about the interaction between an agent and its environment requires distinguishing two distinct subsystems: an agent, and an environment [2, p. 2]:

> The problem of individuality becomes the problem of justifying which one we choose among the large set of possible and arbitrary distinctions between system and environment

Undoubtedly, any theory of agency that omits a treatment of this question is an unsatisfactory one. BDR go on to argue [2, p. 3]:

> A concept of agency that cannot account for the way in which an agent defines itself as an individual requires another agent (the observer) to perform the system-environment distinction. If then we have to justify the identity of this observer agent by means of another one and so on, we enter an infinite explanatory regress.

This conclusion appears to be premature. The scientific theorist does need to justify how they carve the world into agent and environment; but there appears no *a priori* reason to suppose that this cannot, in principle, be done on the grounds of some purely physical distinction that does not invoke a subjective perspective.

If, for some reason, it turns out that a subjective perspective must be invoked, we come readily equipped with one ourselves. Scientists pretend to a 'God's-eye view' [23] that transcends individual subjectivity; but when discussing consciousness this pretense may need to drop (as Nagel points out in [19], we can only imagine what it would be like for ourselves to be a bat, not what it is like for the bat to be a bat).

Hence, I agree with BDR that an agent must be distinguished from its environment in some appropriate way, but disagree that this distinction must be founded on a notion of the agent's phenomenology.

5   Interactional Asymmetry

Characterising an event as an action seems to imply that the agent, not the environment, is responsible for it. BDR describe this as 'interactional asymmetry', and, after rejecting thermodynamic and statistical approaches, attempt to account for it by reference to a notion of modulation.

I will argue that the notion of modulation, first proposed in [11], is ill-defined, and propose an alternative analysis based on modern statistical approaches to causality.

5.1   Modulation

BDR's solution to characterising asymmetry is the notion of *modulation*, possibly following [11]. They state [2, p. 4]:

> The coupling between a system and its environment is, strictly speaking, a symmetrical physical happening [...]. However, an agent is able to modulate some of the parametrical conditions and to constrain this coupling in a way that the environment (typically) does not.

For this approach to work, BDR need to:

1. define explicitly what distinguishes a modulatory parameter from other variables in the system; and
2. show why this definition captures properties essential to agency.

They neither do so, nor cite any work that does so. In [2, p. 4] they refer to *nonholonomy* as a possible distinguishing feature of modulatory parameters, but do not provide any justification for why this arcane mathematical property is relevant to agency, or how it might pick out modulatory parameters. For holonomic systems, path integrals depend only on initial and final states, and not on the particular path taken; the canonical example of a nonholonomic system is the Foucault pendulum.

5.2 Causation and Statistics

It turns out that there is a well-defined mathematical sense in which a subset of variables describing the agent system (let's call them 'actuators') mediate all causal influences of the agent on its environment. Similarly, a subset of environmental variables can be identified with 'sensory input'.

Modern statistical graphical approaches to causality, which seek to characterise the way systems behave in response to external *interventions* (see [12] for a summary), have been applied to complexity science since at least [1].

A Bayesian network describes (statistical) conditional independence relationships between variables, allowing a notion of local dependencies (which form 'Markov blankets' around particular nodes). Causal Bayesian networks [22] extend this idea by describing how probability distributions change in response to external interventions that fix particular variables' values directly, capturing the counterfactual character of causality.

If the time dimension is discretised, the time-varying states of the agent and its environment can then be understood as a series of random variables that are related by a causal Bayesian graph, with states at time t_n being caused by states at time t_{n-1}. It then becomes meaningful to talk about those aspects of the agent's state that have a direct causal influence on the environment's next state, and vice versa; these variables are naturally interpretable as actuators and sensory inputs (see, e.g. [17]).

Limitations. Of course, this characterisation is too inclusive: it defines all causal interactions between the agent and its environment as sensorimotor, while clearly only some of them are (for instance, the environment is changed by the heat radiated from the agent's brain, but we would balk at labelling this a motor effect). Nevertheless, it will serve as a useful starting point.

Note also that there is debate about what probabilities are supposed to represent in the real world [15, 20]; I will not attempt to answer that question here.

I suggest that the asymmetry of the agent's/environment's relationship to symmetric agent-environment interactions is, in fact, not causal at all: rather, it arises simply because the interactions serve some purpose for the agent, and they do not appear to do so for the environment. Hence, causation is relevant only for defining the interface between agent and environment. The more fundamental question of purposes is discussed in the next section.

6 Normativity

Agency involves goals, which in turn involve the ascription of "good" or "bad" valences to outcomes. The term "normativity" denotes the association of (some sort of) value with behaviours. BDR's approach, like other autopoietic accounts, stipulates *a priori* that normativity is founded in survival.

Contra BDR, I believe there are at least three distinct contexts which reasonably call for the attribution of "good" and "bad" valences to the outcomes of a biological organism's actions.

1. An evolutionary context. Is the outcome is evolutionarily adaptive, i.e. does it further the reproduction of the agent's genes? (I'll call this *evolutionary-normativity*.)
2. A survival context. Does the outcome further the survival of the individual agent? (I'll call this *survival-normativity*.)
3. A personal context. Does the outcome further the agent's own[2] goals? (I'll call this *personal-normativity*)

For living organisms, these three contexts usually assign very similar valences to outcomes, and for good reason. Evolution favours the production of organisms which act to promote their own survival, and hence the reproduction of their genes.

However, there are exceptions to this rule which demonstrate that the three normative contexts are non-identical. Social insects will sometimes engage in self-destructive behaviour, such as the 'suicide bomber' phenomenon known as *autothysis* [18,24]. This behaviour is typically evolutionarily adaptive (because their clones will be more likely to reproduce).

In extreme cases, the actions of humans run counter to both evolutionary fitness and personal survival; for instance, murder-suicides in which a person kills their own children before killing themselves. Therefore, personal-normativity is not identical to survival-normativity or evolutionary-normativity. Since autothysis establishes that survival-normativity is not equivalent to evolutionary-normativity, we have identified three nonequivalent normative schemes.

It seems that while agency must be founded in normativity, there are multiple normative schemes that it can be related to. The most important of these three is the least well-defined one: personal-normativity. In the next section, I will explain why neither evolutionary-normativity nor personal-normativity can be reduced to survival-normativity in the case of the individual agent.

6.1 Actions by Agents

A theory of agency needs to account for more than just why particular events constitute actions rather than mere happenings; it needs to account for why those events constitute actions performed by particular agents. Otherwise, it posits a world in which some events are actions rather than mere happenings, but those actions are performed by nobody in particular.

There have been some attempts by autopoietic cognitive scientists to account for behaviours such as injecting heroin, which do not seem to be survival-normative, as stemming from the self-maintenance of some higher-level process. The claim is that survival-threatening behaviour maintains some sort of organisation or identity at a different level than the biological organism as a whole: for instance, a habit or a cultural institution, or some stable pattern in the organism's internal dynamics. However, this solution is deeply problematic.

---

[2] At present, there is no scientific consensus on what this represents in physical terms. For the purposes of discussion, we will have to rely on the meaning of the words in ordinary English.

Consider a bacterium which through a point mutation has a tendency to exhibit chemotaxis towards a toxic substance. The relations of toxin and nutrient to the bacterium's metabolism are different, but the relation to the bacterium's short-term locomotive behaviour may be the same for toxin and nutrient[3].

Proponents of the autopoietic account need to do one of two things:

1. Account for why the mutant's chemotaxis constitutes active behaviour on the part of the very entity whose existence is threatened by that behaviour (the entire bacterium); or
2. deny that the mutant's chemotaxis constitutes active behaviour on the part of the bacterium itself (either by denying that it constitutes active behaviour of any sort, or by asserting that it constitutes active behaviour on the part of some other level of identity).

It is hard to see how the first can be done while still maintaining that the intentional nature of acts performed by an agent is grounded purely in the survival-normativity of that very same agent (this being what sets the autopoietic approach apart from other schools of cognitive science).

The second option is more internally consistent, but it seems to fly in the face of what we mean by active behaviour. In particular, it renders the notion of performing intentionally self-destructive actions literally contradictory: either the events are not actions at all, or they are the actions of some entity that is not destroyed by them.

The next section presents my proposal for an alternative solution, based on a novel approach that cuts the Gordian knot and simplifies the question.

7   An Alternative: As-If Theories

If the enactivist approach is unsatisfactory, what alternatives are there? I believe there is a more promising avenue, that begins with a much simpler question: what does it mean for a system to behave *as-if* it were an agent (from an observer's perspective)?

While this fits well with ascriptive theories of cognition such as Dennett's 'intentional stance' [9] (which, roughly speaking, deny that there is any difference between behaving like a cognitive agent and being a cognitive agent), it does not represent any such philosophical commitment. It can be seen merely as an attempt to deal with a theoretical question closely related to the topic of agency *per se*.

Presumably a scientifically-understood agent should appear to behave like an agent, at least from the perspective of the scientist; in other words, every genuine agent (if such a distinction makes sense) is also an as-if agent. Hence, a satisfactory scientific theory of as-if agency may not be able to describe sufficient conditions for real agency, but it seems guaranteed to describe some necessary conditions.

---

[3] Of course, in the long term, the toxin fatally disrupts the bacterium's locomotive behaviour.

Usually, we do not bother constructing as-if theories, because they come 'for free' from a direct theory of the phenomenon in question: for instance, once we know how ballistic trajectories work, we know what it means for a powered object in zero gravity to behave as if it is following a ballistic trajectory. However, there are some reasons to believe that an as-if theory of agency would at least function as a useful preliminary to a full theory of agency:

1. The hard problem of phenomenology does not affect as-if theories.
2. An as-if theory does not need to tackle the problem of justifying
   (a) what the agent-environment boundary is taken to be,
   (b) on which side of the boundary the agent is taken to lie, or
   (c) what the agent's purposes are taken to be
   because its remit is to explain whether some system behaves as though it were an agent, after all the parameters that make this question meaningful have been specified.
3. An as-if theory can treat a candidate agent as a black box, although it can also ask questions about the system's internal state if necessary.

8   What Theories of Agency Should Look Like?

The BDR treatment of agency is welcome for several reasons: it recognises the need to provide an explicit definition of agency within cognitive science; it iden-tifies several relevant features which distinguish actions from mere happenings; and it is a clear statement of the enactivist conception of agency.

I have argued that the BDR definition is inadequate, for reasons directly related to the assumptions of the phenomenological-autopoietic strand of enac-tivism; in any case, I propose that a proper theory of agency, enactivist or otherwise, should meet at least the following criteria:

1. It does not have to address phenomenological concerns, but it may legitimately do so (in which case it is a theory both of agency and phenomenology).
2. It does not have to distinguish between voluntary and automatic actions, but may legitimately do so (in which case it is a theory both of agency and of volition).
3. It should provide an account of how some physical phenomena constitute *active behaviour* (or for an as-if theory, as-if active behaviour) that is
   (a) *performed by* (c.f. asymmetry)
   (b) particular *agents* (c.f. identity),
   (c) in pursuit of particular *goals* or *values* (c.f. normativity),
   in a way that identifies the particular behaviour, agent and reasons for action (see Sect. 6.1).
4. The theory should be *semantically appropriate*:
   (a) It should correctly classify as many as possible of the phenomena we ordi-narily view as active behaviour, or provide a new insight that persuades us the ordinary view is wrong. (For instance, it should preferably not render the notion of an intentionally self-destructive act logically contradictory.)

(b) if it is a direct theory, it should not misclassify phenomena we ordinarily view as inanimate and purely mechanical, without good reason;

(c) if it is an as-if theory, and it classifies a 'purely mechanical' phenomenon as as-if active behaviour, it should describe a convincing perspective from which the phenomenon appears to be such.

5. It should (at least eventually) be formalisable as a *mathematical theory*, and one that is commensurate with the mathematical language of the physical sciences.

9   A General As-If Theory

The minimal requirements for a theory of agency would seem to be a distinction between the agent and its environment, a specification of what variables are taken to be under the control of the agent, and some notion of purpose or normativity. I propose that these can be captured along the following lines:

1. Formally define the agent, the environment, their sensorimotor interface, and a normative standard:

   (a) (Arbitrarily) distinguish a subsystem X within a Universe Ω, and define X's environment Y as everything in Ω that is not in X.

   (b) Define the system's *actuators* A and *sensors* S as the variables mediating the causal interaction between X and Y over time (as in Sect. 5.2).

   (c) Define some theory of *embodied rationality* R_C that characterises how the actuators of an ideally rational agent should vary, in the context of a particular sensorimotor history, given certain notional 'cognitive' parameters C such as desires.

2. Define a sub-trajectory A_T of A over a time interval T as being *as-if active behaviour* by X, **with respect to** R_C, if and only if A_T largely matches the constraints specified by R_C.

Definition 1b is a first approximation that blurs the distinction between 'true' sensorimotor variables and mere interactional variables, as discussed in Sect. 5.2; this issue does not seem insuperable in principle and can be addressed in future work.

In its central invocation of rationality, this definition is similar to Dennett's formulation of the intentional stance [10]:

> The intentional stance is the strategy of interpreting the behavior of an entity (person, animal, artifact, whatever) by treating it as if it were a rational agent who governed its 'choice' of 'action' by a 'consideration' of its 'beliefs' and 'desires.'

However, the definition given here is even more general: it does not assume the notion of belief (although if needed beliefs can appear in C), or presuppose a unique Platonic standard of rationality.

Let us consider how this definition relates to the criteria in Sect. 8. The definition is a theory of 'bare' agency that does not address phenomenological (criterion 1) or volitional (criterion 2) concerns. It fulfills criterion 3: since this is an as-if theory, it can be applied to arbitrarily-distinguished agents (criterion 3b) with arbitrarily-posited goals (criterion 3c). The asymmetry required by condition 3a arises because we identify active behaviour with actuator channels A that are internal to the agent; in the case where the environment is also an as-if agent with respect to some theory of rationality R_D, the environment's actions will then correspond to sub-trajectories of S, not A.

Semantic appropriacy (criterion 4) is what makes an abstract formulation into a theory of agency rather than a theory of some other phenomenon. However, it is the hardest one to evaluate, since it requires subjective judgements about agency and explanatory adequacy to be applied to all possible systems in all possible environments. Therefore, it must remain a topic of active discussion.

Regarding criterion 5, the choice of R_C will evidently be crucial. The mathematical framework of Bayesian inference is an excellent candidate: it formalises ideal empirical reasoning under uncertainty [7,15]; can be extended in various various ways to describe ideal embodied behaviour [14,21]; and is completely interoperable with the causal Bayesian network formalism in Sect. 5.2. The use of a quantitative, rather than qualitative, theory of rationality will allow the 'largely' in definition 2 to be given a precise meaning, by assigning numerical magnitudes to deviations from ideal rationality.

10   Conclusion

Cognitive science, particularly of the embodied sort, needs a naturalistic definition of agency. I have summarised the most comprehensive attempt to date: Barandiaran, Di Paolo and Rohde's [2], which is strongly enactivist in character, and have argued that autopoietic-enactivism is the wrong foundation for agency. Instead, I have proposed the notion of an 'as-if' theory, as a less problematic starting point for naturalising agency.

The criteria defined in [2] have been reframed, and extended with some finer distinctions (theories of phenomenology and volition), and notions of semantic appropriacy and formalisability. These extended criteria are proposed as a minimal standard for future theories of agency.

Finally, I have sketched out a general 'as-if' theory of agency, founded in an abstract notion of rationality, and suggested that Bayesian inference forms a good candidate for a formal theory of embodied rationality.

Acknowledgments. Nathaniel Virgo, Pedro Martínez Mediano, and Paulo De Jesus provided invaluable feedback on early versions of this article.

References

1. Ay, N., Polani, D.: Information flows in causal networks. Adv. Complex Syst. **11**(01), 17–41 (2008)
2. Barandiaran, X.E., Di Paolo, E., Rohde, M.: Defining agency: individuality, normativity, asymmetry, and spatio-temporality in action. Adapt. Behav. **17**(5), 367–386 (2009)

3. Benner, S.A.: Defining life. Astrobiology **10**(10), 1021–1030 (2010)
4. Boly, M., Seth, A.K., Wilke, M., Ingmundson, P., Baars, B., Laureys, S., Edelman, D.B., Tsuchiya, N.: Consciousness in humans and non-human animals: recent advances and future directions. Front. Psychol. **4**, 625 p. (2013). doi:10. 3389/fpsyg.2013.00625
5. de Bruin, L.C., Kästner, L.: Dynamic embodied cognition. Phenomenol. Cogn. Sci. **11**(4), 541–563 (2012)
6. Chalmers, D.J.: Facing up to the problem of consciousness. J. Conscious. Stud. **2**(3), 200–219 (1995)
7. Cox, R.T.: Probability, frequency and reasonable expectation. Am. J. Phys. **14**(1), 1–13 (1946)
8. De Jesus, P.: Autopoietic enactivism, phenomenology and the deep continuity between life and mind. Phenomenol. Cogn. Sci. **15**(2), 265–289 (2016)
9. Dennett, D.: The Intentional Stance. MIT Press, Cambridge (1987)
10. Dennett, D.: Intentional systems theory. In: Beckermann, A., McLaughlin, B.P., Walter, S. (eds.) The Oxford Handbook of Philosophy of Mind, pp. 339–350. Oxford University Press, Oxford (2009)
11. Di Paolo, E.A.: Autopoiesis, adaptivity, teleology, agency. Phenomenol. Cogn. Sci. **4**(4), 429–452 (2005)
12. Eichler, M.: Causal inference in time series analysis (2012)
13. Franklin, S., Graesser, A.: Is it an agent, or just a program? a taxonomy for autonomous. In: Jennings, N.R., Wooldridge, M.J., Müller, J.P. (eds.) ECAI-WS 1996 and ATAL 1996. LNCS, vol. 1193, pp. 21–35. Springer, Heidelberg (1997)
14. Hutter, M.: Universal algorithmic intelligence: a mathematical top→down approach. In: Goertzel, B., Pennachin, C. (eds.) Artificial General Intelligence, pp. 227–290. Springer, Heidelberg (2007)
15. Jaynes, E.: Probability theory as logic. In: Fougère, P. (ed.) Maximum Entropy and Bayesian Methods, pp. 1–16. Springer, Heidelberg (1990)
16. Juarrero, A.: Dynamics in Action: Intentional Behavior as a Complex System. MIT Press, Cambridge (1999)
17. Klyubin, A.S., Polani, D., Nehaniv, C.L.: Representations of space and time in the maximization of information flow in the perception-action loop. Neural Comput. **19**(9), 2387–2432 (2007)
18. Maschwitz, U., Maschwitz, E.: Platzende arbeiterinnen: eine neue art der feindabwehr bei sozialen hautflüglern. Oecologia **14**(3), 289–294 (1974)
19. Nagel, T.: What is it like to be a bat? Philos. Rev. **83**(4), 435–450 (1974)
20. Nau, R.F.: De finetti was right: probability does not exist. Theor. Decis. **51**(2–4), 89–124 (2001)
21. Ortega, D.A., Braun, P.A.: Information, utility and bounded rationality. In: Schmidhuber, J., Thórisson, K.R., Looks, M. (eds.) AGI 2011. LNCS, vol. 6830, pp. 269–274. Springer, Heidelberg (2011)
22. Pearl, J.: Causality: Models, Reasoning and Inference. Cambridge University Press, New York (2000)
23. Putnam, H.: Reason Truth and History, vol. 3. Cambridge University Press, Cambridge (1981)
24. Šobotník, J., Bourguignon, T., Hanus, R., Demianová, Z., Pytelková, J., Mareš, M., Foltynová, P., Preisler, J., Cvačka, J., Krasulová, J., et al.: Explosive backpacks in old termite workers. Science **337**(6093), 436 (2012)

A Biologically Inspired Soft Robotic Hand Using Chopsticks for Grasping Tasks

Mariya Chepisheva[1], Utku Culha[1,2], and Fumiya Iida[1(✉)]

[1] Biologically Inspired Robotics Laboratory, Department of Engineering,
University of Cambridge, Cambridge, UK
{mkc40,fi224}@cam.ac.uk, utku.culha@mavt.ethz.ch
[2] Department of Mechanical and Process Engineering,
ETH Zurich, Zurich, Switzerland

Abstract. In this paper we investigate the dexterity of human manipulation capabilities by using a soft robotic hand. We built a robotic hand based on our inspiration from the real human's, which is capable of handling chopsticks for grasping variations of objects. The robotic hand is made of soft structures, by using anthropomorphic configurations of bones, joints, ligaments, and tendons, that are connected to a minimum set of motor components, i.e. only four servomotors. By developing a minimalistic physics model of chopstick handling and its simulation experiments, we have identified one of the necessary conditions of actuation which enables the robot to grasp variations of small objects, those with different shape, size and weight.

Keywords: Biomimetics · Robot hand · Soft Robotics

1 Introduction

Nowadays, there are many robotic hands available on the market that compete with each other's design and ceaselessly claim to be one step closer to anthropomorphism. Roboticists have long been looking at the extremity of the upper limb in order to produce a more realistic representation of it- one that is flexible, skilful and sensitive enough to perform fine motor skills. Despite being successful to a great extent, widely used robotic joint mechanisms with fixed axis of motion, still cannot capture the passive compliance of the human hand which depends on the elasticity of the tissues that build up the joints [1]. Consequently, although there are many scientists showing very advanced innovations in the field [2–18] further research is needed since the medical sector is still not ready to provide amputees with reliable, human-like hands. An important factor that has affected the progress in building capable robotic hands is the lack of easily obtainable, low cost experimental robotic hands that can be used as test beds [19]. That is the reason why many scientists prefer to use simulations as a single source of information when investigating real world objects although it has long been known that the combination of real models and simulations proves to be the best

© Springer International Publishing Switzerland 2016
E. Tuci et al. (Eds.): SAB 2016, LNAI 9825, pp. 195–206, 2016.
DOI: 10.1007/978-3-319-43488-9_18

and most complete approach. Barbara Webb's "Can robots make good models of biological behaviour?" [20] suggests valuable examples to support this point of view. In our work we chose to apply the "build a real model" approach because systems for the real world must be developed in the real world, because the complexity of interactions available for exploitation in the real world cannot be matched by any practical simulation environment [21].

The robotic hand we built is a simplified model of a 5-finger-human hand that uses four motors controlled through microprocessors. There is an increasing interest in the use of unconventional materials and morphologies in soft robotic systems because the underlying mechanical properties (such as body shapes, elasticity, viscosity, softness, density and stickiness) are crucial research topics for our in-depth understanding of embodied intelligence [22]. While there are many challenges in these research topics, the technological innovations usually originate from the fact that we employ soft materials for constructing the robotic platforms. The use of soft materials requires a certain control architecture regulating a large number of degrees of freedom (often infinite), which is a significant challenge from a control systems engineering viewpoint. Nevertheless, we aim to make use of the mechanical dynamics through a unique bio-inspired actuation method based on the tendon-driven drives, in order to manipulate a pair of chopsticks to handle variations of objects. This case study will not only demonstrate the usefulness of soft materials in robotics but also contribute to our better understanding of dexterous manipulation in humans (Fig. 1).

So far we have developed a few five-finger robotic hands, and the latest prototype demonstrated successful grasps with variations of objects by using a pair of chopsticks held in three fingers (i.e. thumb, index, and middle fingers). For investigating the stability performance of this platform, we tested objects with different shapes, sizes, and weights (including different material properties).

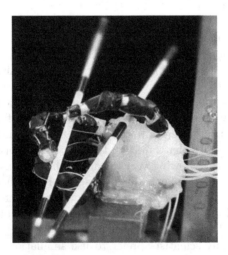

Fig. 1. A picture of the built soft robotic hand.

In this paper we discuss how we took inspiration from the human hand to build a soft robotic one and investigate its dexterity through manipulation of chopsticks in a tendon-driven motor-controlled soft robotic hand. We propose a minimalistic model of the human hand that although being operated only by four motors (in comparison to real human hand that has more than 30 muscles) is capable of performing object grasping by using chopsticks and firmly holding objects of different shape and size.

The use of chopsticks is not a new idea as studied and reported in the previous literature [16,23–28]. However none of the previous works has explored the anthropomophic configuration of robotic hand in the level we report in this paper.

Section 2 will explain in more detail the process of building the soft robotic hand and Sect. 4 will present the whole experimental set-up. Section 3 will concentrate on the mathematical model we suggest and Sect. 5 will show theoretical and practical results which we discuss in Sect. 6.

2   Hand Model

It is a common belief that the dexterity of human hands is the reason for our success as a biological species and is also a matchless characteristic making us defer from apes. Although "each of the features forming the human morphological pattern appears variably in at least one or more non-human primate species" [29], even primates such as the chimpanzees are not capable of delicately coordinating the knapping movement the way Homo Sapiens is. Consequently, human hand still remains a reason for admiration and inspiration for research for many scientists.

To explore this fascinating research topic, we developed an anthropomorphic soft robotic hand (see Fig. 2) has taken inspiration from the design proposed in [1]; however, as stated, the number of tendons and their location in the currently discussed robotic hand are different from the tendons proposed in the article and the tendons from the real human anatomy. The reason why we chose this design of the tendons is connected to a trial in which we look for an optimization and simplicity in comparison to the real human hand.

2.1   Materials

In order to build our soft robotic hand we used a variety of materials to represent its soft and rigid nature. The combination of different materials did not hinder the performance of the hand and allowed for it to show skilful and flexible performance with and without the chopsticks and also bend properly when the tendons were pulled by the motors. Thus, the chosen set of materials proved to be an appropriate one.

For the palm we used silicon (EcoFlex® 20) and hot melt adhesive (HMA, Pattex, Henkel, UK). When heated up, the HMA turns into a viscous liquid and fills the gap between two complex surfaces to make a strong bond when

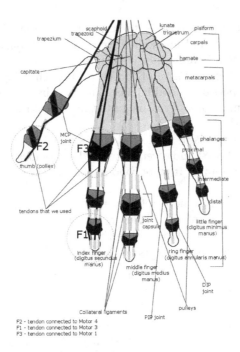

Fig. 2. Drawing of the built soft robotic hand. The picture shows an anterior view (palmar view) of the built hand. With grey colour we have drawn the joint capsules, with black the collateral ligaments, with dark blue the tendons and with yellow-the pulleys. MCP stands for metacarpophalangeal joints, DIP - distal interphalangeal joint, PIP - proximal interphalangeal joints. Additionally, we show where the points of contact between the top chopstick and the two fingers (index finger and thumb) are: F_2, F_1 and F_3. F_2 is the force acting on the thumb and is controlled via a tendon by motor 4; F_1 is acting on the tip of the distal phalanx of the index finger and is controlled by motor 3; F_3 is acting on the proximal phalanx and is controlled by motor 1. (Color figure online)

cooled down [1]. It usually starts to cool down and form a strong bond with the surface to which it is applied within 20 s and becomes stiff and with an ambient temperature after a minute. To build the fingers we used anatomically correct plastic bones by 3B Scientific GmbH, Germany. They helped us retain the accuracy and qualities of the real human hand. For the joint capsule we used black nitrile rubber (NBR sheet, White Cross Rubber Products, UK) which covers the whole joint and keeps it tightly attached. The material can also elongate under applied torque to generate the bending motion of the joints [1]. For collateral ligaments we used black butyl rubber (Butyl IIR sheet, White Cross Rubber Products, UK) that winds around at the intersection between two phalanges and contributes to additional stability of the joint.

The tendons which carry the output force to the bones are made of 0.55 mm diameter Dyneema® PE braided fishing lines with 3.1 GPa tensile strength.

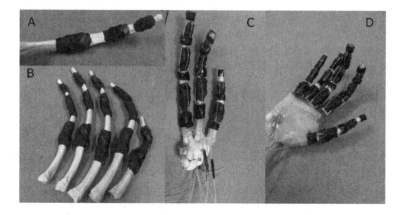

Fig. 3. Manufacturing of the hand: showing the process and the final result.

The pulleys which the tendons go through are made of Polytetrafluoroethylene (PFTE tubes, Farnell, UK) with Teflon coating which generates a low friction inner surface [1]. In order to assemble and glue the required materials to each other, we used the hot melt adhesive mentioned before.

2.2 Fabrication of the Hand

Due to the complexity of the anatomically correct pieces and continuum surfaces we assemble our fingers by hand. Exact process of the fabrication and pictures can be seen in [1]. In brief, we dissembled the plastic hand to the state where we had each bone separately. Using the black nitrile rubber, cut into rectangular shaped pieces, we covered the joints (MCP, PIP and DIP) and secured the newly gainted structure with the black butyl rubber as collateral ligaments.

After we were ready with the assembling of the capsule ligaments and the collateral ligaments, the fingers looked like the ones shown on Fig. 3(A) and (B). The next step involved the adding of the tendons and pulleys. In our robotic hand, the index finger and the middle finger have four tendons each, located on the anterior side, the right and left side and the posterior side of the finger. For the thumb, we decided that the minimum required number of tendons we will need is two and so located one on the anterior and one on the posterior side. The ring finger and little finger have only one tendon each, located on the anterior side as these fingers do not contribute to the movement of the hand and the manipulation of the chopsticks. There are four sets of pulleys that the tendons go through (see Fig. 3(D)). The pulleys are secured with tape (to mimic the function of the human ligaments for keeping the tendons to the bones) for additional stability.

Once the fingers were ready, they were placed back to their anatomically correct locations with regard to the carpal bones (Fig. 3(C)). After all fingers were connected to the carpal bones and glued to them with HMA, we decided to build a palm-like soft structure using again the hot melt adhesive fluid and a certain amount of silicon as to cover the hand as much as possible from all sides. The silicon was prepared in advance, 24 h before the fabrication of the hand. In the end, the result was a fully assembled hand as shown on Fig. 3(D). After the assembly we glued a pair of chopsticks to four contact points of the hand.

3 Chopstick Model

In this paper, we demonstrate the capacity of our fingers by holding two glued chopsticks and use them to grab small sized objects. Figure 4 shows the model we are using to express the forces acting on the chopsticks by our fingers. Here, forces F_1, F_2 and F_3 are applied by the fingers on the top chopstick and F_{act} is the total force generated at the tip of the chopsticks we call it activation force. We assume that a physical rigid object in between the sticks transfers the Fact force so that the bottom chopstick reflects the same force, but in opposite direction.

In our paper, we only actuate the top chopstick with the index finger and the thumb. Forces F_1 and F_3 are generated by the distal and proximal phalanges of the index finger, respectively and F_2 is generated by the distal phalanx of the thumb. Given these forces and the distances on the top chopstick depicted by a_1, a_2 and a_3, the force and moment equalities for our model are given as below:

$$F_{act} + F_1 + F_3 - F_2 = 0 \tag{1}$$

$$F_1 a_1 + F_3(a_1 + a_2 + a_3) - F_2(a_1 + a_2) = 0 \tag{2}$$

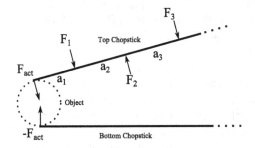

Fig. 4. A free body diagram of the forces acting on the top and bottom chopsticks. In our paper we only concentrate on the forces on the top chopstick.

4 Experimental Setup

The experimental setup consisted of three parts: actuation mechanism, measuring scales and the robotic hand itself.

Fig. 5. Experimental set-up. (A) forces that we measure (B) experimental set-up (C) motors, power supply and measuring scales. (Color figure online)

The actuation mechanism of our robot hand consists of four tendon driven modules which can be controlled independently from each other. Each module has a microcontroller, a motor driver, a 100:1 gear ratio Pololu® 6 V DC motor with 0.22 Nm stalling torque output, and a motor encoder for position feedback inside a $30 \times 40 \times 50$ mm box [1]. There is a pulley with a circumference of 22 mm attached to the motor shaft, which is connected to the free end of a tendon. These modules are connected to each other over a master communication unit with a I^2C bus. Each module runs a PD controller loop whose target position can be set by computer and transferred to the master communication unit with a USB connection [1]. The modules are connected to an Arduino® Duemilanove board and a power circuit. Through a USB connection the Arduino board connects to a computer with Matlab that operates the movements of the chopsticks with the help of a set of commands. A power supply is connected to the computer to give electricity to the system.

The second part of the experimental set is represented by three measuring scales by the company Ajax Scientific (Plastic Tubular Spring Scale, 2000 g/20 N Weight Capacity, Red) and one spring scale by Pesola (Medio-Line Spring Scale, Newton, 25 N). The robotic hand was placed on a stand at the same height level as the modules and the red spring scales as to allow accurate measurements and free motion of the chopsticks in the air. The complete platform is shown on Fig. 5.

5 Experiments and Results

5.1 Simulation Results

Figure 6 shows the numerical solutions to the force equilibrium depending on the Eqs. (1) and (2). In Fig. 6(a), we have set F_{act} with its minimum and maximum

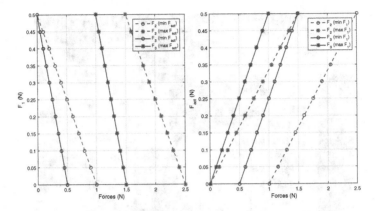

Fig. 6. Numeric solutions of the force equilibrium given in Eqs. 1 and 2. (a) Relation between F_1 and F_2 and F_3 when F_{act} is kept constant. (b) Relation between F_{act} and F_2 and F_3 when F_1 is kept constant. In both figures lines with circles represent the values when the fixed force is at its minimum, and lines with asterisks represent values when the fixed force is at its maximum value.

values (0 and 0.5 N respectively) and observed the relation between F_1 versus F_2 and F_3. As expected, both F_2 and F_3 have an inverse relation with F_1 while F_{act} is fixed at either 0 or 0.5N. We also notice that F_2 has a higher magnitude and a larger range of values compared to F_1 and F_3 because it is the counteracting force to the sum of F_1, F_3 and F_{act}. In Fig. 6(b) we observed the relation between forces F_2 and F_3 versus F_{act} when F_1 is fixed at either 0 or 0.5 N. As F_{act} is the resulting force on the tip of the chopstick, we naturally observe a direct relationship between F_{act}, F_2 and F_3. Similar to Fig. 6(a), we notice that F_2 has a higher magnitude and a larger range of values as it is the counteracting force to the sum of the rest of the forces.

We start our experiments with force equilibrium by numerically solving the equations presented in the chopstick model in Sect. 3. As we have only two equations for four unknowns, i.e. F_1, F_2, F_3 and F_{act}, we provided a fixed range of 0 to 0.5 N for F_{act} and F_1 to observe the relation of the two other forces with respect to these ranges. We have chosen equal distances between force points shown in Fig. 4, i.e. a_1, a_2 and a_3, and set them to be 45 mm, in order for the sake of simplicity and to explore the basic characteristics of the model.

5.2 Experimental Results

As we saw from the chopstick model on Fig. 4, there are three points of contact between the fingers (index finger and thumb) and the top chopstick and consequently three points of possible force application – F_1, F_2, F_3. In addition, there is the activation force F_{act} between the two chopsticks that reflects the stability of the grasp. In this section of the paper we are presenting the experimental results of the measurements of these four forces. As shown on Fig. 5(A), we built a specific construction in order to be able to measure all forces in their plane of action: F_1, F_2, F_3 and F_{act}.

F_1 is the force acting on the inner tip of the distal phalanx of the index finger. The tendon that is located on the inner middle side of the index finger (as shown on Fig. 2-tendons used are highlighted in black) connects the area where F_1 acts to motor 3. F_2 is the force coming from the inner part of the tip (distal phalanx) of the thumb and is connected via a tendon with motor 4. Lastly, F_3 is the finger force acting on the proximal phalanx of the index finger and is connected to motor 1. Since the index finger has two finger forces - F_1 and F_3 each connected to a motor: motor 3 and motor 1, respectively, it becomes obvious that f.ex. motor 3 does not only influence the performance of F_1, but also of F_3. The same holds true for motor 1: the force that we apply in motor 1 not only triggers a motion in the area where F_3 is located, but also influences the F_1 area. This is why, when measuring the finger forces F_1 and F_3, we took into account both motors: for F_1 – motor 3 and motor 1 and for F_3 – motor 1 and motor 3. For finger force F_2 we measured the influence of only one motor motor 4.

Controlling the amount of force we were applying to the modules (where motor 1, 3 and 4 are located), we measured the force of the motors and force of the fingers for every different amount of output force we were applying. The range of force values we applied was different for F_1, F_3 and F_2. They were not picked randomly but according to previous measurements showing in which range we will experience the most noticeable changes. For example, when measuring finger force F_2, we used 10 different values of the force we applied via Matlab (in the range between 4.75 N and 8.97 N), wrote down the values that the measuring scale connected to motor 4 and the measuring scale connected to the thumb showed and performed the same measurements three times. So, in the end only for F_2 we had three sets of 30 measurements, i.e. 90 data points. We took the average values for F_2 and for the force of motor 4 and plotted the values as shown on Figs. 7 and 8.

In order to check the stability of the grasp, we tested the hand with objects of different shape, size and weight (see Fig. 9). The objects used for this grasping test were: wooden bar (0.7 g), paper frog (0.8 g), plastic butterfly (2.0 g), paper box (9.0 g), embroidered textile ball (19 g), raven-plastic toy (10 g), Pink plastic toy (20 g), plastic ball (20 g), spool with thread (0.7 g), paracetamol tablet (0.6 g). The maximum weight that we tested was 20 g. In addition, we see that the hand

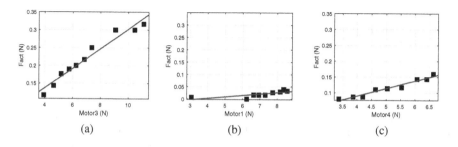

Fig. 7. Experimental results showing the relationship between the activation force F_{act} and the motors: motor 3, motor 1 and motor 4.

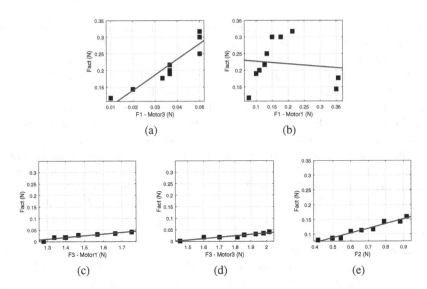

Fig. 8. Experimental results showing the relationship between the activation force F_{act} and the finger forces: F_1, F_2 and F_3

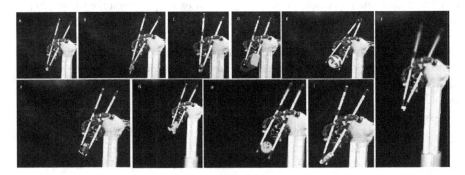

Fig. 9. Holding of 10 different object to show stability of the grasp: (A) wooden bar (B) paper frog (C) plastic butterfly (D) paper box (E) embroidered textile ball (F) raven plastic toy (G) pink plastic toy (H) plastic ball (I) spool with thread (J) paracetamol tablet. (Color figure online)

is holding not only big objects such as the paper box or embroidered textile ball, but also delicate ones such as a tablet or a plastic butterfly.

6   Conclusion

In this paper, we presented an approach to design, fabricate, and control anthropomorphic robotic hand that is capable of using chopsticks to manipulate various objects. Unlike conventional rigid grippers, our platform consists of a number of soft components, which is, on the one hand, advantageous for manipulation dexterity, but on the other hand, challenging to perform motor control. This paper presented the first experimental result based on the minimalistic actuation components to identify its basic handling capabilities of chopsticks. Through the investigation with the simple chopstick physics model, we found how to provide constraints to chopstick motions, and generate necessary forces at the tips of them for manipulation tasks. After all we demonstrated that, with the pertinent constraints, it is sufficient for this robot to control only one motor to adjust forces necessary to grasp variations of objects. In the future, we plan to extend this project with more challenging tasks such as holding of chopsticks without gluing them on hands, and controlling the chopstick forces more dynamically to negotiate with deforming objects, and so on. With these investigations, we envision to understand the nature of grasping in biological and artificial soft hands, as well as to develop more dexterous manipulators for robotic applications.

Acknowledgement. This research was supported by the RoboSoft: Coordination Action for Soft Robotics, funded by the European Commission under the Future and Emerging Technologies (FP7-ICT-2013-C project No 619319), and the Cambridge Commonwealth, European and International Trust.

References

1. Culha, U., Iida, F.: Design of biomimetic robotic fingers with compliant anthropomorphic joints. Bioinspiration Biomimetics **11**(2), 026001 (2016)
2. Salisbury, J.K., Craig, J.J.: Articulated hands force control and kinematic issues. Int. J. Robot. Res. **1**(1), 4–17 (1982)
3. Townsend, W.: The barretthand grasper-programmably flexible part handling and assembly. Industr. Robot Int. J. **27**(3), 181–188 (2000)
4. Kawasaki, H., Komatsu, T., Uchiyama, K.: Dexterous anthropomorphic robot hand with distributed tactile sensor: Gifu hand II. IEEE/ASME Trans. Mechatron. **7**(3), 296–303 (2002)
5. Lovchik, C.S., Diftler, M.A.: The Robonaut hand: a dexterous robot hand for space. In: IEEE International Conference on Robotics and Automation, pp. 907–912 (1999)
6. Jacobsen, S.C., Iversen, E.K., Knutti, D.F., Johnson, R.T., Biggers, K.B.: Design of the Utah/MIT dextrous hand. In: IEEE International Conference on Robotics and Automation, pp. 1520–1532 (1986)
7. Liu, H., Wu, K., Meusel, P., Seitz, N., Hirzinger, G., Jin, M.H., Chen, Z.P.: Multisensory five-finger dexterous hand: the DLR/HIT hand II. In: IEEE/RSJ International Conference on Intelligent Robots and Systems, pp. 3692–3697 (2008)
8. Deshpande, A.D., Xu, Z., Vande Weghe, M.J., Brown, B.H., Ko, J., Chang, L.Y., Matsuoka, Y.: Mechanisms of the anatomically correct testbed hand. IEEE/ASME Trans. Mechatron. **18**, 238–250 (2013)
9. Hirose, S., Umetani, Y.: The development of soft gripper for the versatile robot hand. Mech. Mach. Theor. **13**(1), 351–359 (1978)
10. Catalano, M.G., Grioli, G., Farnioli, E., Serio, A., Piazza, C., Bicchi, A.: Adaptive synergies for the design and control of the Pisa/IIT softHand. Int. J. Robot. Res. **33**(5), 768–782 (2014)
11. Gaiser, I., Schulz, S., Kargov, A., Klosek, H., Bierbaum, A., Pylatiuk, C., Dillmann, R.: A new anthropomorphic robotic hand. In: IEEE-RAS International Conference on Humanoid Robots, pp. 418–422 (2008)

12. Dollar, A.M., Howe, R.D.: The highly adaptive SDM hand: design and performance evaluation. Int. J. Robot. Res. **29**(5), 585–597 (2010)
13. Odhner, L.U., Jentoft, L.P., Claffee, M.R., Corson, N., Tenzer, Y., Ma, R.R., Dollar, A.M.: A compliant, underactuated hand for robust manipulation. Int. J. Robot. Res. **33**(5), 736–752 (2014)
14. Manti, M., Hassan, T., Passetti, G., D'Elia, N., Laschi, C., Cianchetti, M.: A bioinspired soft robotic gripper for adaptable and effective grasping. Soft Robot. **2**(3), 107–116 (2015)
15. Chen, W., Xiong, C., Yue, S.: Mechanical implementation of kinematic synergy for continual grasping generation of anthropomorphic hand. IEEE/ASME Trans. Mechatron. **20**(3), 1–15 (2014)
16. Fukaya, N., Asfour, T., Dillmann, R., Toyama, S.: Development of a five-finger dexterous hand without feedback control: the TUAT/Karlsruhe humanoid hand. In: IEEE International Conference on Intelligent Robots and Systems, pp. 4533–4540 (2013)
17. Xu, Z., Kumar, V., Todorov, E.: A low-cost and modular, 20-DOF anthropomorphic robotic hand: design, actuation and modeling. In: IEEE-RAS International Conference on Humanoid Robots, pp. 368–375 (2013)
18. Jiang, L., Low, K., Costa, J., Black, R.J., Park, Y.L.: Fiber optically sensorized multi-fingered robotic hand. In: IEEE/RSJ International Conference on Intelligent Robots and Systems, pp. 1763–1768 (2015)
19. Miller, A., Allen, P., Santos, V., Valero-Cuevas, F.: From robotic hands to human hands: a visualization and simulation engine for grasping research. Industr. Robot Int. J. **32**(1), 55–63 (2005)
20. Webb, B.: Can robots make good models of biological behaviour? Behav. Brain Sci. **24**(6), 1033–1050 (2001)
21. Beckers, R., Holland, O.E., Deneubourg, J.L.: From local actions to global tasks: stigmergy and collective robotics. Artif. Life IV **181**, 189 (1994)
22. Iida, F., Laschi, C.: Soft robotics: challenges and perspectives. Procedia Comput. Sci. **7**, 99–102 (2011)
23. Ramadan, A.A., Takubo, T., Mae, Y., Oohara, K., Arai, T.: Developmental process of a chopstick-like hybrid-structure two-fingered micromanipulator hand for 3-D manipulation of microscopic objects. IEEE Trans. Industr. Electron. **56**(4), 1121–1135 (2009)
24. Joseph, R.A., Goh, A.C., Cuevas, S.P., Donovan, M.A., Kauffman, M.G., Salas, N.A., Dunkin, B.J.: "Chopstick" surgery: a novel technique improves surgeon performance and eliminates arm collision in robotic single-incision laparoscopic surgery. Surg. Endosc. **24**(6), 1331–1335 (2010)
25. Hsu, S.H., Wu, S.P.: An investigation for determining the optimum length of chopsticks. Appl. Ergon. **22**(6), 395–400 (1991)
26. Yamazaki, A., Masuda, R.: Autonomous foods handling by chopsticks for meal assistant robot. In: German Conference on Robotics, pp. 1–6 (2012)
27. Chang, B.C., Huang, B.S., Chou, C.L., Wang, S.J.: A new type of chopsticks for patients with impaired hand function. Arch. Phys. Med. Rehabil. **87**(7), 1013–1015 (2006)
28. Park, J., Moon, W.: The systematic design and fabrication of a three-chopstick microgripper. Int. J. Adv. Manuf. Technol. **26**(3), 251–261 (2005)
29. Shrewsbury, M.M., Marzke, M.W., Linscheid, R.L., Reece, S.P.: Comparative morphology of the pollical distal phalanx. Am. J. Phys. Anthropol. **121**(1), 30–47 (2003)

Linguistic Primitives: A New Model for Language Development in Robotics

Alessio Mauro Franchi[(⊠)], Lorenzo Sernicola, and Giuseppina Gini

DEIB Department, Politecnico di Milano, Milano, Italy
{alessiomauro.franchi,giuseppina.gini}@polimi.it

Abstract. Often in robotics natural language processing is used simply to improve the human-machine interaction. However, language is not only a powerful communication tool: it is deeply linked to the inner organization of the mind, and it guides its development. The aim of this paper is to take a first step towards a model of language which can be integrated with the diverse abilities of the robot, thus leading to its cognitive development, and eventually speeding up its learning capacity. To this end we propose and implement the Language Primitives Model (LPM) to imitate babbling, a phase in the learning process that characterizes a few months old babies. LPM is based on the same principles dictated by the Motor Primitives model. The obtained results positively compare with experimental data and observations about children, so confirming this interest of the new model.

Keywords: Emergence of vocalization · Babbling · Motor primitives

1 Introduction

Recently Natural Language Processing (NLP) has developed many voice recognition technologies, such as Apple Siri [17], mostly used for simple tasks like sending a message. Limitations emerge also in other applications; video games and robots are often able to recognize a few words, mainly related to a specific task. Instead language plays an important role in intelligent behaviours, as initially indicated by Alan Turing in his "Imitation Game" [19]. His final considerations was that language manipulation is a necessary condition for a machine to be intelligent.

In biology the ability of communicating through sounds is present in several animal species. However language has evolved differently in humans, mainly due to the fact that it is more than an external instrument for communicating; it is intrinsic to the mind itself [3]. Spokeng language is thus the epiphenomenon of the deep link existing between brain and language. It is known that cerebral areas dedicated to language are highly connected with motor ones; when one elaborates a sentence or produces a word both areas are activated [14]. This is a clue of the presence of common mental mechanisms both for motor or linguistic skills.

© Springer International Publishing Switzerland 2016
E. Tuci et al. (Eds.): SAB 2016, LNAI 9825, pp. 207–218, 2016.
DOI: 10.1007/978-3-319-43488-9_19

To recreate in artificial agents such an ability, natural language and perceptions should be linked together; the comprehension of natural language by robots should be based on sensory-motor experiences and not on a sort of hard coded semantics [2]. In a longer time perspective, a language based on the experience would help robots to autonomously extract knowledge about the environment, integrating also this information with those from its own actions and related sensorial feedbacks [12].

Our research mainly focuses on this relationship between motor learning and mental abilities development in humans as a way to improve the robot learning system.

We draw inspiration both from humans and from decades of studies in NLP, that despite impressive results [17] has still many problems to solve. We start from the hypothesis that the linguistic apparatus in robotics should be part of several other biologically inspired mechanisms, cooperating together towards the cognitive development of the artificial agent. We take inspirations from newborns, focusing in particular on the evolutive steps of language. Starting from data collected during the Speechome Project at M.I.T. [13], we have designed and implemented a model called the Linguistic Primitive Model (LPM). It aims at imitating babies in a specific moment of language exploration, the babbling phase, that takes place from the sixth to the tenth month and is the way they imitate sounds and words on purpose.

This new model re-uses several concepts typically associated in robots with movements, creating a parallel between motor and linguistic mechanisms that is known to exist in humans brain. Learning starts from a simple hard coded dataset of linguistic primitives; the agent tries to imitate an heard word continuolsy composing the primitives, and producing new sounds until it succeeds. Newly learned words are added to the set of primitives ready to be used or composed again to form more complex sounds. Other primitives become useless and are discarded.

In the rest of the paper we shortly review the related works and introduce our model of Linguistic Primitives. We make experiments using some data from the mentioned Speechome data. Results of our experiments are not easily comparable with state of the art, but they demonstrate that our hypotheses about language development are correct and that LPM is a basis for further researches. They highlight also that the use of a typical model for movements is a new promising point of view for the development of linguistic skills in robotics.

2 Related Works

As we have briefly seen language is strictly connected with mind; its learning helps the cognitive development, and viceversa [3]. From studies about babies it is clear that cognitive development in humans is a process parallel to language learning. Words are used by infants as powerful instrument for building an internal representation of the external world; they act as labels for objects in the environment [11]. New grammatical constructs interact with sensory-motor

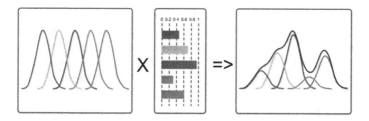

Fig. 1. A schema of the motor primitive composition mechanism

apparatus at a neuronal level [21]: when somebody listens to verbs like "walk" or "see" its brain activates also neurons of the cortical motor areas. Motor and sensors areas are thus linked togheter: language learning depends strictly on physical and sensorial experiences, and viceversa. This concept is known as embodiment: intelligence needs a body and an environment to develop [16].

A biologically inspired approach for language development should help robots in autonomously extracting simple semantic information from the context; it is the case of [10] where a moving robot is able to correctly interpret navigation commands expressed in natural language. Another challenge is the symbol grounding problem, that concerns the relation between words or symbols with their meaning [18]. An interesting study showed that sensory-motor integration can improve symbol grounding processes, just like humans do [9].

The main idea is thus that robots, just like living beings, must play an active role in their cognitive development and learning, interacting through their body with the environment. Also language emergence should follow this paradigm and should be grounded on sensorial experiences. Several evidences show that motor and linguistic learning share the same mechanisms. Nowadays a validated theory for movement learning is the motor primitive mechanism [7]; motor primitives are the "smallest" entity of voluntary movement, that activate a single muscle. Composition and coordination of several motor primitives, one for each muscle involved, result in a final complex movement Fig. 1. This theory seems to clearly explain how infants go from instinctive to voluntary movements, and may also hold for language development: babbling is for babies the mechanism to start from simple innate sounds and get to complex and intentional words by their composition [20].

3 Our Approach: Language Primitives

Understanding and producing language is a multisensory process; it is grounded on the visual, musculoskeletal and proprioceptive systems; we use our ears to listen to spoken words but several studies demonstrated that we also exploit sight for facial expression analysis or body movements recognition [1]. In the same way the production of language involves the muscular and proprioceptive systems; these should be seen as two significant hints of the relation between linguistic and motor skills.

In their first months of life, babies are not able to pronounce and to distinguish words, but can determine their phonetic differences. This mechanism leads to the so called "phonetic attunement", that is a greater sensitivity to the contrasts and to the specific tones of a particular language, that eventually leads babies to distinguish the first words. In the same time they start also to distinguish the repeated language patterns, mainly by a statistical approach. It is not necessary for a child to segment a sentence, but he is able to create early phonetic categories simply listening to sounds. This statistical approach is part of the distributional learning mechanism and it represents the origin of language learning: the information concerning the distribution of the frequencies of tones is merged with the visual information, contributing to the creation of a speech context.

This first stage paths the way for the following ones in language learning: the recognition of vowels (6–8 month), of consonants (8–12 month) and finally of phonemes duration. These phases in children follow very rapidly one another, more quickly than the only auditory inputs would allow; this gap may be explained by cross-modal association [4]. Language development is a very complex phenomenon, but also a universal process and it is the same across different environmental condition and experiences [6].

We propose a model focused mainly on the basic mechanism through which words are formed in the first months of life; the term "babbling" refers to the sounds uttered by newborns when they still aren't able to pronounce complete words. Researchers agree that this phenomenon plays a key role in the correct cognitive development of the baby. Actually, the first movements of the limbs and of the mouth of newborns are the product of involuntary reflexes. During the first two months of life, the baby utters sounds that are called protophones, which already have some features of vowels; these develop until, around the sixth month, babbling starts.

With time the protophones become no longer involuntary sounds and are intentionally produced. This voluntary act is part of a more global cognitive development of the baby, which maps the movements of the vocal tract and the resultant sounds, allowing babies to replicate a sound. This mapping leads them to voluntarily utter a word [8]. Other researches have highlighted how these basic mechanisms for language learning are in common with those for movement learning and both modules communicate to strengthen each other [13].

The Speechome Project is our main inspiration. Among the huge amount of collected data, several audio files recorded a baby repeating the same word in different instants and house places, starting from the very first trials of imitation to its voluntary pronunciation. As an example we report a brief transcription of the word "water":

"gaga" - "gata" - "wata" - "wate" - "water"

From the analysis of these registrations has emerged that each single consonant-vocal couple may be considered as the most similar particle to a linguistic primitive we can extract. In nature a baby tries to imitate the sound he is listening to composing all the "linguistic primitives" he has, in a similar way to motor learning mechanism. In the above example the baby starts repeating the innate "ga" particle; as his vocal tract and facial muscles modify in time he learns more complex sounds such as "ta" or "wa", replacing simpler particles and resulting in a more accurate reproduction of the target word. The baby finally learns the "r" and succeeds in pronouncing "water".

Our linguistic primitives model aims at reproducing this process of imitation of a spoken word starting from a hard coded dataset of linguistic primitives; this set has a direct equivalent in humans as the internal mapping between a sound and a specific movement of the mouth and of the diaphragm. We consider linguistic primitives as innate, as they are a direct consequence of non-voluntary changes, and are independent from the language family and context.

To generate the primitives dataset we have analyzed various registrations reproducing sounds made by babies during their babbling stages. We have first discarded videos not tagged with the age of the baby and then classified those selected into the five different stages of language learning [8]:

1. Cooing (1st–4th month), repetition of single sound, e.g.: ooooooo, aaaaaaah;
2. Consonant-Vowel (CV) or Vowel-Consonant (VC) sounds combinations (4th–6th month), e.g.: maaaa, uuuum, baaaa ;
3. Reduplicated babbling (6th–10th month), e.g.: babababa, gagagaga, dadadada;
4. Non-reduplicated babbling (6th–10th month), e.g.: bama, gagamee
5. Quasiwords (10th–12th month), e.g.: watee.

Stages 4 and 5 see the first attempts to compose these primitives intentionally. Since during these stages the dataset of primitives is quite limited, babies are not able to compose real words but only simple terms such as "mama" or "dad", made of two or three primitives concatenated. The continuous enrichment of this internal dataset eventually leads to the production of complex sounds.

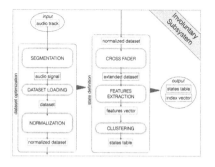

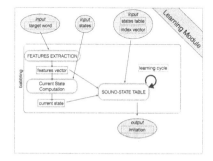

Fig. 2. The involuntary subsystem.   **Fig. 3.** The voluntary subsystem.

4   The Implemented System

An artificial architecture able to simulate the language development skills as seen above should comprehend both the innate mental abilities and all the mechanisms of voluntary learning that rely on multi-modal sensorial inputs. Such an architecture is a long term goal; in our model we will consider only those aspects related to canonical babbling and to the auditory stimulus processing.

Two subsystems compose our model: the involuntary (ISS) Fig. 2 and voluntary (VSS) Fig. 3. The first reproduces all the aspects related to the physiologic growth of the body, starting from the earlier months of life until first voluntary mechanisms of imitation starts. It receives as input several examples of babbling and extracts the linguistic primitives; all the possible combinations of two primitives are then generated, a mechanism that corresponds to the innate development of the proto-word. A Sound-State table is generated, which recreates the natural mapping between "words" and "states" each baby learns during time.

The second subsystem deals with babbling, a phase of learning that emerges in parallel to the acquirement of new words and to the first voluntary imitations of heard sounds. The VSS receives as input a sound representing the word to be learned and the architecture starts to "babble", i.e. it produces sounds by composing linguistic primitives. The first type of composition we implemented consists in the concatenation of two or more linguistic primitives; more advanced mechanism may be added in the future. These sounds are compared with the target input and the learning process is stopped when the similarity is greater than a fixed threshold; this event triggers the activation of the Sound-State Table, mimicking the neural activation it is known to appear when a baby accomplishes his imitation task [15].

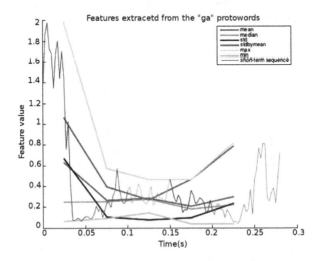

Fig. 4. The six features extracted in the short-term processing from the sound "ga"

4.1   Involuntary Subsystem

The main task accomplished by the ISS is the generation of the "hard-coded" dataset of linguistic primitives. The ISS receives as input several segmented audio signals, each containing exactly one "babble", i.e. a vocal-consonant couple. Every signal is processed with the following filters: stereo-to-mono converter, sampling frequency normalizator, pitch shifter and an RMS equalizer. This process equalizes signals coming from different sources. A second module is responsible for the concatenation of these primitives by a cross-fading technique. This process can be considered part of the involuntary subsystem as in babies the generation of first linguistic primitives appears as a direct consequence of their physical development more than of an a-posteriori learning.

The last step is the selection of the "States" for the table. A state is a compact representation of the environment; it is actually composed by the sound the robot has listened to. For state selection we perform two kinds of elaboration on the signals, mid-term windowing and short-term processing: both make use of a framing mechanism for trimming primitives into very short segments which are then analyzed independently from each other. Several features are extracted; their mean and variance form the vector of features we use in classification for the state selection and for similarity computation Fig. 4.

4.2   Voluntary Subsystem

The second module deals with the babbling and learning phase; it receives in input a target word, the Sound-State Table and the dataset of primitives. The features vector of the input word is computed and projected onto the collection of states and the most similar one is selected.

The States-Sounds Table is used as a sort of neural network to register each tentative of imitation; rows are dedicated to states, columns correspond to produced sounds. For each tentative the system will do, the similarity values between the target and the produced sound is computed and stored in the corresponding entry of the table; this process is repeated until the imitation performance is satisfying. As the number of trials grows, the mean number of tentatives needed by the agent significantly decreases, indicating that the system is learning new words.

5   Experimental Results

For validating the proposed model we defined different experiments; stated the innovative approach here presented a direct comparison with other works is very difficult. Our goal is not to improve others' models, but to propose a new point of view for language learning that is bio-inspired, grounded on the agent's experience, and that shares its mechanisms with those of the motor system.

Experiments are intended to evaluate the ability of the system both to correctly imitate an input sound and to learn them as the number of tentatives grows. Two metrics are evaluated. The first is similarity, that describes how much the produced word is similar to the listened one and is computed as the distance between the features vectors of both sounds, normalized in the range [0..1]:

$$similarity = \tanh \left(\frac{1}{vectorsDistance} \right) \tag{1}$$

where vectorsDistance is the squared norm of the difference between the two vectors; similarity is thus the probability that two sounds represent the same word.

The second is the number of cycles the system needs to produce a "good" output, where good means above a predefined similarity threshold we empirically evaluated. For all the following experiment we split our dataset of sounds into training and testing subset, composed of 600 and 300 signals respectively.

5.1 Preliminary Step

In a preliminary step we had to optimize the open parameters of the system; the most fundamental is the similarity threshold, that is the minimum value of similarity we require to consider an imitation as valid.

The setup for this preliminary experiment is:

– training dataset: 600 words;
– testing dataset: 300 words;
– number of tests: 20;

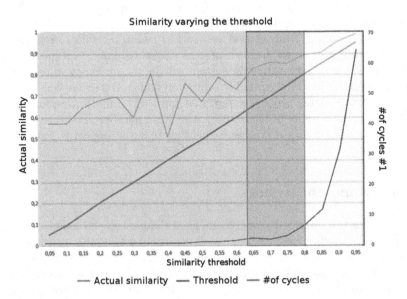

Fig. 5. The graph shows the combined result and the optimal values for the similarity threshold is highlighted

- threshold value step: 0.05 (from 0.05 to 0.95);
- input words per test: 200 words (selected randomly from the 300 words).

For each threshold value in the range, the mean number of cycles necessary to correctly imitate the input word is logged; as Fig. 5 shows this value is low (<15) for threshold lower than 0.85, a value corresponding to a very accurate imitation of the input word. Moreover the mean value of the actual similarity is always greater that the defined treshold. The combination of these two considerations defines a range of optimal similarity threshold in [0.65, 0.8], a good trade-off that guarantees a similarity above 0.8 and a mean number of cycles lower than 10.

5.2   First Experiment

We firstly evaluated the importance of the number of words in input to the system; by this parameter we can copy the natural tendency of caregivers to use a simplified lexicon, with non-conjugate verbs and a restricted vocabulary.

We thus reduced the number of words in the testing dataset down to only 20, keeping other parameters unaltered:

- training dataset: 600 words;
- testing dataset: 20 words;
- number of tests: 19;
- threshold value step: 0.05 (from 0.05 to 0.95);
- input words per test: 200 words (selected randomly from the 20 words).

By comparing experimental data with previous results it emerges that our system is able to correctly imitate and learn words in a lower number of cycles, especially in cases of high similarity threshold values Fig. 6. Moreover the quality of learning is good even if the number of input word decreases Fig. 7.

This behavior is biologically validated by results from the Speechome Project: in nature the learning of a new word happens as caregivers repeat it more frequently and homogeneusly.

5.3   Second Experiment

The second experiment is mostly focused on the ability of the system to learn new words. We have analyzed the trend of the learning rate as input words follow each other and we expect it to decrease in time.

The parameters for this second experiment are:

- training dataset: 600 words;
- testing dataset: 300 words;
- number of test: 1;
- threshold values: 0.8;
- input words per test: 200 words (selected randomly from the 300 words).

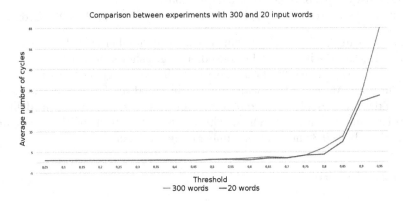

Fig. 6. The number of cycles needed to reproduce a word decrease if a reduced input set of word is used

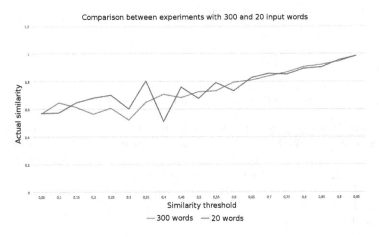

Fig. 7. The trend of the similarity values is not affected by the number of input words

From this experiment we have extracted the number of cycles necessary to imitate each single word sent as input to the system, computing then the moving average to remove noise in data. The decreasing mean number of cycles and the frequency of input words requiring a single tentative to be correctly imitated show an ongoing learning of novel words or proto-words Fig. 8. This result is supported by scientific evidence showing that babies speed up language learning by memorizing the correct imitation tentatives they make and reusing words already learned.

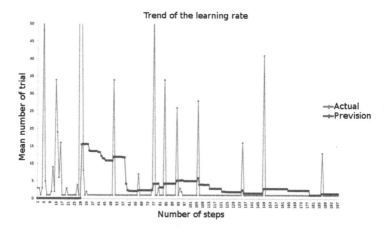

Fig. 8. The moving average of the mean number of tentatives the system need to imitate the target word

6   Conclusion

The use of natural language in robotics has always been an independent field of research that was born with the aim to obtain intelligent and immediate interaction between men and machines. However, the importance of language does not exclusively lie in the field of communication: it actually represents the very image of the mind, it is deeply linked to its inner structure, and it guides its development through innumerable phases.

The aim of this work is to take a first step towards a model of language that can be integrated with the other cognitive abilities of the robot, with the purpose of contributing and collaborating towards a faster and more reliable development of its mind and of its learning ability.

We focused our attention on the initial stages of language development, which takes place in babies during their first years of life during which they switch from an involuntary production of sounds to the voluntary use of vowels and syllables: the babbling phase. We consequently elaborated the Model of Language Primitives (LPM), which is based on the same principles lying under the motor primitives, transposed into the language learning process.

In order to test the LPM we performed some experiments with the aim to evaluate its imitation ability and to test whether the system is effectively able to learn. The obtained results not only validate this model, but also show a behavior very similar to the one observed in babies. This supports the idea of the strict parallelism between language and motor primitives, the core of the proposed model.

This preliminary results are encouraging but several open problems still exist. The next step we want to explore is the integration of this model into our intentional architecture IDRA [5], to exploit its potentiality in processing different types of sensorial input, in learning associations, and in the autonomous generation of new objectives starting from innate instincts. The integration of the LPM in IDRA should strengthen their learning abilities.

References

1. Calvert, G., Spence, C., Stein, B.E.: The Handbook of Multisensory Processes. MIT Press, Cambridge (2004)
2. Cangelosi, A.: Grounding language in action and perception: from cognitive agents to humanoid robots. Phy. Life Rev. **7**, 139–151 (2010)
3. Dominey, P.F.: How are grammatical constructions linked to embodied meaning representations? AMD Newslett. **10**, 3 (2013)
4. Erneling, C.E.: Understanding Language Acquisition: The Framework of Learning. Cambridge University Press, Cambridge (1993)
5. Franchi, A.M., Mutti, F., Gini, G.: From learning to new goal generation in a bioinspired robotic setup. In: Advanced Robotics (in press, 2016). doi:10.1080/01691864.2016.1172732
6. Gleitman, L.R., Newport, E.L.: The invention of language by children: environmental and biological influences on the acquisition of language. In: Gleitman, L.R., Liberman, M. (eds.) An Invitation to Cognitive Science, 2nd edn, pp. 90–116. MIT Press, Cambridge (2005)
7. Konczak, J.: On the notion of motor primitives in humans and robots. In: Proceedings of the Fifth International Workshop on Epigenetic Robotics: Modeling Cognitive Development in Robotic Systems, pp. 47–53 (2005)
8. Kuhl, P.K., Meltzoff, A.N.: Infant vocalizations in response to speech: vocal imitation and developmental change. J. Acoust. Soc. Am. **100**, 2425–2438 (1996)
9. MacDorman, K.F.: Grounding symbols through sensorimotor integration. J. Robot. Soc. Jpn. **17**, 20–24 (1999)
10. Matuszek, C., Herbst, E., Zettlemoyer, L., Fox, D.: Learning to parse natural language commands to a robot control system. In: Desai, J.P., Dudek, G., Khatib, O., Kumar, V. (eds.) Experimental Robotics. Springer Tracts in Advanced Robotics, vol. 88, pp. 403–415. Springer, New York (2013)
11. Pastra, K.: Autonomous acquisition of sensorimotor experiences: any role for language? AMD Newslett. **25**, 12–13 (2013)
12. Popescu, A.M., Etzioni, O., Henry, K.: Towards a theory of natural language interfaces to databases, vol. 1, pp. 149–157 (2013)
13. Roy, D., Patel, R., DeCamp, P., Kubat, R., Fleischman, M., Roy, B., Mavridis, N., Tellex, S., Salata, A., Guiness, J., Levit, M., Gorniak, P.: The human speechome project, vol. 1, pp. 192–196 (2006)
14. Saffran, J.R., Pollak, S.D., Seibel, R.L., Shkolnik, A.: Dog is a dog is a dog: infant rule learning is not specific to language. Cognition **105**, 669–680 (2007)
15. Scott, M., Yeung, H.H., Gick, B., Werker, J.F.: Inner speech captures the perception of external speech. J. Acoust. Soc. Am. **133**, 2425–2438 (2013)
16. Spenko, M.J., Haynes, G.C., Saunders, J.A., Cutkosky, M.R., Rizzi, A.A., Full, R.J., Koditschek, D.E.: Biologically inspired climbing with a hexapedal robot. J. Field Robot. **25**, 223–242 (2008)
17. Stern, J.: Apple's siri: loved, but underused. The ABC News, pp. 83–92 (2012)
18. Taddeo, M., Floridi, L.: Solving the symbol grounding problem: a critical review of fifteen years of research. J. Exper. Theor. Artif. Intell. **17**, 419–445 (2005)
19. Turing, A.M.: Computing machinery and intelligence. Mind **59**, 433–460 (1950)
20. Vihman, M.M.: Phonological Development: The Origins of Language in the Child. Wiley, Chichester (1996)
21. Weng, J.: These questions arose because you used symbolic representations. AMD Newslett. **25**, 11 (2013)

Learning to Synchronously Imitate Gestures Using Entrainment Effect

Eva Ansermin[✉], Ghiles Mostafaoui, Nils Beaussé, and Philippe Gaussier

Neurocybernetic Team, ETIS Laboratory, CNRS, ENSEA,
University of Cergy-Pontoise, Cergy, France
{eva.ansermin,ghiles.mostafaoui,nils.beausse,philippe.gaussier}@ensea.fr

Abstract. Synchronisation and coordination are omnipresent and essential in humans interactions. Because of their unavoidable and unintentional aspect, those phenomena could be the consequences of a low level mechanism: a driving force originating from external stimuli called the entrainment effect. In the light of its importance in interaction and wishing to define new HRI, we suggest to model this entrainment to highlight its efficiency for gesture learning during imitative games and for reducing the computational complexity. We will put forward the capacity of adaptation offered by the entrainment effect. Hence, we present in this paper a neural model for gesture learning by imitation using entrainment effect applied to a NAO robot interacting with a human partner.

Keywords: Entrainment · Synchrony · Gesture learning · Human robot interaction · Neural network

1 Introduction

Humans tend to be set in motion by strong or rhythmical stimuli [12]. This driving force, which allows us to be reactive and adaptive, is called the *entrainment effect*. This phenomenon, also called magnet effect, is strongly linked to our ability to be synchronized and coordinated with external stimuli. Under some conditions, one can consider that synchrony is caused by the entrainment effect. For example, a synchronous interaction between two partners can be seen as the result of a mutual and bi-directional entrainment. In fact, entrainment can be observed with different modalities in various human-human interactions and plays an obvious role in social coordination (walking together, playing music, dancing, imitating etc.) [18]. This influence on our motor control have been largely analysed by psychological studies about interpersonal coordination. Varlet et al. [21] revealed that the continuity of the stimuli rhythms has a fundamental role in influencing the visual and auditory motor coordination, Lagarde and Kelso [15] found similar results by studying the multi-modal coordination dynamics between the senses (sound and touch) and human movements.

This work is funded by the DGA and the DIRAC project.

E. Tuci et al. (Eds.): SAB 2016, LNAI 9825, pp. 219–231, 2016.
DOI: 10.1007/978-3-319-43488-9_20

Another interesting characteristic of entrainment and synchrony is their unintentional aspect. Indeed, we can distinguish intended and unintended synchrony. In the first case, synchronisation is aimed whether in the second, it is spontaneous and occurs without the subject noticing. Numerous researches found out that two subjects interacting with each other tend to unintentionally synchronise [10]. This mutual unintended convergence toward a similar interacting rhythm can occur when the subject's own frequencies are close (supposedly a difference of more or less 10 %), otherwise, it may be difficult for the interacting partners to be "unintentionally" synchronized. Nevertheless, even in this case one can notice the presence of mutual unintentional entrainment (each partner driving the other toward his own motion dynamic) [8]. In fact, as demonstrated in [10], this phenomenon is such that unintentional entrainment cannot be willingly avoid. It is precisely this unavoidable aspect which makes the entrainment effect very interesting to model for Human-Robot Interactions (HRI). We believe that rhythmic adaptation does not only sustain the interaction but also is caused by the interaction through mutual entrainment.

More precisely, in this paper we address the question of integrating the so called entrainment (or magnet effect) in a neural model for HRI. Indeed, despite its importance in social interactions, this phenomenon is seldom taken into account when modelling those interactions. Yet, as we will show in this study, modelling the entrainment effect can make human/robot interacting tasks easier thanks to the adaptability its offers. This aspect will be highlighted through an experimental study presenting an example of a neural network model based a on low level entrainment and designed for learning gestures during an imitative games between a human and a NAO robot. We will demonstrate that integrating the entrainment effect simplifies drastically the computational complexity.

2 Related Works and Positioning

Broaching the subject of interpersonal coordination (entrainment, synchronisation) during interactions involves addressing the issue of gaining sensory motor abilities to be able to adapt our motion dynamics and behaviour according to external stimuli.

A classical way to approach this question is to consider a sensory motor system capable of predicting and adapting its behaviour after analysing the observed stimuli. Several efficient bio-inspired computational models have been proposed in this line. As examples, Demiris et al. performed experiments in which a robotic head equipped with a pair of cameras observed and imitated the head movements of a human demonstrator [4], Blanchard and Canamero proposed the basis of a simple algorithm generating explorative and imitative behaviours [2], Jenkins et al. described an imitation model based on a set of perceptuo-motor primitives. A simple version of the model was validated on a 20 DOF simulated humanoid using real vision data to imitate movements from athletics and dance [11].

Despite their promising results, those approaches imply a relative high level of processing (observing, analysing, predicting and adapting at each time) which does not explain the unintentional aspect of entrainment and synchronization in human-human interactions. In fact, recent works of Dumas et al. using hyper-scanning has revealed the emergence of millisecond inter-brain synchronization across multiple frequencies bands during social interactions (spontaneous exchanges between two participants of intransitive bi-manual movements [5]). Moreover, Varlet et al. investigated social motor coordination of patients suffering from schizophrenia. The results demonstrated that patients intentional motor coordination was altered while their unintentional low level motor coordination was retained implying that unintentional and intentional coordination are not part of the same process [22]. We can conclude that these inter subject synchronizations are not planned as high level processing but result in low level analogical synchronization of neural populations from the sensory flow (vision, audition...). Otherwise millisecond synchronization would not be obtained. Another way to model and explain interpersonal coordination is to considered the two interacting agents as *dynamical systems* influencing each other. Their behaviours can be considered as Hugens metronomes [17] cross influencing each other in a "mechanical way" via several signals (audition, vision etc.). In this case, subjects (or their limbs) can be modelled by oscillatory systems *entraining* each other. This mutual driving force can lead to synchronisation. Hence synchronisation would only be a particular case where the entrainment effect is strong enough (depending on the range between the partner frequencies) to reach a stable convergent state where the frequencies of the partners are equal and in phase. This type of approaches is clearly a better way to explain human tendencies to be unintentionally and unavoidably entrained by others without noticing or without "predicting" it.

2.1   Modelling Sensori-Motor Coordination in Dynamical Systems

As previously mentioned, the interacting partners behaviours are modelled by rhythmic or oscillatory systems in a dynamical system approach. In other words, the motor controllers of the partner's body parts are often described as a set of oscillators. This way to define motor controllers is inspired by the fact that body parts can be seen as oscillatory systems (pendulums for example) due to their physiognomy and capacity of movement [7]. Furthermore, several neuro-biological studies highlighted the presence of a strong oscillatory component in human and animal motor control. In fact, researches on the locomotion of several species has allowed to put forward the existence of a neural network located in the spine and enabling a minimal rhythmic autonomous motor control [6]. This set of oscillators is called *Central Pattern Generator* (CPG) and is supposed to be involved in several task such as breathing, eating or walking. Other recent studies suggest that motor cortex responses during non oscillatory movements (reaching) contain a brief but strong oscillatory component [3]. For those reasons, oscillators are often used to define the motor behaviour of interacting agents in a dynamical system approach.

To model the mutual exchange of informations (entrainment) between the interacting systems (agents) those oscillators are often coupled in a non linear way as in the well known Haken Kelso Bunz model (HKB) [13] where a Van Der Pol oscillator is coupled with a Rayleigh oscillator. This mathematical model permits to report the effect of using the energy of an oscillator to entrain the other. From a neural point of view, oscillators are often modelled as two linked neurons which inhibit and stimulate each other to maintain an oscillatory behaviour. The way they are linked and the behaviour of the neurons are depending on the type of oscillators: Wilson- Cowan [23], Terman-Wang [20], Revel [19]etc. Indeed *echo state networks* are used to get a complex response to a precise entry. Thus, rhythmical complex and adaptive movements can be obtained from such networks [16].

2.2   Positioning on Entrainment Model and its Advantage

Being interested in modelling entrainment effects for HRI, we will adopt an approach using dynamical systems as this is an efficient way to describe the possible unconscious or unpredictable aspects of this low level phenomenon (see above for the justifications). The models based on dynamical systems theories presented above are effective but possess some limitations because of their computational complexity or the obligation to have access to the parameters of both oscillators (agents motor controllers) which is not always possible if we consider the practical case of a robot interacting with a human.

  In our previous works, we proposed a solution to overcome those limitations by endowing a NAO robot with a neural model which uses the energy of the optical flow (visual stimuli) induced by the human partner movements to "directly" entrain the robot's motor controller [9]. This model, which permits to modify the dynamic of a given movement, was tested and validated with one oscillator as a motor controller and a very simple gesture (one arm moving up and down) and will be more precisely described below Sect. 5.2. Here we propose the same approach using this entrainment model to study its possible use for learning (by imitating) more complex gestures and trajectories. We will prove that the use of entrainment in the neural model proposed in this paper can not only enhance the adaptability of a humanoid robot interacting with a human but also simplifies the computational complexity.

3   System Workflow and Experimental Setup

Fig. 1. Experimental set-up: Example of an imitation game between NAO and a human partner

We used a minimal set-up for our experiments as shown in Fig. 1. The components include a NAO robot, an external camera to avoid the limitations of NAOs camera and a human partner. The frame rate is 30 images per second. During the experiments, the human partner faces the robot as shown in Fig. 1 and moves rhythmically his arm. Our objective is to build a model based on entrainment effect in order to give the robot the ability to imitate synchronously

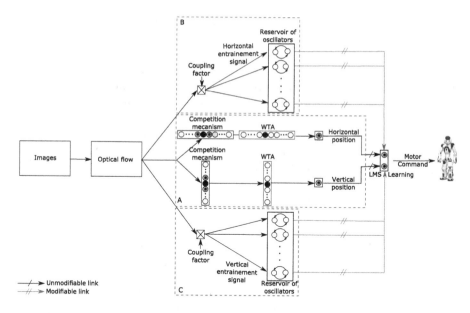

Fig. 2. Structure of the imitation model

the human gesture. Only the NAO's shoulder articulation is used and controlled by the model (2 degrees of freedom: up and down/left and right). As we wish the robot to be able to reproduce a rhythmical movement shown by an interacting partner, the NAO's motor controller will be generated by a reservoir of oscillators (see Fig. 2). The idea is to define the desired motor signal as a weighted sum of oscillators at different frequencies (such as in Fourier series). Hence reproducing a movement or a trajectory means finding the right combination within a set of oscillators. The general workflow of our model, illustrated Fig. 2, can be summarized as follow:

- The images of the camera capturing the human movements are used to compute the optical flow
- The so resulted optical flow is then used to:
  - Extract the X and Y coordinates of the human movement trajectory (A block in Fig. 2).
  - Build the X entrainment signal (B block in Fig. 2) and the Y entrainment signal (C block in Fig. 2) which will influence (entrain) and modify the frequencies and phases of the oscillators in the reservoir which commands the motor controller of the robot.
- By modifying the weight of each oscillator of the reservoir, the Least Mean Square (LMS) algorithm will learn the combination of oscillators describing the X and Y desired trajectory extracted from the human motion by the A block.
- Finally, the outputs of the two LMS neurons are used directly as the final motor controller signals leading the robot to imitate the human 's gestures.

Each part of the model will now be detailed in sections below.

4   Extracting the Trajectories to Imitate

As mentioned above, the robot aims at imitating the gestures of the human partner. The trajectory to learn corresponds consequently to the one described by the human's moving arm, and more precisely by the human's hand (see the experimental set-up Sect. 3). Rather than performing a complex image processing to recognize and localize the moving hand, we based upon the fact that this hand is the body part which moves the most comparing to the rest of the arm. Consequently, the trajectory to learn and imitate will be defined, at each time, by the x and y coordinates of the point in the image having the higher optical flow. To do so, we first measure the optical flow using the hierarchical algorithm described by Amiaz et al. [1]. At each time t, the optical flow is computed for all the image pixels and projected to a set of 240 neurons, 120 for the horizontal component and 120 for the vertical one. In order to filter the noise, a simple competition mechanism is used. Each neuron is stimulated by its closest neighbours and inhibited by the distant neurons. This process is equivalent to a convolution by a Difference of two Gaussians filter highlighting consequently the local maxima of the optical flow by taking into account its local distribution. A *Winner Takes All* (WTA) is then used to extract the x and y coordinates of the point (with a higher filtered optical flow) describing the human hand trajectory to imitate (see A block in Fig. 2). Two examples of extracted trajectories are illustrated in Fig. 6 in the case of a human moving his hand (circular and infinite shape movement).

5   Modelling the entrainment effect

5.1   The Reservoir of Oscillators

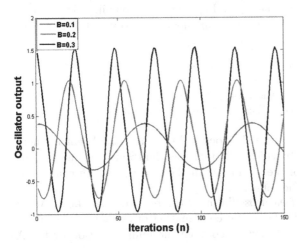

Fig. 3. 3 Oscillator outputs for different values of β

Our reservoir of oscillators is composed by two sets of 8 oscillators which will respectively describe the x and y motor controllers of the NAO's arm. Each oscillator is made using a simple neural model introduced by Revel et al. [19]. This oscillator model shown in the A Block of the Fig. 4 is made of two neurons $N1$ and $N2$, fed by constant signals $\alpha1$ and $\alpha2$ (to start the oscillator and change its average). These two neurons inhibit each other proportionality to the parameter β. The frequency and amplitude of the oscillator depend on the β parameter. It has a stable limit cycle, however, it can saturate when coupled with another signal with a too large dynamic. We choose this oscillator because of its easy implementation and the facility it gives to obtain an oscillatory behaviour. The resulting signals are defined by the equations below:

$$N_1(n+1) = N_1(n) - \beta N_2(n) + \alpha 1 \tag{1}$$

$$N_2(n+1) = N_1(n) + \beta N_2(n) + \alpha 2 \tag{2}$$

By modifying the β parameter, we defined our two sets of 8 oscillators whose own frequencies are between 0.5 Hz and 2.6 Hz. We heuristically choose these frequencies to cover a large range of possible rhythms reachable by the human and mechanically plausible for the NAO. Figure 3 illustrates the oscillatory signals obtained for three different values of β.

5.2   The Entrainment Model

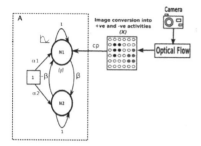

Fig. 4. Hasnain et al. entrainment model

As previously detailed, the usual methods to model entrainment impose to have access to both oscillating systems. To avoid this limitations, we proposed in our previous works a simple neural model where the interacting agent (a robot and a human) are coupled via low level visual information. For clarity sake, this model will be summarized in this section but we invite the reader to refer to [9] for a detailed description. We took inspiration from interpersonal coordination studies demonstrating that unintended motor entrainment can not be avoided (see Sect. 3). This observation implies a strong and direct link between the external stimuli and the motor controller. Starting from these conclusions, the model presented in [9] and illustrated in Fig. 4 propose to use the energy induced by the optical flow of the human partner movement to entrain the robot motor controller. The oscillatory signal controlling the robot's arm (Eq. 1) can be rewritten as fellow (Eq. 3):

$$N1(n+1) = N1(n) - \beta N2(n) - \alpha 1 + cp * f(n) \tag{3}$$

with $f(n)$ the entrainment signal and cp the coupling factor. $f(n)$ is deducted at each time by a spatial integration of the optical flow. As the optical flow can be either positive or negative according to the movement direction, $f(n)$ oscillates in the case of rhythmic movements. This resulted signal is modulated by a coupling factor cp (see Fig. 4) and added to the oscillator to modify its dynamic and hence the robot behavior. The coupling factor cp is included into 0 to 1, it allows to modulate the energy brought in the oscillator: the higher it is, the more important the entrainment is. This implies that the range of frequencies in which the oscillators are able to synchronise can change according to cp and be larger for a higher coupling factor. Using this model we demonstrated that a synchronous interaction can emerge considering the fact that humans will also be entrained by the modifications of the robot 's behaviours. Those results were validated by experimental studies in psychology with naive subjects [8].

6   Learning by Imitating

To learn the desired movement sequence and to decompose it in an oscillatory base, we use a Least Mean Square algorithm network (see Fig. 2). This algorithm is a supervised learning where we aim at reducing the square error between a required sequence and the different available input signals whose weight can be modified (cf Fig. 5). At each iteration, the algorithm compares the error with the precedent and changes the weights in function. Those modifications are made according to the following equations:

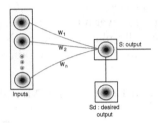

Fig. 5. Structure of the LMS Network

$$
\begin{cases}
S(n) = \sum_{i=1}^{p}(w_i * b_i) \\[2em]
W_i(n+1) = W_i(n) - \epsilon \Delta e(n) \\[2em]
e(n) = (Sd - S)^2
\end{cases}
\tag{4}
$$

with:

- ϵ the learning step. A higher ϵ permits to modify the weights quickly but makes it more sensitive to noise. ϵ is set to a fixed value of 0.1 here.
- Sd an S respectively the desired signal to learn and the output of the LMS.

With this model we try to learn a rhythmical motion sequence. As we wish to reproduce any rhythmical signal and because of the nature of the algorithm, the learning is possible only if we can find a set of oscillators with adequate frequencies and phases to describe the desired signal. In this context, this implies to have a very high number of oscillators. To resolve this problematic we will use the entrainment model presented earlier to change the set of oscillators behaviours (amplitude, frequency and phase) to better fit the desired trajectories without adding computational complexity.

Let's consider now the complete model as presented Fig. 2. We add the entrainment effect (presented in the previous section) to our reservoir of oscillators (part B and C of the Fig. 2).

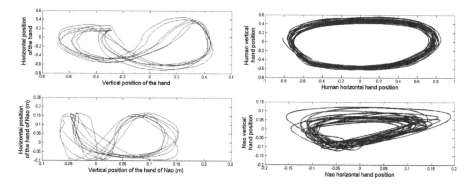

Fig. 6. Human and Robot hand trajectories during learning a round and an infinite gesture during imitation games

The oscillators will now be entrained by the optical flow induced by the human movements in both x and y directions (respectively B and C paths in Fig. 2). We distinguish the horizontal and vertical component of the movement for entrainment because different studies suggest that visual entrainment can be segmented into several directions. For example, Kilner et al. showed that we tend to be entrained vertically by a vertical stimuli when making an horizontal movement [14].

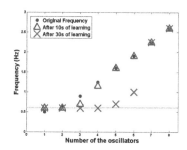

Fig. 7. Frequency of the oscillators before and after $10s$ and $30s$ learning of a $0.6\,\mathrm{Hz}$ sinus.

The model is tested in real conditions to make the NAO robot imitate the human performing two different gestures: a circle and an infinite shape trajectory. It is worth noticing that the set of initial oscillators and the parameters used are exactly the same for the two conditions. Figure 6 illustrates the efficiency of this simple model. The robot is able to imitate the two different gestures after less then 30 seconds of learning thanks to the entrainment effect which facilitate the adaptation in amplitude, frequency and phase of the initial oscillators. Videos of these experiments can be seen here[1].

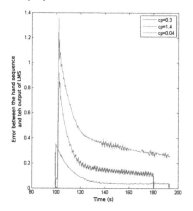

Fig. 8. Influence of the coupling factor on the convergence speed.

---

[1] www.etis.ensea.fr/neurocyber/Videos/authors/ansermin/sab2016.

To clarify this mechanism, we consider the learning of a simple simulated sinus of 0.6 Hz. The added entrainment effect permits a quick convergence of some of the oscillators to the frequencies sought by the signal to learn (0.6 Hz). This fast adaptation of the reservoir of oscillators to the desired signal proves the fact that using entrainment can avoid the complex problem of defining a too large number of oscillators at different frequencies and phases. The Fig. 7 allows us to observe the frequency after 10 s and 30 s of learning and put forward the fact that the oscillators do not synchronise at once and that the learning is consequently progressive.

The coupling factor can modify the range of frequencies we can define with our reservoir of oscillators. Higher values of cp permit a bigger influence of the entrainment signal (optical flow of the moving partner) on the oscillators which can lead to drive them to farthest frequencies and phases (comparing to their initial status).

6.1   Influence of the Coupling Factor

Consequently, the results and the convergence speed of the LMS algorithm are dependent on the cp value. The Fig. 8 shows the reconstruction error computed by the LMS for different values of cp while learning a sinus of 1 Hz. We can observe that indeed, a higher cp means a quicker learning but also more oscillators synchronised on the same harmonic of the signal as shown in Fig. 9. Nevertheless, a high value of cp can lead to an exaggerated entrainment which implies several synchronized oscillators (toward the fundamental frequency) leading to a synchronized behaviour but a less defined reconstruction of the desired trajectories (less harmonics).

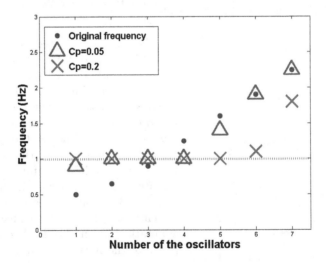

Fig. 9. Observation of the frequencies of the oscillators during the learning of an 1 Hz sinus for different coupling factors.

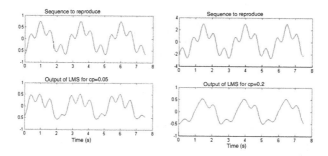

Fig. 10. Learning of a complex simulated signal (sum of 3 sinus) for different coupling factors

This phenomenon is illustrated in Fig. 10 where the simulated trajectory to learn is better explained (after learning) with a lower coupling factor.

7   Conclusion

The entrainment effect has been proven to be very present in human behaviour during our interaction with the environment or in social interplays where it plays an important role in interpersonal coordination. Yet, it has been rather neglected by many research which tried to model interactions in HRI. In this paper we presented a model based upon low level entrainment using visual stimuli (optical flow). We proved with both simulated and real experimental tests, that despite its relative simplicity, our model is able to give the robot abilities to imitate synchronously different gestures in real time while using exactly the same parameters.

Yet, this model presents some limits. Indeed, the system is unable to perform the learned movement alone, without entrainment effect. When there is no entrainment, the oscillators will return to their original frequency. Thus, if more than one oscillator have been synchronised with a harmonic of the signal and learned by the LMS, the learned signal would be deformed without the entrainment. Moreover, the phase between the different part of the movement (vertical and horizontal) cannot be maintained without entrainment. The questions of how memorizing the gestures and what information to memorize (the entrainment signal? the oscillator weights? etc.) are our near future perspectives. It is worth noticing that the principal limitations of the model is in its definition itself. In fact our objective here is to prove the efficiency of using low level entrainment of the motor controller (by the external visual stimuli) to adapt the behaviour and synchronize it with the interacting partner. We argue that learning to imitate or reproduce more complex, refined and non rhythmic gesture sequences needs a higher level of treatment including a more "predictive" aspects.

Nevertheless, regarding the fact that the entrainment was proved to be unintentional in human behaviour, our position on the matter is that learning and imitating gestures imply merging a very low level sensory motor processing (entrainment) for a fast adaptation of the motions dynamics and to eases a higher level which deals with more complex sequences, refined trajectories, social contexts etc. Such an association is clearly in our perspectives.

References

1. Amiaz, T., Lubetzky, E., Kiryati, N.: Coarse to over-fine optical flow estimation. Pattern Recogn. **40**(9), 2496–2503 (2007)
2. Blanchard, A., Canamero, L.: Modulation of exploratory behavior for adaptationto the context. In: Proceedings of Biologically Inspired Robotics Symposium 2006, pp. 131–137 (2006)
3. Churchland, M.M., Cunningham, J.P., Kaufman, M.T., Foster, J.D., Nuyujukian, P., Ryu, S.I., Shenoy, K.V.: Neural population dynamics during reaching. Nature **487**(7405), 51–56 (2012)
4. Demiris, J., Rougeaux, S., Hayes, G., Berthouze, L., Kuniyoshi, Y.: Deferred imitation of human head movements by an active stereo vision head. In: 6th IEEE International Workshop on Robot and Human Communication, RO-MAN 1997, Proceedings, pp. 88–93. IEEE (1997)
5. Dumas, G., Nadel, J., Soussignan, R., Martinerie, J., Garnero, L.: Inter-brain synchronization during social interaction. PLoS ONE **5**, 1–10 (2010)
6. Grillner, Z.: On the central generation of locomotion in the low spinal cat (1979)
7. Haken, H., Kelso, J.A.S., Bunz, H.: A theorical model of phase transition in human hand movements. Biolog. Cybern. **51**, 347–356 (1985)
8. Hasnain, S.K., Mostafaoui, G., Salesse, R., Marin, L., Gaussier, P.: Intuitive human robot interaction based on unintentional synchrony: a psycho-experimental study. In: 2013 IEEE Third Joint International Conference on Development and Learning and Epigenetic Robotics (ICDL), pp. 1–7, Aug 2013
9. Hasnain, S.P., Mostafaoui, G., Gaussier, P.: A synchrony-based perspective for partner selection and attentional mechanism in human-robot interaction. Paladyn J. Behav. Robot. **3**(3), 156–171 (2012)
10. Issartel, J., Marin, L., Cadopi, M.: Unintended interpersonal co-ordination: "can we march to the beat of our own drum?". Neurosci Lett. **411**(3), 174 (2007)
11. Jenkins, O.C., Mataric, M.J., Weber, S.: Primitive-based movement classification for humanoid imitation. In: Proceedings, First IEEE-RAS International Conference on Humanoid Robotics (Humanoids-2000), pp. 1–18 (2000)
12. Kay, B.A., Kelso, J.A.S., Saltzman, E.L.: Space-time behaviour of single and bimanual rythmical movments. J. Exper. Pysychol. Hum. Percept. Perform. **13**, 178–192 (1987)
13. Kelso, J.A.S.: Haken-Kelso-Bunz model. Scholarpedia **3**(10), 1612 (2008). revision 91336
14. Kilner, J., Paulignan, Y., Blakemore, S.: An interference effect of observed biological movement on action. Curr. Biol. **13**(6), 522–525 (2003)
15. Lagarde, J., Kelso, J.: Binding of movement, sound and touch: multimodal coordination dynamics. Exper. Brain Res. **173**(4), 673–688 (2006)
16. Mannella, F., Baldassarre, G.: Selection of cortical dynamics for motor behaviour by the basal ganglia. Biol. Cybern. **109**(6), 575–595 (2015)
17. Pataleone, J.: Synchronization of metronomes. Am. J. Phy. **70**, 992–1000 (2002)
18. Phillips-Silver, J., Aktipiz, A.: Bryant., G.A.: The ecology of entrainment: Foundations of coordinated rhythmic movement. Music Perception **28**(1), 3–14 (2010). PMC. Web. 9 Sep 2015

19. Revel, A., Andry, P.: Emergence of sturctured interactions: from theoretical model to pragmatic robotics. Neural Netw. **22**, 116 (2009)
20. Terman, D., Wang, D.: Global competition and local cooperation in a network of neural oscillators. Phys. D Nonlinear Phenom. **81**(1–2), 148–176 (1995)
21. Varlet, M., Marin, L., Issartel, J., Schmidt, R., Bardy, B.G.: Continuity of visual and auditory rhythms influences sensorimotor coordination. PloS one **7**(9), e44082 (2012). doi:10.1371/journal.pone
22. Varlet, M., Marin, L., Raffard, S., Schmidt, R.C., Capdevielle, D., Boulenger, J.P., Del-Monte, J., Bardy, B.G.: Impairments of social motor coordination in schizophrenia. PloS one **7**(1), e29772 (2012). doi:10.1371/journal.pone
23. Wilson, H.R., Cowan, J.D.: Excitatory and inhibitory interactions in localized populations of model neurons. Biophys. J. **12**, 1–24 (1972)

Time-Informed, Adaptive Multi-robot Synchronization

Michail Maniadakis[✉] and Panos Trahanias

Foundation for Research and Technology Helloas (FORTH), Heraklion, Crete, Greece
{mmaniada,trahania}@ics.forth.gr

Abstract. Timely interaction is a key topic for multi-robot systems operating in the real world. The present work puts forward a new approach for multi-robot synchronization that is based on representing temporal constraints as fuzzy numbers. By using fuzzy arithmetic it is possible to process temporal constraints, analyze their relations, detect temporal gaps, and additionally develop corrective measures that minimize these gaps. The present study addresses temporal planning by directing the robotic agents to (i) adapt their speed to accomplish task execution and, (ii) carry out simplified, yet acceptable, versions of the assigned tasks at faster speeds. The latter adaptations fit particularly well with the fuzzy theoretic approach that enables the direct calculation of their effects on the temporal plan. Accordingly, more efficient synchronization is accomplished in multi-robot coordinated task execution.

Keywords: Sense of time · Time-based adaptation · Fuzzy time

1 Introduction

Behavior plans for agents acting in the real world combine both spatial and temporal information. Despite the fact that the majority of contemporary works on robot planning has mainly focused on the spatial aspects of planning, in recent years there is an increasing interest on the temporal properties of motion plans. Typically, Simple Temporal Networks ($STNs$) are used to represent temporal constraints in planning systems. To allow fast checking of temporal consistency, such networks are mapped to equivalent Distance Graphs (DGs) [5] to check the existence of no negative cycles and thus prove the consistency of the plan. Multi-robot synchrony using $STNs$ is achieved by introducing constraints that maximize coincidence in the parallel activities of independent robots [9–11,13]. Since there is no attempt to speed up execution, the pace of the slower robot defines in practice synchronization of the multi-robot team.

The present work follows an alternative approach to accomplish synchrony that enforces the slower agent to achieve goals faster and thus realize synchrony that is more adapted to the faster agent. To this end, we introduce a new approach that deals with adaptive temporal plans in multi-robot systems by representing temporal constraints with fuzzy numbers. Interestingly, fuzzy times are

© Springer International Publishing Switzerland 2016
E. Tuci et al. (Eds.): SAB 2016, LNAI 9825, pp. 232–243, 2016.
DOI: 10.1007/978-3-319-43488-9_21

used for many years in job scheduling problems [2,6]. It is therefore surprising that it is the first time they are employed in dynamic task assignment problems that consider multi-robot synchrony.

The fuzzy time assumption fits perfectly to STNs keeping the representation of the original problem simple and easily manageable. In the current work we introduce fuzzy $STNs$ ($fSTNs$) together with the procedures for performing fuzzy calculations to examine the temporal properties of the plan. We demonstrate that the proposed formulation has the expressive power to address all temporal issues considered by previous works. Due to the simplicity of fuzzy number calculus, the current approach does not introduce any workload compared to contemporary approaches, resulting in an easily implemented and particularly fast solution for time-constrained robot planning problems.

At the same time, the $fSTN$ approach offers certain advantages for the solution of planning problems, which include: (i) a more complete definition of constraints with both lower and upper bounds, (ii) the suggestion of concrete time moments for triggering actions, (iii) the formulation of time-equations that enable detecting latency in robot actions, and (iv) the ability to develop corrective measures to minimize time gaps across multiple robots. The paper focuses mainly on the last two issues, which, to the best of our knowledge, have not been considered thus far in the literature. The introduction of a new Expected Latency measure enables temporal adaptations early in the plan execution, therefore maximizing the chances to achieve the desired synchrony among agents.

2   Robot-Robot Coordination Scenario

The proposed fuzzy-time approach aims at enforcing coordination in multi-robot setups. Without loss of generality, and for the sake of simplicity, we confine the current presentation to the case of two cooperating robots. We note however, that the proposed methodology is readily applicable to the case of multiple cooperating robots. In this section we summarize the cooperative exploration scenario that will be used as a motivating example for the rest of the paper.

The scenario assumes that two NAOs cooperatively explore an office environment to find and take pictures of two rooms identified by a blue and a red box on their walls. NAO 1 navigates to Room 1 where it is informed of the color of the room it has to search (blue or red). NAO 2 moves to Room 2 to be also informed of the color of the room it has to search (different than NAO 1). Then they start exploration to identify the assigned rooms. After finding the rooms, the two humanoids need to take pictures that allow synthesizing a 360° view of each room (in the current experiment only left-eye robot images are used). Ideally, robots should rotate in-place and take a snapshot (picture) of the room every 10°. This assumes the collection of 36 pictures that can be stitched together to produce the panoramic view of the rooms. However, it is possible to reduce the quality of the 360° view by taking a smaller number of pictures. The lowest allowed panoramic-quality dictates that 15 pictures are taken at approximately every 24°. When the two robots take the pictures necessary to construct the

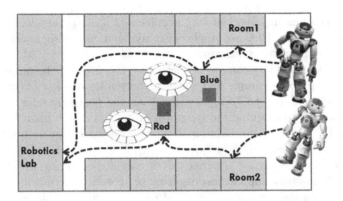

Fig. 1. A schematic representation of the exemplar scenario considered throughout the paper. (Color figure online)

360° view, they rendezvous at the premises of the Robotics Lab. A graphical interpretation of the scenario is shown in Fig. 1. For the sake of presentation we assume that the two robots run different versions of gating controllers and thus they proceed at different paces.

The action execution plan corresponding to this scenario involves uncontrollable events, because the two robots are not informed of the location of the blue and red rooms and thus, they need to explore the office environment to localize the rooms. Additionally, the scenario involves two alternative options that enable the faster accomplishment of tasks. The first option regards motion speed up that can be decided by the central planner when one of the robots is delayed. The second option regards a simplified, suboptimal, but faster execution of tasks with a reduced cost for the completion of the global cooperative goal. Switching from a detailed to a simplified execution of tasks is a particularly common approach for humans in everyday cooperative tasks.

3   Literature Review

A Simple Temporal Network consists of a set of variables $E_1, ..., E_n$ representing executable events linked with edges $E_i \rightarrow E_j$ indicating that E_i is a prerequisite for the occurrence of E_j. Each edge $E_i \rightarrow E_j$ is labeled by an interval $[a_{ij}, b_{ij}]$ which represents that passing from E_i to E_j takes minimum a_{ij} and maximum b_{ij} moments. If we represent with t_{E_i}, the time of occurence of E_i and with t_{E_j}, the time of occurrence of E_j, then they are constrained as follows:

$$a_{ij} \leq t_{E_j} - t_{E_i} \leq b_{ij} \tag{1}$$

To model the fact that an agent can only control the timing of the plan's events fully executed by itself but not the timing of events driven by external parameters, we employ Simple Temporal Networks with Uncertainty ($STNU$) that distinguishes between controllable and uncontrollable events. To represent

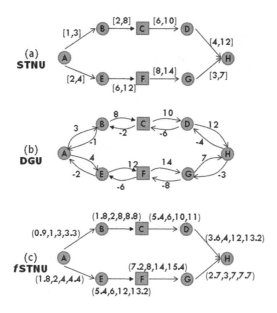

Fig. 2. The robot-robot coordination plan illustrated as (a) an STNU form, (b) DGU form, and (c) a fuzzy STNU form.

plan uncertainty, $STNU$ links are divided into two classes, contingent links and requirement links. Contingent links can be thought of as representing uncontrollable processes whose uncertain duration is determined exogenously by the environment of the agent. Requirement links represent processes controlled by the agent who is capable to complete processes satisfying the time bounds on the links. The $STNU$ graph of the plan coordinating agents' activities in the robot-robot coordination task is shown in Fig. 2(a). NAO 1 moves to Room-1 (link A-B) then it searches for the Blue Room (link B-C), it collects room pictures (link C-D) and navigates to the Robotics Lab (link D-H). NAO 2 follows a similar task sequence that is represented by the $STNU$ path A-E-F-G-H. Note that we use rectangles to represent contingent events (explore the environment to localize the blue and red rooms) and a different type of edges to represent contingent links (see edges BC and EF).

To manage temporal constraints, $STNU$s are typically mapped to the equivalent Distance Graphs with Uncertainty (DGUs) [11]. A DGU has the same vertices as the corresponding $STNU$ but the lower and upper bounds of $STNU$ are now separated and represented with two distinct edges. The edge in the forward direction is labeled with the value of the upper time bound and the edge on the reverse direction is labeled with the negative of the lower time bound. The DGU that corresponds to the example under investigation is shown in Fig. 2(b).

Checking the DGU for negative cycles provides information on the consistency of the plan [5]. The non-existence of negative cycles in the DGU indicates that the $STNU$ is consistent and thus dispatchable, meaning that (i) there are no temporal conflicts and (ii) there is enough time for all events to occur. Following this formulation, previous works have considered back propagation rules to dynamically preserve dispatchability of plans [9,11], address temporal problems with choice [12], or reason between interacting agents [3].

4   Fuzzy Times

In contrast to the ordinary approaches that assume the mapping of STN to DG, therefore separating the lower and upper limits of temporal constraints, the current work proposes using a fuzzy theoretic approach to address time processing and plan adaptations. The key idea is to keep coupled the lower and upper bounds of temporal constraints, exploiting at the same time fuzzy number calculus to analyze the plan and explore the effect of alternative adaptations.

Fuzzy sets were introduced by Lotfi A. Zadeh [14] as an extension of the classical notion of sets to include elements that have degrees of membership.

In the present work we use trapezoidal[1] fuzzy numbers to represent the time boundaries an action may take to complete and we use fuzzy arithmetic to develop multi-criteria measures that enable comparing alternative planning scenarios. A fuzzy number in trapezoidal form is represented by the quadruplet (p, m, n, q).

Fig. 3. Schematic representation of a fuzzy number representing the duration "approximately 4 to 6 min".

Lets assume that a given action takes approximally a to b moments to complete. To represent this duration with a fuzzy number, we assign the lower bound of the time interval to m (i.e. $m = a$) and the upper bound of the time interval to n (i.e. $n = b$). Subsequently, we define $p = 0.9m$ and $q = 1.1n$. A graphical representation of the fuzzy time "approximately 4 to 6 min" represented by the trapezoid (3.6,4,6,6.6) is shown in Fig. 3.

The most common approach to process fuzzy numbers is following the L-R calculus [7]. The addition of two fuzzy numbers $F1 = (p1, m1, n1, q1)$ and $F2 = (p2, m2, , n2, q2)$ is a new trapezoid fuzzy number of the form $F1 + F2 = (p1 + p2, m1 + m2, n1 + n2, q1 + q2)$. The difference between two trapezoid fuzzy numbers is again a fuzzy number defined as $F1 - F2 = (p1 - q2, m1 - n2, n1 - m2, q1 - p2)$.

---

[1]   The trapezoid representation of fuzzy numbers is not mandatory but simplifies calculations and therefore it is adopted in the present work.

Following the formulation introduced above, a classic STN is transformed into its fuzzy form $fSTN$ by representing any edge labeled with $[a, b]$ in the original network, with a similar edge labeled with the fuzzy trapezoidal number $(0.9a, a, b, 1.1b)$. The fuzzy version of the exemplar $STNU$ in Fig. 2(a), is shown in Fig. 2(c).

5   Time-Informed Planning Features

The discussion above shows that the fuzzy theoretic approach has the expressive power to address the temporal planning problems considered in the literature so far [9–11]. Interestingly the proposed approach provides new additional features that may significantly facilitate multi-agent planning and synchronization. These are summarized below:

• By using the fuzzy equations approach to explore the association of event triplets, it is straightforward to obtain information on both the lower and "upper" bounds of temporal constraints. For example, consider the case of tightening the edge $D - H$ in Fig. 2(a), from $[4, 12]$ to $[8, 12]$ (similar to the example in [11]). This change affects the execution of G because by considering the triangular association of the three events, writing down the equation $DG + GH = DH$, which indicates:

$$DG + (2.7, 3, 7, 7.7) = (3.6, 4, 12, 13.2) \Rightarrow DG = (-4.1, -3, 9, 10.5)$$

The above introduces a constraint on the temporal relation of events D and G, which assumes that G should preferably start 3 time moments after D (this is similar to [11]) with a hard constraint of 4.1 moments after D. The same calculations reveal that G should preferably start not latter than 9 moments after D (the worst acceptable time is 10.5 moment). This is an important piece of information not discussed in the previous works [10, 11], but is readily available in the proposed formulation.

• Capitalizing on the well known defuzzifiction process, the result of fuzzy equations can be easily defuzzified into crisp values that suggest specific times for triggering the occurrence of events. In the example mentioned above, besides constraining the occurrence of D at "some time, 3 moments after D", the defuzzification of the fuzzy DG value may suggest when exactly G must start. Following the classic graded mean integration representation [8], a fuzzy number (p, m, n, q) can be represented by the crisp value $v = (p + 2m + 2n + q)/6$. In the example, we defuzzify $DG = (-4.1, -3, 9, 10.5)$ to get the crisp value $v = 3.06$, which suggests that event G to start 3.06 moments after D.

• By using fuzzy equations the planner can be readily informed about the current state in plan execution, detect emergency situations and undertake appropriate corrective actions. We introduce a new measure named Expected Latency as an estimate of the temporal gap between two agents that need to synchronize their activities. The Expected Latency (EL) is based on the difference between the times that remain for each agent until their coincidence. Consider the case that NAO 1 proceeds very fast and after 9 time moments it has already accomplished the events B, C, D and has already started moving towards H. NAO 2 moves rather slow and it completes events E and F after 11 moments. At that time, we want to estimate whether NAO 2 is late in comparison to NAO 1. The time remaining for NAO 2 to reach event H is $(7.2, 8, 14, 15.4) + (2.7, 3, 7, 7, 7)$. The time remaining for NAO 1 to reach event H is $(3.6, 4, 12, 13.2) - 2$, where $2 = 11 - 9$, represents the fact that NAO 1 has already started progressing towards H, two moments earlier than the time of the current calculations. Assuming a latency X for NAO 2, the synchronization of the two agents on event H assumes that:

$$(7.2, 8, 14, 15.4) + (2.7, 3, 7, 7, 7) =$$
$$X + (3.6, 4, 12, 13.2) - 2] \Rightarrow$$
$$X = (-1.3, 1, 19, 21.5)$$

The defuzzification of X provides an estimate of NAO 2's latency, that is $EL = 10.03$ time moments. The planner may exploit this information to undertake corrective actions that will reduce the foreseen problem as explained below.

6   Enforcing Synchrony

When the central planner detects the latency of a participating agent using the EL measure described above, it is possible to initiate corrective actions that minimize synchronization gaps. These may regard either (i) ordering an agent to slow down, or (ii) ordering an agent to speed up, or (iii) ordering an agent to simplify the execution of an event so that it is completed faster. In the current work we consider the last two options to achieve multi-agent synchronization (the implementation of the first option is straightforward and thus it is not considered in the present work).

A work sharing similar ideas is presented in [1], which considers temporal constrained relaxation and violation without however following the fuzzy time assumption and without being applied in a robotic domain.

We separate tasks in two classes depending on how agents may complete their execution faster than expected. The first class includes Adaptive Speed (AS) events which assumes activities that must be fully completed, but this can be done at varying speeds. For example, robot's navigation towards a specific location, is successful only when the robot reaches this location. This is an AS task because the robot may move at various speeds towards the target. When we consider an AS task as a part of a global multi-robot synchronization scenario, we assume that the lower temporal bound regards maximum speed and perfect, convenient conditions for task execution, and the upper temporal bound regards minimum speed and inconvenient conditions for task execution. Therefore, when a task with an associated fuzzy time (p, m, n, q) is executed at the maximum allowed speed, e.g. 20 % faster than normal, the upper temporal bound can be reduced by a factor of $100/120$. This results into a new fuzzy number to describe the time of event execution that is $(p, m, n * 100/120, q * 100/120)$.

The second class named Imperfection Enabled (IE) tasks, assumes actions that can be accomplished in a suboptimal manner, without this having any crucial effect on the global goal targeted by multi-robot coordination (i.e. instead of sacrificing the big goal, we may partially sacrifice a non-crucial partial goal). For example, when an agent does not have enough time to prepare an omelet, he may whisk the eggs for only 20 s rather than 60 s assumed by the majority of recipes, still producing an acceptable meal. For IE tasks, the lowest temporal bound regards the simplest possible execution of the task while the upper temporal bound regards the most sophisticated, optimal execution of the task. Any IE task is implemented to the highest possible quality, i.e. consuming the time specified by the upper temporal bound. To accomplish the task faster, the upper temporal bound must be reduced at a lower value. For example, consider there is an estimated positive latency EL, and the execution of an IE task assigned the fuzzy time (p, m, n, q) must be simplified. The suboptimal completion of the task assumes a new fuzzy time (p, m, n', q'), where:

$$
\begin{aligned}
n' &= m, && \text{if } n - EL < m \\
&= t - EL, && \text{if } t - EL >= m
\end{aligned}
\tag{2}
$$

$$
\begin{aligned}
q' &= m, && \text{if } q - EL < m \\
&= q - EL, && \text{if } q - EL >= m
\end{aligned}
\tag{3}
$$

During the plan setup, each edge representing the process of accomplishing an event is classified as either an Adaptive Speed (AS) task or an Imperfection Enabled (IE) task. In the current example (see Fig. 2), edges A-B, D-H, A-E, G-H represent AS events, and edges C-D and F-G represent IE events. As already noted, edges B-C and E-F represent contingent processes whose time of execution is not controlled by the planner and thus remain unaffected during plan adaptations.

In the case of a positive EL greater than a threshold $\theta > 0$, we consider adapting the temporal properties of the forthcoming task of the given agent. If it is not a contingency task, (i.e. it is either AS or IE) we apply the appropriate latency reduction procedure, and we re-estimate EL. In the case of a contingency task, the execution proceeds as normal, and the latency of the agent is re-estimated after the end of the task, considering the possibility of a new corrective action.

Following our running example, we consider the example case of $EL = 10$ for NAO 2 as described in section V. The robot has just completed event F and is now ready to proceed towards G, which regards the IE task of 360° photoing. Following the IE time adaptation procedure described above and given that $EL = 10$, the time of the edge is modified to $(7.2, 8, 8, 8)$ which assumes the task shall be executed in its simplest possible form. After this change the expected latency is estimated again resulting to the new fuzzy value $(-1.3, 1, 13, 14.1)$ which is defuzzified to $EL = 6.8$.

Just for demonstration purposes, we consider the case that edge F-G represents an AS task rather than an IE task as discussed above. We assume that the robot can speed up execution by 20 % which results into changing the fuzzy time of F-G from $(7.2, 8, 14, 15.4)$ to $(7.2, 8, 11.2, 12.32)$. This would reduce the expected latency for NAO 2 to $(-1.3, 1, 16.2, 18.42)$, which is deffuzified according to the graded mean integration representation to $EL = 8.58$.

7 Results

The advanced planning features introduced by the fuzzy perspective of temporal constraints is demonstrated by a realistic version of the exemplar scenario used throughout the paper. We use two Aldebaran NAO humanoids, one of them running a home-made gating controller that enables NAO 1 move with an average speed of 13 cm/s, and the built-in open-loop Aldebaran gating that furnishes NAO 2 with the ability to move with an average speed of 10.5 cm/s. The times used by the robots to complete each action in the cooperative exploration task are shown in the $fSTNU$ that represent the overall plan and is illustrated in Fig. 4. The computational implementation of the $fSTNU$ is based on the graph analysis package IGRAPH [4] that provides all basic features for implementing and processing graph-represented robot plans.

The implementation of the plan by the two NAOs is monitored by a central planner that is responsible for taking corrective actions that minimize the expected latency for the robot with positive EL, and therefore enforce synchrony between the two agents. Corrective actions are undertaken only when EL is greater than the threshold $\theta = 15$. Moreover, corrective actions are undertaken only at the commence of events (sub-tasks) and they cannot change during execution.

The evolution of robots' activities and plan adaptations is described below and is depicted in Fig. 5. Prior to any movement, the planner estimates EL values for both robots. This results to $EL_1 = -53.93$ for NAO 1 and $EL_2 = 53.93$ for NAO 2, indicating that NAO 2 will probably be late if the plan proceeds with the normal, currently scheduled execution of events. To minimize this latency, the planner undertakes a corrective action that regards navigating to Room2 at a higher speed. NAO 2 will move 10 % faster than normal which implies changing the labeling of $Start- > Room2$ edge to $(57.6, 64, 80, 88)$. The expected latency for NAO 2 is re-estimated to $EL_2 = 49.8$.

The two robots start with the assigned tasks. After 63 s, NAO 1 reaches Room1. We estimate the expected latency for NAO 1 which is $EL_1 = -48.16$. NAO 1 is not late, and thus it proceeds with a normal speed to explore the environment and identify the Blue Room.

At time 70, NAO 2 arrives at Room2. The new value for EL_2 is now estimated at 45.9 s. Ideally, this would imply a corrective action on the procedure represented by edge EF, which however can not implemented because it is a contingent link representing a procedure that temporally, is not under the full control of the robot. NAO 2 proceeds to identifying the Red Room without any corrective action.

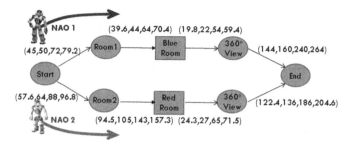

Fig. 4. The $fSTNU$ describing the real robot scenario explored in the present study.

At time 121, NAO 1 identifies the Blue Room and is ready to take the pictures that enable synthesizing the 360° view of the room. Its latency is estimated to $EL_1 = -42.23$ and since it is not late, it proceeds taking a large sequence of 36 pictures every 10°, in the Blue Room.

After 175 s NAO 1 completes photoing, and is ready to depart towards the Robotics Lab. Its latency is estimated to $EL_1 = -26.76$ and it thus moves at a normal speed. Note that the collection of 36 photos took 54 s to complete, therefore the synchronization gap between the two robots has been slightly reduced.

At time 199, NAO 2 reaches the Red Room. The latency for NAO 2 is now estimated to $EL_2 = 31.13$. To speed up execution the planner decides to develop the 360° view of the Red Room with the smallest possible number of photos. NAO 2 initiates the simplified mode of photoing, 15 pictures every 24°, which changes labeling of edge $RedRoom-> 360View$ to $(24.3,27,27,27)$.

After 226 s, NAO 2 completes photoing the Red Room. Its latency in comparison to NAO 1 is estimated to $EL_2 = 11.5$. This is below the threshold $\theta = 15$,

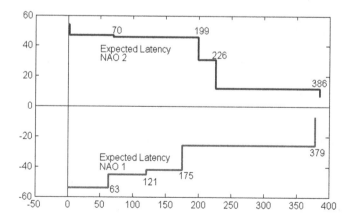

Fig. 5. The evolution of expected latency for each robot, during the implementation of the plan.

and thus for the last event assigned to NAO 2, no corrective action is initiated. NAO 2 navigates to the Robotics Lab at a normal speed.

After 379 s NAO 1 arrives at the Robotics Lab, ready to be assigned a new task. NAO 2 arrives at sec 386, having a small difference of 7 s from the previous robot.

Overall, the proposed method has successfully enforced synchronization between the two robots making appropriate corrective actions that incrementally minimize the latency gap between their actions.

8   Conclusions and Future Work

The present work introduces a new approach for multi-robot synchrony in time-informed planning that is based on representing temporal constraints with fuzzy numbers. This is an alternative to the contemporary approaches that consider constraint handling by means of $STNU$ and DGU networks. We show that the proposed approach is able to handle constraints in the same way as previous works. Moreover, the use of fuzzy calculus facilitates the detection of problematic situations which in turn enables taking early corrective measures to enforce synchrony of participating agents. To this end, we explore how action simplification and motion speed up may strengthen coordination in multi-agent setups. To the best of our knowledge this is the first time that this is issue is explored in the literature. While existing works introduce constraints that mainly delay the faster agent in order to match with the slower agent, we follow an opposite approach which aims at speeding up the slower agent to catch up with the faster agent, without harming the execution of the global plan.

In the future we plan to enrich the newly introduced fuzzy time planning method with additional features that will enhance further its ability to adapt and correct plans. Our priorities include analog speed adaptations (current implementation assumes binary choice between normal and fast speed), the ability to slow-down, consider subtasks temporally evolving non-linearly, and dynamically estimate threshold θ depending on the task at hand.

While the present work considers the synchronization of two robots, the proposed methodology is readily applicable to the case of multi-robot setups. The systematic assessment of the method in coordinating robot-teams that include three or more agents is among our immediate plans. Finally, we are particularly keen in testing the implemented methodology in human-robot cooperation setups where the robot will act as a slave synchronized to human actions.

Acknowledgment. This work has been partially supported by the EU FET grant (GA: 641100) TIMESTORM - Mind and Time: Investigation of the Temporal Traits of Human-Machine Convergence.

References

1. Akhil, K., Sharat, S., Russell, B.: Managing controlled violation of temporal process constraints. In: Motahari-Nezhad, H.R., Recker, J., Weidlich, M. (eds.) BPM 2015. LNCS, vol. 9253, pp. 280–296. Springer, Heidelberg (2015)
2. de la Asunción, M., Castillo, L., Fernández-Olivares, J., García-Pérez, O., González, A., Palao, F.: Handling fuzzy temporal constraints in a planning environment. Ann. Oper. Res. **155**(1), 391–415 (2007)
3. Boerkoel, J., Durfee, E.: Distributed reasoning for multiagent simple temporal problems. J. Artif. Intell. Res. **47**, 95–156 (2013)
4. Csárdi, G., Nepusz, T.: The igraph software package for complex network research. Inter. J. Complex Syst., 1695 (2006)
5. Dechter, R., Meiri, I., Pearl, J.: Temporal constraint networks. Artif. Intell. **49**, 61–95 (1991)
6. Dubois, D., Fargier, H., Prade, H.: Fuzzy constraints in job-shop scheduling. J. Intell. Manuf. **6**(4), 215–234 (1995)
7. Dubois, D., Prade, H.: Possibility Theory: An Approach to Computerized Processing of Uncertainty. Plenum Press, New York (1988)
8. Khadar, B.A.R., Madhusudhan, R., Ramanaiah, M., Karthikeyan, K.: Statistical optimization for generalised fuzzy number. Int. J. Mod. Eng. Res. **3**(2), 647–651 (2013)
9. Morris, P.: Dynamic controllability and dispatchability relationships. In: Simonis, H. (ed.) CPAIOR 2014. LNCS, vol. 8451, pp. 464–479. Springer, Heidelberg (2014)
10. Morris, P., Muscettola, N., Vidal, T.: Dynamic control of plans with temporal uncertainty. In: International Joint Conference on AI (IJCAI) (2001)
11. Shah, J., Stedl, J., Williams, B., Robertson, P.: A fast incremental algorithm for maintaining dispatchability of partially controllable plans. In: Proceedings of the 18th International Conference on Automated Planning and Scheduling (2007)
12. Shah, J., Williams, B.: Fast dynamic scheduling of disjunctive temporal constraint networks through incremental compilation. In: Proceedings of the 19th International Conference on Automated Planning and Scheduling (2008)
13. Smith, S., Gallagher, A., Zimmerman, T., Barbulescu, L., Rubinstein, Z.: Distributed management of flexible times schedules. In: International Conference on Autonomous Agents and Multiagent Systems (AAMAS) (2007)
14. Zadeh, L.: The concept of a linguistic variable and its application to approximate reasoning. Inform. Sci. **8**, 199–249 (1978)

Co-exploring Actuator Antagonism and Bio-inspired Control in a Printable Robot Arm

Martin F. Stoelen[1]([✉]), Fabio Bonsignorio[2], and Angelo Cangelosi[1]

[1] Centre for Robotics and Neural Systems, Plymouth University, Plymouth, UK
{martin.stoelen,a.cangelosi}@plymouth.ac.uk
[2] The BioRobotics Institute,
Scuola Superiore Sant'Anna, Pisa and Heron Robots, Genova, Italy
fabio.bonsignorio@sssup.it

Abstract. The human arm is capable of performing fast targeted movements with high precision, say in pointing with a mouse cursor, but is inherently 'soft' due to the muscles, tendons and other tissues of which it is composed. Robot arms are also becoming softer, to enable robustness when operating in real-world environments, and to make them safer to use around people. But softness comes at a price, typically an increase in the complexity of the control required for a given task speed/accuracy requirement. Here we explore how fast and precise joint movements can be simply and effectively performed in a soft robot arm, by taking inspiration from the human arm. First, viscoelastic actuator-tendon systems in an agonist-antagonist setup provide joints with inherent damping, and stiffness that can be varied in real-time through co-contraction. Second, a light-weight and learnable inverse model for each joint enables a fast ballistic phase that drives the arm close to a desired equilibrium point and co-contraction tuple, while the final adjustment is done by a feedback controller. The approach is embodied in the GummiArm, a robot which can almost entirely be printed on hobby-grade 3D printers. This enables rapid and iterative co-exploration of 'brain' and 'body', and provides a great platform for developing adaptive and bio-inspired behaviours.

Keywords: Bio-inspiration · Learnable models · Agonist-antagonist joints · Variable stiffness · 3D printing · Targeted movements

1 Introduction

This paper concerns a bio-inspired robot arm, the GummiArm. See Fig. 1. The robot is based on a set of principles drawn from the human and animal sensori-motor system. These principles include:

1. *Agonist-antagonist actuators* with control of joint equilibrium point and co-contraction. The equilibrium point hypothesis has been used to predict multi-joint human trajectories [1], and has been shown to lead to fast point-to-point movements in biomechanical simulations [2].

© Springer International Publishing Switzerland 2016
E. Tuci et al. (Eds.): SAB 2016, LNAI 9825, pp. 244–255, 2016.
DOI: 10.1007/978-3-319-43488-9_22

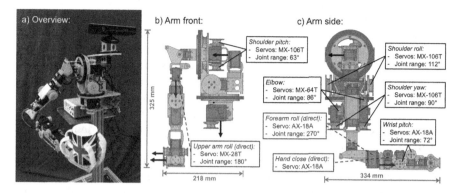

Fig. 1. The GummiArm v2.1.0. All light green parts are printable on hobby-grade 3D printers, while the joints are actuated by Dynamixel (Robotis Inc, Irvine, CA, USA) digital servos. The 5 agonist-antagonist joints provide inherent damping, impact robustness, and stiffness adjustment in real-time, through the composite viscoelastic tendons seen in orange and white. 3 further joints are directly driven by servos, the *upper arm roll, forearm roll,* and *hand close.* (a): The arm mounted on an aluminium frame, with a Kinect sensor (Microsoft, Redmond, WA, USA) on a pan mechanism. (b) and (c): Annotated front and side views, respectively. Thick filled-in arrows indicate the joint $\hat{z}$ axes.

2. *Viscoelastic actuator-tendon system.* Humans exploit co-contraction of the viscoelastic muscle-tendon system both during movements and after movement completion for achieving accuracy [3]. Here we show that we can adjust stiffness through co-contraction of rubber tendons with non-linear stiffness, and use movement-dependent excitation of co-contraction to further control unwanted end-point oscillations. The viscoelasticity provides damping.

3. Learnable *inverse joint models* for feedforward control of rapid point-to-point movements in joint-angle space. There is extensive work on inverse models for movement control in the brain [4]. We here use learnable inverse models for the joints to generate a ballistic phase of movement towards a given joint angle and co-contraction level. A second phase uses a feedback controller to compensate for any model deviations.

4. A *concurrent approach to the design of 'brain' and 'body',* enabled by a printable platform with open-source hardware and software. The robot structure is printable on hobby-grade 3D printers, and the overall platform cost is reasonably low (less than $5000) for a 7+1 Degree Of Freedom (DOF) arm with variable stiffness. The passive compliance makes it robust to impacts, and a broken part can be 3D printed (and potentially improved upon) quickly.

2   Related Work

Soft materials can afford new capabilities in safety, speed and agility of robotic agents [5]. Soft materials also have the potential to reduce the algorithmic complexity if the 'body' and 'brain' are developed together [6]. On one end of the 'soft' spectrum we find artificial octopus arms [7], providing extreme dexterity and compliance. On the other end are robots with stiff links, but elastic elements connecting the links and actuators. That is, series elastic actuators [8]. As an example, a low-cost compliant actuator was developed by Quigley, Asbeck and Ng [9], with a series elastic setup for the main actuators. The Polyurethane elastic elements provided compliance and some damping, but could not be varied in real-time. Another example is the Baxter light industrial robot (Rethink Robotics, Boston, USA). The inability to increase physical stiffness (and damping) can make such robots hard to control on fast point-to-point movements.

However, Variable Stiffness Actuators (VSA) are gradually becoming commonplace [10]. Benefits over traditional stiff robot actuators include safety, for humans, robots and the environment, but also performance [11]. The VSA-Cubebot [12] is a great example of a low-cost and flexible VSA. The standard modular design can simplify the design of a VSA arm, but it also means the actuators will typically have to be placed at the joints. The DLR hand arm system is a full size VSA arm with extensive use of tendons [13]. It is aimed at human levels of scale and performance, and therefore also has a high complexity. A key issue with introducing elastic elements into the actuation loop is that end-point oscillations can be hard to dampen. Advanced torque control strategies is one way to approach this problem [14], but typically requires an accurate robot model. Variable damping can also be achieved through physical means in the actuator. For example an electrically damped actuator [15]. The CompAct anthropomorphic actuator is also able to vary the physical damping, through piezo-electric clutches and an advanced sliding-mode control [16].

If exact models of the body cannot easily be pre-defined by the designer, such models can perhaps be learnt as part of the 'development' of the robot [17]. Among the platforms exploring this general direction is Roboy [18], a tendon-driven humanoid robot with passive compliance and force sensing directly in the muscle units. The iCub [19], one of the most popular platforms for developmental robotics, is also tendon-driven. However, it lacks passive compliance, and is aimed at a much higher cost and complexity level. A model-free approach for damping VSAs with a step change at just the right point in the oscillations shows promise [20], and should be possible to combine with the work presented here in the future.

3   The GummiArm

3.1   An Easily Evolvable Arm

The GummiArm is a 7+1 DOF robot arm, and is an open-source project available at: http://mstoelen.github.io/GummiArm/. See Fig. 1. The structure of the GummiArm consists of plastic parts connected to Dynamixel digital servos of Robotis Inc (Irvine, CA, USA). This design feature was inspired by the Robotis Bioloid robots and the Poppy Project [21], but with the addition of variable stiffness. The proportions of the arm (except the current hand) are equivalent to a 50th percentile female human [22]. The servos are joined by PLA-based plastic parts that can be printed on hobby-grade 3D printers. PLA is safe and cheap, and the parts can be made surprisingly light and strong due to the matrix-like internal structure. The total mass of the 7+1 DOF arm below the shoulder is 1.1 kg (excluding the hand), and the total mass of the arm is around 3 kg. Less than 1 kg of PLA plastic is needed to print the current version of the arm (v2.1.0).

The combination of fully open source software and hardware (with the exception of the servos) makes it possible to do a concurrent design of the soft arm itself with the control and adaptation algorithms. For example by quickly modifying the 3D printed parts of a joint to handle bigger tendons, while making corresponding changes to accommodate the higher stiffness in the arm control. Such changes can be made on the order of minutes and hours, leading to fast iterative improvements that explore the full design space of hardware and software. A bit like evolution on a small scale, with the designer in the loop.

3.2   Agonist-Antagonist Joints

Agonist-antagonist joints have been explored extensively for bio-inspired robotic arms. For example with two opposing pneumatic actuators, such as the McKibben type [23]. Such actuators require an external compressor however, and can be hard to control. The GummiArm has 5 agonist-antagonist joints with electric actuation, see Fig. 1. Each agonist-antagonist joint has two Dynamixel servo actuators operating the uni-directional tendons via pulleys, and one encoder on the joint axis. The tendons are based on a Filaflex 2.85 mm filament from Recreus (La Torreta, Spain), and their elasticity provide the arm passive compliance.

A quadratic force-length relationship is desirable in tendons used for agonist-antagonist joints. This allows independent control of stiffness and equilibrium without sensory feedback, as shown in [24]. To approach such behaviour we emulated typical rubber compensators for mooring lines on boats. That is, a much

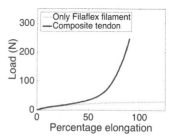

(a) 2 composite tendons on the *biceps* servo pulley.

(b) Load (y-axis) vs elongation (x-axis) of tendons.

Fig. 2. The composite tendon design, based on a soft 2.85 mm Filaflex filament (Recreus, La Torreta, Spain) and a stiff 1.5 mm nylon thread twinned around it.

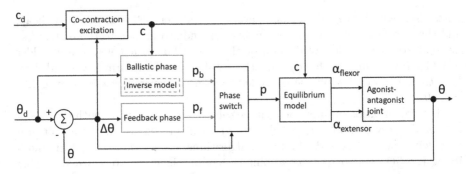

Fig. 3. The control architecture for the agonist-antagonist joints. The joint controller is provided with a desired joint angle θ_d and co-contraction level c_d (from 0 to 100 %). For large desired changes in joint angle (here $|\Delta\theta| > 15°$) a switching mechanism activates the ballistic phase. The co-contraction c is also excited proportionally to the desired change in joint angle $\Delta\theta$, to provide stabilization towards the end of the movement. The ballistic phase aims for a high percentage of the desired joint angle change (here 85 %), and aims to get there with the excited co-contraction level. A desired equilibrium point p_b is generated with an inverse joint model and fed forward. An equilibrium model relates the equilibrium point and co-contraction to the required actuation commands, which are here the angles of the actuator pulleys (α_{flexor} and $\alpha_{extensor}$). When a threshold percentage of $\Delta\theta$ is passed (here 50 %) the feedback controller takes over, correcting for discrepancies between the model and the real situation of the joint.

less flexible nylon line was twinned around the Filaflex filament, as seen in Fig. 2a. As can be seen in Fig. 2b this composite tendon design has an increase in stiffness with elongation, as the nylon line gradually straightens out. The tensile testing was performed on a Instron (Wycombe, United Kingdom) 5582 frame with a static 100kN load cell (Instron UK195) on a 190 mm specimen. For the tensile testing a pitch of 0.1 per mm was used.

3.3   Combined Ballistic/Feedback Control

A dual-phase control architecture is used for controlling the GummiArm on fast point-to-point joint movements. See Fig. 3. Referring to the 'Equilibrium model' box, the two servo actuator angles α_{flexor} and $\alpha_{extensor}$ for a joint are assumed to scale linearly with equilibrium point p and co-contraction c. See Eq. 1.

$$\alpha_{\text{flexor}} = p\frac{\gamma}{4} - c\frac{\pi}{2},$$
$$\alpha_{\text{extensor}} = p\frac{\gamma}{4} + c\frac{\pi}{2}. \tag{1}$$

Note that the equilibrium point here is a virtual joint feature, and any deviations from this assumption is attempted corrected through the joint calibration. For simplicity we here assume step-changes to equilibrium point in joint-space, rather than the task-space trajectories with explicit velocity profiles used by among other Flash [1]. The equilibrium point p ranges from -1 to 1, and is assumed to influence half the actuator range γ. This range was 270° for the wrist joint (AX-18 servos), 360° for the *elbow* (MX-64T servos) and *shoulder pitch* (MX-106T servos), and 720° for the remaining joints (MX-106T servos). The co-contraction c ranges from 0 to 1 (0 % to 100 %), corresponding to ±90° of range on the actuator servos.

The co-contraction was set according to the desired c_d, but was also excited by large commanded changes in joint angle from the actual, when a distinct point-to-point command was received. Refer to the 'Co-contraction excitation' box in Fig. 3. As can be seen in Eq. 2 the ballistic component c_b was scaled proportionally with the absolute value of $\Delta\theta$.

$$c_b = k|\Delta\theta|,$$
$$c_e = c_b - c_d. \tag{2}$$

The co-contraction c was set according to: $c = c_d + c_e$. Here c_e was reduced every iteration by the factor μ, with $0 < \mu < 1$, according to: $c_e = c_e\mu$. Thus the co-contraction is gradually reduced to the desired value c_d, relaxing the joint after the movement. The constants k and μ were adjusted for this to occur, with $k = 0.035$ and $\mu = 0.0015$ for a 60 Hz update rate of the control system.

As described in Fig. 3, the ballistic phase was initiated if $|\Delta\theta| > 15°$. Ballistic movements, with little or no online sensory feedback, have been widely studied in humans. They typically exhibit a characteristic 'triphasic' burst of activity in agonist and antagonist muscles, for example in fast thumb flexion [25]. In our current work the inverse model, described in Sect. 3.4, was used to obtain the equilibrium point for the ballistic movement, given the co-contraction c. The feedback phase (see corresponding box in Fig. 3) was set to take over when more than 50 % of the joint angle movement had been completed. See 'Phase switch' box in Fig. 3. A PID feedback controller was used, tuned to provide reasonable performance over the full range of co-contraction levels available. To help reduce overshoot, the ballistic phase was aimed at 85 % of the actual $\Delta\theta$ required.

3.4   Inverse Joint Model for Ballistic Phase

The term 'inverse model' is used to denote transformations from desired object movements to motor commands [4]. The ballistic phase described above requires a mapping from a desired joint angle and co-contraction to the corresponding equilibrium point p_b. That is, what muscle lengths (here the servo actuator angles α_{flexor} and $\alpha_{extensor}$) are required to reach a certain joint pose with a given amount of stiffness. This mapping would in general depend on the forces acting on the joint, and thus also the pose of the full arm, any payload held in the hand, any interaction with the environment, and the dynamics of the movement. We here assume a much simpler model, which provides a mapping under quasi-static conditions around the resting pose of the arm seen in Fig. 1. We show that such a simple model is sufficient in many cases, when combined

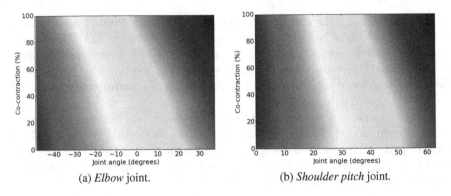

(a) *Elbow* joint.   (b) *Shoulder pitch* joint.

Fig. 4. The mappings for the inverse models of the *elbow* and *shoulder pitch* joints. Colour represents the output of the model, the equilibrium point p. (Color figure online)

with a feedback phase, the intrinsic damping of the viscoelastic tendons used, and the movement-dependent excitation of co-contraction.

The inverse model for the *elbow* and *shoulder pitch* joints are visualized in Fig. 4. The inverse models were aquired using a calibration procedure for each joint. The joint was moved through the full joint range, stopping at 7 quasi-static poses (joint angles), each at 7 different levels of co-contraction (from 0 to 100 %). A linear interpolation could then be used to obtain values for p_b spanning the convex hull of the 49 calibration points. That is, the model assumes linearity between the 49 points obtained, although a finer sampling scheme could be used if required. The Python *scipy.interpolate.griddata* function was used. The full calibration procedure takes less than 5 min for each joint. An estimate for the appropriate p_b value could be obtained in less than 1 ms for each joint, on an Intel i7 5960X running at 3 MHz. An interesting feature of these inverse models is that they can be adjusted in real-time, during quasi-static poses. Such learning could help adjust the arm performance to the task context, for example if always holding an object of a certain mass on a given task.

4   Experimental Results

4.1   Exploring Co-Contraction

The ability to co-contract opposing actuators is the key feature of agonist-antagonist joints. A quasi-static loading setup was created for the *elbow* joint. The upper arm was locked in place, while the lower arm was replaced with a rigid beam with multiple attachment points for weights, from 70 mm to 200 mm from the joint axis, and at 10 mm intervals. The actuator was commanded to a passive horizontal pose. Three different weights (0.1 kg, 0.5 kg, and 1.5 kg) were then attached at different distances from the joint axis to generate a set of torques up to almost 3 Nm. The passive deflection of the joint was then recorded with the AX-12A encoder. This process was repeated three times for the 3 weights and

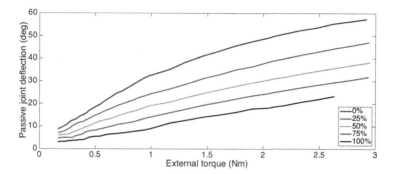

Fig. 5. Passive joint deflection (y-axis) of the *elbow* joint from applying an external torque (x-axis) under quasi-static conditions, for different values of commanded co-contraction. Deflection corresponding to elbow extension.

the 14 distances. The same procedure was repeated for 5 different stiffness levels, from 0 % to 100 %. See Fig. 5 for the results. The maximum torque feasible for the *elbow* joint with the MX-64T servo was close to 3 Nm, reducing somewhat with the highest stiffness setting. It can be seen that the amount of deflection for a given external torque can be changed considerably by the co-contraction. The deflections possible are also quite high for a VSA [26], exceeding 45° at high external torques with the 0 % stiffness setting. Such 'softness' is an interesting feature when having robots explore autonomously the physical world in developmental experiment paradigms. A 100 % change in stiffness can for most joints be done in less than 0.5 s.

4.2   Fast Joint-Space Movements

The step response of the *shoulder pitch* joint was explored, with feedback control only, and with the bio-inspired two-phase ballistic/feedback control. The joint was mounted as part of the full arm, and all other joints were kept passively at the resting pose (see Fig. 1). The *shoulder pitch* joint was moved through 3/5 of full joint range, from close to body to shoulder abduction, and back again. As can be seen in Fig. 6, both controllers showed good tracking of the desired joint angle with 100 % co-contraction, and little overshoot and oscillations. The ballistic/feedback controller did show a superior response time, but the difference was small and requires further investigation. However the ballistic/feedback controller was able to provide very good tracking also for down to 0 % co-contraction at start, while the feedback controller showed increasing levels of oscillations. For both cases a PID-type feedback controller was used, but a simpler PD controller would likely suffice, as there is little steady-state error.

The full arm was also assessed on point-to-point movements, to compare the controllers when there are un-modelled interactions between the moving joints. All joints were commanded to move as fast as possible to the joint angles corresponding to a finish pose. Note that no inter-joint coordination was performed,

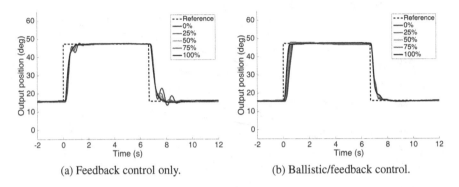

Fig. 6. Step responses of the *shoulder pitch* joint with *elbow* at resting pose in Fig. 1(b), for different levels of co-contraction. Zero degrees corresponds to resting pose for *shoulder pitch* joint. Average of 3 attempts for each trajectory shown.

each joint moved as quickly as possible. Such a movement can cause large inter-acting forces between joints, making it harder for the joint-level controllers. As can be seen in Fig. 7, the feedback controller suffered from these interactions during the movement, and had a considerable amount of oscillations towards the end of the movement. The ballistic/feedback controller performed better, also with 0 % co-contraction at start (not shown). The achievable speed of movement was also higher for the ballistic/feedback controller. This can be evaluated visually by the fewer 'shadows' seen in the intermediate stages of movement in the long-exposure image in Fig. 7b. Further tests are required to generalise about these results, and to better understand the factors influencing performance.

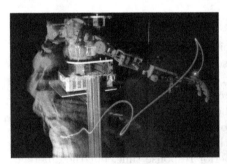 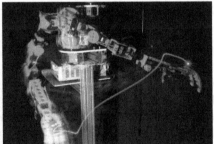

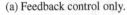

(a) Feedback control only.   (b) Ballistic/feedback control.

Fig. 7. Fast point-to-point movement in joint space with the whole arm, with 100 % co-contraction. Note that the movements are generated in joint-space, not as a straight-line Cartesian trajectory. The goal is to achieve the movement as fast as possible, settling within a minimum tolerance of the desired finish pose. Images created with a long-exposure of 6 s, and strobe lighting at 8.5 Hz. Red LED mounted on hand. (Color figure online)

4.3   Teleoperation with Physical Interaction

The GummiArm is utilising the Robot Operating System (ROS) for all its functionality. A differential inverse kinematics solver based on the OROCOS [27] KDL library is also implemented, allowing teleoperation of the arm. While teleoperating the co-contraction can be adjusted freely by the operator, making the arm joints loose or stiff. The arm can also be commanded in a passive mode, where the equilibrium position of each joint is moved without controlling for the exact joint angle. This is very useful when interacting with physical objects, as the arm complies naturally to the forces experienced. Figure 8 shows screenshots of a continuous sequence where the robot shows its ability to absorb impacts, to be teleoperated accurately with high stiffness, to write on a keyboard, and to open a drawer while moving in the passive mode. The full video can be accessed here: https://youtu.be/_syFAQBrgio.

(a) Absorbing physical impacts. (b) Performing a precision move. (c) Typing on a computer keyboard. (d) Opening an office drawer.

Fig. 8. Example teleoperation task with physical interaction.

5   Conclusions

Co-exploring 'body' and 'brain' seems fruitful when investigating adaptive behaviours. We believe the GummiArm platform is highly suitable for this purpose, and can be of use to researchers at the intersection of biology, cognitive science and human motor control with robotics. The arm has a high robustness and a low lifetime cost, given the low-cost printable PLA structure, the passive compliance of the tendons, and since a non-specialist user can quickly fix and improve any pieces that do break. A key element is the agonist-antagonist joints driven by accurate digital servos, and with viscoelastic composite tendons. The inherent damping and the ability to adjust stiffness in real-time helps simplify joint control. The dual phase ballistic/feedback controller was inspired by the way humans can quickly move the hand close to a target with a ballistic movement, then refine the pose with sensory feedback. It has a low algorithmic complexity, in essence relying on distributed and learnable inverse models in the joints, and simple switches, but enables the GummiArm to perform fast and accurate joint movements. Together with the ability to interact safely with the physical environment, this makes for interesting possibilities in robot self-exploration. We hope to exploit this, and to integrate more adaptive and context-sensitive behaviours in the arm, in the near future. We would also like to explore scalable equilibrium point trajectories in task space [1].

Acknowledgments. This work was funded by a Marie Curie Intra-European Fellowship within the 7th European Community Framework Programme (DeCoRo FP7-PEOPLE-2013-IEF).

References

1. Flash, T.: The control of hand equilibrium trajectories in multi-joint arm movements. Biol. Cybern. **57**(4–5), 257–274 (1987)
2. Kistemaker, D.A., Van Soest, A.K.J., Bobbert, M.F.: Is equilibrium point control feasible for fast goal-directed single-joint movements? J. Neurophysiol. **95**(5), 2898–2912 (2006)
3. Gribble, P.L., Mullin, L.I., Cothros, N., Mattar, A.: Role of cocontraction in arm movement accuracy. J. Neurophysiol. **89**(5), 2396–2405 (2003)
4. Wolpert, D.M., Miall, R.C., Kawato, M.: Internal models in the cerebellum. Trends Cogn. Sci. **2**(9), 338–347 (1998)
5. Rus, D., Tolley, M.T.: Design, fabrication and control of soft robots. Nature **521**(7553), 467–475 (2015)
6. Pfeifer, R., Lungarella, M., Iida, F.: The challenges ahead for bio-inspired 'soft' robotics. Commun. ACM **55**(11), 76–87 (2012)
7. Mazzolai, B., Margheri, L., Cianchetti, M., Dario, P., Laschi, C.: "Soft-robotic arm inspired by the octopus: II. From artificial requirements to innovative technological solutions. Bioinspiration Biomimetics **7**(2), 025005 (2012)
8. Pratt, G.A., Williamson, M.M.: Series elastic actuators. In: IEEE/RSJ International Conference on Intelligent Robots and Systems (IROS), vol. 1, pp. 399–406 (1995)
9. Quigley, M., Asbeck, A., Ng, A.: A low-cost compliant 7-DOF robotic manipulator. In: IEEE International Conference on Robotics and Automation (ICRA), pp. 6051–6058, May 2011
10. Vanderborght, B., et al.: Variable impedance actuators: a review. Robot. Auton. Syst. **61**(12), 1601–1614 (2013)
11. Bicchi, A., Tonietti, G., Bavaro, M., Piccigallo, M.: Variable stiffness actuators for fast and safe motion control. In: Dario, P., Chatila, R. (eds.) The Eleventh International Symposium on Robotics Research. STAR, vol. 15, pp. 527–536. Springer, Heidelberg (2005)
12. Catalano, M.G., Grioli, G., Garabini, M., Bonomo, F., Mancini, M., Tsagarakis, N., Bicchi, A.: VSA-CubeBot: a modular variable stiffness platform for multiple degrees of freedom robots. In: IEEE International Conference on Robotics and Automation (ICRA), Shanghai, China, pp. 5090–5095 (2011)
13. Grebenstein, M., et al.: The DLR hand arm system. In: IEEE International Conference on Robotics and Automation (ICRA), pp. 3175–3182 (2011)
14. Petit, F., Dietrich, A., Albu-Schäffer, A.: Generalizing torque control concepts: using well-established torque control methods on variable stiffness robots. IEEE Robot. Autom. Mag. **22**(4), 37–51 (2015)
15. Radulescu, A., Howard, M., Braun, D.J., Vijayakumar, S.: Exploiting variable physical damping in rapid movement tasks. In: IEEE/ASME International Conference on Advanced Intelligent Mechatronics (AIM), pp. 141–148 (2012)

16. Kashiri, N., Tsagarakis, N.G., Van Damme, M., Vanderborght, B., Caldwell, D.G.: Proxy-based sliding mode control of compliant joint manipulators. In: Filipe, J., Gusikhin, O., Madani, K., Sasiadek, J. (eds.) Informatics in Control, Automation and Robotics. Lecture Notes in Electrical Engineering, vol. 370, pp. 241–257. Springer, Heidelberg (2016)

17. Cangelosi, A., Schlesinger, M.: Developmental Robotics: From Babies to Robots. MIT Press, Cambridge (2015)

18. Pfeifer, R., Marques, H.G., Iida, F.: Soft robotics: the next generation of intelligent machines. In: Proceedings of the Twenty-Third International Joint Conference on Artificial Intelligence, pp. 5–11 (2013)

19. Metta, G., Sandini, G., Vernon, D., Natale, L., Nori, F.: The iCub humanoid robot: an open platform for research in embodied cognition. In: Proceedings of the 8th Workshop on Performance Metrics for Intelligent Systems, pp. 50–56 (2008)

20. Petit, F., Ott, C., Albu-Schäffer, A.: A model-free approach to vibration suppression for intrinsically elastic robots. In: IEEE International Conference on Robotics and Automation (ICRA), pp. 2176–2182 (2014)

21. Lapeyre, M., Rouanet, P., Grizou, J., Nguyen, S., Depraetre, F., et al.: Poppy Project: Open-Source Fabrication of 3D Printed Humanoid Robot for Science, Education and Art, Digital Intelligence 2014, September 2014, Nantes, France, p. 6 (2014). https://hal.inria.fr/hal-01096338

22. NASA, Man-Systems Integration Standards - Revison B. National Aeronautics, Space Administration: Houston, USA (1995). http://msis.jsc.nasa.gov/

23. Chou, C.P., Hannaford, B.: Measurement and modeling of McKibben pneumatic artificial muscles. IEEE Trans. Rob. Autom. **12**(1), 90–102 (1996)

24. Ham, R.V., Sugar, T.G., Vanderborght, B., Hollander, K.W., Lefeber, D.: Compliant actuator designs. IEEE Rob. Autom. Mag. **16**(3), 81–94 (2009)

25. Hallett, M.A.R.K., Marsden, C.D.: Ballistic flexion movements of the human thumb. J. Physiol. **294**, 33–50 (1979)

26. Grioli, G., et al.: Variable stiffness actuators: the user's point of view. Int. J. Rob. Res. **34**(6), 727–743 (2015)

27. Bruyninckx, H.: Open robot control software: the OROCOS project. In: IEEE International Conference on Robotics and Automation (ICRA), pp. 2523–2528 (2001)

Modelling the Effect of Dorsal Raphe Serotonin Neurons on Patience for Future Rewards

Marc Sutherland and Bernd Porr$^{(\boxtimes)}$

University of Glasgow, University Avenue, Glasgow, Scotland
Bernd.Porr@glasgow.ac.uk

Abstract. Serotonin is a neurotransmitter that is implicated in many basic human functions and behaviours and is closely associated with happiness, depression and reward processing. In particular it appears to be involved in suppressing responses to distracting stimuli while waiting for a delayed reward. Here we present a system level model of the limbic system which is able to generate a serotonin (5-hydroxytryptamine [5HT]) signal so that a simulated animal waits for a delayed reward. We propose that the 5HT signal is computed by a network involving the medial Orbital Frontal Cortex (mOFC), medial Pre Frontal Cortex (mPFC), Dorsal Raphe Nucleus (DRN)and the Nucleus Accumbens Core (NAcc). The serotonin signal encodes pre-reward liking, motivation throughout the trial and delayed reward waiting. We have successfully replicated the behaviour and dynamics of laboratory studies. With the help of this model we can predict that low levels of serotonin indirectly cause less encountered rewards because the animal gives up too early.

Keywords: Serotonin · Dopamine · Reward · Inhibition · Waiting

1 Introduction

The neurotransmitter serotonin is considered to be involved in the regulation of a number of behaviours principally involving aggression, aversive learning, impulsivity, attention, decision making, and reward [2]. It is implicated in many psychiatric disorders including depression, panic attacks, anxiety and obsessive compulsions [3]. In spite of serotonin's implication in a wide array of fundamental behaviours, the explicit circuitry that regulates serotonin producing neurons continues to be insufficiently understood [4]. And despite a considerable amount of research, the challenge of creating a unified theory of serotonin function persists [5].

We present a biologically inspired, systems level model which combines dopamine and serotonin networks to actualize learning and reversal learning in a simulated reward seeking task. Higher levels of serotonin allow the agent to remain at the reward site long enough to receive the reward without being distracted by competing attractions. Lower levels of serotonin mean that the agent does not wait long enough for the reward if it is delayed, and thus receives less rewards [1].

© Springer International Publishing Switzerland 2016
E. Tuci et al. (Eds.): SAB 2016, LNAI 9825, pp. 256–266, 2016.
DOI: 10.1007/978-3-319-43488-9_23

2   Task and Simulated Agent

The model is tested on a food and water seeking task based on the experiment conducted by Miyazaki [1]. A straightforward scenario is used in which an agent has a choice of two potential reward sites, see Fig. 1. The reward is only present at one site, see Fig. 1 "cake". The animal is simulated to move based on Braitenberg behaviour, calculated from distance from left and right eye to the Conditioned Stimulus (CS). At the beginning of the task the agent wanders around the designated area and approaches the different sites by chance. Once the agent has learned where the reward is located it will consistently go to that reward site. If the reward is toggled to the other site, reversal learning will lead the agent to eventually return to the haphazard wandering stage, until it happens on the reward again by chance. The reward is not presented at the site immediately in all cases, the agent may have to wait until it is delivered.

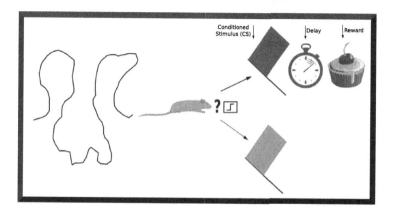

Fig. 1. Simulation environment

Mouse Simulation Environment: At the beginning of the task, approach behaviour is governed by a proximal signal which is determined by the angle of sight and distance between the rat and a red or blue flag. As the rat learns which flag harbours the reward, the flags become conditioned stimuli and approach behaviour is governed by a distal signal when the rat has the flag in its line of vision. When the rat is in position to receive the reward it must wait until the reward is delivered. A learning weight related to reward delivery increases as the reward is delivered consistently and diminishes as the reward is omitted. If the reward weight falls back to zero, the agent returns to its wandering activity and approach behaviour is again governed by a proximal signal.

3   The Role of Serotonin

The DRN signal in our model is composed of three main aspects. First, serotonin neurons signal pre-reward motivation to access the reward associated with a CS. Nakamura argues that the DRN signals reward value associated with current behaviour and that the reaction to CS signals motivation to access the received reward [21]. Bromberg-Martin et al.'s 2010 study found that DRN neurons systematically encoded behaviour tasks in terms of their capacity to provide future rewards [22]. A view supported by Homberg who argues that there is some evidence that 5HT could signal the possibility of future reward [18] (see Fig. 2A). Secondly, serotonin also signals reward receipt. Nakamura's posits that the reaction to the received reward demonstrates appreciation with some neurons exhibiting a preference for large rewards while other neurons exhibit a preference for smaller rewards [21,25] (see Fig. 2C). Lastly specific DRN neurons fire when the agent is in position, waiting to receive the reward (see Fig. 2B). These neurons fire until the completion of the task, when the reward is finally presented to the subject. If the level of neuronal firing diminishes before the agent has received the reward, the agent will leave the site to start a new search [1]. Therefore, the agent's ability to wait is dependent on its serotonin level. Lower firing rates mean that the agent will move away before the reward is presented.

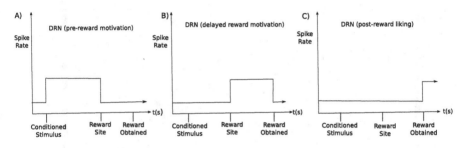

Fig. 2. DRN serotonin signals

4   Model Description

Limbic System Model: The model consists of a serotonin pathway which encodes pre-reward liking, motivation throughout the trial and delayed reward waiting. Dopamine (DA) pathways have also been created according to the standard model of DA action. These consist of reward, reward prediction and reward omission pathways which are capable of generating a dopamine liking signal to promote reward seeking action and also a dopamine reward prediction error.

Abbreviations: l-OFC - lateral Orbital Frontal Cortex, m-OFC - medial Orbital Frontal Cortex, m-PFC - medial Pre-Frontal Cortex, DRN - Dorsal Raphe Nucleus, l-shell - lateral shell of the Nucleus Accumbens, m-shell - medial shell of the Nucleus Accumbens, core - core of the Nucleus Accumbens, dl-VP - dorso-lateral Ventral Pallidum, m-VP - medial Ventral Pallidum, EP - Entopenduncular Nucleus, LHb - Lateral Habenula, RMTg - Rostral Medial Tegmental Nucleus, LH - Lateral Hypothalamus, VTA - Ventral Tegmental Area.

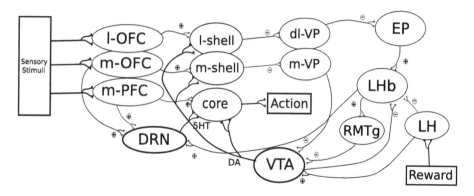

Fig. 3. Limbic system model

4.1 Reward Circuit

The dopamine circuits presented below are based on the standard prediction error paradigm by Schultz, Montague and Dayan [28]. The reward pathway is activated when the agent receives a primary reward (see Fig. 4A). This is modelled as beginning from the Lateral Hypothalamus (LH) which sends a strong inhibitory projection to the Lateral Habenula and an excitatory projection to the Ventral Tegmental Area (VTA) [6,7] (see Fig. 3).

4.2 Reward Prediction Circuit

The reward prediction circuit is activated when a conditioned stimulus (CS) associated with reward is observed (see Fig. 4B). The circuit creates a dopamine burst in response to the CS and suppresses the dopamine burst that would be

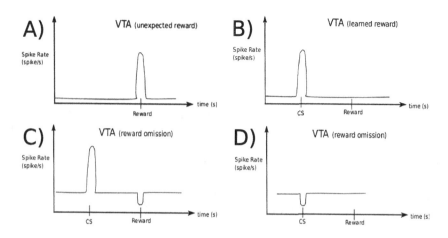

Fig. 4. Reward omission circuits

created by the LH upon reward receipt. The circuit starts at the mOFC, which generates persistent activity in response to each CS (see Fig. 1). An excitatory efferent from the m-OFC to the m-shell is modelled to undergo long term potentiation (LTP) if a dopamine burst coincides with the falling edge of activity on this connection [8]. If a dopamine dip coincides with the falling edge then long term depression (LTD) is modelled to take place. LTP allows the CS signal to pass through the inhibitory m-shell to the m-VP connection [9] and from there to the disinhibitory m-VP to VTA projection [7] (see Fig. 3). After sufficient LTP this will cause a DA burst when the CS is observed. Sustained CS activity also creates a sustained increase in GABAergic projections [10] which suppress DA bursts in the VTA due to reward receipt, as the reward is now predicted.

4.3 Reward Omission Circuit

This circuit is activated when a forecasted reward is omitted (see Fig. 4C) and also when a CS which is associated with reward omission is observed (see Fig. 4D). The signal starts from the lOFC, top left of the diagram, and comprises a range of signals depending on learning weight wlOFC, ranging from a short burst at learning weight zero to persistent activity at learning weight one. The appearance of a CS creates lOFC activity which projects to the l-shell [11] and is modelled to experience LTP due to a combination of the falling edge of the lOFC signal and a DA burst. This excludes activation of the circuit by a novel stimulus or a stimulus that has not previously led to a reward. When a CS that is associated with reward is presented, the signal is passed to the EP via the vl-VP by inhibition/disinhibition [9,12]. If no reward is delivered as expected, the VTA DA activity falls. The EP projects to the LHb [13,14] at the falling edge of the signal. The EP innervates the LHb which sends a glutamergic signal to the RMTg [15] which then inhibits the VTA [16], causing a dip in DA projections (see Fig. 3). The signal is also propagated when a CS that predicts omission is observed.

4.4 Serotonin Circuit

Serotonin is widely implicated in reward seeking behaviour. Nakamura et al.'s 2008 study of the primate dorsal raphe nucleus found that DRN responded tonically to both stimulus and reward and reliably encoded the value of the received reward, whether it was expected or not [21]. Based on Nakamura we proffer that the 5HT signal is computed by a network involving the medial Orbital Frontal Cortex (mOFC), medial Pre Frontal Cortex (mPFC), Dorsal Raphe Nucleus (DRN) and the Nucleus Accumbens Core (Core) (see Fig. 3). The lateral Orbital Frontal Cortex (lOFC) links specific stimuli to certain reward and failure results whereas the mOFC and mPFC are involved in appraising reward value, decision making, inhibition and choice across subsequent decisions [8]. Observance of the conditioned stimulus causes the signal to start at the lOFC and then transfer through the mOFC to the mPFC [17]. The mPFC in turn innervates the DRN [18,19]. Finally the signal terminates at the NAcc Core, controlling actions [20].

5   Results

We first present the DA signal results and then the 5HT results.

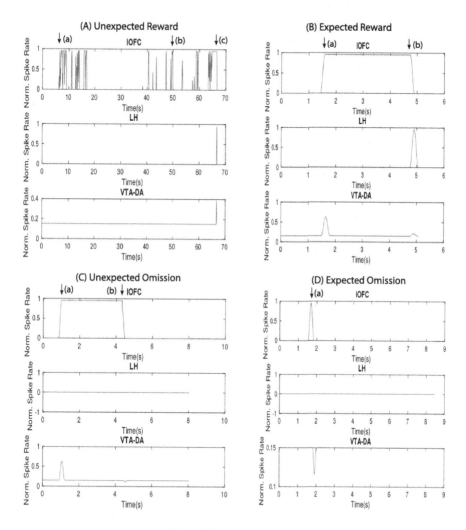

Fig. 5. Dopamine results

5.1   Dopamine Results

Unexpected Reward: At the start of the trial the agent wanders around the task area in a haphazard manner. In this wandering phase the stimulus comes in and out of view. Viewing the stimulus causes the lOFC spike rate to increase, examples of which are points (a) and (b) in Fig. 5A. As the stimulus is not yet associated with reward the agent does not move towards it when it is viewed. Eventually the agent's wandering leads it by chance to the stimulus where it finds there is a reward. At point (c) in Fig. 5A LH spikes at reward presentation causing VTA DA to also increase it's spike rate as presented in Fig. 4A.

Expected Reward: At the start of the task the agent begins its wandering phase, to examine the site. At point (a) in Fig. 5B there is visual onset of the Conditioned Stimulus. As the CS is at this point associated with reward VTA DA increases its spike rate and the agent moves towards the CS to obtain the reward. At point (b) the agent receives the reward causing LH to increase its spiking rate. VTA GABA inhibits the release of VTA DA at reward presentation, hence the rate of spiking has diminished at this point as presented in Fig. 4B.

Unexpected Omission: The agent has now learned to associate the Conditioned Stimulus with reward. After the initial wandering stage, at point (a) in Fig. 5C, it sees the CS and moves towards it. At point (b) it arrives at the CS and when that reward is unexpectedly omitted, it causes a dip in the base firing rate of the VTA DA as displayed in Fig. 4C.

Expected Omission: The agent has now learned to associate the Conditioned Stimulus with an omission of reward. At the start of the task there is the initial wandering stage, then at point (a) in Fig. 5D, the agent sees the CS. This causes a dip in the VTA DA spiking rate, as presented in Fig. 4D.

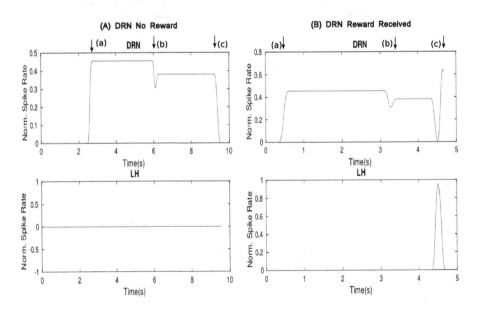

Fig. 6. DRN results

5.2   DRN Results

DRN No Reward: The task starts with the agent wandering around the task area. At point(a) in Fig. 6A the agent sees the conditioned stimulus and moves towards it. The DRN neurons increase spiking related to pre-reward motivation to achieve a reward (see Fig. 2A). At point (b) the agent is at the reward site. DRN spiking is maintained to inhibit leaving the site before the reward is delivered (see Fig. 2B). Eventually spiking reduces and as no reward has been provided, the agent leaves the site to begin a new reward search, point (c).

DRN Reward Received: The task starts with the agent wandering around the task area. At point (a) in Fig. 6B the agent sees the conditioned stimulus and moves towards it. DRN neurons increase spiking related to pre-reward liking (see Fig. 2A). At point (b) the agent is at the reward site. DRN spiking is maintained to inhibit leaving the site before the reward is delivered (see Fig. 2B). When the reward is delivered at point (c), the neurons which maintained delayed reward waiting cease firing and an alternative set of serotonin neurons fire, signalling post-reward liking (see Fig. 2C) [1].

6   Discussion

The work we present here builds on the limbic model inspired by the seminal work of Papez, Yakovlev and MacLean. Current dominant models of serotonin function focus on reward seeking behaviour, inhibition, perseveration and the processing of aversive cues. Nakamura argues that the DRN signals reward value associated with current behaviour and that the reaction to CS signals motivation to access the reward and the reaction to the received reward demonstrates appreciation [21,25]. Dayan's model proposes that a reduction in 5HT leads to behavioural disinhibition which is interconnected to an increased sensitivity to aversive cues and large negative prediction errors [2]. Cools asserts that serotonin has the opposite function to dopamine in that it deals with aversive cues and inhibiting behaviour [27]. Seymour argues that the depletion of serotonin produces perseverative responding, inducing the agent to persistently respond to a previously rewarding stimulus that offer diminishing returns, no returns or even negative outcomes [29].

The novel model of serotonin function we propose builds on the models above. We have shown that serotonin plays a critical role in reward seeking activity; enhanced spiking rates signal motivation to achieve a reward, motivation to wait for a reward and also appreciation of the achieved reward. Lower levels of serotonin in the agent would mean less motivation, less patience and lower reward appreciation, therefore less rewards, which would have a significant impact on the agent's well-being and mood. Bromberg-Martin et al.'s 2010 study asserts that serotonin controls motivation and reward seeking. High levels of serotonin led the case studies to wait for larger delayed rewards. Lower levels made the monkeys impulsively choose the smaller more readily available reward [22]. Higher 5HT helps the agent to stay focussed and become less distracted, allowing them to exploit a resource rather than set off to explore before it has been fully exploited [18]. Robinson et al. state that different subtypes of serotonin receptor control varying forms of impulsive behaviour. They claim there are at least 15 subtypes. Their study found that a reduction of forebrain 5HT led to impulsive responding in rats and argue that their findings add to a growing body of evidence for multiple neurotransmitter systems that regulate impulsive behaviour which includes serotonin, dopamine, noradrenergic and histaminergic systems [26]. In a 2011 paper Cools et al. discuss the fact that the depletion of 5HT is characterised by both impulsive behaviour and depression. They consider this fact incongruous as depression is associated with reduced behavioural vitality. They posit that 5HT's link to depression may be indirect and caused by associative learning or the disinhibition of unpleasant thoughts [27]. It would appear that serotonin does have an indirect effect on depression as anti-depressants that target depression only start to affect mood after a considerable length of time. One could also argue that increased impulsivity could lead to a negative mood if the impulsive behaviour was having negative outcomes.

7   Model Equations

The following equations show how the signals are generated in different sections of the limbic system model.

G(t) is a Gaussian filter which smooth out transitions in the raw signals.

$$LH(t) = G(t) * rewardSet(t) \tag{1}$$

$$VTA_{DA}(t) = \begin{cases} \frac{LH(t)}{VTA_{GABA}(t)} + EP(t) + G(t) * reward_{LTP} * w_{mshell}(t), & mOFC_{diff}(t) > 0 \\ \frac{LH(t)}{VTA_{GABA}(t)} + EP(t), & mOFC_{diff}(t) < 0 \end{cases} \tag{2}$$

$reward_{LTP}$ denotes when the long term potentiation in the reward prediction circuit has reached a level significant enough to allow the signal to pass through the circuit.

w_{mshell} is the learning weight associated with reward prediction.

$mOFC_{diff} > 0$ denotes a rising edge of the mOFC signal.

$mOFC_{diff} < 0$ denotes a falling edge of the mOFC signal.

$$EP(t) = \begin{cases} G(t) * -0.2 * omission_{LTP}(t) * LH_{inhibition}(t), & lOFC_{diff}(t) < 0 \,\&\, lOFC(t) < 0.1 \\ 0, & lOFC_{diff}(t) > 0 \,\|\, lOFC(t) > 0.1 \end{cases} \tag{3}$$

$omission_{LTP}$ denotes when the long term potentiation in the reward omission circuit has reached a level significant enough to allow the signal to pass through the circuit.

$lOFC_{diff} > 0$ denotes a rising edge of the lOFC signal.

$lOFC_{diff} < 0$ denotes a falling edge of the lOFC signal.

$$lOFC(t) = lOFC_{pa}(t) * w_{lOFC}(t) * G(t)(lOFC_{burst}(t) * (1 - w_{lOFC}(t))) \tag{4}$$

The lOFC signal is a combination of a permanent lOFC signal and a lOFC burst signal, controlled by an omission learning weight.

$$mOFC(t) = delay(lOFC_{pa}(t)) \tag{5}$$

The mOFC signal originates in the lOFC and is therefore a delayed version of that signal.

$$mPFC(t) = \begin{cases} G(t) * 0.5 + LH, & mOFC_{diff}(t) > 0 \\ LH(t), & mOFC_{diff}(t) < 0 \end{cases} \tag{6}$$

$$DRN(t) = G(t) * (mOFC(t) + mPFC(t)) \tag{7}$$

References

1. Miyazaki, K., Miyazaki, K.W., Doya, K.: Activation of dorsal raphe serotonin neurons underlies waiting for delayed rewards. J. Neurosci. **31**(2), 469–479 (2011)
2. Dayan, P., Huys, Q.J.M.: Serotonin, inhibition, and negative mood. PLoS Comput. Biol. **4**(2), e4 (2008)
3. Dorocic, I.P., Furth, D., Xuan, Y., Johansson, Y., Pozzi, L., Silberberg, G., Carlen, M., Meletis, K.: A whole-brain atlas of inputs to serotonergic neurons of the dorsal and median raphe nuclei. Neuron **83**, 663–678 (2014)
4. Sparta, D.R., Stuber, G.D.: Cartography of serotonergic circuits. Neuron **83**(3), 513–515 (2014)
5. Ranade, S.P., Mainen, Z.F.: Transient firing of dorsal raphe neurons encodes diverse and specific sensory, motor, and reward events. J. Neurophysiol. **102**(5), 3026–3037 (2009)
6. Nakamura, K., Ono, T.: Lateral hypothalamus neuron involvement in integration of natural and artificial rewards and cue signals. J. Neurophysiol. **55**(1), 163–181 (1986)
7. Sesack, S.R., Grace, A.A.: Cortico-basal ganglia reward network: microcircuitry. Neuropsychopharmacology **35**(1), 27–47 (2010). Official publication of the American College of Neuropsychopharmacology
8. Noonan, M.P., Kolling, N., Walton, M.E., Rushworth, M.F.S.: Re-evaluating the role of the orbitofrontal cortex in reward and reinforcement. Eur. J. Neurosci. **35**(7), 997–1010 (2012)
9. Humphries, M.D., Prescott, T.J.: The ventral basal ganglia, a selection mechanism at the crossroads of space, strategy, and reward. Progress Neurobiol. **90**(4), 385–417 (2010)
10. Van Bockstaele, E.J., Pickel, V.M.: GABA-containing neurons in the ventral tegmental area project to the nucleus accumbens in rat brain. Brain Res. **682**(1–2), 215–221 (1995)
11. Brog, J.S., Salyapongse, A., Deutch, A.Y., Zahm, D.S.: The patterns of afferent innervation of the core and shell in the 'accumbens' part of the rat ventral striatum. J. Comp. Neurol. **338**, 255–278 (1993)
12. Basar, K., Sesia, T., Groenewegen, H., Steinbusch, H.W.M., Visser-Vandewalle, V., Temel, Y.: Nucleus accumbens and impulsivity. Progress Neurobiol. **92**(4), 533–557 (2010)

13. Rajakumar, N., Elisevich, K., Flumerfelt, B.A.: Compartmental origin of the striato-entopeduncular projection in the rat. J. Comp. Neurol. **331**(2), 286–296 (1993)
14. Hong, S., Hikosaka, O.: The globus pallidus sends reward-related signals to the lateral habenula. Neuron **60**(4), 720–729 (2008)
15. Barrot, M., Sesack, S.R., Georges, F., Pistis, M., Hong, S., Jhou, T.C.: Braking dopamine systems: a new GABA master structure for mesolimbic and nigrostriatal functions. J. Neurosci. **32**(41), 14094–14101 (2012). The Official Journal of the Society for Neuroscience
16. Bourdy, R., Barrot, M.: A new control center for dopaminergic systems: Pulling the VTA by the tail. Trends Neurosci. **35**(11), 681–688 (2012)
17. Hoover, W.B., Vertes, R.P.: Projections of the medial orbital and ventral orbital cortex in the rat. J. Comp. Neurol. **519**(18), 3766–3801 (2011)
18. Homberg, J.R.: Serotonin and decision making processes. Neurosci. Biobehav. Rev. **36**(1), 218–236 (2012)
19. Juckel, G., Mendlin, A., Jacobs, B.L.: Electrical stimulation of rat medial prefrontal cortex enhances forebrain serotonin output: implications for electroconvulsive therapy and transcranial magnetic stimulation in depression. Neuropsychopharmacology **21**(3), 391–398 (1999)
20. Vertes, R.P., Linley, S.B.: Efferent, afferent connections of the dorsal, median raphe nuclei in the rat. In: Monti, J.M., Pandi-Perumal, S.R., Jacobs, B.L., Nutt, D.J. (eds.) Serotonin, Sleep: Molecular, Functional and Clinical Aspects. Birkhäuser, Switzerland (2008)
21. Nakamura, K., Matsumoto, M., Hikosaka, O.: Reward-dependent modulation of neuronal activity in the primate dorsal raphe nucleus. J. Neurosci. **28**(20), 5331–5343 (2008). The Official Journal of the Society for Neuroscience
22. Bromberg-Martin, E.S., Hikosaka, O., Nakamura, K.: Coding of task reward value in the dorsal raphe nucleus. J. Neurosci. **30**(18), 6262–6272 (2010). The Official Journal of the Society for Neuroscience
23. Cardinal, R.N.: Neural systems implicated in delayed and probabilistic reinforcement. Neural Netw. **19**, 1277–1301 (2006)
24. Evenden, J.: Impulsivity: a discussion of clinical and experimental findings. J. Psycopharmacology **13**(2), 180–192 (1999)
25. Nakamura, K.: The role of the doral raphe nucleus in reward-seeking behaviour. Front. Integr. Neurosci. 60 (2013)
26. Robinson, E.S.J., Dalley, J.W., Theobald, D.E.H., Glennon, J.C., Pezze, M.A., Murphy, E.R., Robbins, T.W.: Opposing roles for 5-HT2A and 5-HT2C receptors in the nucleus accumbens on inhibitory response control in the 5-choice serial reaction time task. Neuropsychopharmacology **33**(10), 27–47 (2010). Official Publication of the American College of Neuropsychopharmacology
27. Cools, R., Nakamura, K., Daw, N.D.: Serotonin and dopamine: unifying affective, activational, and decision functions. Neuropsychopharmacology **36**(1), 98–113 (2011). Official publication of the American College of Neuropsychopharmacology
28. Schulz, W., Dayan, P., Montague, P.R.: A neural substrate of prediction and reward. Science **275**, 1593–1599 (1997)
29. Seymour, B., Daw, N., Roiser, J., Dayan, P., Dolan, R.: Serotonin selectively modulates reward value in human decision-making. J. Neurosci. **32**(17), 5833–5842 (2012)

A Model of Artificial Genotype and Norm of Reaction in a Robotic System

Angel J. Duran$^{(\boxtimes)}$ and Angel P. del Pobil

Robotic Intelligence Lab, Universitat Jaume I, Castellon, Spain
{abosch,pobil}@uji.es

Abstract. The genes of living organisms serve as large stores of information for replicating their behavior and morphology over generations. The evolutionary view of genetics that has inspired artificial systems with a Mendelian approach does not take into account the interaction between species and with the environment to generate a particular phenotype. In this paper, a genotype model is suggested to shape the relationship with the phenotype and the environment in an artificial system. A method to obtain a genotype from a population of a particular robotic system is also proposed. Finally, we show that this model presents a similar behavior to that of living organisms in what regards the concept of norm of reaction.

Keywords: Bio-inspired · Genotype · Phenotype · Norm of reaction

1 Introduction

Nature has created a mechanism for transmission of information that allows organisms to improve throughout the process of evolution. This information is encoded in their genetic material. The way in which this information is decoded in living organisms can be considered from distinct abstraction levels. The low level regards the biochemistry and molecular reactions involved. Hence, a *gene* is a section of a threadlike double-helical molecule called deoxyribonucleic acid [6]. The genes dictate the inherited properties of a species and allelic variations cause hereditary variation within the species. The main elements of form in organisms are proteins. The main task of the living system is to convert the information contained in the DNA of genes into proteins [7].

A higher abstraction level considers how to connect the genetic information (genotype) stored in the DNA molecules with a specific characteristic of a living organism (phenotype). In the theoretical scheme proposed by evolutionary genetics, development is the function that maps the genotype onto the phenotype $(G \rightarrow P)$. It is known that the relationship genotype-phenotype is not one-to-one at the lowest levels. At higher levels of interaction, such as morphological traits, the genotype-phenotype relationship is even more complex [1]. Genes can not generate the structure of an organism by themselves. For a gene to have any influence on a phenotype it must act in concert with many other

E. Tuci et al. (Eds.): SAB 2016, LNAI 9825, pp. 267–279, 2016.
DOI: 10.1007/978-3-319-43488-9_24

genes and with the external and internal environment. Hence, the $G \to P$ map is really $G \xrightarrow{E} P$ (**GEP**) map. For an understanding of this concept it is fundamental to consider the role of phenotype plasticity and the idea of reaction norm, which are introduced as the basic link relating the three variables (**GEP**). *Phenotype plasticity* is the property of a given genotype to produce different phenotypes in response to distinct environmental conditions. The fundamental conceptual research tool in phenotypic plasticity is the idea of *norm of reaction* [10]. A norm of reaction is a function that relates the environments to which a particular genotype is exposed and the phenotypes that can be produced. In practice, such a tabulation can only be made for a partial genotype, a partial phenotype, and some particular aspects of the environment [6].

Frequently, this abstraction level has been used to model evolutionary behaviors in artificial systems. The $G \to P$ map is usually the basis of bio-inspired genetic algorithms (GAs). However, such algorithms have been more concerned with imitating the evolution process results in order to solve searching and optimization problems. Genetic algorithms emphasize the use of a "genotype" that is decoded and evaluated. These genotypes are often simple data structures [14]. Genetic algorithms are a simple form of evolutionary algorithms (EAs). These are composed of four components: a genotype, $G \to P$ mapping, a set of variation operators, and a user-defined function to be optimized, called a fitness function. The EAs are often classified as "black-box optimization algorithms" [3]. Overall, this kind of algorithms propose that, although evolution manifests itself as a succession of changes in a species' features, it is the changes in the genetic material that form the essence of evolution [13]. The main idea of these methods is based on the "genetic blueprint" or a "genetic programme". In other words, genes determine phenotypes. This sort of answer bypasses the process of development, which is treated as an incidental blackbox with no direct causal relevance to the evolutionary process [11]. From this point of view, changes in the species are produced by isolated changes in the individuals. In addition, the influence of the environment is limited to be used merely as a testbed to evaluate the phenotype fitness. Evolutionary Robotics (ER) proposes to employ EAs to design robots or, more often, control systems for robots.

Over millions of years of evolution, living organisms have adapted to different environments and have competed for survival, allowing them to improve their phenotypic attributes. From a conceptual standpoint, the information to generate living organisms has been transmitted in successive generations, improving and diversifying in each iteration and generating the particular attributes in each species. Nowadays, any species has the same common phenotype as a result of evolution because this information is transferred to the new members by inheritance. The species' individuals have differences which are usually morphological, but the main mechanism that accounts for these allelic differences is not mutation in genes, as in classical EAs.

The aim of this paper is to propose an artificial genotype data structure which generates a given phenotype conditioned by an environment. In particular, this work is focused on the way the species share functionalities using their genes.

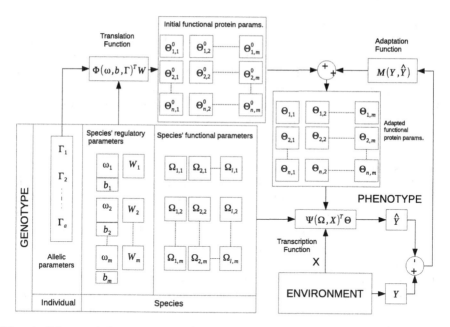

Fig. 1. Schema of the proposed genotype model and the relationship with the environment and phenotype

To evaluate the performance of this proposed artificial genotype, a "species" of robotic system is used. The artificial genotype for each species' individual is obtained and it is used to check the **GEP** model proposed. To do this, the reaction norm of the species' individuals is estimated. The proposed artificial genotype shows the same behavior that a biological genotype does in relation to phenotype plasticity.

2   Model

2.1   Genotype Model

The biochemical information stored in the DNA strings is converted in some way in living organisms with their anatomy, physiology and behaviors. In the proposed model, different types of information are defined according to the way this information is encoded in living organisms. The genotype model proposed transfers this information to a space parameters

- **Allelic Information.** It is the information stored in DNA which encode amino acids and proteins directly, so some phenotypes can be determined directly by this information. This information is encoded by *allelic parameters*: $\Gamma = \{\Gamma_1, \Gamma_2, ..., \Gamma_a\} \mid \Gamma \in \mathbb{R}^a$, where a is the number of encoded allels.

– **Species' Regulatory Information.** It is related to information stored in DNA which does not encode amino acids directly, but is shared by all individuals of the species. This kind of data is encoded by the *species' regulatory parameters*(SRP). There are two kind of SRP parameters: the first class is the *regulatory parameters of transcription function*: $\mathbf{W} = \{\mathbf{W}_1, \mathbf{W}_2, ..., \mathbf{W}_m,\} \mid W_i \in \mathbb{R}^t$ where t is the number of combinations of the encoded proteins from allelic genes, to encode a functional protein. The second class is the *combination parameters from allelic and species' regulatory information*: $\omega = \{\omega_1, \omega_2, ..., \omega_m\} \mid \omega_i \in \mathbb{R}^{a,t}$, $b = \{b_1, b_2, ..., b_n\} \mid b_i \in \mathbb{R}^t$.

– **Species' Functional Information.** It is the information encoded in DNA which is transformed into specific species' phenotypes. The function of this information is regulatory and regards the control of the functional combination of synthesized proteins from allelic information which is encoded by the *species' functional parameters* (SFP): $\Omega \in \mathbb{R}^{l,m}$, where l is the number of the environment modifiers and m is the number of proteins which adjust the obtained phenotype.

– **Functional Protein Configuration.** It is a sequence of proteins that are obtained from the translation function and regulatory species information. These proteins represent a certain phenotype which can be modified by the environment. This kind of information is transferred into parametric space: *initial functional protein parameters* (FPP^0), these parameters represents the initial proteins synthesized from species' genes, but they are going to be modified by the interaction with the environment. $\Theta^0 = \{\Theta_1^0, \Theta_2^0, ..., \Theta_m^0\} \mid \Theta_i^0 \in \mathbb{R}^n$ where n is the number of parameters that define a phenotype. The successive modified sets of functional parameters depend on the consecutive environments where the individual has been adapted. This kind of parameters are named *adapted functional protein parameters*: $\Theta = \{\Theta_1, \Theta_2, ..., \Theta_m\} \mid \Theta_i^0 \in \mathbb{R}^n$ where n is the number of parameters that define a phenotype.

2.2   GEP Mapping Model

So far, we have encoded the information stored in DNA in a parametric space. The parameter space defined above can be considered as a data structure. Several operations can be established for modeling GEP mapping (Fig. 1). Hence, a species' individual has got a genotype defined by the previous structure. One part is specific for this individual (allelic information). In the biological case, this information is represented by allelic genes which can be converted into proteins. The transcription of one gene may be turned on or off by other genes called regulatory genes [6]. In the proposed system, this transcription process is modelled by the *transcription function* (Eq. 1).

$$\Theta^0 = \Phi(\omega, b, \Gamma)^T W \tag{1}$$

In a mathematical way, the transcription function is a regression model that relates the allelic information with initial functional parameters. The SRP fit this model and represent the information shared with every member of this species that accounts for the phenotypic behavior.

Furthermore, proteins encoded by one gene may modify the proteins encoded by a second gene in order to activate or deactivate protein function. The equivalent of the latter proteins are the SFP in the proposed model. These proteins can also be modified by the environment through signal transduction. Moreover, proteins encoded by one gene may bind to proteins from other genes to form an active complex that performs some function. This is modeled by a *transduction function*.

$$\hat{Y} = \Psi(\Omega, X)^T \Theta \tag{2}$$

This function finally generates a phenotype. From a mathematical point of view, the transduction function is a recursive regression model, where there are some input cues (X) that are combined with common fixed parameters (Ω) into a nonlinear function Ψ for all the species individuals and the regression parameters are Θ.

So far, the environment adaptation has not been considered. In 1930, Ronald A. Fisher emphasized [4] that adaptation is characterized by the movement of a population towards a phenotype that best fits the present environment. However, this evolution is produced by changes in the individuals in this population. In the proposed model, this is considered in the *adaptation function*.

$$\Theta_e = \Theta_{e-1} + M(Y, \hat{Y}) \tag{3}$$

where e is the number of interacting successive environments. This equation has to accomplish these limit restraints: when $e = 0 \rightarrow \Theta_e = \Theta^0$ and the difference between $\Theta_e - \Theta_{e-1}$ has to tend to zero. The value Y is the optimal phenotype and $\hat{Y}$ is the current individual phenotype.

Equation 3 expresses a sequence of changes in functional proteins modifying the phenotype showed by the individual. The motor for these changes is the gap between the optimal phenotype and the current phenotype expressed in a functional way in the adaptation function. This had been defined as a first degree dynamic system where its initial condition is defined by the initial functional protein parameters. When the individual is adapted the gap between Y and $\hat{Y}$ has to be minimum (Θ_e^*). Once in this point, there might be another adaptation stage for the individual, so Θ_e^* generates epigenetic changes in SRP. This changes are propagated to the descendants improving Θ^0 estimation. From an information point of view, the environment adaptation is a learning procedure whose goal is to learn the environment model to better predict the response to environmental cues.

3   Case Study

3.1   The Robot Species Description

Of course, the genotype for a robotic system is not defined as a biological system, but from an information point of view the model **GEP** can be considered valid for a robot. In this case, the environment is the part of the universe with which the robot interacts, i.e. it receives information through its sensors and modifies it using its actuators. The phenotype comprises not only its morphology but also its behavior. The genotype as defined above is composed of the allelic information, which are the parameters or design variables of the robot, and the information concerning the species. This last point is a critical question because it is not usual to work with the concept of species in robotics. Two robots belong to the same "species" if they have the same number of design variables and show a similar behavior in a similar environment.

Let us consider a species composed of robot heads. We have selected this species because it presents sensor and actuators to interact with the environment. These sensors and actuators may be different between individuals from the same species. However, this species can show a behavior that is shared by all its individuals, namely saccadic movements. This species is characterized for having two cameras and 3 DOF. One of them for each camera and the other shared. The morphological traits can be described from a robotics point of view as a Denavit-Hartenberg model (Table 1). In addition, the sensor traits, are modelled by the pinhole scheme. So each camera has several characteristics: focal length, pixel size (supposed squared), height and width image resolution. Therefore, the design parameters, which are individual traits into the same species, are defined by $a = 16$ values. This information corresponds to allelic information in the proposed genotype model ($\Gamma \in \mathbb{R}^{16}$). The genotype-phenotype mapping of this allelic information is directly the morphology and sensor properties of each individual in the species and it is not dependent on the environment (Fig. 2).

If other complex phenotypes are defined for every individual of this species, for example, the ability to execute saccadic movements, the environment must be considered. A saccade is a fast eye movement that shifts the gaze to a target point and can be used to scan the visual space [2]. We will focus on the transformation that links the visual position of a stimulus into a target position of the eyes, as well as on *feedback error learning* (FEL) as described in [8]. In this method, there are two inverse controllers. A fixed controller (**B**) that slowly drives the system toward the target and provides a learning signal to a second adaptive

Table 1. Denavit-Hartenberg model of the left side of the head. ρ_p, ρ_t are the revolute joints of the pan and common tilt motors. The right side is the same model and it shares the ρ_t joint

Joint	ρ (rad)	r (m)	a (m)	α (rad)	Offset	Type
q_1	ρ_t	0	0	$\pi/2$	$\pi/2$	R
q_2	0	0	0	$-\pi/2$	0	P
q_3	$\pi/2$	0.055	0	$\pi/2$	0	P
q_4	$\pi/2$	0.055	0	$\pi/2$	0	P
q_5	ρ_p	0	0	$\pi/2$	π	R
q_6	0	0.01	0	$\pi/2$	0	P

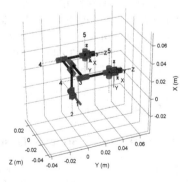

Fig. 2. Example of the head model

controller (C_f). In this case, the phenotype is quantified by the gaze point after a saccade. If the projection of the gaze point were in the center of the two images, the phenotype would be optimal. Therefore, the gap for the adaptation function is the difference between these gaze points.

3.2   The Environment

The environment is a spatial region around the robot head. A virtual object is randomly placed in the vision field of the two robot cameras. This object is static related to the robot frame. To assure that these points cam be watched by the two cameras at the same time, the environment region has been generated from the minimal and maximum tilt, version and vergence angles of the heads. For this reason the resulting region is not regular and the geometrical centroid point is used to represent this spatial region.

3.3   Applying the GEP Model to the Robotic System

To match the **GEP** model with the robot species proposed, it is necessary to identify the transcription, activation and adaptation function. In the proposed case, to adapt the saccadic behavior to the environment, the robot must learn how it has to change the cameras position to gaze the object. The environment transduction cues are the projection of the visual stimulus in the robot camera images. They, combined with the proprioception of the robot, must generate the saccadic behavior. The transduction function is really the system controller. If the robotic system had perfectly adapted to the environment, the projection of the visual point in the images of the cameras would be in the center, exactly. So the distance between the real projection to the image center could be considered as a gap between the optimal phenotype and the showed phenotype. In the **GEP** proposed model, the system controller represented by a transduction function is modified by an adaptation function depending on the phenotype gap, so the proposed system controller represented by a transduction function is really an adaptive controller.

   In the proposed FEL model [2] for one robot, there are two controllers, a fixed one (**B**) and adaptive (**C**$_f$), both contributions are the system controller. As **B** is independent of the environment, it is possible to apply the $G \rightarrow P$ model and **B** can be estimated from allelic information (Γ), directly. The **C**$_f$ controller is implemented by a single-layer neural network, with 7 inputs and 3 outputs. The environment cues are defined by these seven inputs ($l = 7$). Gaussian activations using random space features [12] were used for the hidden layer. If these random space features are the same for every species' individual, they are the species' functional parameters (Ω), because they regulate the phenotype function. The weights in this network combine the activation functions, as the transduction function is modified by functional proteins parameters in the proposed model, hence these weights are Θ. The dimensions of Θ are the number of units in the hidden layer (n) and the number of outputs (m). The adaptation function is equivalent to adapt the weights in the neural network. In [2] the incremental sparse spectrum Gaussian process regression (I-SSGPR) is used.

Finally, the transcription function is another regression model that relates the allelic information with the initial functional parameters (Θ^0). Hence, the regression parameters can be obtained if Γ and Θ^0 are known. The problem is to fix the Θ^0 value for each individual in the species.

3.4 Getting the Robot Genotype

Thus, if a population of robots from the same species is forced to adapt to the same environment and to develop the same behavior, the shared information that defines the behavior of all the species individuals can be extracted. To do this:

1. A robot population is generated, changing their allelic information. The SRP and FPP^0 are initialized randomly but they are the same for all the members of the species.
2. Each individual is immersed into the same environment and it is forced to adapt to get Θ_e^* from (Eq. 3):

$$\frac{dM(\mathbf{Y}, \hat{Y})}{de} \approx 0 \rightarrow \Theta_e = \Theta_e^* \tag{4}$$

3. With the Θ_e^* value for each individual and their allelic information, the transcription function is converted into a regression problem where its parameters are the SRP. A fixed environment is used to obtain these parameters. The species individuals will adapt quickly in similar environments and slowlier in different ones

4   Experimental Results

To validate the model fitting to a population of robots, the shared information by every individual of this population must be known. In the living organism, this information is encoded in DNA, but in robots, we have to set up an environment, a behavior and an allelic encoded morphology for each individual in order to get that shared information.

Once we have the species genotype model, we must check if this model shows the same performance that the living organisms. That is, when an individual's genotype is completely defined and it is placed in different environments, the phenotype has to be changed according to the norm of reaction.

4.1   Generating a Population of Robots

A robot model was used to simulate different robot head setups (44271 individuals were generated) with allelic information as described in the previous section. A reasonable interval is fixed to avoid infeasible configurations. The values of

Table 2. Design parameters to generate the allelic information

Prismatic joints (cm)	
Left size	Right side
$\Gamma^p_{i,1} = q_2 \in [-0.054, 0.054]$	$\Gamma^p_{i,2} = q_2 = \Gamma^p_{i,1} + [0, 0.01]$
$\Gamma^p_{i,3} = q_3 \in [0, 0.07]$	$\Gamma^p_{i,4} = q_3 = \Gamma^p_{i,3} + [0.035, 0.07]$
$\Gamma^p_{i,5} = q_4 \in [-0.02, 0.054]$	$\Gamma^p_{i,6} = q_4 = \Gamma^p_{i,5} + [0, 0.02]$
$\Gamma^p_{i,7} = q_6 \in [0, 0.01]$	$\Gamma^p_{i,8} = q_6 = \Gamma^p_{i,7} + [0, 0.01]$
Cameras parameters: f(px); s(m/px); w(px); h(px)	
Left camera	Right camera
$\Gamma^p_{i,9} = f_l \in [340, 1920]$	$\Gamma^p_{i,10} = f_r = \Gamma^p_{i,9} + [0, 200]$
$\Gamma^p_{i,11} = s_l \in [3. \ 10^{-6}, 7. \ 10^{-6}]$	$\Gamma^p_{i,12} = s_r \in [3. \ 10^{-6}, 7. \ 10^{-6}]$
$\Gamma^p_{i,13} = h_l \in [340, 1920]$	$\Gamma^p_{i,14} = h_r = \Gamma^p_{i,13} + [0, 200]$
$\Gamma^p_{i,15} = w_l \in [340, 1920]$	$\Gamma^p_{i,16} = w_r = \Gamma^p_{i,15} + [0, 200]$
if $\Gamma^p_{i,13} > \Gamma^p_{i,15}$, swap($\Gamma^p_{i,13}, \Gamma^p_{i,15}$)	if $\Gamma^p_{i,14} > \Gamma^p_{i,16}$, swap($\Gamma^p_{i,14}, \Gamma^p_{i,16}$)

the left side of the head are chosen randomly and the right side is defined in a random interval as shown in Table 2.

The generated population is split into three groups: (i) Adaptation group (26500 individuals). This group is used to get an estimation of the transcription function because there is no knowledge about the species regulatory parameters. (ii) Control group (4500 individuals). This group is used to validate the species regulatory parameters obtained from the adaptation group. (iii) Control population (13271 individuals). This group is used to validate the obtained genotype.

4.2 Getting the Genotype Model from the Generated Population of Robots

Each of the individuals in the adaptation group, that were generated previously, is immersed in the same environment and it starts the adaptation process interacting with this environment. The FPP^0 are zero for all individuals because there is no previous information. The SFP are randomly initialized, however they are shared by all the species individuals. Hence, all of them show the same initial degree of adaptation to this environment. The result of this adaptation process is a set of pairs of allelic information (Γ) and Θ^*_c (Eq. 4).

From a robotics point of view, the used neural network controller has the same value for the initial weights (zero) for all training cases. In addition, a unique set of random sparse features are generated for all neural network controllers. Each robot setup is trained with the same environment using the same neural network parameters tuned previously [5]: variance of the model ($\sigma^2_n = 0.1$), signal variance ($\sigma^2_f = 1.0$) and number of projections (m = 300) so the number of neural centers is 600. With these parameters the mathematical dimensions of the proposed genotype are defined as: $\Gamma \in \mathbb{R}^{16}$ and $\Omega \in \mathbb{R}^{3,300}$. The FPP^0

are $\Theta \in \mathbb{R}^{3,600}$. The results of this process are the neural network weights for each robotic head setup that allow the robot head to generate saccadic movements. In Fig. 3a, there is an example of how the phenotype changes with each adaptation. The relationship between the allelic and the species' regulatory information connect the particular traits of an individual with specific traits of the species. After the environment adaptation described previously, a set of allelic information, and species' functional parameters are defined along with a valid set of initial functional protein parameters for each individual. As it is shown in (Eq. 1), the transcription function is a regression model. Hence, it is possible to use any regression method to estimate the parameters (ω, b, Γ). The challenge is to solve the dimensional problem. In particular, the mapping from Γ (16 dimensions) to Θ (1800 dimensions). Fortunately, due to the fact that the weights of a trained network are independent among them, the regression problem can be decomposed into multiple smaller regression problems. Each Θ_i is influenced by Γ independently of the rest of Γ. The problem is transformed into

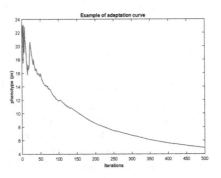

(a) Example of adaptation curve

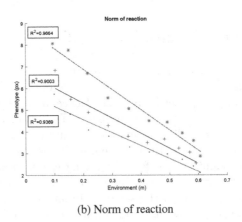

(b) Norm of reaction

Fig. 3. (a) Example of adaptation curve (b) Norm of reaction

solving $1800 = (3 \times 600$ dimensions of Θ) small regression problems. In this way, the SRP are the set of parameters of each regression. The regression tool used is a MLP neural network with 16 inputs, 10 units in the hidden layer and one output. The hyperbolic tangent function was used for the hidden layer and the output layer was linear. The algorithm to train each network was the scaled conjugate gradient descent (SCG) [9]. The performance follows from comparing the weights obtained after training the adaptive controller and those estimated by the neural network stack. The training result for the adaptation group has a mean square error equal to $(2.19 \pm 0.43)10^{-4}$. In this way the SRP are 1800 matrices and vectors: $\omega \in \mathbb{R}^{16,10}$, $b \in \mathbb{R}^{10}$ and $W \in \mathbb{R}^{10}$.

The result of this procedure is a set of 44500 individuals with their own allelic information that generates different traits in the same species. Hence, there are 44500 different genotypes, but every individual has the same SRP and SFP characterized by Ω and (ω, b, Γ).

4.3   The Genotypes' Norm of Reaction

For each individual in the species, one artificial genotype is defined. When the individual is placed in a distribution of environments, a distribution of phenotypes results. This relationship is regulated by the norm of reaction. Therefore, each individual in the control population is characterized by its norm of reaction. The defined environment is a spatial region in front of the robotic system, so one way to create a distribution of environments is to displace this region in one axis direction. Then, the robot system is placed in each environment. The FPP^0 are generated with the allelic information and SRP from its artificial genotype using the transcription function. The robot interacts with the environment using the transduction function and the SFP parameters from its artificial genotype and it adapts to the environment using the adaptation function. The phenotype is measured in this case study as the mean distance to the centers of images. Finally, a set of pairs of phenotype (distance in pixels) and environment variations (exploration space distance in meters) is obtained. For the sake of clarity, we randomly selected three individuals from the control group and we represent the obtained pairs of values PE (Fig. 3b). It can be observed that there is a linear correlation. The mean squared correlation coefficient for the control group is $R^2 = (0.930 \pm 0.034)$ for linear regression of their norms of reaction.

5   Discussion

Figure 3b shows three examples of the proposed genotype model. These samples represent three robotic systems from the same species which show a specific phenotype after an adaptation process using the explained model. These results are similar for every robot in the control group, as the value of R^2 shows. Beyond the shape of the curves, this experiment shows: (i) The proposed genotype model is able to show different behaviors (different curves) for each individual robotic system. (ii) The relationship between environments and phenotype can be handled (linearly in this case) by the proposed model. (iii) For a species individual with its genotype, we obtained different phenotypes in response to distinct environmental conditions, in a certain way, phenotype plasticity is achieved by the proposed model. This differs from classical models used in genetic and evolutionary algorithms, which only consider allelic information for determining an individual's phenotype. This is a key point due to the fact that the plasticity of a robot system is achieved without changing the individual genotype.

6   Conclusions

We proposed an artificial genotype model based on the **GEP** relationship that exists in living organisms. To do this, we extracted the common information from all the individuals in a species and then we used it to define their genotypes by mixing it with the specific individual differences (allelic information). The obtained result is equivalent to norm of reaction behavior in living organisms. Therefore, the proposed model of genotype is able to behave as a biological genotype in relation to phenotype and environment. In the case study, the norm of reaction is able to generate phenotypic plasticity as in living organisms. We tested this artificial genotype in a robot system estimating the species parameters and generating norm of reaction curves similar to those obtained by biologists for living organisms.

Acknowledgements. This paper describes research done at the UJI Robotic Intelligence Laboratory. Support for this laboratory is provided in part by Ministerio de Economía y Competitividad (DPI2015-69041-R), by Generalitat Valenciana (PROMETEOII/2014/028) and by Universitat Jaume I (P1-1B2014-52, PREDOC/2013/06).

References

1. Alberch, P.: From genes to phenotype: dynamical systems and evolvability. Genetica **84**(1), 5–11 (1991)
2. Antonelli, M., Duran, A.J., Chinellato, E., del Pobil, A.P.: Learning the visual-oculomotor transformation: effects on saccade control and space representation. Robot. Auton. Syst. **71**, 13–22 (2015)
3. Doncieux, S., Mouret, J.B.: Beyond black-box optimization: a review of selective pressures for evolutionary robotics. Evol. Intell. **7**(2), 71–93 (2014)
4. Fisher, R.A.: The Genetical Theory of Natural Selection: a Complete, variorum edn. Oxford University Press, Oxford (1930)
5. Gijsberts, A., Metta, G.: Real-time model learning using incremental sparse spectrum Gaussian process regression. Neural Netw. **41**, 59–69 (2013)
6. Griffiths, A.: An Introduction to Genetic Analysis, 8th edn. W.H. Freeman, New York (2005)
7. Griffiths, A.: Introduction to Genetic Analysis, 10th edn. W.H. Freeman, New York (2008)
8. Kawato, M.: Feedback-error-learning neural network for supervised motor learning. In: Eckmiller, R. (ed.) Advanced Neural Computers, pp. 365–372. Elsevier, North-Holland (1990)

9. Møller, M.F.: A Scaled Conjugate Gradient Algorithm for Fast Supervised Learning Supervised Learning. Neural Netw. **6**, 525–533 (1993)
10. Pigliucci, M.: Phenotypic Plasticity: Beyond Nature and Nurture. JHU Press, Baltimore (2001)
11. Pigliucci, M.: Genotype–phenotype mapping and the end of the 'genes as blueprint' metaphor. Philos. Trans. R. Soc. Lond. B Biol. Sci. **365**(1540), 557–566 (2010)
12. Rahimi, A., Recht, B.: Random features for large-scale kernel machines. In: Advances in Neural Information Processing Systems, pp. 1177–1184 (2007)
13. Srinivas, M., Patnaik, L.M.: Genetic algorithms: a survey. Computer **27**(6), 17–26 (1994)
14. Whitley, D., Sutton, A.M.: Genetic algorithms – a survey of models and methods. In: Rozenberg, G., Bäck, T., Kok, J.N. (eds.) Handbook of Natural Computing, pp. 637–671. Springer, Heidelberg (2012)

Abstraction as a Mechanism to Cross the Reality Gap in Evolutionary Robotics

Kirk Y.W. Scheper[✉] and Guido C.H.E. de Croon

Micro Air Vehicle Laboratory,
Delft University of Technology, 2629 Delft, The Netherlands
k.y.w.scheper@tudelft.nl

Abstract. One of the major challenges of Evolutionary Robotics is to transfer robot controllers evolved in simulation to robots in the real world. In this article, we investigate abstraction on the sensory inputs and motor actions as a potential solution to this problem. Abstraction means that the robot uses preprocessed sensory inputs and closed loop low-level controllers that execute higher level motor commands. We apply abstraction to the task of forming an asymmetric triangle with a homogeneous swarm of MAVs. The results show that the evolved behavior is effective both in simulation and reality, suggesting that abstraction can be a useful tool in making evolved behavior robust to the reality gap. Furthermore, we study the evolved solution, showing that it exploits the environment (in this case the identical behavior of the other robots) and creates behavioral attractors resulting in the creation of the required formation. Hence, the analysis suggests that by using abstraction, sensory-motor coordination is not necessarily lost but rather shifted to a higher level of abstraction.

1 Introduction

Evolutionary Robotics (ER) is a field of research which uses Evolutionary Computation techniques to solve robotic tasks without explicit interaction from a human designer. This approach requires a roboticist to define the problem to be solved and the evolutionary optimization determines the behavior required solve it. Early work in this field made quick progress showing that ER could automatically solve tasks such as: obstacle avoidance [10], phototaxis [11] and chemotaxis [2]. Work was not restricted to the evolution of the brain but was also used to evolve the physical body of the robot in a form of co-evolution [4,17]. A comprehensive overview of this early work in ER can be found in the book from Nolfi et al. [21].

Despite this early sprint, the pace of development slowed as researchers attempted more complex tasks. Some of the major challenges encountered include the reality gap, reducing optimization time, fitness function design and behavior representation [3]. Although all these issues must be addressed for ER to be truly successful, in this paper we would like to address the reality gap.

© Springer International Publishing Switzerland 2016
E. Tuci et al. (Eds.): SAB 2016, LNAI 9825, pp. 280–292, 2016.
DOI: 10.1007/978-3-319-43488-9_25

ER typically utilizes simulated environments to evaluate the performance of generated candidate solutions. Although these faster-than-real-time simulations reduce the total optimization time, differences between simulation and reality often result in reduced performance in reality when compared to that seen in simulation. This difference is referred to as the *reality gap*.

The apparent coupling seen between the perceived environment and emergent behavior that causes this reality gap is partly the result of Sensory-Motor Coordination(SMC). This inherent coupling of perception and action with embodied agents results in the observation that an agent can actively influence the perceived environment through its actions [20]. Typical implementations of ER utilize raw sensor inputs to generate low level control commands to the robotic platform. This approach has been shown to be effective in the development of behavior which can solve non-trivial tasks with SMC [1,20]. The evolved SMC will exploit the properties of the low-level sensors and motor actions in the simulated environment. Unfortunately, these properties in general are quite different from those of the real robotic platform, causing a significant reality gap.

Much progress has been made towards solving the reality gap problem most notably by Jakobi et al. [15], Koos et al. [16] and Eiben et al. [8]. Jakobi suggests hiding unnecessary features of the simulation in noise through *minimal simulations*. Koos includes the transferability of the robotic behavior to the agent's fitness evaluated by intermittently testing the simulated behavior on real robots during evolution. Eiben promotes on-line embodied evolution on a swarm of real robotic platforms to remove the reality gap altogether. Some recent work has also suggested that improved insight into the optimized behavior can enable the roboticist to actively reduce the reality gap after optimization [24].

One method which has not been investigated in much detail is the use of *abstraction* to make the robotic control more robust to the reality gap. Generally, real robotic platforms are controlled using closed loop control systems. These systems receive a desired set-point as input and drive the output to reduce the perceived error. Closed loop control has been mathematically proven to make the eventual control system more robust to external disturbances or changes to the environment [18]. With the use of a closed loop low-level control system, evolution would abstract away from the low-level sensor inputs and actuator outputs. Some resent work has shown promising results in bridging the reality gap using abstracted methods [5,7]. This however may come at a price, as abstraction "hides" the properties of the raw sensory inputs and motor actions to the controller, it may have as a disadvantage that the potential for SMC by the robot is reduced.

In this paper we investigate whether abstraction can lead to an easy transfer of an evolved robot controller from simulation to the real world. Moreover, we look into the open question of how abstraction affects the ability of the robot to exploit its environment to solve a seemingly complex task. What happens to SMC when the agent doesn't have access to the raw sensor inputs and the ability to directly control the raw motor outputs?

Fig. 1. Swarm of homogeneous ARDrone 2 quadrotors autonomously used to form an asymmetric triangle using evolved behavior.

To investigate this we implement an experiment based on the work of Izzo et al. [14] to generate an asymmetric formation of a swarm of robots using a homogeneous control system. The task will be discussed in more detail in Sect. 2. The implementation and results of the evolutionary optimization of the robotic behavior is presented in Sect. 3. A brief description of the flight hardware shown in Fig. 1 is given in Sect. 4 followed by a discussion of the behavior on a swarm of real flying robots in Sect. 5. Section 6 dives a bit deeper into the optimized behavior and the effect of abstraction on the SMC. Finally, we summarize and make some conclusions in Sect. 7.

2   Task

In this paper we would like to demonstrate the power of using high level control cues with an underlying closed loop control system to reduce the reality gap. The use of closed loop control systems helps to reject disturbances due to noise or small a mismatches between the dynamics in simulation and that in reality.

To this end we have selected the asymmetric formation flight as demonstrated in simulation by Izzo et al. [14]. That paper described a homogeneous swarm of three SPHERES spacecraft flying in a triangular formation where each side was a different length. Methods have been developed to autonomously form symmetric formations using homogeneous swarms but asymmetric shapes have proven to be more difficult [13]. The design of asymmetric formations using a distributed control system without explicit roles in the formation is a non-trival task for most human designers making it an ideal task for automatic optimization.

The work of Izzo et al. was confined to a simulated environment, in this paper we would like to move to reality to demonstrate the effect of abstraction on crossing the reality gap. Due to the lack of availability of the SPHERES vehicles on the International Space Station, the formation control is implemented on a swarm of Micro Air Vehicles (MAVs). Notably, we constrain the problem to two dimensions to facilitate a more straightforward analysis of the resultant behavior.

The goal of the swarm will be to achieve an asymmetric triangular formation with sides of lengths: 0.7, 0.9 and 1.3 m. The MAVs can observe the relative

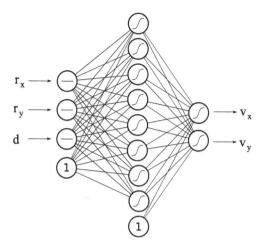

Fig. 2. Single hidden layer Neural Network topology used in this paper. Inputs are the summed Cartesian components of the relative positions to the other vehicles in the formation (**r**) along with the summed absolute distances (*d*).

position of all other members in the formation. The control system should use this information and provide the MAV with a velocity set-point. As in [14], we utilize a single hidden layer Artificial Neural Network (ANN) with three inputs and two outputs as shown in Fig. 2. A *tanh* activation function was used in the neurons. Additionally, a bias neuron is added to the input and hidden layer. The output of the network can be linearly scaled to the limits of the vehicle, which in the case of this paper was set as ± 0.5 m/s. The inputs, outputs and ranges of all parameters were chosen to be as similar to the original values used by Izzo et al. [14] to facilitate a fair comparison of our results with the original work.

The inputs to the ANN are the sum of the Cartesian components of the relative positions of the other members of the formation (**r**) and the sum of absolute distances (d) as given by (1) and (2). Note that **r** is mathematically equivalent to triple the distance from the ownship to the centroid of the formation (**c**).

$$\mathbf{r} = \sum_{i=2}^{k} (\mathbf{p}_i - \mathbf{p}_1) \tag{1}$$

$$d = \sum_{i=2}^{k} |\mathbf{p}_i - \mathbf{p}_1| \tag{2}$$

Where **p** is the position vector of a vehicle and k is the total number of vehicles in the swarm. These inputs are computed for each vehicle where $\mathbf{p}_1$ is the ownship location. Figure 3 illustrates a possible solution to the formation problem. Combining the positions of the other vehicles in this way is essential to ensure the input is invariant to permutations of the vehicles. Adding a separate input for each vehicle would implicitly encode a unique formation identifier for

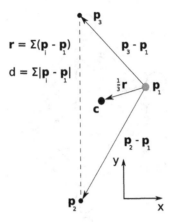

$$r = \Sigma(\mathbf{p}_i - \mathbf{p}_1)$$

$$d = \Sigma|\mathbf{p}_i - \mathbf{p}_1|$$

Fig. 3. Illustration of a possible formation. Vehicles are represented by a filled dot with the ownship in this example highlighted.

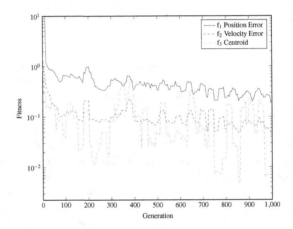

Fig. 4. Progression of the performance of the best individual during evolution validated using 250 initialization points.

each vehicle. Additionally, only the relative positions are required for the input rather than the absolute position, this would facilitate a wide range of real world sensors to be used to provide this information. It should be noted that as this input is from the point of view of each vehicle, a given set of inputs describes a unique formation and is not rotationally invariant.

3   Evolutionary Optimization

There are many forms of evolutionary optimization in literature but they all have a few things in common: a population of candidate solutions; a measure

of fitness; a way of evaluating the individuals on this fitness function; and a
method to change individuals to create the next population [9]. In this paper,
we use a population of 100 candidate solutions expressed as ANNs. The fitness of
an individual is determined with the use of a multi-objective sorting algorithm
based on Nondominated Sorting Genetic Algorithm II (NSGA-II) [6]. Multiple
objective optimization was used to promote effective exploration of the fitness
landscape. Again, to facilitate a fair comparison, the objective functions used in
this paper are based on those used in [14] and are given in (3).

$$f_1 = \sum_{n=1}^{3} |L_n - l_n|$$

$$f_2 = \sum_{n=1}^{3} |\mathbf{v}_n|^2 \qquad (3)$$

$$f_3 = \begin{cases} 0, & |\mathbf{c}| < 2 \\ 1, & \text{else} \end{cases}$$

Where $\mathbf{L}$ is the vector of the required distances, l is the vector of the distances
between the vehicles at the end of the simulation sorted in ascending order.
Sorting the distances makes the computation of the fitness it invariant to the
vehicle order. $\mathbf{v}$ is the velocity vector of the MAV at the end of the simulation
and $\mathbf{c}$ is the location of the centroid of the triangle. The first fitness function
tries to have the MAVs end up in the correct formation. The second promotes
individuals that have a low final velocity. The final function is an augmentation
to the original set from [14] and promotes behavior that results in the centroid of
the formation remaining inside of a 2 m radius of the origin of the axis system.
This requirement was added due to the practical limitation that the vehicles
must operate in a constrained 8×8 m flight arena.

A simulation was used to assign a fitness to the candidate solutions. A simple
Euler integration based kinematic simulation was implemented to ensure that
computational requirements of each simulation would remain low, speeding up
the optimization. This simulator captures the approximate kinematics of the
real MAVs with a simple low pass filtered velocity response with a time constant
determined by performing real world flight tests. Each simulation was initialized
with the three MAVs at a stand still at random locations in a 2×2 m area with
at least 1 m separating each vehicle and the centroid of the initial orientation
located at the origin of the axis system. The vehicles were then allowed to traverse
the room in the $x - y$ plane for a maximum of 50 s. The simulation can be
prematurely terminated if the MAVs come within 30 cm of each other as this
would constitute a collision on the real vehicles. At the end of the simulation
run, the final position and speed of the MAVs is used to assign a value to each
fitness function as given in (3).

Once the population is evaluated, they are sorted using the NSGA-II algorithm. The best individuals are stored in an archive of 100 members. This archive
is also used as the mating pool which is used to generate the population of the
next generation. Members are selected from the mating pool using a tournament

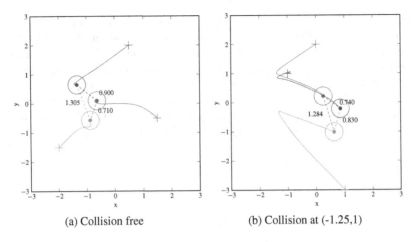

(a) Collision free   (b) Collision at (-1.25,1)

Fig. 5. Ground tracks of a collision free flight and a flight that would have ended in a collision of three ARDrones performing the asymmetric formation task. The length of each side is shown in text, + marks the start location and the circle with the dot in the center marks the end location with the diameter of the vehicle to scale.

selection technique with a size of 8 randomly selected members from the mating pool and the best individual averaged over all fitness dimensions returned as a champion. Mutation was the only evolutionary operator used in this paper as some works have shown that mutation only evolution to be effective [25]. Each weight in the ANN was considered for mutation with a probability of 5%. Mutation consisted of a random perturbation of the previous value by selecting a new value based on statistical acceptance based on the previous value constrained on the range $[-1,1]$.

Figure 4 shows the performance of the best individual from each generation of the evolutionary optimization for this problem. Each individual was evaluated using 250 different combinations of initial conditions with a maximum simulation time of 50 s. This figure shows that evolution gradually reduces the error in the final vehicle distances and the final velocity. This figure also shows that the behavior does not guarantee a collision free flight for all initial conditions. After 1000 generations the average error of each side of the formation is about 5 cm.

The member with the lowest average score over the three fitness functions from the last generation of the evolutionary optimization was selected for further analysis and implementation on the real swarm of three MAVs. Here we will first analyze the behavior exhibited by the ANN controller to gain some insight into the solution to the problem.

The behavior was evaluated by a validation run of 250 different initial conditions. During the validation run, the simulation was not cut short if a collision occurred. A formation is considered accurate when the summed error of the lengths is below 0.15 m or 5 cm average error. The results show that 98% of runs resulted in a successful triangle formation within 50 s of which 14% would have incurred a crash. Of these successful runs, the mean error was 0.0222 m with a standard deviation of 0.0262. In 2 % of the runs the triangle was not formed within 50 s. Figure 5 shows one of the successful runs of the formation behavior and one case where a collision would have occurred.

4   Flight Hardware

The flight tests performed in this paper were conducted using the 420g Parrot ARDrone 2 quadrotor MAV. This vehicle is equipped with a 1 GHz 32 bit ARM Cortex A8 processor running an embedded Linux operating system [22]. The default flight software provided by Parrot was overwritten by custom flight software implemented using Paparazzi, an open-source flight control software [12,23].

5   Flight Tests Results

Moving from the simulated environment to the real world, the behavior shown above was implemented on a swarm of three ARDrones. Flights were performed in an 8×8 m flight arena and the flight path of the vehicles was captured using an Optitrack motion camera system [19]. The position of all vehicles were broadcast at 5 Hz so all vehicles know the relative position of the other swarm members. For the first set of tests, as in simulation, the three vehicles were initialized at random in a 3 × 3 m area in the flight arena with the centroid of the initial formation at the origin of the arena. Figure 6 shows the result of one test performed.

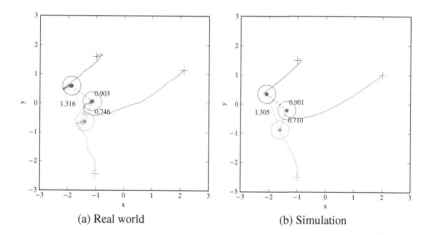

(a) Real world   (b) Simulation

Fig. 6. Ground track of the real world flight test and the simulated flight for the same initial positions. The length of each side is shown in text, + marks the start location and the circle with a dot in the center marks the end location with the diameter of the vehicle to scale.

It was observed that the quadrotors were so close to each other that the downwash from one quadrotor would interact with the other vehicles causing significant external disturbances. Figure 7 shows the commanded velocity of the ANN and the true vehicle velocity along with the result of the simulation. In contrast with the simulation, the real-world quadrotors have clear errors in tracking the desired velocities, in part due to the aerodynamic interactions. These tracking errors represent a significant reality gap.

Despite this apparent mismatch between simulation and reality, the observed behavior is very similar to that seen in simulation with the correct formation achieved with an accuracy of ±0.034.

6   Analysis of the Sensory-Motor Coordination

To analyze the effect of abstraction on the extent to which evolved robots exploit their environment and make use of SMC, we must first diver deeper into the optimized behavior. In Izzo et al., an analysis of the evolved behavior was performed. As a part of the analysis, two robot satellites were fixed at one of the desired distances. The third satellite was left free to move but did not settle into a position which completed the formation. This led them to an interesting hypothesis: perhaps the asymmetric formation could only be reached if all three satellites were free to move. Here we will investigate if we can observe a similar phenomenon for our specific evolved solution, and evaluate whether SMC plays a role in successful formation flight.

In the flight tests performed in this paper, it was observed that all successful formations resulted in a triangular formation with the same rotational orientation to the Cartesian axis system. The orientation can be seen in Figs. 5 and 6.

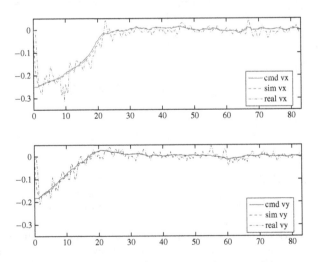

Fig. 7. Tracking performance of the velocity controller on the simulated and real ARDrone 2 given the same velocity command highlighting the reality gap.

As there is a unique set of inputs to describe every possible rotational orientation of the triangle formation, this alludes us to the possibility that the ANN is
trying to solve the formation for a fixed set of sensory inputs (r_x, r_y, d) rather
than a set of linear combinations that would define a rotationally independent
formation. This demonstrates how influential the fitness function is to the final
solution. The function used in this paper requires the formation of a triangle
with three fixed length sides but makes no definition of the required orientation.
Given that freedom, the optimization finds the simplest solution to the problem,
which in this case is a unique formation.

This solution also suggests a level of inherent environmental exploitation,
namely that the other vehicles will comply and also move in such a way to solve
the problem. We can test this by fixing two of the vehicles in an orientation
different to that converged upon when they are all free. If we initialize the third
vehicle at various locations around the other two and allow the vehicle to move
for 500 s we should be able to identify the basin of attraction this configuration.
Figure 8 shows a basin of attraction for the situation when the longest side of
the formation is fixed along the x-axis. This figure shows the magnitude of the
commanded velocity of the free vehicle at all locations in around the other two
fixed vehicles. It also shows that the velocity vector field has three attractor
points, none of which are correct locations to complete the formation. Notably,
although the highlighted spots are stable points when the two other vehicles are
fixed, the commanded velocities of the other two vehicles is non-zero showing
that this formation itself is not stable.

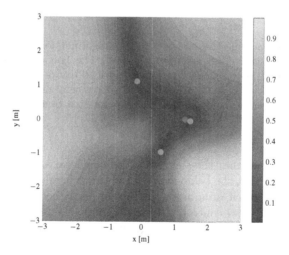

Fig. 8. Basin of attraction showing the velocity magnitude for one vehicle given the
other two vehicles (dark dots) are fixed in space. The hollow circles highlight the
possible solutions to the formation problem and the light dots show the stable attractor
points.

If we repeat this for the case when the two fixed vehicles form the angle which is converged upon when all vehicles are free we are left with the basin of attraction seen in Fig. 9. This analysis shows that in this new configuration there is only one stable attractor in the velocity map which would indeed solve the formation problem. In this location the fixed vehicles have near zero velocity set-points.

We also performed real flight tests with two vehicles fixed along the correct orientation and distance of one side of the formation. Figure 9 shows that the ground tracks of the real flights overlap almost exactly with this velocity field.

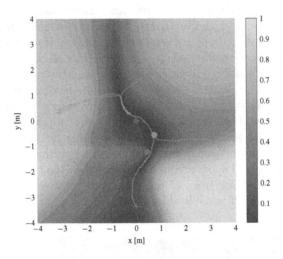

Fig. 9. Basin of attraction showing the velocity magnitude for one vehicle given the other two vehicles (dark dots) are fixed in space. The hollow circle highlights the solution to the formation problem. Overlain are ground tracks of all real world flights with the light dot showing the location the real robots converged toward. This shows that the real world performance mirrors what is expected from simulation quite well despite a clear reality gap.

Nolfi et al. suggest that the emergence of behavioral attractors is indicative of SMC [20]. Given this, the behavior we have shown here would seem to exhibit some form of SMC albeit on a more abstract level. Although the evolution has no access to the low level control or sensory inputs, the resultant behavior was still able to exploit the implicit knowledge that the other members of the swarm would unintentionally cooperate to solve the task.

This result also sheds some light onto the result of Izzo et al. It may not have been necessary for all the vehicles to be moving to achieve the formation but rather the relative orientation of the members must facilitate the behavioral attractor.

7   Conclusions

In this paper we investigated the application of abstraction on the inputs and outputs of a neural network controller within the Evolutionary Robotics paradigm. The evolutionary optimization was tasked with forming an asymmetric triangle with MAVs. The optimized behavior was effective both in simulation and reality suggesting that abstraction can be a useful tool in making evolved behavior robust to the reality gap. We also showed that sensory-motor coordination which is a typical emergent phenomenon of reactive agents is not necessarily lost when abstracting away from the raw inputs and output but is rather shifted to a higher level of abstraction. Future work will implement the task presented here with the control on a lower level of abstraction to more explicitly investigate the influence of abstraction through direct comparison.

References

1. Agmon, E., Beer, R.D.: The evolution and analysis of action switching in embodied agents. Adapt. Behav. **22**(1), 3–20 (2013)
2. Beer, R.D., Gallagher, J.C.: Evolving dynamical neural networks for adaptive behavior. Adapt. Behav. **1**(1), 91–122 (1992)
3. Bongard, J.C.: Evolutionary robotics. Commun. ACM **56**(8), 74–83 (2013)
4. Bongard, J.C., Zykov, V., Lipson, H.: Resilient machines through continuous self-modeling. Science **314**(5802), 1118–1121 (2006)
5. Cully, A., Clune, J., Tarapore, D., Mouret, J.B.: Robots that can adapt like animals. Nature **521**(7553), 503–507 (2015). http://dx.doi.org/10.1038/nature14422, http://www.nature.com/nature/journal/v521/n7553/abs/nature14422.html#supplementary-information
6. Deb, K., Pratap, A., Agarwal, S., Meyarivan, T.: A fast and elitist multiobjective genetic algorithm: NSGA-II. IEEE Trans. Evol. Comput. **6**(2), 182–197 (2002)
7. Duarte, M., Costa, V., Gomes, J., Rodrigues, T., Silva, F., Oliveira, S.M., Christensen, A.L.: Evolution of collective behaviors for a real swarm of aquatic surface robots. PLoS ONE **11**(3), 1–25 (2016)
8. Eiben, A.E., Kernbach, S., Haasdijk, E.: Embodied artificial evolution: artificial evolutionary systems in the 21st Century. Evol. Intell. **5**(4), 261–272 (2012)
9. Eiben, A.E., Smith, J.E.: Introduction to Evolutionary Computing, 2nd edn. Springer, Berlin (2015)
10. Floreano, D., Mondada, F.: Automatic creation of an autonomous agent: genetic evolution of a neural-network driven robot. In: Cliff, D., Husbands, P., Meyer, J.A., Wilson, S. (eds.) Proceedings of the Third International Conference on Simulation of Adaptive Behavior: From Animals to Animats 3, pp. 421–430. MIT Press, Cambridge (1994)
11. Floreano, D., Mondada, F.: Evolution of homing navigation in a real mobile robot. IEEE Trans. Syst. Man Cybern. Part B Cybern. **26**(3), 396–407 (1996)
12. Hattenberger, G., Bronz, M., Gorraz, M.: Using the Paparazzi UAV system for scientific research. In: International Micro Air Vehicle Conference and Competition 2014, IMAV, Delft, Netherlands, pp. 247–252 (2014)
13. Izzo, D., Pettazzi, L.: Autonomous and distributed motion planning for satellite swarm. J. Guidance Control Dyn. **30**(2), 449–459 (2007)

14. Izzo, D., Simões, L.F., de Croon, G.C.H.E.: An evolutionary robotics approach for the distributed control of satellite formations. Evol. Intell. **7**(2), 107–118 (2014)
15. Jakobi, N.: Minimal simulations for evolutionary robotics. Ph.D. thesis, University of Sussex (1998)
16. Koos, S., Mouret, J.B., Doncieux, S.: The transferability approach: crossing the reality gap in evolutionary robotics. Trans. Evol. Comput. **17**(1), 122–145 (2013)
17. Lipson, H.: Evolutionary robotics: emergence of communication. Curr. Biol. **17**(9), 129–155 (2007)
18. Love, J.: Process Automation Handbook, 1st edn. Springer, London (2007). No. 800 in Production & Process Engineering
19. Natural Point Inc: Optitrack (2014). www.naturalpoint.com/optitrack/
20. Nolfi, S.: Power and limits of reactive agents. Neurocomputing **42**, 119–145 (2002)
21. Nolfi, S., Floreano, D.: Evolutionary Robotics: The Biology, Intelligence and Technology. MIT Press, Cambridge (2000)
22. Parrot: ARDrone 2. www.ardrone2.parrot.com/
23. Remes, B., Hensen, D., van Tienen, F., de Wagter, C., van der Horst, E., de Croon, G.: Paparazzi: how to make a swarm of Parrot AR Drones fly autonomously based on GPS. In: Proceedings of the International Micro Air Vehicle Conference and Flight Competition, IMAV, Toulouse, France, pp. 17–20 (2013)
24. Scheper, K.Y.W., Tijmons, S., de Visser, C.C., de Croon, G.C.H.E.: Behaviour trees for evolutionary robotics. Artif. Life **22**(1), 23–48 (2016)
25. Yao, X.: Evolving artificial neural networks. Proc. IEEE **87**(9), 1423–1447 (1999)

Analysis of Social Learning Strategies When Discovering and Maintaining Behaviours Inaccessible to Incremental Genetic Evolution

Ben P. Jolley$^{(\boxtimes)}$, James M. Borg, and Alastair Channon

School of Computing and Mathematics, Keele University, Keele, UK
{b.p.jolley,j.borg,a.d.channon}@keele.ac.uk

Abstract. It has been demonstrated that social learning can enable agents to discover and maintain behaviours that are inaccessible to incremental genetic evolution alone. However, previous models investigating the ability of social learning to provide access to these inaccessible behaviours are often limited. Here we investigate teacher-learner social learning strategies. It is often the case that teachers in teacher-learner social learning models are restricted to one type of agent, be it a parent or some fit individual; here we broaden this exploration to include a variety of teachers to investigate whether these social learning strategies are also able to demonstrate access to, and maintenance of, behaviours inaccessible to incremental genetic evolution. In this work new agents learn from either a parent, the fittest individual, the oldest individual, a random individual or another young agent. Agents are tasked with solving a river crossing task, with new agents learning from a teacher in mock evaluations. The behaviour necessary to successfully complete the most difficult version of the task has been shown to be inaccessible to incremental genetic evolution alone, but achievable using a combination of social learning and noise in the Genotype-Phenotype map. Here we show that this result is robust in all of the teacher-learner social learning strategies explored here.

Keywords: Social learning · Incremental genetic evolution · Learning by imitation · Teacher-learner model · 'who' strategies

1 Introduction

Previous research has shown that with the use of social learning, individuals are able to discover more complex behaviours that are not accessible via incremental genetic evolution alone [3]. In this work, and many other simulation models that explore social learning and culture, social learning itself is often limited. These limitations are often centred around who individuals learn from. Here we expand on previous work to explore whether behaviours inaccessible to incremental genetic evolution alone are still discovered, and maintained, when individuals are permitted to learn from a variety of different individuals. We go on to discuss why these differing teacher-learner social learning strategies solve the task used here in differing ways.

© Springer International Publishing Switzerland 2016
E. Tuci et al. (Eds.): SAB 2016, LNAI 9825, pp. 293–304, 2016.
DOI: 10.1007/978-3-319-43488-9_26

1.1   Incremental Genetic Evolution

Incremental genetic evolution necessarily uses converged populations, which is
often referred to as the Species Adaptation Genetic Algorithm (SAGA) approach
[6]. SAGA impacts on the way populations evolve: recombination will have a far
smaller effect on the motion of the population than in a standard genetic algorithm, as each species is already genetically similar, leaving mutation as the
primary driving force behind evolution. Mutation can be substantially effective
in spaces percolated by neutral networks: pathways of level fitness through the
fitness landscape; in this case genotypes can vary while still producing similar
phenotypes and behaviours. When phenotypes of higher fitness are found the
population converges onto them thus enabling species to discover and converge
upon easily accessible solutions and behaviours. However, if there is no neutral
or incremental path between the corresponding basic behaviour and fitter behaviours, the population will struggle to move away from sub-optimality. Figure 1
depicts a mock example. One approach to solving the problem of suboptimal
convergence is to increase the rate at which mutation is applied, potentially
allowing the population to explore more of the fitness landscape. However, there
are problems with this approach: as mutation rates increase, evolutionary search
begins to resemble random search making it increasingly difficult for the population to maintain solutions. The point at which mutation becomes so large that
favourable structures discovered by evolution are lost more frequently than they
are found is known as the error threshold [10].

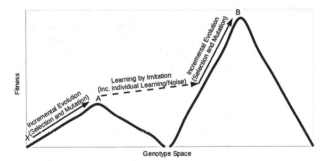

Fig. 1. A species starting from point X on the above mock fitness landscape would
achieve peak A via the hill climbing strategy adopted by incremental genetic evolution
(driven primarily by mutation and selection). The inclusion of noise in the genotype
to phenotype map and social learning (e.g. imitation) can enable the species to bypass
areas of lower fitness.

1.2   Discovering and Maintaining Inaccessible Solutions

To solve the issue of sub-optimal population convergence without crossing the
error threshold, noise can be added to the fitness landscape via the genotype

to fitness map. However, depending on where such noise is in the phenotype to fitness section of that map, its ability to aid in the transition between peaks is limited. By instead incorporating noise into the genotype to phenotype map, behaviours inaccessible to incremental genetic evolution may be exhibited reliably by individuals while leaving the genotype untouched. One method for introducing noise in this way is to introduce transcription errors when writing from the genotype to the phenotype in systems with equivalent genotype and phenotype encodings, such as direct artificial neural network weight encodings [3]. By introducing potentially new behaviours to the phenotype we deny the initial possibility of these behaviours being inherited by new individuals through standard Darwinian evolutionary mechanisms. Therefore in order to maintain successful behaviours in the population, some form of extra-genetic learning needs to take place. The extra-genetic learning employed in this model is a combination of the aforementioned genotype to phenotype noise and social learning through interaction between teachers and learners to facilitate the transmission of learnt behaviours [1,4]. As in Borg et al. [3], learners or pupils follow teachers in a mock evaluation on a set of environments or maps. As both teacher and pupil receive the same environmental input the teacher's output may be used as a target pattern for error back-propagation, reducing the pupil's output error compared to that of the teacher. By learning in this way pupils are able to partially imitate the behaviours exhibited by teachers, thus maintaining aspects of new behaviours in the population that would have been lost by a stand alone evolutionary process.

The use of teacher-learner social learning has been shown to be sufficient for discovering and maintaining behaviours inaccessible to incremental genetic evolution alone in a grounded simulation [3]. However, these simulations only allowed one form of social learning, in which offspring would learn from their fittest parent. Though a valid approach that has been used in previous work [4], there are other theoretical and empirical models that can be adapted to this work to evaluate whether or not other social learning strategies are still capable of achieving these complex behaviours.

Social learning is seen widely in nature [11] and in a range of species as diverse as humans and nine-spined stickleback fish [7]. The mechanisms and processes that underpin social learning are themselves broad, ranging from teaching, imitation and emulation to stimulus enhancement and exposure [5], with any of these mechanisms potentially leading to formation of traditions and cultures [15,16]. However, within each social learning category there is some dependence on who information is obtained from, be it a teacher or which agent is unintentionally (or intentionally) exposing an individual to something new. As social learning is necessarily conformist, a poor learning model may result in the discovery and propagation of sub-optimal behaviours. In this work we assess whether who you are learning from, otherwise known as 'who' social learning strategies [8], can hinder social learning's ability to discover and maintain behaviours inaccessible to incremental genetic evolution alone, thus undermining social learning's adaptive advantage over incremental genetic evolution in complex environments.

Laland [8] assess both 'who' and 'when' social learning strategies, alongside the complexity of social learning in animals, providing evidence to show its adaptive advantages. Laland [8] has a particular focus on conformity: a population's ability to share popular behaviours amongst each other while minimising exploration for new behaviours; the use of conformist social learning can be beneficial or detrimental depending on the environment or task [2, 8, 9]. It has also been suggested that conformist social learning that is not supplemented with non-social exploration can lead to population collapse in temporally varying environments [2], though recent work suggest that conformist learning may be of benefit in spatially varying environments [9]. The 'who' social learning strategies (concerned with who an agent should learn from rather than when learning should take place) inspired by Laland [8] are modelled here as three core social learning strategies: 'Best Parent', 'Oldest' and 'Fittest'. The 'Fittest' strategy selects the fittest individual from the population to be the teacher. The theoretical basis behind this strategy falls partially into the 'Learning from majority' category discussed by Laland [8], but also has a wider basis in nature with many animals being shown to learn from more successful individuals. Learning from older individuals derives from the rationale that older individuals must have exhibited successful behaviours to survive, however this does not have to mean the older individual in question is in fact the fittest individual, due to this the 'Oldest' strategy is likely to provide a broader range of behaviours than the 'Fittest' strategy. The 'Best Parent' strategy (as seen in Borg et al. [3]) sets the teacher to be the parent who has won the right to reproduce in a tournament. This is the least conformist strategy of the three as it allows unfit individuals, relative to the rest of the population, to be parents as tournaments only involve a small number of individuals. Additional to these three core strategies we also introduce social learning strategies for learning from random and young individuals. Though not widely evident in nature, the theoretical benefits of learning from a random individual (sometimes described as unbiased social learning) have been have been discussed in numerous works [9, 12]. The theorised benefits of unbiased social learning arise in temporally varying environments, where learning from a broader set of individuals enables increased access to new behaviours that may be relevant in the specific environmental state being experienced. A 'Youngest' strategy, despite no theoretical basis, is being evaluated as a contrast to the 'Oldest' strategy.

1.3 Neuroevolution of Deliberative Behaviours for an Advanced River Crossing Task

This work uses populations of hybrid neural networks embodied in agents (often referred to as animats). The hybrid networks are comprised of two different neural networks: the first controlling the high level deliberative behaviours of the animat, and the second controlling the animat's reactive capabilities. Hybrid neural network architectures of this sort have demonstrated the ability to seek long term goals whilst also reacting to unforeseen events ultimately enabling the evolution of complex problem solving abilities [3, 13, 14]. To demonstrate these problem solving abilities Robinson et al. [13] developed a complex problem called the 'river crossing' or RC task. The RC task required animats to find a reward-giving Resource in a 2D grid-world environment containing a number of obstacles, including Traps, Water (connected to form an impassable river), and Stones. In order to cross the river animats were required to pick up Stone objects, which could be carried at no cost to the animat, and place them in the same cells as Water thus negating the cell's lethality. Once a continuous bridge of Stones over the river had been built, animats could access the Resource. Despite the RC task being reasonably complex, it has been demonstrated that it could be solved by initially converged populations of animats using only incremental genetic evolution [13]. To test whether social learning could discover and maintain behaviours inaccessible to incremental genetic evolution alone, a more complex version of the RC task, known as the RC+ task, was developed by Borg et al. [3]. A snapshot of the RC+ task can be seen in Fig. 2.

An important aspect of the RC task was that individuals were evaluated on increasingly difficult environments. The RC+ task maintains this principle whilst making the RC task more difficult in regard to both river width and exposure to Stone objects. The number of environments an animat was evaluated on increased from three to five, with environments becoming increasingly difficult to solve due to river width increasing from zero to four cells. To add additional difficulty, the number of Stone objects gradually decreases from twenty in the first environment to zero in the final environment, rendering the bridge building behaviour useless for solving the final environment. In order to make the final environment solvable, two extra objects, Object A and Object B, were introduced into the environment. Object A and Object B were rare objects, with only one instance of each found in each environment. Object A and Object B are moveable at no cost to the animat and may be placed upon any cell or object. If an animat places both Object A and Object B on a cell containing Water, a reward equal to that of the Resource is received and the animat is considered to have successfully solved the map. The RC+ task has been shown to be impossible to solve with incremental genetic evolution alone [3].

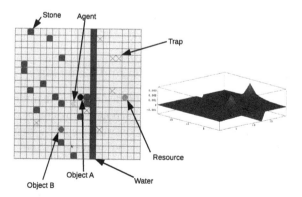

Fig. 2. RC+ environment with accompanying activity (shunting) landscapes.

2   The Model

The hybrid neural network used by Borg et al. [3] and others [13,14], and therefore used here, may be broken down into two network models: a shunting network and a decision network, with the decision network passing information on to the shunting network which in turn controls animat movement. The shunting network is not directly exposed to any evolution or learning. The deliberative network is exposed to both evolution and learning, enabling the evolution and inheritance of behaviour.

2.1   The Shunting Network

The shunting network is a locally-connected, topologically-organised network of neurons that was originally used for collision free motion planning and has already been applied to the river crossing task [13,14] and RC+ task [3]. This network is advantageous as it exhibits computational efficiency by not explicitly searching over all possible paths. The shunting model is used here by mapping the topologically-organised neurons as cells in the RC+ environment's 20 by 20 grid. Using the shunting equation (see Eq. 1) values are to propagate across the neurons/cells using the outputs from the decision network, producing an activity landscape with peaks and valleys representing desirable and undesirable features in the environment. The result is a landscape which allows the animat to follow a route with the higher (iota) values while avoiding undesirable valleys. An example of an activity landscape with a snapshot of the environment it represents can been seen in Fig. 2.

$$\frac{dx_i}{dt} = -Ax_i + \sum_{j \in N_i} w_{ij} [x_j]^+ + I_i \tag{1}$$

In Eq. 1 each neuron/node in the shunting network corresponds to one cell in the RC+ environment; x_i is the activation of neuron i; A is the passive decay rate; N_i in the receptive field of i; w_{ij} is the connection strength from neuron j to i, specified to be set by a monotonically decreasing function of the Euclidean distance between cells i and j; the function $[x]^+$ is $max(0, x)$; and I_i is the external input to neuron i (known as the Iota output).

2.2   The Decision Network, Evolution and Learning

The decision network can inform agents of desirable and undesirable objects in the environment based on the agent's current environmental position. The decision network is a feed-forward neural network, with a single four neuron hidden layer, that inputs information from the animats current location in the RC+ task world to gain an iota value for each possible environmental state, with the exclusion of grass whose value is always set to 0 (to ensure neutral space for activity to propagate through when producing an activity landscape using the shunting model). A hyperbolic tangent activation function is applied at each output node with a boundary of -0.3 to 0.3; values below -0.3 round to -1, above 0.3 rounds to 1 and in between rounds to 0. The output layer contains sixty-seven neurons representing the Iota values of all sixty-four possible environmental states, including inaccessible and redundant combinations, with an additional output neuron for each pick-up/put-down operation on each non-static objects (Stones, Object A, Object B). A standard hyperbolic tangent activation function is applied at each hidden node.

Here error back-propagation is used to simulate learning. The use of error back-propagation to simulate learning has been previously used by Curran et al. [4] to enable pupil outputs to be corrected to more closely resemble the teacher outputs. In Curran et al. [4] multiple learning cycles are conducted, until the error between learner and teacher outputs is minimised to an acceptable level. Here, as in Borg et al. [3], a similar approach is taken, with learning cycles represented by each move in a mock evaluation of the environment by the teacher. However, unlike Curran et al. [4], learning only continues until either the demonstrator completes all five maps or fails, no direct attempt is made to ensure learner outputs were minimised to some arbitrary level. A novel approach is taken in this experiment, that builds on previous work by having different simulations with different teacher-learner social learning strategies.

3   Experimentation

The model used here is fundamentally the same as introduced by Borg et al. [3]. Each iteration/generation has a tournament event in which two individuals from the population of 100 are ran through the RC+ task, with each individual's fitness being determined by the number of maps successfully completed. Each map gets increasingly more complex therefore if an individual is not able to complete a map they are prevented from continuing on to further maps. Each map has seven Trap objects and $20 - (5 \times riverwidth)$ Stone objects, both of which are randomly placed, though never on the same space, one reward-giving Resource on the opposite side of the map to the agent starting position, and one instance each of Object A and Object B. The river width varies from an initial width of zero, increasing by one cell per map. Each individual is evaluated on their ability to reach the resource or place Object A and Object B on to a cell containing Water. Agents fail when they come into contact with an uncovered Water or Trap element. Failing to complete a map within 100 steps is also evaluated as a failed attempt. The two tournament individuals are compared, with the fitter agent reproducing with a randomly selected agent from the population, with the child replacing the weaker of the tournament agents. Each loci in an agent's genotype directly writes to a locus in the agent's phenotype, which itself directly encodes a weight in the decision network, with all genotypes and phenotypes being of length $L = 308$. To ensure network structures from parents are maintained during reproduction, a single point recombination mechanism is applied. Mutation follows recombination; each loci has a probability $P_{mut} = 1/L$ of having a random value from $N(0, 0.4)$ added to it, with the resulting values being bounded within the range [-1,1]. Once the child genotype has been constructed it is written to the child agent's phenotype; this process is referred to as transcription. During transcription two randomly selected connection weights are overwritten with a new random value selected from a discrete uniform distribution $U(-1, 1)$. Directly following reproduction the learning strategy is enforced via back-propagation. A mock evaluation of the RC+ task takes place between the teacher and child (now thought of as the learner), with the learner's inputs being set to those of the teacher. Learning takes place until the teacher either fails or completes all five maps. At each step through the evaluation the learner attempts, via error-back propagation with a learning rate of $\delta = 1$, to imitate the teacher's output for the current inputs.

The model in this work utilities five learning strategies, each with a different way of determining teacher selection. The winner of the reproduction tournament being set as the teacher in the 'Best Parent' strategy, the fittest individual in the population for the 'Fittest' strategy, the individual who has registered the most tournament wins for the 'Oldest' strategy, the last animat to be created before the current reproduction event in the 'Youngest' strategy, and a random individual for the 'Random' strategy. In any case where more than one individual met the criteria to be assigned the role of teacher, an individual from the valid sub-set was chosen at random, this situation only every arose when using the 'Fittest' or 'Oldest' strategies. One hundred populations for each learning strategy were evaluated so the results can be aggregated for an overview of each strategy's performance. Simulations were run for 2,000,000 tournaments, with each simulation recording the fitness of the fittest individual and the mean fitness of the population at every 500th tournament. The highest fitness is five, which indicates an agent completed map five. To indicate the behaviour has not only been achieved but also maintained the fitness of five has to have been recorded a further ten times, without a suboptimal result. Each learning strategy is comprised of 100 populations of agents.

4   Results

Table 1 (top) shows the proportion of populations that were successful in solving each map. The most notable result was that all strategies were able to complete map five, the map which required exhibiting and maintaining a behaviour that in previous work was not obtainable by incremental genetic evolution alone [3], thus demonstrating that discovering and maintaining behaviours inaccessible to genetic evolution alone is possible using various teacher-learner social learning strategies, even those strategies that are either non-conformist (the 'Random' strategy) or contrary to strategies observed in nature (the 'Youngest' strategy). It should be noted that to complete one map, all preceding maps must have also been completed, therefore the ability to solve map five indicates that a population also managed to successfully complete maps 1–4. In Table 1 (top) we do see many instances of learning strategies failing to complete simpler maps; we also see this in Table 1 (bottom), which shows how many populations were successful

Table 1. (Top) % of populations completing each map for each social learning strategy. (Bottom) % of populations achieving each map as their maximum achievement for each social learning strategy. (BP = Best Parent)

Map	BP	Fittest	Oldest	Random	Youngest
1	99 %	99 %	99 %	99 %	99 %
2	71 %	68 %	54 %	74 %	63 %
3	47 %	47 %	37 %	54 %	47 %
4	39 %	46 %	34 %	49 %	38 %
5	8 %	15 %	5 %	10 %	7 %

Map	BP	Fittest	Oldest	Random	Youngest
None	1 %	1 %	1 %	1 %	1 %
1	28 %	31 %	45 %	25 %	36 %
2	24 %	21 %	17 %	20 %	16 %
3	8 %	1 %	3 %	5 %	9 %
4	31 %	31 %	29 %	39 %	31 %
5	8 %	15 %	5 %	10 %	7 %

at completing each map as their maximum achievement, that is to say completed map one or two, ... without going on to complete any later maps. Maps 2–4 were all solvable using either a 'bridge building' strategy or the more advanced Object A + Object B strategy, the suggestion here is that some learning strategies sometimes failed to find the sub-optimal, but more incrementally accessible, 'bridge building' strategy. We would also expect to see populations that were able to complete map two also completing map four as the behaviour required is the same, the only difference being a wider river, however Table 1 (bottom) suggests that all strategies had populations that exhibited flawed behaviours which were not as generally applicable as they should have been. In comparable tests by Borg et al. [3], non-learning populations were shown to achieve above 90 % success on maps three and four, with 100 % success for maps one and two, the failure of the social learning strategies explored here to achieve this rate of success for maps three and four (as indicated by Table 1 (top)) indicates that whilst social learning can enable access to, and maintenance of, behaviours inaccessible to incremental genetic evolution, they are less effective at solving simpler, incrementally accessible, tasks. One explanation for this result is that social learning is necessarily conformist, even when unbiased or random, thus running the risk of sub-optimal behaviours being maintained and dispersed within the population.

The results also offer no definitive best strategy for the solving the RC+ task, as all are able to achieve the final map. However both Table 1 (bottom) and Fig. 3 do allow us to begin seeing the differences between strategies. Performance may be viewed from three differing perspectives: (1) the number of populations achieving map five, (2) the distribution of maps achieved by populations, (3) the speed at which populations were capable of completing maps. Both measure

(1) and (2) may be considered using the data from Table 1 (bottom): from this data we can see that 'Fittest' strategy achieves the highest proportion of populations completing map five, however if we conduct a Chi squared test to find whether the proportion of populations achieving map five is dependent on the social learning strategy applied or not we come our with a p-value of 0.1316, thus indicating that the proportion of populations achieving map five is in fact independent of the strategy applied, therefore we cannot say with any certainty that the ability of the 'Fittest' strategy to achieve map five is significantly better than any other strategy (we do find that a Chi squared test that only considers the 'Fittest' and 'Oldest' strategies does provide a p-value below a significance level of 0.05, but no other pairings do). If we take Table 1 (bottom) to be a contingency table on which a Chi Squared test may be conducted we may be able to derive whether the distribution of maps achieved by populations (measure (2)) is dependent or independent of the social learning strategy used. When such a test is conducted a p-value of 0.04739 is produced, suggesting that the distribution of maps achieved by populations is dependent on the strategy used. This result requires further investigation of the data for each population, for each strategy, in order provide a robust overview of the dynamics each strategy employs to solve the task. Measure (3) may be considered using the graphs seen in Fig. 3. From Fig. 3 it seems that populations employing the 'Best Parent' strategy are able to achieve map five quicker than other strategies, with the 'Youngest' strategy seeming to struggle to achieve map five in any haste. However if we only consider the average number of generations to complete each map both 'Best Parent' and 'Youngest' seem to give an average performance, with 'Random' and 'Oldest' giving the best general performance. It is interesting to note that those populations employing the 'Oldest' strategy who are able to complete map five, do so quicker on average than 'Oldest' strategy populations that complete map two, three or four this result suggests that when individuals in 'Oldest' strategy populations do discover the behaviour required to solve map five, it spreads rapidly through the population. As the 'Oldest' strategy acts somewhat like a 'Dominance' strategy, with only the dominant tournament winning agent acting as the teacher, it is maybe unsurprising that behaviours can spread rapidly, however the random nature of tournament selection can somewhat undermine this strategy's ability to guarantee fit behaviours or a consistent teacher. The best performing populations for the 'Best Parent', 'Oldest' and 'Fittest' strategies (as seen on the left of Fig. 3) also seems to indicate that once a favourable behaviour is discovered using these strategies it is able to spread reasonably quickly. This is unsurprising as each of these strategies can be highly conformist, with successful individuals potentially having a monopoly on being the teacher for new agents. With the 'Youngest' strategy, the high turnover of teachers provides little opportunity for beneficial behaviours to take hold, though these teaching agents are the progeny of tournament winning parents, so can be expected to be reasonably fit. The most surprising result is the general performance of the 'Random' strategy, given that unlike the other strategies there is no guarantee of the teacher being either consistent nor particularly fit. One reason for the

'Random' strategy performing at least as well as the other strategies is the nature of the RC+ task itself. If a population only discovers the 'bridge-building' behaviour needed for maps 2–4, whilst forming a dislike for Object A and/or Object B, any conformist strategy will struggle to discover the behaviour required for map five, as the population will tend to conform to the sub-optimal behaviour. However, the very nature of the 'Random' strategy allows for a variety of individuals to fulfil the role of teacher, regardless of fitness, thus enabling newer ideas to potentially establish themselves and sub-optimal behaviours to be lost. However, maintaining these newly found optimal behaviours may be difficult in such a strategy. This does suggest that a hybrid approach may be beneficially, whereby numerous conformist and non-conformists strategies may exists within a population thus enabling both innovation and rapid behavioural convergence to occur.

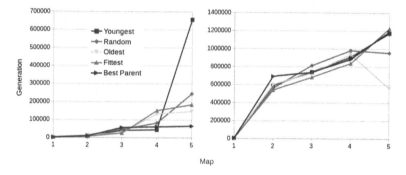

Fig. 3. (Left) Graph showing the first time any population achieved each map. (Right) Graph showing the average generation populations achieved each map.

5 Conclusions and Further Work

The aim here was to demonstrate that multiple, varied, social learning strategies would be capable of discovering and maintaining behaviours that are inaccessible to hill-climbing strategies such as incremental genetic evolution. The results presented here echo previous work [3], while extending the research to show that various social learning strategies are capable of both discovering and maintaining inaccessible behaviours. Due to each strategy applied being highly abstracted from behaviours seen in nature, along with the task being highly artificial, this work is unable to draw strong parallels to observed social behaviours in nature. Achieving a comparable status will require a more complex use of social learning, a sensible progression would be the inclusion of synchronous, distinct learning styles into a single population. A model that allows for multiple social learning strategies to be employed along side genetic evolution has compelling implications for agents, i.e. choosing optimal learning styles for the appropriate task. Going forward, additional tests will explore the dynamics between multiple learning strategies and incremental genetic evolution when included in the same population.

References

1. Acerbi, A., Parisi, D.: Cultural transmission between and within generations. J. Artif. Soc. Soc. Simul. **9**(1) (2006). http://jasss.soc.surrey.ac.uk/9/1/9/citation.html
2. Borg, J.M., Channon, A.: Testing the variability selection hypothesis - the adoption of social learning in increasingly variable environments. In: The Thirteenth Conference on the Synthesis and Simulation of Living Systems, ALIFE 13, pp. 317–324. MIT Press (2012)
3. Borg, J.M., Channon, A., Day, C.: Discovering and maintaining behaviours inaccessible to incremental genetic evolution through transcription errors and cultural transmission. In: Proceedings of the Eleventh European Conference on the Synthesis and Simulation of Living Systems, ECAL 2011, pp. 101–108. MIT Press (2011)
4. Curran, D., O'Riordan, C.: The effects of cultural learning in populations of neural networks. Artif. Life **13**(1), 45–67 (2007)
5. Galef, B.G.: Social learning and traditions in animals: evidence, definitions, and relationship to human culture. Wiley Interdisc. Rev. Cogn. Sci. **3**(6), 581–592 (2012)
6. Harvey, I.: Artificial evolution: a continuing SAGA. In: Gomi, T. (ed.) ER-EvoRob 2001. LNCS, vol. 2217, pp. 94–109. Springer, Heidelberg (2001)
7. Kendal, J.R., Rendell, L., Pike, T.W., Laland, K.N.: Nine-spined sticklebacks deploy a hill-climbing social learning strategy. Behav. Ecol. **20**(2), 238–244 (2009)
8. Laland, K.N.: Social learning strategies. Anim. Learn. Behav. **32**(1), 4–14 (2004)
9. Nakahasi, W., Wakano, J.Y., Henrich, J.: Apative social learning strategies in temporally and spatially varying environments. Hum. Nat. **23**(4), 368–418 (2013)
10. Ochoa, G., Harvey, I., Buxton, H.: Error thresholds and their relation to optimal mutation rates. In: Floreano, D., Mondada, F. (eds.) ECAL 1999. LNCS, vol. 1674. Springer, Heidelberg (1999)
11. Reader, S.M., Biro, D.: Experimental identification of social learning in wild animals. Learn. Behav. **38**(3), 265–283 (2010)
12. Rendell, L., Boyd, R., Cownden, D., Enquist, M., Eriksson, K., Feldman, M.W., Fogarty, L., Ghirlanda, S., Lillicrap, T., Laland, K.N.: Why copy others? insights from the social learning strategies tournament. Sci. **328**(5975), 208–213 (2010)
13. Robinson, E., Ellis, T., Channon, A.: Neuroevolution of agents capable of reactive and deliberative behaviours in novel and dynamic environments. In: Almeida e Costa, F., Rocha, L.M., Costa, E., Harvey, I., Coutinho, A. (eds.) ECAL 2007. LNCS (LNAI), vol. 4648, pp. 345–354. Springer, Heidelberg (2007)
14. Stanton, A., Channon, A.: Incremental neuroevolution of reactive and deliberative 3D agents. In: Proceedings of the Thirteenth European Conference on the Synthesis and Simulation of Living Systems, ECAL 2015, pp. 341–348. MIT Press (2015)
15. Whiten, A., Van Schaik, C.P.: The evolution of animal cultures and social intelligence. Philos. Trans. R. Soc. B Biol. Sci. **362**(1480), 603–620 (2007)
16. Zwirner, E., Thornton, A.: Cognitive requirements of cumulative culture: teaching is useful but not essential. Scientific Reports 5 (2015). Article no. 16781

Simulating Chemical Reactions Using a Swarm of Miniature Robots

Audrey Randall, John Klingner, and Nikolaus Correll[✉]

Department of Computer Science, University of Colorado at Boulder,
Boulder, USA
ncorrell@colorado.edu

Abstract. We wish to simulate basic rules of chemistry using a swarm of miniature robots, which mimic atoms and forming molecules. Atomic scale interactions are difficult to observe and computer simulations or ball-and-stick models capture either behavioral or embodied aspects, but not both. Miniature robots that are able to determine their orientation and position with respect to each other and provide audible, visual, and tactile feedback to a user could make such simulations both interactive and tangible. We describe a working prototype of our swarm-robotic chemistry simulation which demonstrates concepts including electronegativity, reaction spontaneity, the octet rule, and hybridization. Here, the key challenge is that once we go beyond the most simple set of atoms, the outcome of reactions cannot be calculated from first principles. We solve this problem by letting robots exchange local measurements, the nearby atoms, their geometry, and molecules that have formed and then using a compact look-up table implementation, which suggests avenues of further studies for both physical chemistry and swarm robotics. We also present preliminary data recorded from a high-school demonstration evaluating using a tangible simulation of chemistry reactions as a teaching tool.

Keywords: Chemistry · Swarm · Simulation

1 Introduction

We are interested in simulating the basic rules of chemistry in a swarm of miniature robots for two reasons: First, we wish to encourage chemists to think about atomic interactions in terms of distributed systems and self-organization. Second, we hope to produce a teaching tool for chemistry students. While the latter use case might justify a simulation that is not perfectly faithful to the functioning of the physical system as long as it produces the correct phenomenological results, our long term goal is for those two applications of chemistry simulation to merge, thereby advancing our understanding of both chemistry and education (Fig. 1).

This research has been supported by NSF grant #1150223.

E. Tuci et al. (Eds.): SAB 2016, LNAI 9825, pp. 305–316, 2016.
DOI: 10.1007/978-3-319-43488-9_27

Chemistry simulations fall broadly into two categories: teaching tools and research tools. From an educational perspective, interactive simulations of chemical processes are interesting as they may improve visual-spatial cognition [16,22,23,25]. In order to improve the pedagogical value of 3D simulations of molecular interactions, educators have begun embracing augmented reality [10] that combines tangible devices (some of which include olfactory and auditory sensations) [19], with simulations to improve learning [9]. Most teaching tools, such as those collected in MERLOT's database [1], are divided into lessons, each of which demonstrates one chemistry concept. A tool might create molecules that perform an acid-base reaction, but be incapable of a reduction-oxidation reaction. We have not seen any interactive teaching tools designed to imitate the behavior of real atoms and molecules in all situations, and we believe such a simulation could be extremely useful and interesting for students.

A similar gap exists in the area of chemistry simulations for research. Most chemistry research simulations do not simulate individual particles (either atoms or molecules), trading the extreme level of detail for computational expediency. These simulations are also usually optimized toward representing a single environment, such as a specific set of reactions in the troposphere [24] or the interaction of amino acids and mild steel [7], to name just two examples from a very large body of work in computational chemistry [14].

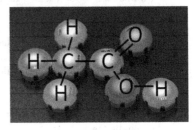

Fig. 1. This figure shows an example of Acetic Acid ($C_2H_4O_2$) in the formation our algorithm would dictate.

The closest example of research similar to our own uses physical concepts to simulate particles [20] as an interactive homogeneous swarm, which demonstrates the emergence of macroscopic patterns from microscopic particles. However, this simulation is composed of only one type of particle, and does not simulate different elements [20]. It is also implemented on a traditional centralized computing platform, not on a physical swarm of individual robots.

2   Background

The study of how and when atoms bond dates back to the 1800s, and between then and now, increasingly complex models have emerged to explain molecular and atomic behavior. The simplest atomic models, such as the Bohr model invented in 1913 by Niels Bohr, are sufficient to explain only the behavior of a small subset of atoms, with irregularities and exceptions. As our understanding of what atoms are and how they function has improved, better behaved models have emerged that can explain the behavior of a wider range of chemical species. But even today, chemistry has not advanced to the point where chemical reactions can be accurately simulated from physical principles. Our models are only as good as our understanding of the atom itself. Chemical physicists, in their attempts to create truly accurate models of the atom, are now delving into the realms of quantum physics and chemistry, which are developing fields that are not yet fully understood. In our attempt to implement the most accurate possible model for chemical reactions on a miniature robot, we found that all non-quantum models based on physical properties eventually break down. For example, the octet rule, which is often presented as the sole explanation for why atoms bond in the first weeks of a chemistry class, states that the valence shell of an atom can have up to eight valence electrons, and is not stable until it has eight. Students often ask why elements in the alkaline and alkaline-earth groups are "satisfied" with two valence electrons, and cannot have more. To solve this problem, the Lewis and Bohr models of the atom are introduced, but they cannot explain bonding between metals, which is why introductory chemistry classes often leave the subject of metallic bonding for the second class. The most complex non- quantum-based model taught to students to explain why atoms form bonds in the shapes they do is called hybridization, which we have chosen as a starting point for a distributed simulation presented here. But even this method is described in a textbook as existing only to predict molecular shapes we have no other explanation for [3]. Chemists doubt that it is an accurate model of what is truly happening.

For some purposes, look-up tables of experimental data are sufficient. Introductory chemistry classes across the world teach the use of tables of enthalpy, entropy, and Gibbs Free Energy values to determine reaction spontaneity. If the set of atoms in question is reduced to only a few specific, well-behaved species, the look-up tables have few enough exceptions that students can get a good idea of how the reactions work without confusion. We therefore believe that our initial attempt on a distributed, swarm robotic implementation described in this paper can convey information at the level of an introductory chemistry course very well, and might lead to similar insights as swarm robotics has afforded for the study of social insects [6,12], another natural system relying on self-organization [2].

3   Mapping Basic Chemistry Concepts to Distributed Embodied Swarms

The Octet Rule: The Bohr atomic model describes electrons as nearly weightless particles arranged in a series of shells around the nucleus, and is considered the simplest possible abstraction of an atom. Within each shell, electrons are divided into orbitals, regions wherein electrons can probably be found. Each orbital contains at most two electrons. As distance from the nucleus increases, successive electron shells do not contain the same number of orbitals, and orbitals themselves have several different shapes. In this model, the outermost or "valence" shell determines how the atom will bond. It contains at most eight electrons. This is called the "octet rule," and though it doesn't always apply for larger atoms, it does apply for the nonmetals in the subset of elements we model.

Students are taught that atoms bond when each has an orbital with a single, unpaired electron in it. Those orbitals then overlap, allowing the atoms to share the electrons within them. This means that both orbitals effectively contain two electrons, which puts them both in a more stable state. If an atom has more than one orbital with an unpaired electron, it can bond with multiple other atoms. If two atoms have more than one orbital with an unpaired electron, they might form a double or triple bond. This model is the basis for our implementation of inter-atomic bonding, requiring individual robots to advertise their own number of unpaired electrons and listen to their neighbors. We assume that all individual atoms have a neutral formal charge. Ions are not currently implemented.

Electronegativity: Students are also taught that atoms can form two types of bonds: *covalent* (where electrons are shared) and *ionic* (where electrons are taken by one atom from the other). Covalent bonds are divided into categories based on strength: the more polar the bond, the stronger it generally is. Polarity measures the difference in partial charge between bonded atoms. Students usually memorize the many types and strengths of covalent bonds, but there is a simpler model to determine bond type: electronegativity. Electronegativity is a property of an atom that determines its tendency to attract shared electrons. By this model, ionic bonds are simply covalent bonds that are so polar, one atom has full control of the electrons. This is reflected by our implementation, where the more electronegative atom has control of the electrons.

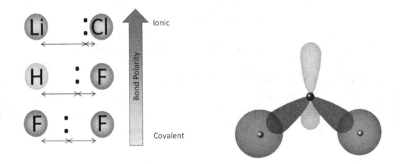

Fig. 2. Left: An increasing difference in electronegativity yields a bond where electrons are held more closely by one atom than the other, until the electrons transfer atoms entirely and the bond becomes ionic in character. Right: Water shown with four orbitals on the central oxygen. Light blue represents an orbital that does not contain bonded electrons (although it does contain a lone pair of unbonded electrons). Dark blue represents the two orbitals that form bonds with hydrogen. Since hydrogen only has one orbital, its shape is different from the orbitals of oxygen. (Color figure online)

We use Mulliken-Jaffe electronegativity values on a Pauling scale [13] for our treatment of this concept. These values are given by the equation:

$$\chi = 3.48\left((IE_v + EA_v)/2 - 0.602\right)$$

EA_v is the electron affinity of the atom and IE_v is the first ionization energy. The electron affinity is the change in energy of an atom when an electron is added to it in its neutral state, and the first ionization energy is the energy required to take an electron away from the atom in its neutral state. Using χ values on a Pauling scale gives values that are between approximately 0 and 4. A larger χ means a stronger tendency to attract shared electrons. While attempting to form bonds, an atom will bond ionically if the difference in χ values between it and its potential partner is greater than 1.70 [3], and covalently otherwise. In a robotic implementation, it is sufficient to simply exchange the χ value between robots and choose bonding behavior accordingly.

Reaction Spontaneity and Thermodynamics: The concept of reaction spontaneity is used to tell students whether, without outside influence, a reaction will occur. Initially, students learn about enthalpy (ΔH). Enthalpy is a quantity related to the heat that a reaction requires or releases. However, the exceptions to this rule lead to misconceptions. In the interest of avoiding these, we chose to implement the more complicated concept of Gibbs Free Energy (ΔG). ΔG values represent the difference in free energy between a reaction's products and reactants.

Reactions between atoms and molecules occur only when the products of the reaction have a lower energy level than the reactants. Thus, we calculate the difference between the sum of the ΔG values for the products and the sum of the ΔG values for the reactants, which gives us an overall ΔG for the reaction:

$$\Delta G_{rxn} = \sum \Delta G_{products} - \sum \Delta G_{reactants}$$

If ΔG_{rxn} is negative, then we say that the reaction occurs spontaneously. Reactions with $\Delta G_{rxn} \geq 0$ do still occur, but only when energy is added to the system. In practice, enough energy can be added by kinetic interactions between molecules for such reactions to occur 'spontaneously'. However, due to the scale of our chemistry simulation, such effects are difficult to model, and thus our simulation only allows reactions with $\Delta G_{rxn} < 0$ to occur. Both individual molecules and reactions have ΔG values. In the case of individual molecules, the implied equation is the formation of that molecule from its most basic components. In a robotic implementation, the ΔG of a molecule can be determined in two ways: either by looking up a table of experimentally determined values or by using this equation [21] (Fig. 3):

$$\Delta G = \Delta H - T \Delta S$$

ΔH is the enthalpy of formation of that molecule, ΔS is the entropy of formation, and T is the temperature (assumed to be 298K). Most of our thermodynamic values were obtained from the DIPPR Chemical Database [18], which provides ΔG data for more than 2000 compounds. This database was selected due to its size and accessibility. We filled in gaps in this database, which were mostly radicals, with data from the NIST Chemistry WebBook [5].

In a robotics context, Gibbs Free Energy calculations require each robot to store the knowledge of the molecule it belongs to. When considering a reaction, the robot calculates the ΔG_{rxn}. It uses its own molecule and the other robot's molecule as reactants, and using its own molecule with the other atom added and the other robot's molecule without that atom as products. Only single atom

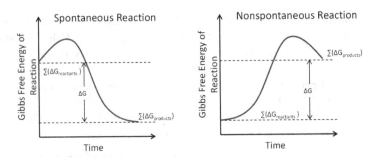

Fig. 3. Difference in Gibbs Free Energy for spontaneous and nonspontaneous reactions.

addition reactions are considered, meaning that the two robots considering reacting are the only ones that might switch molecules. In order to make the look-up of these ΔG_{rxn} values fast enough to run on our platform's microprocessor, we store a list of all possible molecules the robots could form as a prefix tree. More details on this implementation can be found in Sect. 4.

One value of using this system for determining if bonds form is that the robots can also demonstrate the basic principles of reaction direction: specifically, if a reaction occurs in the forward direction, it will never occur in the reverse direction unless energy is added to the system.

Hybridization and Molecular Geometry: Hybridization theory determines the shape that molecules should form. Since electrons repel each other, the placement of the full or partially full orbitals around the atom can explain the shape that bonds make. For example, water has its v-shaped structure because of the placement of the four orbitals on the central oxygen in a tetrahedral shape (Fig. 2, right). These orbitals have an angle to each other of approximately 109.5° [3]. Two out of the four have paired electrons and therefore do not form bonds, and the remaining two singly occupied orbitals bond with hydrogen, resulting in water's bent geometry.

As well as accurately predicting molecular geometry, hybridization gives a more accurate prediction of bond number than any other theory, since it was invented to explain bond structures that other theories couldn't account for. For a second example, according to Lewis bond theory, beryllium (Be) cannot bond because it has two electrons in its s orbital and thus has no orbitals with one unpaired electron that can overlap to form a bond. But *Be* can in fact form two bonds; hybridization theory explains this by stating that an electron gets "promoted" from the s orbital to an empty p orbital. The s orbital and p orbital, both now singly occupied, no longer have the character of an s and p orbital. They will each form a hybridized orbital denoted as sp^1 or simply sp. The hybridized orbitals now can form bonds in the same manner as ordinary orbitals. The repulsion of the hybridized orbitals gives the explanation for the molecule's shape, since the angle of the overlapping orbitals is also the angle between the bonded atoms.

In conjunction with the robotic platform's range, bearing, and heading measurement of the atoms to which it is bonded, hybridization is used in the code so that, for example, the two hydrogen atoms in H_2O are both constantly assessing and adjusting their position relative to the oxygen atom. This simulates traditional two-dimensional representations shown in textbooks such as Burdge and Overby's [4].

4   Implementation

The Droplets are an open-source swarm robotic platform, with source code and manufacturing information available online[1]. Each Droplet is roughly cylindrical with a radius of 2.2 cm and a height of 2.4 cm. The Droplets use an Atmel xMega128A3U micro-controller, and receive power via their legs through a floor with alternating strips of $+5V$ and GND. Each Droplet has six infrared emitters, receivers, and sensors, which are used for communication, collision detection, and for the range and bearing system [8]. The top of each board has a light and color sensor, as well as an RGB LED. Each Droplet has three extended headers for legs located symmetrically around itself. The legs are spaced 120° apart and 1.5 cm from the center. Mounted symmetrically opposite from two of the legs are coin-type vibration motors of the type commonly used in cell phones and pagers. These motors are used as a low-cost locomotion method [15]. The third leg has a speaker mounted opposite it. Each Droplet has a unique ID number.

Our implementation of these chemistry concepts centers around a 'state message',' which each Droplet broadcasts periodically. This message includes:

– The IDs of each Droplet the sender is bonded to.
– A list of the atoms in the sender's molecule.
– The sender's atomic number.
– The state of the sender's valence shells.

A Droplet also receives updated measurements for the sender's range, bearing, and heading with this message [8]. If the Droplet receiving this message is bonded to the sender already, then the Droplet checks where it should move to maintain the appropriate molecular geometry as determined by hybridization. It also updates its list of atoms in its molecule based on the sender's other bonds.

The Droplet's color indicates what atom it is. Bonds are represented visually by the bonded Droplets all blinking red together. The simultaneous blinking occurs because all of the Droplets' clocks are synchronized with a firefly synchronization algorithm [17]. To avoid multiple Droplets trying to communicate simultaneously, their state messages are sent out with a fixed period, but with phase determined by their ID number. Since every Droplet knows the ID number of every other Droplet in its molecule, we use the lowest ID number amongst the Droplets in a given molecule to determine the phase of the blink.

If the receiving Droplet (call it 'C') is not bonded to the sender (call it 'O'), then it considers whether or not it should be. A change in bond status represents a reaction, so the first consideration $\mathbf{C}$ makes is whether the reaction would be spontaneous; whether $\Delta G_{rxn} < 0$. To do so, it must search the list of more than

---

[1] https://github.com/correlllab/cu-Droplet.

350 molecules to find each product and reactant. For a modern desktop, such a search could be performed linearly, but on the Droplet's small and low-cost hardware we wanted the performance benefits of storing the list as a prefix tree. The downside of such a data structure, however, is its large memory footprint, as we have a node for every prefix of a molecule and each node has to store a number of pointers in addition to the values. Using the method described in [11], we packed the prefix tree (which contains 659 nodes with pointer size of two bytes, value size of two bytes, and key size of one byte) as a single byte array with memory footprint of 2719 bytes

Assuming **C** has determined a spontaneous reaction should occur, it then checks its valence shell and that of **O**, to ensure that bonding wouldn't violate the octet rule and, if it doesn't, to determine which orbitals to bond to as determined by hybridization. If these and the other pre-bond checks are passed, **C** updates its state: valence shell, molecule, and bonded atoms.

The next time **C** sends out its own state message, **O** will see that **C** is trying to bond to it, and perform all of the above checks again. This is important because there may be some reason (specifically, due to interactions between **O** and a third Droplet) that **O** can't bond with **C**. If **O** confirms with its checks that a bond should occur, then it updates its own state, and the bond is formed. Otherwise, when **C** gets a new state message from **O** and sees that **O** isn't bonded to it, **C** gives up on the bond and fixes its own state accordingly.

5   Experiments and Results

Our molecule-forming algorithm reaches one or more of several stable states for every combination of atoms in the environment. We tested the algorithm by timing how long it took for one of these states to be reached for a certain number of individual atoms. In order to reduce the chance of error due to missing information, only hydrogen, oxygen, and carbon were used to test timing. These elements are the basic components of simple organic molecules, which means that there is a great deal of information available about the various molecules they form. Since the robots' IDs define the order in which they send messages, we switched the atomic identity of each robot to determine if a bias toward a particular state might be induced by having a predictable message ordering. We didn't find any obvious bias.

The total number of bonds present in all molecules usually increases with, but is not a direct function of, the number of atoms present. For example, if four hydrogen atoms and an oxygen atom are placed on the board, the total number of bonds in the stable state will be three, because these atoms will form a water molecule (H_2O) and

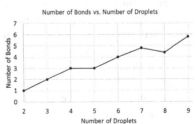

Fig. 4. The average number of bonds formed as a function of the number of Droplets.

dihydrogen (H_2). The maximum number of bonds we observed being formed from our choice of individual atoms was six, when nine atoms were present. Figure 4 shows this relationship.

The notable exception to this rule is when eight atoms are present. If we look at the average number of bonds present in stable configurations as a function of the number of atoms, we see a marked decrease for eight robots (Fig. 4). This likely explains why the time to reach a stable state seems to scale predictably with the number of atoms present, with one exception in the case of eight atoms: the important factor in time-to-stability is actually the total number of bonds in the stable configuration, as shown in Fig. 5.

While we could theoretically form any of the 659 encoded molecules, various factors make this difficult in practice. Specifically, as the size of the molecule increases, the likelihood that its components will form multiple, independently-stable smaller molecules increases as well. This is a consequence of the greedy nature of our molecule-forming algorithm (Fig. 6).

We also presented the Droplet Chemistry Simulation to a group of ten students in grades 10–12. All students are in the St. Vrain School District in Longmont, Colorado. We split the students into three groups and gave each group a board with several chemistry Droplets, as well as several other Droplets with nothing but synchronization code (these extra Droplets help maintain the synchronization, which loses stability for small numbers of robots). The session began with a brief introduction to how the Droplets worked: both hardware and software. We explained that the Droplets communicate using IR sensors and emitters, that they can determine range and bearing based on their communication, and that they walk using vibration motors. We also presented a modified chart of the periodic table that only included our subset of atoms. This chart showed which color corresponded to which atom, as well as the Lewis dot structure of each atom. The information given allowed students to predict which bonds would form by looking at the chart, and then test their prediction by observing the Droplets. The students observed the rate at which bonds formed, the rate at which they broke, and which atoms bonded when, by observing the

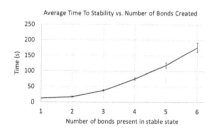

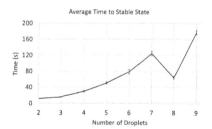

Fig. 5. Time to reach a stable state versus the number of bonds present in the stable state. Error bars represent standard error of the mean.

Fig. 6. Time to reach a stable state from unbonded component atoms. Error bars represent standard error of the mean, and sample size is 5.

pattern of synchronized blinks as well as the Droplets' motion. After a period of interacting with the hardware, we asked them a series of qualitative questions, that are omitted here for brevity, to probe the Droplet's qualities as a teaching tool.

The overall reaction we observed was very positive. Many students expressed the opinion that the Droplets would help or would have helped them to better understand chemistry at the time of their first class in the subject. All agreed that the Droplets would have increased their interest in introductory chemistry. Five students had taken a chemistry class before. When we asked them to rate their previous chemistry class, two students rated their class as a four and three students gave it a three. However, students did not express enthusiasm about the idea of chemistry when we asked them about their experiences with their first class. The Droplets, on the other hand, produced a significant amount of interest. Students were engaged and asked questions, volunteering ideas about other simulations the Droplets could perform. The students seemed in particular to appreciate the tangibility of the Droplets, as compared to what they had experienced in class.

6   Conclusion

Modeling the attractions that cause bonds between atoms intuitively seems like a trivial problem: perhaps one that is computationally expensive, but trivial nonetheless. However, it is important to remember that our ability to model physical forces is only as good as our knowledge of the forces themselves. Chemistry does not have an entirely accurate understanding of the atom yet, which makes modeling its behavior based on physical forces extremely difficult. The Droplets present a solution to this problem by using electronegativity to predict bond type, hybridization theory to predict molecular shape, and Gibbs Free Energy to predict reaction spontaneity. From a computational perspective, this is much more complicated than using the same concepts on a single computer. Instead of one "puppet-master" program controlling a set of virtual constructs in a perfect environment, the Droplets each have their own constant calculations running to determine their position in space relative to the robots around them.

Future work will include expanding the ability of the Droplets to be used as a teaching tool. Based on the positive reaction of the ten students who saw the chemistry simulation prototype, we think that it is worth performing a more formal educational study to judge the Droplets' efficacy in promoting interest in and understanding of chemistry. Our most immediate plans for future work are to conduct a larger scale controlled study of this in classrooms. The data from such a study would help guide which aspects of the simulation should be improved. One such aspect would be to use electronegativity for intermolecular interactions: causing the Droplets to move as if experiencing a force from surrounding molecules. This would allow the Droplets to demonstrate formation of lattice structures.

We also plan to expand the list of elements the Droplets can simulate. In particular, we would include metals, which have much more complicated interactions due to a more advanced orbital configuration. This would require restructuring the valence shell model and removing the assumption that the octet rule applies. We would also like to implement more complicated reactions using the atoms that we already simulate.

Although accurately modeling atomic and molecular interactions is an extremely difficult task, we are confident that the Droplets succeed in demonstrating atomic behavior with reasonable accuracy. Implementing a chemical simulation on a swarm platform also offers other advantages, such as interactivity and scalability.

References

1. Merlot II: Multimedia educational resource for learning and online teaching. http://tinyurl.com/j6686uz. Accessed 4 Jun 2016
2. Bonabeau, E., Dorigo, M., Theraulaz, G.: Swarm Intelligence: From Natural to Artificial Systems, vol. 1. Oxford University Press, Oxford (1999)
3. Burdge, J., Overby, J.: Chemistry Atoms First, Chap. 7.1, vol. 1. McGraw-Hill Learning Solutions, New York (2011)
4. Burdge, J., Overby, J.: Chemistry: Atoms First. McGraw-Hill, New York (2012)
5. Burgess, D.: NIST Chemistry WebBook. National Institute of Standards and Technology, Gaithersburg, MD (2005, 2008, 2009, 2010, 2011, 2012). http://webbook.nist.gov
6. Correll, N., Martinoli, A.: Modeling and designing self-organized aggregation in a swarm of miniature robots. Int. J. Robot. Res. **30**(5), 615–626 (2011)
7. Eddy, N.O., Awe, F.E., Gimba, C.E., Ibisi, N.O., Ebenso, E.E.: Qsar, experimental and computational chemistry simulation studies on the inhibition potentials of some amino acids for the corrosion of mild steel in 0.1 m HCL. Int. J. Electrochem. Sci **6**, 931–957 (2011)
8. Farrow, N., Klingner, J., Reishus, D., Correll, N.: Miniature six-channel range and bearing system: algorithm, analysis and experimental validation. In: 2014 IEEE International Conference on Robotics and Automation (ICRA), pp. 6180–6185. IEEE (2014)
9. Fjeld, M., Fredriksson, J., Ejdestig, M., Duca, F., Bötschi, K., Voegtli, B., Juchli, P.: Tangible user interface for chemistry education: comparative evaluation and redesign. In: Proceedings of the SIGCHI Conference on Human Factors in Computing Systems, pp. 805–808. ACM (2007)
10. Fjeld, M., Voegtli, B.M.: Augmented chemistry: an interactive educational workbench. In: 2002 Proceedings of the International Symposium on Mixed and Augmented Reality, ISMAR 2002, pp. 259–321. IEEE (2002)
11. Germann, U., Joanis, E., Larkin, S.: Tightly packed tries: how to fit large models into memory, and make them load fast, too. In: Proceedings of the Workshop on Software Engineering, Testing, and Quality Assurance for Natural Language Processing, pp. 31–39. Association for Computational Linguistics (2009)
12. Halloy, J., Sempo, G., Caprari, G., Rivault, C., Asadpour, M., Tâche, F., Said, I., Durier, V., Canonge, S., Amé, J.M., et al.: Social integration of robots into groups of cockroaches to control self-organized choices. Science **318**(5853), 1155–1158 (2007)
13. Hinze, J., Jaffe, H.H.: Electronegativity. I. orbital electronegativity of neutral atoms. J. Am. Chem. Soc. **84**(4), 540–546 (1962)

A. Randall et al.

14. Jensen, F.: Introduction to Computational Chemistry. Wiley, New York (2013)
15. Klingner, J., Kanakia, A., Farrow, N., Reishus, D., Correll, N.: A stick-slip omni-directional powertrain for low-cost swarm robotics: mechanism, calibration, and control. In: 2014 IEEE/RSJ International Conference on Intelligent Robots and Systems (IROS 2014), pp. 846–851. IEEE (2014)
16. Limniou, M., Roberts, D., Papadopoulos, N.: Full immersive virtual environment CAVE TM in chemistry education. Comput. Educ. **51**(2), 584–593 (2008)
17. Mirollo, R.E., Strogatz, S.H.: Synchronization of pulse-coupled biological oscillators. SIAM J. Appl. Math. **50**(6), 1645–1662 (1990)
18. Design Institute for Physical Properties, S.b.A.: DIPPR Project 801 - Full Version. Design Institute for Physical Property Research/AIChE (2005, 2008, 2009, 2010, 2011, 2012). http://app.knovel.com/hotlink/toc/id:kpDIPPRPF7/dippr-project-801-full/dippr-project-801-full
19. Richard, E., Tijou, A., Richard, P., Ferrier, J.L.: Multi-modal virtual environments for education with haptic and olfactory feedback. Virtual Reality **10**(3–4), 207–225 (2006)
20. Sayama, H.: Seeking open-ended evolution in swarm chemistry. In: 2011 IEEE Symposium on Artificial Life (ALIFE), pp. 186–193. IEEE (2011)
21. Silberberg, A.: Chemistry: The Molecular Nature of Matter and Change, Chap. 20.3, 7th edn. McGraw-Hill Education, New York (2015)
22. Stieff, M., Wilensky, U.: Connected chemistry-incorporating interactive simulations into the chemistry classroom. J. Sci. Educ. Technol. **12**(3), 285–302 (2003)
23. Vavra, K.L., Janjic-Watrich, V., Loerke, K., Phillips, L.M., Norris, S.P., Macnab, J.: Visualization in science education. Alberta Sci. Educ. J. **41**(1), 22–30 (2011)
24. Wang, Y., Jacob, D.J., Logan, J.A.: Global simulation of tropospheric O3-NOx-hydrocarbon chemistry. 1: model formulation. J. Geophys. Res. Atmos. **103**(D9), 10713–10725 (1998)
25. Wu, H.K., Shah, P.: Exploring visuospatial thinking in chemistry learning. Sci. Educ. **88**(3), 465–492 (2004)

Adaptive Combinatorial Neural Control for Robust Locomotion of a Biped Robot

Giuliano Di Canio$^{(\boxtimes)}$, Stoyan Stoyanov, Ignacio Torroba Balmori,
Jørgen Christian Larsen, and Poramate Manoonpong$^{(\boxtimes)}$

Embodied AI and Neurorobotics Lab, Centre for BioRobotics,
Mærsk Mc-Kinney Møller Institute, University of Southern Denmark,
Odense, Denmark
`giuliano.dicanio@gmail.com, poma@mmmi.sdu.dk`

Abstract. Humans can perform natural and robust walking behavior. They can even quickly adapt to different situations, like changing their walking speed to synchronize with the speed of a treadmill. Reproducing such complex abilities with artificial bipedal systems is still a difficult problem. To tackle this problem, we present here an adaptive combinatorial neural control circuit consisting of reflex-based and central pattern generator (CPG)-based mechanisms. The reflex-based control mechanism basically generates energy-efficient bipedal locomotion while the CPG-based mechanism with synaptic plasticity ensures robustness against loss of global sensory feedback (e.g., foot contact sensors) as well as allows for adaptation within a few steps to deal with environmental changes. We have successfully applied our control approach to the biomechanical bipedal robot DACBOT. As a result, the robot can robustly walk with energy efficiency and quickly adapt to different speeds of a treadmill.

Keywords: Locomotion control · Motor control · Artificial neural networks · Sensory-motor coordination · Humanoid robotics · Adaptive behavior · Central pattern generator · Bio-inspired robots

1 Introduction

Human locomotion is a complex process that results from the interaction of neural control and biomechanics [1,2]. While biomechanics allows for natural movements, neural control, on the other hand, plays a role in generating different locomotion patterns with energy efficiency as well as assuring that a proper pattern can be quickly employed to, for instance, adapt to terrain change. This process is fast and adaptive which leads to the generation of natural robust locomotion and adaptation. During the last few decades, roboticists have tried to imitate such complex abilities with artificial bipedal systems. Although different bipedal robot systems have been developed, most of them is based on engineering control techniques like trajectory-based methods with precise joint-angle control [3–6]. This results in non human-like locomotion (i.e., walking with

© Springer International Publishing Switzerland 2016
E. Tuci et al. (Eds.): SAB 2016, LNAI 9825, pp. 317–328, 2016.
DOI: 10.1007/978-3-319-43488-9_28

bending knee) and high energy consumption. Others use biologically-inspired control mechanisms where global sensory feedback, like foot contact signals, is continuously used for generating coordinated walking behavior [7–10]. Thus, the absence of the feedback can lead to unstable locomotion or failure. If learning mechanisms for adaptation are applied, then conventional machine learning techniques are normally employed [11–15]. Such learning techniques are usually complex and require an off-line learning process.

To tackle this problem, we present here a minimal adaptive combinatorial neural control approach coupled with biomechanics of our bipedal robot DACBOT. This control approach combines two main control modules: Reflex-based and CPG-based control modules. While the reflex-based control module [9] generates natural and energy-efficient locomotion, the CPG-based control module with synaptic plasticity allows for fast online adaptation to walk on different treadmill speeds as well as ensures robust locomotion against loss of (global) sensory feedback (e.g., foot contact sensors).

The paper is organized as follows. First, we describe the adaptive combinatorial neural control approach. Second, we present a setup of the biomechanical bipedal robot DACBOT. Third, we illustrate the performance of the control approach focusing on robust and adaptive walking on a treadmill at different speeds. Finally, we provide conclusion and discuss future work.

2 Adaptive Combinatorial Neural Control

The adaptive combinatorial neural control (Fig. 1) with a modular architecture consists of two main neural modules: CPG-based and reflex-based neural control modules (see subsections below for the details of each module). The idea behind this control approach is to first use the reflex-based control module to find and generate a proper walking frequency of a bipedal robot with respect to its property and the environment. Simultaneously, the CPG-based control module with synaptic plasticity learns the generated walking frequency and can later control the robot for robust walking behavior even without sensory feedback.

According to this concept, at the beginning the reflex-based control generates locomotion based on joint angle and foot contact sensory feedback for the biomechanical bipedal robot DACBOT. While the robot is walking, the CPG-based control uses only hip angle feedback to adapt its internal frequency to match the walking frequency generated by the reflex-based control. When the reflex-based control is disconnected (manually or due to sensory failure), the CPG-based control can still drive the robot. As long as the hip angle feedback is applied to the CPG-based control, the control can adapt its internal frequency to walking behavior with respect to the environment. If the feedback is removed from the CPG-based control, the robot will still be able to stably walk with the adapted walking frequency.

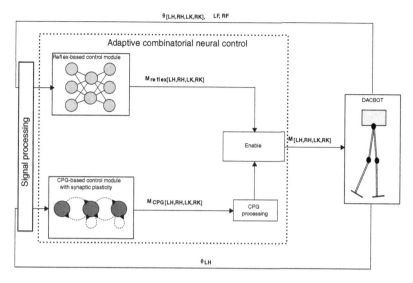

Fig. 1. The adaptive combinatorial neural control uses reflex-based neural control and CPG-based neural control with synaptic plasticity to generate energy-efficient, robust, and adaptive locomotion of a biped robot, like DACBOT. The reflex-based control generates the motor outputs ($M_{reflex[LH,RH,LK,RK]}$) by using all sensory information: Left/right hip angle feedback ($\theta_{LH,RH}$), left/right knee angle feedback ($\theta_{LK,RK}$), and left/right foot contact feedback (LF, RF). When the reflex-based control drives the robot system, the CPG-based control uses only hip angle feedback (e.g., the left hip (θ_{LH})) to adapt its internal frequency to generate the motor outputs ($M_{CPG[LH,RH,LK,RK]}$). A CPG processing unit is used to shape the CPG motor outputs by using threshold functions to obtain proper patterns for locomotion control. The shaped patterns follow the ones generated by the reflex-based control. An enable unit selects (manually or due to sensors failure) either the reflex motor outputs or the CPG motor outputs and transmits the selected motor outputs ($M_{[LH,RH,LK,RK]}$) to finally control the robot. Note that raw sensory signals are firstly preprocessed at a signal processing unit and then transmitted to the reflex-based and CPG-based control units. We use a low pass filter to remove sensory noise at the processing unit.

2.1 Reflex-Based Neural Control

The reflex-based neural control, developed in our previous study [9] for biped locomotion, is a sensor-driven neural network with a hierarchical design. It is simulated as mono-synaptic connections containing motor neurons for hip and knee joints ($M_{reflex[LH,RH,LK,RK]}$, see Fig. 2(a)). The motor neurons are linear and can send their signals unaltered to the motors of a biped robot. Furthermore, there are several local non-spiking sensory neurons (rate coded neurons), which by their conjoint reflex-like actions trigger the walking pattern. These local sensor neurons are for joint control, intrajoint control and leg control. Joint control arises from sensors at each joint (ES, FS), which measure the joint angle and influence only their corresponding motor neurons. Intra-joint control is achieved

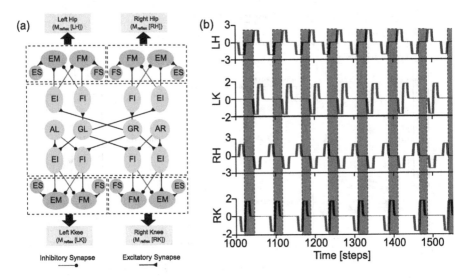

Fig. 2. (a) The reflex-based neural control coupled with biomechanics for generating energy-efficient locomotion of the bipedal robot DACBOT. $AL(AR)$ refers to stretch receptor for anterior extreme angle of left (right) hip. $GL(GR)$ refers to ground contact sensor neuron of left (right) foot. $EI(FI)$ refers to extensor (flexor) reflex interneuron. $EM(FM)$ refers to extensor (flexor) motor neuron and $ES(FS)$ is extensor (flexor) sensor neuron. (b) Energy-efficient walking of DACBOT. The motor outputs ($M_{reflex[LH,RH,LK,RK]}$) are directly sent to the robot through amplifiers. Gray areas indicate when all four motor outputs (corresponding to motor voltage) remain zero during part of every step cycle; i.e., DACBOT walks passively.

from sensors, which measure the anterior extreme angle (AL, AR) at the hip and trigger an extensor reflex at the corresponding knee. Leg control comes from ground foot contact sensors (GL, GR), which influence the motor neurons of all joints. In general, the reflexive locomotion generation works as follows: When one foot touches the ground, the hip extensor and knee flexor of the other leg (swing leg) are triggered, as well as the hip flexor and knee extensor of the stance leg. When the hip stretch receptor of the swing leg is activated, the extensor of the knee joint in this leg is triggered. Finally the foot of the swing leg touches the ground and the swing leg and the stance leg swap their roles thereafter. The generated motor patterns of the controller can be seen at Fig. 2(b).

Further details of the controller are not subject of this study, but can be found in [9]. Although the reflex-based neural control coupled with biomechanics of DACBOT can generate energy-efficient locomotion (see Fig. 2(b)), it fails if sensory feedback is not provided. Thus, here we apply the CPG-based neural control (Fig. 3) to overcome this problem. For energy-efficient locomotion in our study here, we implies that the robot does not require energy all the time during walking; i.e., it has partly passive locomotion (here, approx. 32 % of one gait cycle, see gray areas in Fig. 2(b)) where all actuators are not actively actuated (receiving zero voltage).

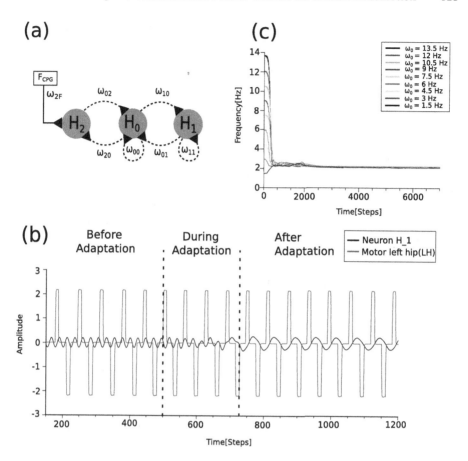

Fig. 3. (a) The CPG-based neural control with synaptic plasticity. The neurons ($H_{0,1,2}$) are connected through synaptic plasticity ($\omega_{00,01,10,11,20,02}$) to generate a periodic pattern with its internal frequency. The internal frequency can be entrained by an external feedback through the synaptic weight (ω_{2F}). By using the Hebbian-type learning rules (Eqs. 2, 3, and 4) and the frequency adaptation rule (Eq. 5) for synaptic plasticity, the CPG-based neural control can be entrained to quickly adapt its output frequency to the external frequency of sensory feedback and can memorize the adapted frequency although the feedback has been removed. (b) CPG and hip motor signals before, during, and after adaptation. The CPG-based control can quickly change its frequency within about 3–4 walking cycles. (c) Time series of the internal frequency changes during walking for different initial frequencies (ω_0). It finally converts to a proper walking frequency of DACBOT which is originally generated by the reflex-based control.

2.2   CPG-based Neural Control

The CPG-based neural control (Fig. 3(a)), developed in our previous study [16], consists of three rate coded neurons with a hyperbolic tangent (tanh) transfer function. The two neurons ($H_{0,1}$) are fully connected with the four synapses

$(\omega_{00}, \omega_{01}, \omega_{10}, \omega_{11})$. This forms an oscillator if the synaptic weights are chosen according to an SO(2)-matrix [17]:

$$\mathbf{W} = \begin{pmatrix} w_{00} & w_{01} \\ w_{10} & w_{11} \end{pmatrix} = \alpha \cdot \begin{pmatrix} cos(\varphi) & sin(\varphi) \\ -sin(\varphi) & cos(\varphi) \end{pmatrix}. \tag{1}$$

With $-\pi < \varphi < \pi$ and $\alpha > 1$, the oscillator generates sine-shaped periodic outputs $(o_{0,1})$ of the neurons $(H_{0,1})$ where φ defines a frequency of the signals. The third neuron (H_2) receives sensory feedback (F_{CPG}) through the plastic synapse (ω_{2F}) and connects to the oscillator through the other plastic synapses $(\omega_{02}, \omega_{20})$. For convenience, we use here the left hip angle signal (θ_{LH}) of DACBOT as the feedback. These plastic synapses are governed by Hebbian-type learning rules based on correlation and relaxation terms driving the weights towards given relaxation values $(\omega_{2F_{relax}}, \omega_{02_{relax}}, \omega_{20_{relax}})$. The parameters A, $B > 0$ determine the influence of the individual terms [16]:

$$\omega_{2F}(t+1) = \omega_{2F}(t) + A \cdot F_{CPG}(t) \cdot o_2(t) - B \cdot (\omega_{2F}(t) - \omega_{2F_{relax}}), \tag{2}$$

$$\omega_{02}(t+1) = \omega_{02}(t) - A \cdot o_0(t) \cdot o_2(t) - B \cdot (\omega_{02}(t) - \omega_{02_{relax}}), \tag{3}$$

$$\omega_{20}(t+1) = \omega_{20}(t) - A \cdot o_2(t) \cdot o_0(t) - B \cdot (\omega_{20}(t) - \omega_{20_{relax}}). \tag{4}$$

The parameter $(\varphi$, Eq. 1) is adapted based on the following frequency adaptation rule:

$$\varphi(t+1) = \varphi(t) + \mu \cdot \omega_{02}(t) \cdot o_2(t) \cdot \omega_{01}(t) \cdot o_1(t), \tag{5}$$

where μ is a learning rate, o_1 and o_2 are the outputs of the neurons $(H_{1,2})$, and ω_{01} and ω_{02} are synaptic weights (Fig. 3(a)). With an appropriate choice of the control parameters [16], the CPG-based control governed by above equations is able to adapt to sensory feedback (F_{CPG}) within a wide frequency range. As soon as the controller has adapted to the external frequency of the sensory feedback (F_{CPG}), the average correlation of o_2 (sensory feedback) and o_1 (controller output) is equal to zero. After adaptation, the sensory feedback can be removed from the controller while it maintains to oscillate at the adapted frequency.

Here, the output (o_1) of the CPG neuron (H_1) is used for controlling the hip and knee joints of DACBOT since after the adaptation process the output will be in phase with the reflex motor command. This will lead to smooth switching between the reflex-based and CPG-based control; thereby the dynamical stability of the system is still maintained. The final CPG output (o_1) is post-processed at a CPG processing unit to obtain the hip and knee motor patterns $(M_{CPG[LH,RH,LK,RK]}$, e.g., red line in Fig. 3(b)) that have exactly the same motor patterns $(M_{reflex[LH,RH,LK,RK]}$, see Fig. 2(b)) of the reflex-based control. The CPG-based control can quick adapt to the proper walking frequency of DACBOT and is not sensitive to an initial internal frequency (Fig. 3(c)).

3   Setup of the Biomechanical Bipedal Robot DACBOT

DACBOT (Dynamic, Adaptive, Compliant walking robot) is a biomechanical bipedal robot which has been developed based on RunBot [9]. It is a 600 g robot,

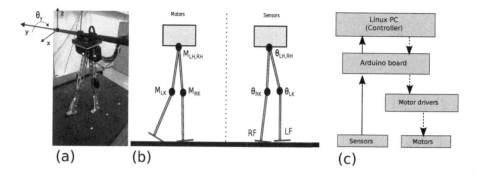

Fig. 4. (a) The planar bipedal robot DACBOT. For our experiments here, we constrain the robot such that it can only rotate along the y-axis. (b) Motors and sensors of DACBOT. (c) Schematic of the DACBOT setup.

26 cm tall from foot to hip. Since the robot is designed for two-dimensional motion, a rod is used to constrain its movement and prevent lateral displacement; therefore, the robot can only rotate along the y-axis (Fig. 4(a)). DACBOT consists of two legs, where each leg is actuated by hip and knee joints. With a special design based on a human leg, each leg of DACBOT consists of a compliant ankle connected to a flat foot. It is mainly employed to realize dynamic and robust self-stabilization in a passive compliant manner. In addition, each foot has one switch sensor for ground detection as a binary feedback. The left and right hips are actuated by HS-624MG servomotors while the left and right knees are actuated by HS-85BB+ micro servomotors. The built-in controller of each servomotor was removed in order to directly control its DC motor and be able to read the angle feedback via its internal potentiometer sensor.

The motor commands ($M_{LH,LK,RH,RK}$, Fig. 4(b)), generated by the adaptive combinatorial controller, are sent to the DACBOT motors through an Arduino UNO board and the Groove I2C Motor drivers. The sensory signals ($\theta_{LH,LK,RH,RK}, LF, LH$, Fig. 4(b)) are also digitized using this board for the purpose of feeding them into the controller. The schematic of the DACBOT setup can be seen at Fig. 4(c). A treadmill used to carry out our robot walking experiments has been modified so that its speed can be controlled through a computer.

4   Experiments and Results

Several experiments were carried out to show the performance of the adaptive combinatorial neural control. For the first experiment, we let DACBOT walk with the reflex-based control while the CPG-based control was disabled (Fig. 5). During walking, we then disabled a foot sensor at around 300 time steps. Since the CPG-based control was not activated, DACBOT failed to walk without foot contact feedback. In general, the reflex-based control can generate proper walking

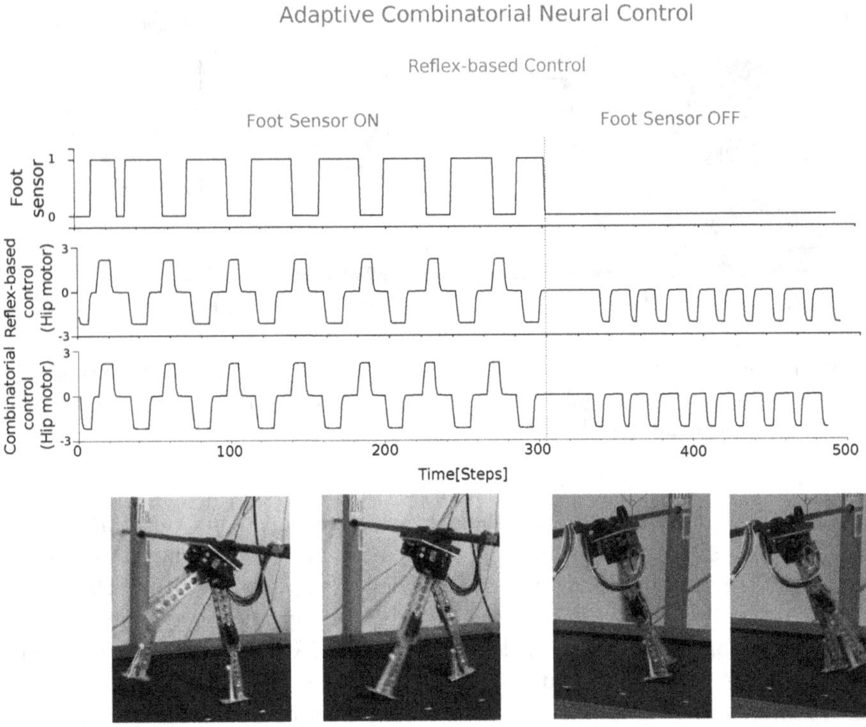

Fig. 5. DACBOT locomotion driven by only the reflex-based control of the adaptive combinatorial neural control. At the first period, all sensors were provided to the system. Therefore, the controller generated stable locomotion. Once a foot sensor has been disabled at around 300 time steps, the controller cannot generate proper motor signals. The top panel shows the left foot sensor signal. The middle panel shows a motor signal of the reflex-based control. The bottom panel shows the final motor signal controlling the left hip of DACBOT from the adaptive combinatorial control. In this case, since only the reflex-based control is used to drive the system, the combinatorial control has the same output as the reflex-based control. We encourage readers to watch the video clip of this experiment at http://manoonpong.com/SAB2016/M1.mp4.

behavior when all sensory feedback ($\theta_{LH,RH,LK,RK}$, LF, RF) are provided, while it fails if any sensory feedback (e.g., foot sensor signal) is missing.

For the second experiment, we let DACBOT walk with a combination of the reflex-based and CPG-based control (Fig. 6) where the reflex-based control drove DACBOT first and then the CPG-based control took over as soon as its frequency adapted to the walking frequency generated by the reflex-based control. Afterwards, we disabled a foot sensor at around 1000 time steps. Since DACBOT was driven by the CPG-based control after the frequency adaptation, it can still stably walk without foot contact feedback.

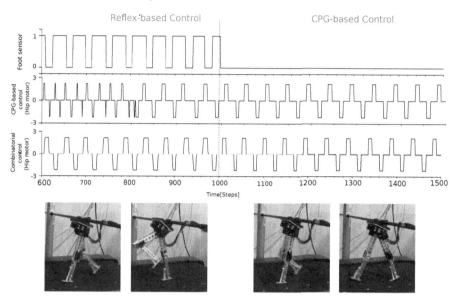

Fig. 6. Robust locomotion of DACBOT driven by the adaptive combinatorial control. Initially, the system was driven by the reflex-based control and simultaneously the CPG-based control adapted its internal frequency using the frequency adaptation mechanism with hip angle feedback to synchronize with the generated walking frequency. At around 1000 time steps, a foot sensor was disabled but DACBOT still performed robust locomotion driven by the CPG-based control. We encourage readers to watch the video clip of this experiment at http://manoonpong.com/SAB2016/M2.mp4.

The last experiment shows adaptive locomotion of DACBOT on different speeds of the treadmill. DACBOT was driven by the combinatorial control. The same procedure as the second experiment was performed with an extension of changing the speed of the treadmill after DACBOT was controlled by the CPG-based control where foot contact feedback was also disabled. We increased the speed of the treadmill from 0.09 m/s to 0.15 m/s and finally to 0.23 m/s. Figure 7 shows frequency adaptation and a hip motor signal with respect to the different situations. It can be seen that the controller can quickly react and adapt its output frequency to generate proper locomotion behavior. Recall that we used only a hip angle signal for the frequency adaptation process.

Adaptive Combinatorial Neural Control

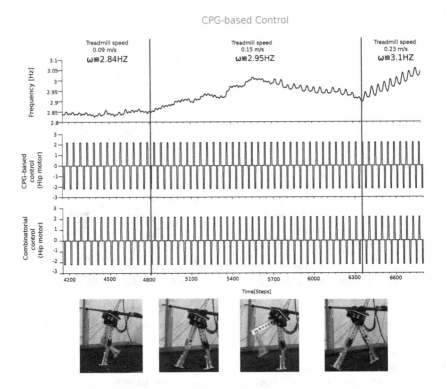

Fig. 7. Adaptation to three different speeds of the treadmill. Here DACBOT was controlled by the combinatorial control where the reflex-based control drove the system first and then the CPG-based control took over. Walking frequency was adapted according to the speed of the treadmill. The online frequency adaptation is obtained from the adaptation process of the CPG-based control with hip angle feedback. The top panel shows the internal frequency of the CPG-based control adapting to the different speeds of the treadmill. The middle panel shows a motor signal of the CPG-based control. The bottom panel shows the final motor signal controlling the left hip of DACBOT from the adaptive combinatorial control. This adaptation leads to different walking behaviors; i.e., DACBOT performed about six walking cycles within 300 time steps at 0.09 m/s, about seven walking cycles within 300 time steps at 0.15 m/s, and about eight walking cycles within 300 time steps at 0.23 m/s. Note that due to the robot dynamics, the CPG frequency can slightly increase and decrease although the treadmill is constant. We encourage readers to watch the video clip of this experiment at http://manoonpong. com/SAB2016/M3.mp4.

5   Conclusion and Future Work

This paper presents the development of adaptive combinatorial neural control for a biped robot, like DACBOT. It combines reflex-based and CPG-based control mechanisms. Based on our control strategy, the reflex-based control firstly drives the robot system by exploiting sensory feedback and biomechanics of the robot to obtain proper walking frequency and leg coordination which results in energy-efficient locomotion. In parallel, the CPG-based control adapts its internal frequency to the actual walking frequency. Once the internal frequency of the CPG-based control has matched to the actual walking frequency or the CPG output has become in phase with the reflex output, the CPG-based control can be switched to control the system. Due to synaptic plasticity and a frequency adaptation mechanism embedded in the CPG-based control, DACBOT can quickly adapt its walking frequency to a change of the speed of a treadmill. For the adaptation, only a hip angle signal is required as sensory feedback to the CPG-based control while other sensory signals (e.g., knee and foot sensor signals) can be removed (as shown in the last experiment). This way, DACBOT performs adaptive locomotion with minimal feedback requirement. Furthermore, DACBOT can still perform robust locomotion at a certain walking speed even the hip angle signal has been removed from the CPG-based control. Such adaptive and robust locomotion cannot be achieved by purely reflex-based control [9] while proper initial walking frequency and leg coordination cannot be achieved by purely CPG-based control.

Some works combined CPG-based control with adaptive mechanisms (like, reinforcement learning [13] and evolutionary algorithms [14,15]) for robust locomotion. However, such adaptive mechanisms need long learning time. In contrast, our control strategy with synaptic plasticity and the frequency adaptation mechanism can generate robust locomotion and online adaptation within a few steps to deal with environmental changes. Thus, this study shows that this novel and simple combinatorial control approach -presented here for the first time- may be a way forward to solve coordination problems and to achieve fast online adaptation with minimal feedback in other complex motor tasks for active prosthetic and orthotic devices. In the next step, we will implement a 2DOF upper body component on DACBOT and develop adaptive body control to allow DACBOT to walk with minimal movement constraints and to deal with large disturbance.

Acknowledgments. This research was supported partly by Bernstein Center for Computational Neuroscience II Goettingen (BCCN grant 01GQ1005A, project D1) and Center for BioRobotics (CBR) at the University of Southern Denmark (SDU).

References

1. Orlovsky, G.N., Deliagina, T.G., Grillner, S.: Neuronal Control of Locomotion: From Mollusk to Man. Oxford University Press, Oxford (1999)
2. Dickinson, M.H., Farley, C.T., Full, R.J., Koehl, M.A.R., Kram, R., Lehman, S.: How animals move: an integrative view. Science **288**(5463), 100–106 (2000)
3. Okada, k., Ogura, T., Haneda, A., Kousaka, N.H., Inaba, M., Inoue, H.: Integrated system software for HRP2 humanoid. In: Proceedings of IEEE International Conference on Robotics and Automation, pp. 3207–3212 (2004)

4. Ogura, Y., Kondo, H., Morishima, A., Lim, H., Takanishi, A.: Development of a new humanoid robot WABIAN-2. In: Proceedings of IEEE International Conference on Robotics and Automation, pp. 76–81 (2006)
5. Kajita, S., Kanehiro, F., Kaneko, K., Fujiwara, K., Harada, K., Yokoi, K., Hirukawa, H.: Bipedal walking pattern generation by using preview control of zero-moment point. In: Proceedings of IEEE International Conference on Robotics and Automation, pp. 1620–1626 (2003)
6. Chevallereau, C., Djoudi, D., Grizzle, J.: Stable bipedal walking with foot rotation through direct regulation of the zero moment point. IEEE Trans. Robot. **24**(2), 390–401 (2008). IEEE
7. Endo, G., Nakanishi, J., Morimoto, J., Cheng, G.: Experimental studies of a neural oscillator for biped locomotion with QRIO. In: Proceedings of IEEE International Conference on Robotics and Automation, pp. 596–602 (2005)
8. Woosung, Y., Chong, N.Y., Ra, S., Chang, H.K., Bum, J.Y.: Self-stabilizing bipedal locomotion employing neural oscillators. In: Proceedings of IEEE International Conference on Humanoid Robots, pp. 8–15 (2008)
9. Manoonpong, P., Geng, T., Kulvicius, T., Porr, B., Woergoetter, F.: Adaptive, fast walking in a biped robot under neuronal control and learning. PLOS Comput. Biol. **3**(7), e134 (2007)
10. Pratt, J., Chew, C.-M., Torres, A., Dilworth, P., Pratt, G.: Virtual model control: an intuitive approach for bipedal locomotion. Int. J. Robot. Res. **20**, 129–143 (2001)
11. Calandra, R., Gopalan, N., Seyfarth, A., Peters, J., Deisenroth, M.P.: Bayesian gait optimization for bipedal locomotion. In: Pardalos, P.M., Resende, M.G.C., Vogiatzis, C., Walteros, J.L. (eds.) Lion 8. LNCS, vol. 8426, pp. 274–290. Springer, Switzerland (2014)
12. Nakanishi, J., Morimoto, J., Endo, G., Cheng, G., Schaala, S., Kawato, M.: Learning from demonstration and adaptation of biped locomotion. Robot. Auton. Syst. **47**, 79–91 (2004)
13. Matsubara, T., Morimoto, J., Nakanishi, J., Sato, M.A., Doya, K.: Learning CPG-based biped locomotion with a policy gradient method. Robot. Auton. Syst. **54**(11), 911–920 (2006)
14. Reil, T., Husbands, P.: Evolution of central pattern generators for bipedal walking in a real-time physics environment. IEEE Trans. Evol. Comput. **6**(2), 159–168 (2002)
15. Dip, G., Prahlad, V., Kien, P.D.: Genetic algorithm-based optimal bipedal walking gait synthesis considering tradeoff between stability margin and speed. Robotica **27**, 355–365 (2009)
16. Nachstedt, T., Wörgötter, F., Manoonpong, P.: Adaptive neural oscillator with synaptic plasticity enabling fast resonance tuning. In: Villa, A.E.P., Duch, W., Érdi, P., Masulli, F., Palm, G. (eds.) ICANN 2012, Part I. LNCS, vol. 7552, pp. 451–458. Springer, Heidelberg (2012)
17. Pasemann, F., Hild, M., Zahedi, K.: SO(2)-networks as neural oscillators. In: Mira, J., Álvarez, J.R. (eds.) IWANN 2003. LNCS, vol. 2686, pp. 144–151. Springer, Heidelberg (2003)

Generalising Predictable Object Movements Through Experience Using Schemas

Suresh Kumar[1,2]([✉]), Patricia Shaw[1], Daniel Lewkowicz[1], Alexandros Giagkos[1], Mark Lee[1], and Qiang Shen[1]

[1] Department of Computer Science, Aberystwyth University, Aberystwyth, UK
{suk9,phs,dal46,alg25,mhl,qqs}@aber.ac.uk
[2] Sukkur Institute of Business Administration-Sukkur IBA, Sukkur, Pakistan
suresh@iba-suk.edu.pk

Abstract. In humans, repeated exposure to the effects of events can lead to anticipation of these effects. This behaviour has been observed in infants from as young as 3 months old. During infant experiments, the infants have been observed to predict either by pre-saccadic movements or reach actions according to the expected future outcome of the event. Event anticipation or prediction is necessary for such behaviours. In this paper we demonstrate prediction of object motion events using the adaptive learning tool Dev-PSchema. Results shows that the system is able to predict the linear motion outcome of the visual event using generalised schemas.

Keywords: Developmental robotics · Psychologically inspired · Action prediction

1 Introduction

Humans can be seen as complex cognitive systems with the capability to make anticipatory behaviours prior to the event outcome. Even human infants, as young as 3 months old, have been observed to show anticipatory behaviours [3]. This anticipatory behaviours plays an important roll in the infants' learning process [12]. Such behaviours help to build and demonstrate an understanding of repeatable events and the agents causing the events or the objects involved in such events.

Psychologists have been investigating anticipatory behaviours and event predictions for many years. The prediction of spatio-temporal information of an event or agent and tracking the moving objects are the main interests in such investigations. There are many evidences of the anticipatory behaviours in humans observed using visual attention and motor control. Schlesinger and Casey in [14] found that 6 months old infants look longer at impossible events than possible events. Longer looking time is obtained when infants observe a new event or an event does not meet expectations. Similarly, Alder and Haith found that 3 months old babies can predict visual events [1].

This evidence suggests that infants possess visual anticipation capability even at early infancy. Infants have been found to use such visual anticipation

© Springer International Publishing Switzerland 2016
E. Tuci et al. (Eds.): SAB 2016, LNAI 9825, pp. 329–339, 2016.
DOI: 10.1007/978-3-319-43488-9_29

in their behaviours. Claxton [5] found that around 10 months old, infants possess some representation of future state of events and use that representation for anticipatory behaviour. Similarly, Hofsten et al. found that 6 months old can predict the position of a moving object and use that information to reach for and intercept the object [9]. This demonstrates that infants possess visual event anticipation as well as anticipatory behaviours. These anticipatory behaviours consist of two main sequential steps; (i) Observing – predicting – expecting the future outcome of an event occurring within a static or dynamic scenario, and (ii) Planning and executing the behaviour based on the anticipated outcome.

For example if a subject wants to catch an object, he/she will need to anticipate the outcome of an objects motion in spatio-temporal space. For static objects, the subject will expect that the object will remain at the same position while in a dynamic situation the change in an objects position is predicted over time. This prediction is the result of an inference made by comparing the current situation with that of previous experiences [11]. An action is then planned taking into consideration the anticipated outcome of the motion [5] and finally it is executed. Similarly Canfield and Haith [3] found that 3.5 months old infants are not only able to anticipate symmetric visual events but they can anticipate asymmetric event as well.

In robotics applications, a robot may need to act in a dynamic environment where objects may change in spatio-temporal space. These changes may be connected with the robot's actions, triggered by another agent in the environment, or be part of the environment itself. An intelligent robotic system should not only be able to infer about anticipated states of the world and actions but also learn relationships between the states and, where the robot is the cause, the associated actions as well. Such relationships will help to predict the future state of a given variable for a particular action. Then, once able to predict, these behaviours can also be applied as goal directed behaviours to achieve the desired effect [12].

Considering event prediction as an initial step of anticipatory behaviours, in this paper we demonstrate the capability of the schema system, *Dev-PSchema*, for learning movements of objects following an action. The schema system then makes initial predictions about the changes by applying mathematical functions to the variables of properties used in states and action. In Sect. 2 we will discuss the psychological and robotic studies relevant to the topic. In Sect. 3 we will discuss the methodology used in this study and present results obtained from experiments. Finally in Sect. 4 we will discuss the implications of the results and future work.

2   Background

The world is full of objects and agents, which are dynamic and change their spatio-temporal position. These changes can be related with the other objects or agents in the environment. Where these changes are predictable, an intelligent system must be able to learn these relations and be able to anticipate the outcome of dynamic objects based on those relations.

Considering anticipation as an important part of learning, developments in artificial intelligence are shifting towards systems which infer according to the predicated outcome of an action on a given environmental state rather than solely based on the environmental state itself [12]. Researchers in robotics, in this regard, are working to develop learning systems which can be used for anticipation in robots.

Geib et al. [7] proposed a learning model based on action and high level perceptual information; Object-Action-Complexes (OACs). Learning was represented in 'Instantiated State Transition Fragments' (ISTF) containing action and perceptual information before and after the action. The model also provides mechanism for extending the learning by generalised ISTF, referred to as OACs. OACs also helps to plan the action for a given perceptual state.

An extension to the OACs model was proposed by Worgotter et al. [18]. This incorporated the ability to calculate and adjust predictability of outcomes. They believed that the OACs system could be extended to find the change between the state before and after actions, which can be used to predict the outcome of actions on novel situations. The proposed extension involved a supervisory mechanism which was used to guide the unpredictability.

Similarly, Hermans et al. [8] demonstrated object affordance prediction using OACs. Affordance prediction was tested on six different object classes and demonstrated significant accuracy. However, supervised learning methods, such as Support Vector Machines (SVMs) and k-Nearest Neighbours (k-NNs) were used to learn affordances, which requires a large number of training examples to learn. The model has shown a good level of accuracy for the objects which belonged to the object class used for the training purpose, however a large error rate was obtained for novel objects. In general the OACs model requires a supervisory learning mechanism to learn predictions along with the intermediate system to link high level system and low level sensory and motor control.

In developmental robotics, researchers aim to develop on-line and open ended learning system inspired from the psychology [4]. Aguilar [2] proposed another goal based behavioural unsupervised learning system. The system is based on Piaget's theory of sensorimotor learning [13]. The learning outcomes of this are the schemas, containing context, action and expectations. This system posesses the capability for on-line learning. However, the type generalisation used in the system is deductive. A very abstract schema is created with very first experience and accommodated to create concrete schema.

In this paper we demonstrate the anticipation capability of a schema system, Dev-PSchema, an extended version of PSchema [17]. This system is a tool for on-line learning and posses inductive generalising capability, creating abstract schema after certain experiences. In the following section, we discuss the extensions made for Dev-PSchema.

3   Methodology

We are using the adaptive behaviour learning tool, *Dev-PSchema*, an enhanced version of the original *PSchema* system developed by Sheldon [17]. Following Piaget's sensorimotor learning paradigm, this tool enables artificial agents to learn dynamically and behave according to their learning experiences. The learning outcome is represented in a schema format, consisting of sensory states before and after action, referred to as pre-conditions and post-conditions respectively, along with the associated action.

The system creates a new schema when a new sensory state is obtained in response to any motor action. In this work we are using the same schema building algorithm as introduced in [16]. The system has an excitation calculator which is responsible for selecting appropriate action schemas, from available schemas, for a given sensory state. The mechanism for the excitation calculation of a schema in for a given state is outlined in Algorithm 1.

Algorithm 1. Excitation algorithm

```
1:  procedure get_excitation(State new, Schema S)
2:      if S has preconditions then
3:          if preconditions in S are similar to new then
4:              predictions = preconditions of S
5:          else
6:              Return 0
7:          end if
8:      else
9:          predictions = postconditions of S
10:     end if
11:     calculate similarity between predictions and new
12:     Return similarity
13: end procedure
```

This system is also capable of generalising learning outcomes, i.e. schemas, using inductive inference. We have extended the generalisation mechanism in *Dev-PSchema*. Where the properties of pre and post-conditions are numeric, the generalising mechanism determines the mathematical relation between the variables used in preconditions, post-conditions and actions. Previously in PSchema [17], the generalisation was limited to recognising change in these values, but not identifying relationships in terms of how the values may have changed. The new schema generalising mechanism for *Dev-PSchema* is illustrated in Algorithm 2.

In a generalised schemas, variables of properties to define sensory states and actions are replaced with "$" plus a unique random character. The mechanism attempts to identify if the change in the values can be described by a repeatable mathematical function. If this is the case, then the function representing the change will also be included as part of the generalised variable. Currently, the system is limited to the additive relation $(+/-)$ between two variables. A generalising example is illustrated in Fig. 1.

Figure 1 shows that two schemas, schema 1 and 2, of the same action type are used to make a generalised schema where variables which appeared with different values or which are of less importance in the action of the schema are

---

Algorithm 2. Generalisation algorithm

 1: **procedure** GENERALISE(*Schema* **new**, **old_schemas**)
 2:     **if** "new" don't have preconditions **then**
 3:         *return*
 4:     **end if**
 5:     **for** each schema **S** in *old_schemas* **do**
 6:         **if S** not generalised *AND* size and type of preconditions, postconditions and action of **S** are same as **new then**
 7:             *Add "S" in List* **similars**
 8:         **end if**
 9:         **if** action in **S** and **new** are similar *AND* postconditions in **S** are less than postconditions in **new then**
10:             *Add postcondition properties in* **old_props**
11:         **end if**
12:     **end for**
13:     **trial_schema** = *copy of new*
14:     *add empty set* "**Var**"
15:     **for** each property **P** in precondition of **S** in **similars do**
16:         **if P** not in **second elements** of set **var then**
17:             **if P** has two different values *OR* is in **old_props then**
18:                 *add set (random character, P) in* **vars**
19:             **end if**
20:         **end if**
21:     **end for**
22:     **for** each property **P** in preconditions of **trial_schema do**
23:         **if P** is in second elements of set **Vars then**
24:             *replace* **P** *with first element of set* "**Vars**"
25:         **end if**
26:     **end for**
27:     **for** each property **P** in postconditions & actions of **trial_schema do**
28:         *Find fucntion* **F** *between* **P** & *second element of set* "**Vars**"
29:         **if** function exists **then**
30:             *replace* **P** *with first element(of Vars)* + **F**
31:         **else**
32:             *replace* **P** *with first element(of Vars)*
33:         **end if**
34:     **end for**
35: **end procedure**

---

replaced with a generalised variable, "$" plus a unique random character, along with a function if identified.

3.1 Experiment

We used a simple simulator for our experiment. The simulator contains 25 (5×5) visual spaces and the capability to saccade, and fixate, to any of these position. Each visual space consist of 32×32 pixels, with objects fully contained in a single

Schema 1		
⊟ Preconditions	⊟ Action	⊟ Postconditions
Colour 'Red' at 1,1 Shape 'Sphere' at 1, 1	Reach 1, 1	Colour 'Red' at 1, 1 Shape 'Sphere' at 1, 1 Touching object at 1, 1

Schema 2		
⊟ Preconditions	⊟ Action	⊟ Postconditions
Colour 'Red' at 2,2 Shape 'Cube' at 2, 2	Reach 2, 2	Colour 'Red' at 2, 2 Shape 'Cube' at 2, 2 Touching object at 2, 2

Generalised Schema		
⊟ Preconditions	⊟ Action	⊟ Postconditions
Colour '$a' at $b, $c Shape '$d' at $b, $c	Reach $b, $c	Colour '$a' at $b, $c Shape '$d' at $b, $c Touching object at $b, $c

Fig. 1. Generalised schema obtained from Schema 1 and Schema 2

position at any point in time. When fixating on a given position the rest of the visual space can be considered as peripheral regions. The simulator provides high level perceptual information about the visual scene to the *schema* system, which uses this information to create learning outcomes, schemas, and simulate play behaviour. Figure 2 shows the simulator environment (left) and current sensory state of it (right). The "X" mark shows the current fixated position, while the red and green shapes are the objects shown in peripheral visual space.

At the start of the experiment, the system is bootstrapped to fixate on each of the visual spaces before any objects are introduced. This process helps the system to build the basic schemas corresponding to the primitive actions that it can perform and corresponds to the random motor babbling in very early infants, building up the sensorimotor control. It is worth mentioning that in this

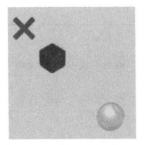

Fixate at 0, 0
Colour "Red" at 1,1
Shape 'Cube' at 1, 1
Colour "Green" at 3,3
Shape 'Sphere' at 3, 3

Fig. 2. Simulator and sensory information

experiment, the system does not observe the environment continuously but only before and after the execution of any action.

When an object is introduced in the simulator, the excitation system activates the action schema relevant to the current sensory state. For example an object at position (1, 1) will trigger the system to fixate at that position, due to recalling the schema where it previously fixated that position. It will also excite the reach action schema to that position, where it remembers seeing its own hand, although only one schema is executed at a time and the reach action is not used in this experiment.

In order to investigate prediction of visual events, an object is moved one position to the right when the system executes an action schema to fixate on the object. Two objects will be introduced at different positions in visual space and through play, new schemas will be obtained. Both concrete (with specific values describing an experience) and generalised schemas, will be used to evaluated the performance of the system in term of finding the functions between the variables.

Finally to test the anticipation, another object is introduced into the environment and the system predicts the movement of the object in response to the action.

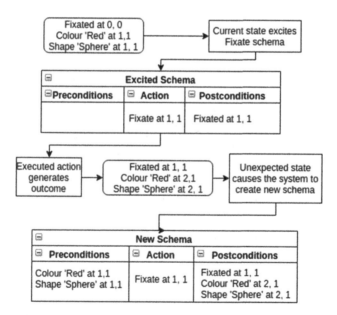

Fig. 3. Schema created while fixating on the first object

3.2   Results

Introducing the first object, referred to as object 1, at a particular position in visual space reminds the system about previously fixating at that position during the bootstrap process. This results in the corresponding saccade action schema being selected for execution by the excitation calculator. After the action is executed the system creates a new schema describing the differences in pre and post conditions from the basic action schema generated during bootstrapping. Figure 3 show the process of obtaining a new saccade schema following the fixation on the first object.

Following the creation of the new schema, the first object was removed from the simulated environment. A second object, object 2, which possessed the same movement property, but was of a different shape and colour, was introduced at a different position. Following the same process, as shown in Fig. 3, a new schema is created for fixating on the object with the concrete details associated with this experience. The similarity of the new schema compared with the previous schema, created for object 1, triggered the generalisation process, resulting in the creation of a new generalised schema. Figure 4 shows the generalised schema along with the schemas used to create it.

⊟	Schema 1	
⊟ **Preconditions**	⊟ **Action**	⊟ **Postconditions**
Colour 'Red' at 1,1 Shape 'Cube' at 1,1	Fixate at 1, 1	Fixated at 1, 1 Colour 'Red' at 2, 1 Shape 'Cube' at 2, 1

⊟	Schema 2	
⊟ **Preconditions**	⊟ **Action**	⊟ **Postconditions**
Colour 'Green' at 2,3 Shape 'Sphere' at 2,3	Fixate at 2, 3	Fixated at 2, 3 Colour 'Green' at 3, 3 Shape 'Sphere' at 3, 3

⊟	Generalised Schema	
⊟ **Preconditions**	⊟ **Action**	⊟ **Postconditions**
Colour '$a' at $b, $c Shape '$d' at $b, $c	Fixate at $a, $b	Fixated at $b, $c Colour '$a' at $b+1, $c Shape '$d' at $b+1, $c

Fig. 4. Schema for object 1 (top), object 2 (middle) and generalised schema (bottom)

Variables in both schemas for object 1 and 2 are of the same type but have different values. As the values for position are numeric, the quantity of change in them can also be considered. The generalisation mechanism recognises the matching change in the values and is able to apply this as a function on the positional values in the new generalised schema.

To test this, a third new object was presented in the environment. The new object excites the new generalised schema, which is instantiated from the observed state. Variables with $ signs are replaced with specific values from the current state, resulting in the action to fixate on the object, whilst also predicting the outcome of the action. Figure 5 shows the state of the simulator (left) and instantiated generalised schema from that state.

The post-condition of the instantiated generalised schema shows that the object is expected to move across one position after fixating on it at its current position.

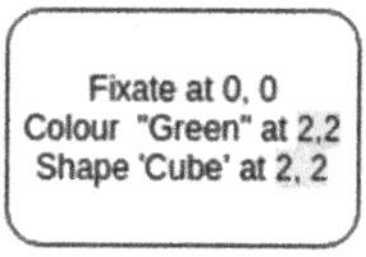

Fixate at 0, 0 Colour "Green" at 2,2 Shape 'Cube' at 2, 2

⊟	Instantiated Generalised Schema		
⊟ **Preconditions**		⊟ **Action**	⊟ **Postconditions**
Colour 'Green' at 2, 2 Shape 'Cube' at 2, 2		Fixate 2, 2	Fixated at 2, 2 Colour 'Green' at 3, 2 Shape 'Cube' at 3, 2

Fig. 5. State for 3rd object (left) and instantiated generalised schema (right)

Thus, the system shows the capability of predicting the future state by making inferences for the current state using previous experiences.

4   Conclusions and Future Work

In this work, we demonstrated the ability of the PSchema system, *Dev-PSchema*, to anticipate the outcome of the action and events related to it. For extending the learning to novel situations, generalised schemas are created. After creating a generalised schema, the system extends this knowledge to novel situations, the third object in this case. Based on previous experiences, the system predicts the outcome of an action on an object, irrespective of object's visual features. This result is consistent with the results obtained in [1]. Adler found that infants anticipate the object movement irrespective of an object's visual features.

This system, *Dev-PSchema*, is also able to find the linear mathematical relation between the property variables for the generalised schema. This capability may be considered as the causal perceptual anticipation as the system finds the causal relation between the action and its outcome. Schlesinger believes that development of causal activity helps the infants to form causal perceptual anticipations [15]. Similarly, it is believed that human actions do not depend upon the current observations but depend upon the anticipated future state of the observation and actions to be acted upon them [6,12]. Thus, human action can be seen as goal directed, even in early infancy [1], which may be considered as causality.

Learning models discussed in Sect. 2 have shown significant achievements for learning and anticipation capability in robotics. However, these learning models use either supervisory learning or learning by demonstrating. The extension proposed in [18] in the OAC model [7] have shown the capability of anticipation. The proposed extension also involves the relation between the pre and post action states in OACs. However, the OACs learning model involves supervisory learning [10] and the proposed extension uses supervisory mechanism to incorporate the unexpected states.

The anticipation mechanism in the Dev E-R model proposed in [2] is very similar to the model used in this work. However, Dev E-R model does not deal with the mathematical relation between properties present in schemas. The schema system used in this work is able to find the mathematical relation between properties in the schemas. We believe this capability will help to develop the system for finding causal relations in the schemas.

The system discussed in this paper is an extension of unsupervised, on-line and continual learning mechanism. It does not require large numbers of training sets of a fixed target. However, it does need a low level sensory and control system to abstract the raw sensory information and represent it at a high symbolic level. Similarly, actions in schemas are in high level definition and a low level control system is responsible for the robotic kinematics to execute actions.

With the extension in the system, it is now capable of finding relation between the numerical values of the sensory state variables. The current system is only able to find the additive function $(+/-)$ between the variable of the properties present in the action and states, pre-conditions and post-condition. In the future, we will consider further extensions to the system allowing it to deal with more complex mathematical functions in schemas. Through building up these predictive schemas, it is possible to learn behaviours such as object tracking where the motion of the eyes is matched to that of the object, along with predictive reaches to where the object will land. Finally, through understanding these changes, the system can exploit these changes to achieve goals involving moving objects to target positions.

This experiment is an example of using *Dev-PSchema* for generalisation and finding functional relation between numerical values of the sensory state variables only. The system can be used as a general learning mechanism and play behaviour generator. In the future, we are interested in extending this event anticipatory mechanism to incorporate anticipatory behaviours. We are also interested in implementing this model on an embodied humanoid robot, such as the iCub. Moreover, we are also aiming to extend the generalisation mechanism to deal with the failure of generalisation.

Acknowledgements. This research is supported by the Aberystwyth University Doctoral Training Programme, Sukkur IBA (Pakistan) Faculty Development Program and the UK Engineering and Physical Sciences Research Council (EPSRC), grant No. EP/M013510/1. We are grateful for contributions from our recent research colleagues, in particularly Dr. Michael Sheldon, for the development of the PSchema tool.

References

1. Adler, S.A., Haith, M.M.: The nature of infants' visual expectations for event content. Infancy **4**(3), 389–421 (2003)
2. Aguilar, W., y Pérez, R.P.: Dev ER: a computational model of early cognitive development as a creative process. Cogn. Syst. Res. **33**, 17–41 (2015)
3. Canfield, R.L., Haith, M.M.: Young infants' visual expectations for symmetric and asymmetric stimulus sequences. Dev. Psychol. **27**(2), 198 (1991)
4. Cangelosi, A., Schlesinger, M., Smith, L.B.: Developmental Robotics: From Babies to Robots. MIT Press, Cambridge (2015)
5. Claxton, L.J., Keen, R., McCarty, M.E.: Evidence of motor planning in infant reaching behavior. Psychol. Sci. **14**(4), 354–356 (2003)
6. Demiris, Y.: Prediction of intent in robotics and multi-agent systems. Cogn. Process. **8**(3), 151–158 (2007)

7. Geib, C., Mourao, K., Petrick, R., Pugeault, N., Steedman, M., Krueger, N., Wörgötter, F.: Object action complexes as an interface for planning and robot control. In: IEEE RAS International Conference on Humanoid Robots (2006)
8. Hermans, T., Rehg, J.M., Bobick, A.: Affordance prediction via learned object attributes. In: IEEE International Conference on Robotics and Automation (ICRA): Workshop on Semantic Perception, Mapping, and Exploration. Citeseer (2011)
9. von Hofsten, C., Vishton, P., Spelke, E.S., Feng, Q., Rosander, K.: Predictive action in infancy: tracking and reaching for moving objects. Cognition **67**(3), 255–285 (1998)
10. Krüger, N., Geib, C., Piater, J., Petrick, R., Steedman, M., Wörgötter, F., Ude, A., Asfour, T., Kraft, D., Omrčen, D., et al.: Object-action complexes: grounded abstractions of sensory-motor processes. Robot. Auton. Syst. **59**(10), 740–757 (2011)
11. Paulus, M., Hunnius, S., van Wijngaarden, C., Vrins, S., van Rooij, I., Bekkering, H.: The role of frequency information and teleological reasoning in infants' and adults' action prediction. Dev. Psychol. **47**(4), 976 (2011)
12. Pezzulo, G.: Coordinating with the future: the anticipatory nature of representation. Minds Mach. **18**(2), 179–225 (2008)
13. Piaget, J., Cook, M., Norton, W.: The Origins of Intelligence in Children, vol. 8. International Universities Press, New York (1952)
14. Schlesinger, M., Casey, P.: Visual Expectations in Infants: Evaluating the Gaze-Direction Model. Lund University Cognitive Studies (2003)
15. Schlesinger, M., Langer, J.: Infants' developing expectations of possible and impossible tool-use events between ages 8 and 12 months. Dev. Sci. **2**(2), 195–205 (1999)
16. Sheldon, M.: Intrinsically motivated developmental learning of communication in robotic agents. Ph.D. thesis, Aberystwyth University (2013)
17. Sheldon, M., Lee, M.: Pschema: A developmental schema learning framework for embodied agents. In: 2011 IEEE International Conference on Development and Learning (ICDL), vol. 2, pp. 1–7. IEEE (2011)
18. Wörgötter, F., Agostini, A., Krüger, N., Shylo, N., Porr, B.: Cognitive agents-a procedural perspective relying on the predictability of Object-Action-Complexes (OACs). Robot. Auton. Syst. **57**(4), 420–432 (2009)

Evolving Controllers for Robots with Multimodal Locomotion

Rita Ramos[(✉)], Miguel Duarte, Sancho Moura Oliveira,
and Anders Lyhne Christensen

BioMachines Lab, Instituto de Telecomunicações & Instituto Universitário
de Lisboa (ISCTE-IUL), Lisbon, Portugal
rita_parada@iscte.pt

Abstract. Animals have inspired numerous studies on robot locomotion, but the problem of how autonomous robots can learn to take advantage of multimodal locomotion remains largely unexplored. In this paper, we study how a robot with two different means of locomotion can effective learn when to use each one based only on the limited information it can obtain through its onboard sensors. We conduct a series of simulation-based experiments using a task where a wheeled robot capable of jumping has to navigate to a target destination as quickly as possible in environments containing obstacles. We apply evolutionary techniques to synthesize neural controllers for the robot, and we analyze the evolved behaviors. The results show that the robot succeeds in learning when to drive and when to jump. The results also show that, compared with unimodal locomotion, multimodal locomotion allows for simpler and higher performing behaviors to evolve.

Keywords: Evolutionary Robotics · Multimodal locomotion · Navigation task

1 Introduction

Animals' ability to move efficiently in complex environments is crucial for key activities related to their survival, such as finding food and escaping predators. As a means to efficiently move through complex and unstructured environments, various animals exploit different modes of locomotion [11]. Birds, for example, use the aerial mode when traveling long distances, whereas the terrestrial mode is chosen for activities that require covering small distances, such as when feeding [14]. Crocodiles use terrestrial locomotion, a quadrupedal gait, when nesting and sunbathing, whilst for hunting, they rely on aquatic locomotion, primarily using undulation of the tail for propulsion [14].

Besides animals, multimodal locomotion has an important role in the field of robotics, particularly in tasks where robots may encounter distinct types of environments. Indeed, in some tasks, such as navigation, and search and rescue, it may be necessary to explore various types of terrains, which requires an adaption of movement modes, rather than just relying on one locomotion strategy [10].

© Springer International Publishing Switzerland 2016
E. Tuci et al. (Eds.): SAB 2016, LNAI 9825, pp. 340–351, 2016.
DOI: 10.1007/978-3-319-43488-9_30

Although some multimodal robots have been developed with distinct combinations of locomotion modes [1,3,20], the majority of them lacks the capacity for autonomous decision-making and are unable to decide when to use each means of locomotion.

Evolutionary Robotics (ER) is a field in which controllers for autonomous robots are synthesized by means of evolutionary computation techniques without the need for manual and detailed specification of behavior. In ER, there have been numerous studies on the evolution of controllers for robots with distinct means of locomotion, ranging from terrestrial and aerial robots, to aquatic robots [4,16,21]. Evolved controllers, however, have so far only made use of one means of locomotion. In this study, we evolve control systems for robots that have the capacity to exploit two modes of locomotion during task execution, namely driving and jumping.

For our study, we use a robot model based on the *Jumping Sumo*, a low-cost robotic platform made by Parrot. The robot has to perform a navigation task in different environments with obstacles. In order to successfully perform the task, the robot must reach a predefined destination as quickly as possible. The Jumping Sumo has a jumping mechanism that has to charge for 1 s before a jump can be executed. The need to charge prior to jumping and the fact the robot rolls stochastically after landing, make jumping slower than driving. There is thus a tradeoff, because the robot has to go around obstacles when driving, whereas the jumping locomotion, although slower, enables the robot to jump over obstacles. Taking into account the tradeoff between the two means of locomotion, we evolve control in a balanced set of environments that is fair for both locomotion modes. We compare results obtained in three distinct setups in which a robot has access to different modes of locomotion, in (i) the robot can only drive, not jump, in (ii) the robot can only jump, not drive, and in (iii) the robot is capable of both driving and jumping. We then analyze the performance and behavior of the controllers evolved in each setup. The contribution of our study is fourfold: (i) we evolve controllers that can take advantage of jumping locomotion; (ii) we demonstrate how controllers can be synthesized for multimodal locomotion, in particular, jumping and driving; (iii) we show that simpler strategies can be evolved for robots with multimodal locomotion capabilities compared with strategies evolved for robots with unimodal locomotion, and (iv) we find that the navigation strategies evolved for multimodal robots outperform strategies evolved for unimodal robots – even when only one mode of locomotion is used.

2   Related Work

In this section, we present prominent multimodal robots and discuss work related to autonomous navigation in the field of ER.

2.1   Multimodal Robots

Robots equipped with more than one means of locomotion have the potential to select which mode to use depending on the types of environment encountered, which is particularly important in tasks where terrains may not be entirely characterized prior to deployment [10]. With the growing interest in using robots for search and rescue tasks, environmental monitoring, and so forth, it is increasingly important to have robots with the capacity to exploit a variety of locomotion strategies.

Of the limited number of multimodal robots that have been developed so far, most combine aquatic and terrestrial locomotion. Examples include Aqua [8] and Salamandra Robotica I and II [3]. There is also a number of robots that combine aerial and terrestrial locomotion, such as MALV [1] and BOLT [17].

Some multimodal robots rely on the combination of jumping and wheeled locomotion, in which wheeled locomotion is the primary means of locomotion and jumping is used as a secondary means. Tsukagoshi et al. [19] developed a wheeled robotic platform with a jumping mechanism for rescue operations. The jumping mechanism uses a pneumatic cylinder and a specially designed valve that allows energy efficient and high jumps. The Jumping Sumo is another example of a wheeled robot capable of jumping that Parrot has recently developed[1], along with other multimodal robots. Other examples include the miniature Scout robot [18], a cylindrical robot with two wheels, and the mini-whegs [13].

Besides the mentioned examples, a recent survey on robotic systems equipped with multimodal locomotion can be found in [15]. Despite the interesting work done so far, most of multimodal robots are unable to autonomously decide when and how to exploit the different locomotion modes during task execution; in fact, the majority of current multimodal robots lack the capacity for autonomous decision-making altogether. In this paper, we study how to automatically synthesize controllers for a robot equipped with multimodal locomotion so that it effectively chooses which mode of locomotion during task execution based only on limited information from onboard sensors.

2.2 Evolved Navigation Behaviors

Terrestrial Robots. Several ER studies on wheeled robots have been carried out since the pioneering real-robot studies by Floreano and Mondada [6] and Jakobi et al. [12]. In [6], the authors evolved behavioral control that enabled a Khepera robot to locate a battery charger and periodically return to it. In [12], the authors managed to successfully evolve artificial neural network-based control for obstacle-avoidance and light-seeking tasks for a Khepera robot. Many others examples of evolved behaviors for terrestrial robots can be found in [16].

Besides wheeled robots, legged robots have also been controlled by evolved behavior. Gallagher et al. [7], for instance, carried out experiments using a neural network to control the locomotion of a real six-legged robot. Gruau and Quatramaran [9] attempted to evolve an artificial neural network with cellular encoding to control the locomotion of OCT-1, an eight-legged robot.

---

[1] Parrot MiniDrone Jumping Sumo, URL: http://www.parrot.com/usa/products/jumping-sumo/.

Aerial and Aquatic Robots. One example of ER in aerial robots includes evolving spiking neural controllers for a flying robot which had to perform a vision-based navigation task [21]. In terms of the aquatic environment, control was recently evolved for a swarm robotics system composed of 10 surface robots, in a study that demonstrated evolved swarm control outside of controlled laboratory conditions [4].

As it is the case for all the studies discussed above, evolution of control has almost exclusively been applied to robots with one type of locomotion. In this study, we evolve control for robots capable of multimodal locomotion, in particular, jumping and driving. It should be noted that, to the best of our knowledge, no controllers have been evolved for robots capable of jumping prior to this study.

3   Robot Model and the Task

In this section, we describe the navigation task and the robot model used in our experiments. We conducted our experiments in JBotEvolver, a Java-based open-source, multirobot simulation platform and neuroevolution framework [5].

3.1   Navigation Task

In our task, the robot must navigate to a predefined target destination in an environment with different obstacle configurations. The configuration of obstacles is random, but generated according to a predefined *ratio* that determines the optimal time to complete the task by driving relative to the optimal time to complete the task by jumping. For instance, if an environment has a ratio of 2, a configuration of obstacles will be generated in such a way that the time to reach the destination will be twice as long when driving than when jumping if the respective optimal paths are followed.

We use five different types of environment with the following ratios: 1/4, 1/2, 1, 2, and 4, during the evolutionary process. In the first two types of environment, the robot can potentially reach the destination faster by driving than by jumping (ratios 1/4 and 1/2), while the opposite is true in the two final types of environment (ratios 2 and 4). In the environment with a ratio of 1, the two means of locomotion potentially allow the robot to reach the target destination equally fast. Solutions are thus evaluated in a balanced set of environments with respect to the two means of locomotion. All environments are bounded and square-shaped, with a side length of 10 m. An example of a random configuration of the five environments can be seen in Fig. 1.

3.2   The Robot Model

The robot model is based on an existing physical multimodal robot, the Jumping Sumo, a differential wheeled robot capable of jumping (see Fig. 2). The robot

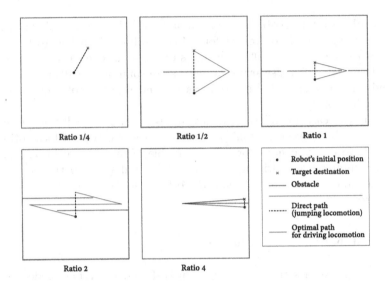

Fig. 1. Examples of configurations of the five types of environment with the respective optimal paths for driving and jumping highlighted.

Fig. 2. Left: Jumping sumo. Right: Jump trajectory.

is equipped with two wheels, can move at up to 7 km/h, is able to prioritizing either height or length, and has a size of 18.5 × 15 x 11 cm.

We conducted a series of empirical tests to assess the jumping characteristics of the robot in order to model the Jumping Sumo in simulation. The jump mode with height prioritization was chosen for our experiments since it allows the robots to overcome tall obstacles. A total of 45 jumps were executed, and both the time and distance covered were recorded. In the empirical tests, we observed a jump length of 85 ± 4 cm, and a roll distance of 16 ± 7 cm after the jump. In simulation, the dynamics were modeled using two Gaussian distributions. The jumping mechanism has to charge for 1 s before a jump is executed, which was also modeled in simulation.

In our experiments, the robot was equipped with two actuators: two wheels and a jump actuator. A Gaussian noise component with a mean of 0 and a standard deviation of 5 % was added to the two wheels to simulate real-world phenomena, such as imperfect motors and wheel slippage. The set of sensors includes eight destination sensors, which have a maximum range of 10 m, and eight obstacle sensors, which have a range of 4 m. The destination sensors are distributed around the chassis of the robot and the obstacle sensors are distributed on the front of the robot. All sensors have an opening angle of 60°. The robot was further equipped with a proprioceptive sensor that indicates if the robot is currently jumping or not.

For our experiments, we use three setups in which the robot has access to distinct locomotion capabilities: (i) Drive, where the robot is only capable of driving, (ii) Jump, where the robot can only jump and rotate on its axis, and (iii) Drive-and-Jump, where the robot is capable of multimodal locomotion, and thus can both jump and drive. In the Jump setup, the robot is considered to have reached the destination when it is within 30 cm of the target, instead of the 10 cm used for the other two setups, given that jumping is less precise than driving.

4   Control Synthesis

We evolve continuous-time recurrent neural networks [2] to control the robot. Each neural network has three layers of neurons: a reactive input layer, a fully connected hidden layer, and an output layer. The input layer is fully connected to the hidden layer, which, in turn, is fully connected to itself and to the output layer. The input layer has one neuron per input sensor and the output layer has one neuron per actuator output.

We use a simple generational evolutionary algorithm to synthesize control for the robot. Each generation is composed of 100 genomes that correspond to artificial neural networks with the topology outlined above. Genomes are evaluated over 25 samples with different initial random seeds (5 samples in each type of environment) and the average fitness is used for selection. Each sample can last up to 750 simulation time steps (19 s), or terminates once the robot reaches the destination. The five highest-scoring genomes are selected to become part of the next generation and to populate it. Each of the top genomes becomes the parent of 19 offspring. The genotype of an offspring is the result of applying a Gaussian noise to each gene with a probability of 10 %.

The fitness function is defined as follows:

$$F(i) = R_i + P_i \tag{1}$$

where R_i is a reward component and P_i a penalty component. Value of R_i depends on whether the robot succeeded or failed to navigate to the target destination:

$$R_i = \begin{cases} 1 + (T - t)/T & \text{if robot reached the destination} \\ 1 - d/D & \text{otherwise} \end{cases} \tag{2}$$

If the robot did not reach the target destination, the fitness function has a value in $[0, 1]$ depending on how close the robot got to the destination during the experiment. By means of this bootstrapping component, a faster convergence to the destination is expected. The term D represents the initial distance between the robot and the target destination, and d is the closest distance the robot came to the destination. If the robot is successful, its fitness will be in the interval $[1, 2]$, depending on how long the robot took to reach the target destination. The term T is the maximum time available for the task (750 simulation steps) and t corresponds to the time needed to reach the destination.

P_i is the penalty component which is used to promote obstacle avoidance:

$$P_i = \begin{cases} nc \times -0.01 & \text{if robot reached the destination} \\ nc \times -0.001 & \text{otherwise} \end{cases} \tag{3}$$

The term nc denotes the number of collisions with obstacles. P_i also depends on whether or not the robot managed to reach the destination. A lower penalty is given when the robot was unable to reach the target destination in order to bootstrap the evolutionary process.

5   Results

A total of 30 evolutionary runs were conducted for each setup (Drive, Jump, and Drive-and-Jump), each lasting 500 generations. For the highest-scoring controller evolved in each run, we conducted a post-evaluation with 100 samples for each of the five environment types used during evolution. In this section, we present the results obtained in each setup, and we analyze the performance and behaviors of the evolved solutions.

5.1   General Performance

Figure 3(left) shows the distribution of fitness scores achieved by the highest-scoring controllers for the different experimental setups. The highest-scoring controller was found in the Drive-and-Jump setup (1.84 ± 0.06), followed by the similar performance of the Drive setup and the Jump setup $(1.71 \pm 0.15$ and 1.71 ± 0.14, respectively). Figure 3(right) shows the distribution of the time to reach the target destination by those highest-scoring controllers. As mentioned in Sect. 3.1, the experiments were conducted in five types of environments that equally favor the driving locomotion and the jumping locomotion. The results show that the highest-scoring controllers evolved in the Drive setup and the Jump setup obtained a similar performance. The highest-scoring controller of the Drive setup reached the destination within a mean time of $5.69 \pm 2.80\,\text{s}$, and the best controller of the Jump setup reached the destination with a mean time of $5.54 \pm 2.96\,\text{s}$. The highest-scoring controller evolved in the Drive-and-Jump setup successfully reached the destination faster than controllers evolved in the other setups $(3.10 \pm 1.20\,\text{s})$. The results demonstrate that robots with

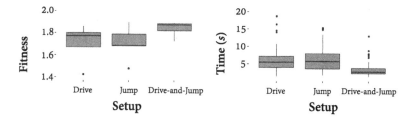

Fig. 3. Left: distribution of fitness scores achieved by the highest-scoring controllers of the three setups (higher is better). Right: distribution of the time to reach the destination by the highest-scoring controllers of the three setups (lower is better).

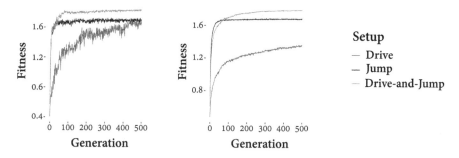

Fig. 4. Left: fitness trajectories of the highest-scoring controllers in each generation. Right: average fitness trajectories of the highest-scoring controllers in each of the 30 runs.

multimodal locomotion capabilities can effective learn when to use each mode of locomotion based on the limited information they can obtain through their onboard sensors.

The simplicity of evolving successful behaviors with multimodal locomotion can be seen in Fig. 4(left): the evolutionary process found successful solutions around the 80th generation, after which fitness only slightly increased. The relatively low average performance displayed by the controllers evolved in the Drive setup (Fig. 4(right)), can be explained by the fact that the majority of them did not succeed in reaching the destination in the final two environments (ratio 2 and 4). It is thus more challenging to evolve effective Drive behaviors than multimodal behaviors.

5.2 Behavioral Analysis

In this section, we analyze the performance and behaviors of the highest-scoring controllers for the first (ratio 1/4), middle (ratio 1) and last environment (ratio 4). Examples of evolved behaviors can be seen in Fig. 5. The highest scoring controller of the Drive setup, Jump setup and Drive-and-Jump setup are hereinafter referred to as *Drive Controller*, *Jump Controller* and *Drive-and-Jump Controller*, respectively.

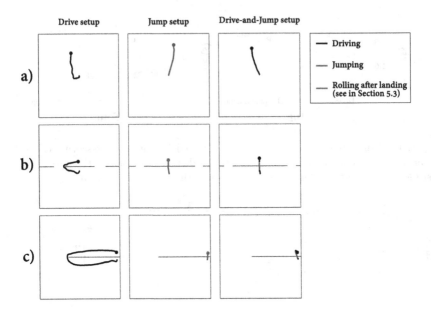

Fig. 5. Example of behaviors in the environments with (a) ratio 1/4, (b) ratio 1, and (c) ratio 4.

Ratio 1/4. The *Drive Controller* reached the destination with a mean time of 2.99 ± 1.33 s, while the *Jump Controller* achieved a mean time of 7.49 ± 1.82 s and the *Drive-and-Jump Controller* outperformed both with a mean time of 1.90 ± 0.28 s. The *Drive Controller* was not as fast as the *Drive-and-Jump Controller*, due to the fact that the controller has the general behavior of turning on the spot to find a way around potential obstacles, as can be seen in Fig. 5(a), which is necessary in order to solve the navigation task in more complex environments. Whereas the *Drive-and-Jump Controller* has a more general behavior, since it is not limited to just one locomotion strategy. Successful behaviors leveraged the ability to overcome obstacles in the other environments by jumping over them, thereby using a simpler strategy in which the robots moves directly toward the destination in the environments.

Ratio 1. This environment has a ratio of 1, thus, the robot can potentially reach the destination in the same amount of time whether it drives or jumps. The *Drive Controller* reached the destination within a mean time of 4.49 ± 1.77 s, similar to the *Jump Controller* that achieved a mean time of 4.11 ± 2.11 s. As to the *Drive-and-Jump Controller*, once again outperformed the other two, achieving a mean task-completion time of 2.59 ± 0.28 s.

We observed the *Drive-and-Jump Controller* successfully combining both modes of locomotion by driving toward an obstacle, jumping over it and then driving again to the destination, therefore achieving a even better performance when compared with using just one of the locomotion strategies.

Ratio 4. The *Drive Controller* reached the destination within a mean time of 8.91 ± 3.47 s, while the *Jump Controller* achieved a mean time of 2.13 ± 0.72 s. In the Drive-and-Jump setup, the mean time to navigate to the destination was 2.83 ± 1.62 s. The reason why the *Jump Controller* had a better performance than the *Drive-and-Jump Controller* is only due to the fact that the robot is considered to reach the destination at a greater distance with the Jump setup than with the Drive-and-Jump setup, as explained in Sect. 3.2. The robot, therefore, needs to drive a short distance after jumping, whereas in the Jump setup, the robot reaches the destination immediately upon landing.

5.3   Generalization

In order to assess how general the evolved strategies are, we conducted an additional set of post-evaluation experiments using the highest-scoring controllers of each setup in 12 additional environments, which were not used during evolution. The distribution of ratios for the new environments were chosen to uniformly fill the gaps between the ratios of the five original environment types. Each controller was evaluated 100 times in each of the 17 environments. The distribution of how long it took to complete the task in each of the 17 environments, using the *Drive Controller* as baseline, can be seen in Fig. 6.

The results show that, as one might expect, the *Drive Controller* outperformed the *Jump Controller* when the ratio was less than 1. With ratios higher than 1, the *Jump Controller* achieve a higher performance than the *Drive Controller*. The *Drive-and-Jump Controller* outperformed both *Drive Controller* and *Jump Controller* in the majority of the environments.

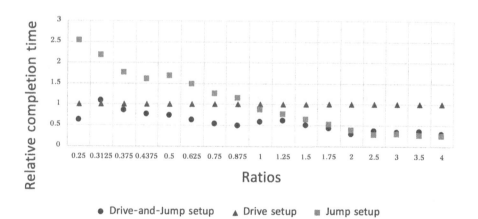

Fig. 6. Distribution of task completion times of the highest-scoring controllers evolved in a range of different environments. Highest-performing controller from the Drive setup is used as baseline

6 Conclusions

In this study, we evolved control for robots with multimodal locomotion. To conduct our experiments, the robot had to perform a navigation task in which it had to reach a target destination as quickly as possible. The navigation task was conducted in different environments, and we compared three modes of locomotion: (i) driving locomotion, (ii) jumping locomotion, and (iii) multimodal jumping and driving locomotion.

In our simulation-based experiments, the robot equipped with multimodal locomotion, was able to adapt its locomotion strategy to a broad range of different environments. Depending on the environment, the robot navigated to the target destination either by combining jumping and driving locomotion or by exploiting the one that best suited the environment. Multimodal locomotion enabled the robot to reach the destination faster than when limited to just one locomotion strategy. The evolved behavior shows that even in environments in which only one type of locomotion is necessary, the robot can be faster by relying on a general behavior.

The concept of evolving robotic control systems that have the capacity to exploit driving and jumping locomotion opens several possibilities for others combinations of two (or more) modes of locomotion, such as jumping and flying. In our ongoing work, we are studying large-scale systems of autonomous robots with multimodal locomotion capabilities.

Acknowledgments. We would like to acknowledge the financial support of ISCTE-IUL. Also, this work was partly supported by FCT – Foundation of Science and Technology under grant UID/EEA/50008/2013.

References

1. Bachmann, R.J., Boria, F.J., Vaidyanathan, R., Ifju, P.G., Quinn, R.D.: A biologically inspired micro-vehicle capable of aerial and terrestrial locomotion. Mech. Mach. Theor. **44**(3), 513–526 (2009)
2. Beer, R.D., Gallagher, J.C.: Evolving dynamical neural networks for adaptive behavior. Adapt. Behav. **1**(1), 91–122 (1992)
3. Crespi, A., Karakasiliotis, K., Guignard, A., Ijspeert, A.J.: Salamandra robotica II: an amphibious robot to study salamander-like swimming and walking gaits. IEEE Trans. Rob. **29**(2), 308–320 (2013)
4. Duarte, M., Costa, V., Gomes, J., Rodrigues, T., Silva, F., Oliveira, S.M., Christensen, A.L.: Evolution of collective behaviors for a real swarm of aquatic surface robots. PLoS ONE **11**(3), e0151834 (2016)
5. Duarte, M., Silva, F., Rodrigues, T., Oliveira, S.M., Christensen, A.L.: JBotEvolver: a versatile simulation platform for evolutionary robotics. In: International Conference on the Synthesis and Simulation of Living Systems (ALIFE), pp. 210–211. MIT Press (2014)
6. Floreano, D., Mondada, F.: Evolution of homing navigation in a real mobile robot. IEEE Trans. Syst. Man Cybern. Part B Cybern. **26**(3), 396–407 (1996)

7. Gallagher, J.C., Beer, R.D., Espenschied, K.S., Quinn, R.D.: Application of evolved locomotion controllers to a hexapod robot. Rob. Auton. Syst. **19**(1), 95–103 (1996)
8. Georgiades, C., German, A., Hogue, A., Liu, H., Prahacs, C., Ripsman, A., Sim, R., Torres, L.A., Zhang, P., Buehler, M., et al.: AQUA: an aquatic walking robot. In: IEEE/RSJ International Conference on Intelligent Robots and Systems (IROS), vol. 4, pp. 3525–3531. IEEE Press (2004)
9. Gruau, F., Quatramaran, K.: Cellular encoding for interactive evolutionary robotics. In: European Conference on Artificial Life (ECAL), pp. 368–377. MIT Press (1997)
10. Ijspeert, A.J.: Biorobotics: using robots to emulate and investigate agile locomotion. Science **346**(6206), 196–203 (2014)
11. Ijspeert, A.J.: Central pattern generators for locomotion control in animals and robots: a review. Neural Netw. **21**(4), 642–653 (2008)
12. Jakobi, N.: Minimal simulations for evolutionary robotics. Ph.D. thesis, University of Sussex (1998)
13. Lambrecht, B.G., Horchler, A.D., Quinn, R.D.: A small, insect-inspired robot that runs and jumps. In: IEEE International Conference on Robotics and Automation (ICRA), pp. 1240–1245. IEEE Press (2005)
14. Lock, R., Burgess, S., Vaidyanathan, R.: Multi-modal locomotion: from animal to application. Bioinspiration Biomimetics **9**(1), 011001 (2013)
15. Low, K., Hu, T., Mohammed, S., Tangorra, J., Kovac, M.: Perspectives on biologically inspired hybrid and multi-modal locomotion. Bioinspiration Biomimetics **10**(2), 020301 (2015)
16. Nolfi, S., Floreano, D.: Evolutionary Robotics: The Biology, Intelligence, and Technology of Self-organizing Machines. MIT Press, Massachusetts (2000)
17. Peterson, K., Fearing, R.S.: Experimental dynamics of wing assisted running for a bipedal ornithopter. In: IEEE/RSJ International Conference on Intelligent Robots and Systems (IROS), pp. 5080–5086. IEEE Press (2011)
18. Stoeter, S.A., Papanikolopoulos, N.: Autonomous stair-climbing with miniature jumping robots. IEEE Trans. Sys. Man Cybern. Part B: Cybern. **35**(2), 313–325 (2005)
19. Tsukagoshi, H., Sasaki, M., Kitagawa, A., Tanaka, T.: Design of a higher jumping rescue robot with the optimized pneumatic drive. In: IEEE International Conference on Robotics and Automation (ICRA), pp. 1276–1283. IEEE Press (2005)
20. Woodward, M.A., Sitti, M.: Multimo-bat: a biologically inspired integrated jumping-gliding robot. Int. J. Robot. Res. **33**(12), 1511–1529 (2014)
21. Zufferey, J.-C., Floreano, D., van Leeuwen, M., Merenda, T.: Evolving vision-based flying robots. In: Bülthoff, H.H., Lee, S.-W., Poggio, T.A., Wallraven, C. (eds.) BMCV 2002. LNCS, vol. 2525, pp. 592–600. Springer, Heidelberg (2002)

Conditions of Depleting Offender Behavior in Volunteering Dilemma: An Agent-Based Simulation Study

Kashif Zia[1(✉)], Momina Shaheen[1], Umar Farooq[2], and Shahid Nazir[1]

[1] Bahria University, Shangrilla Road, Sector E-8, Islamabad, Pakistan
zia@bui.edu.pk
[2] University of Science and Technology, Bannu, Pakistan

Abstract. In this paper, an agent-based model of bystanders effect on volunteering in a crime situation is presented. The model is pivoted on the results of a game-theoretic experimentation of the volunteering dilemma [18], emphasizing the role of guilt in increasing the volunteering tendency. An analytical model of bystanders effect on volunteering [8] is extended so that it incorporates multiple interventions and changes in agents' beliefs to be used in subsequent interactions. However, the main contribution is the model extension including the guilt propagation, subsequently responsible for increases in volunteering tendency. We also introduce a new model of offender behavior, that operates in conjunction with the model of volunteering. The model is simulated asking interesting "what-if" questions with particular focus on decreasing offending tendencies. The results of the simulation reveal that, the model we have proposed, validates the theoretical foundations of bystanders effect on volunteering and importance of guilt in increasing the volunteering tendency.

Keywords: Volunteering filemma · Bystanders effect · Game theory · Agent-based model · Simulation

1 Introduction

Agent-based Modelling (ABM) is a computational method based on autonomous decision-making entities; called agents; interacting with each other locally [9]. Exploiting the bottom-up approach (the essence of the modeling approach), ABM is used to perform (pseudo-) experiments, highlighting the interplay of agents' influence on others. This often helps us understand the root cause of the emergence of a global phenomena and the co-evolution of various behavioral streams in sub-populations of an overall population, thus validating and/or refining the theoretical foundations of it.

Exploiting the advantages stated above, ABM is a helpful tool to analyze the emergence of norms and customs in a society [6]. More recently, ABM has been used to analyze different aspects influencing the dynamics of crimes in a social setting [8]. In criminology, ABM has been used to explore spatio-temporal

© Springer International Publishing Switzerland 2016
E. Tuci et al. (Eds.): SAB 2016, LNAI 9825, pp. 352–363, 2016.
DOI: 10.1007/978-3-319-43488-9_31

dynamics of crime, with focus on spatial as well as behavioral aspects. For example, the model presented in [3] explores the dynamics of displacement of crime places based on diffusion of reputation about those places. At the behavioral level, the relationship between the behavior of offenders, targets and guardians is modelled and simulated. Similarly, in [17], the behaviors of offenders, targets and crime places are modelled based on routine activities theories and the results of the simulation are validated against real data.

Using ABM, the criminologist research has investigated various violent crimes, such as, street robbery [10,11], gang rivalries [12] and civil violence [14–16]. At the same time, research has also been done on society's reaction to a crime situation, which corresponds to the norms prevalent in the society [8]. One of these situations is the bystander effect [8], which refrains a person to volunteer her effort against a crime which she observes. Gerristen in his article [8], referenced the work by [13], explaining the possible reasons for such a behavior, namely, *audience inhibition, social influence,* and *diffusion of responsibility.*

The mere presence of *audience inhibits* a person to intervene or volunteer due to possibility of her to misinterpret the situation resulting into an embarrassment. In addition to that, people are *socially influenced* by others; when she sees others not intervening, she also does the same. The third factor is also associated with a social dilemma (the Volunteer's dilemma (VD)) indicated by Diekmann [5] as "It is appreciable that *somebody* volunteers, but it is best if that somebody is not me", thus, *shifting the responsibility* from her own shoulders to the others. Looking at these factors in combination, it is often argued that the *audience inhibition* and the *social influence* are consequences of the *diffusion of responsibility.* Hence, in literature, the bystander effect / volunteer's dilemma is seen as a consequence of the *diffusion of responsibility,* in which an increase in the size of the group of bystanders lowers the rate of volunteering [18].

However, in practical situations, the volunteering dilemma does not always guarantee a negative result (a person not volunteering). People cooperate and volunteer so often. It is evidenced [18] that the cooperative behavior in humans is driven by many aspects of social interaction, including the aspects tightly integrated with the cognitive behavior of *guilt,* such as "reciprocal altruism" and "conflict resolution". Guilt is a negative value resulting due to inconsistency between the adopted and the desired behavior. Hence, to get rid of sense of guilt and act *responsibly,* it may lead to an altruistic volunteering from an individual, in conflict situations requiring a cooperative decision making. In fact, responsibility is a function of guilt [2] (both terms thus qualify to be used interchangeably). In other words, volunteering in the volunteer's dilemma can be ensured, if an individual tries to be responsible to get rid of state of guilt.

Results of a careful experimentation of the VD have revealed that 'no-intervention' due to bystanders effect often leads to guilt which, as a consequence, persuades the participants to volunteer [18]. However, the study does not provide an analytical model of volunteering. A model of volunteering (whether a person volunteers or not), having an underpinning on three human behavior theories (stated above), is presented by Gerritsen in [8]. Although, this model presents a sophisticated, yet simplistic example of application of social theories within an agent's behavior, it is restricted along two dimensions. First, the model supports only one volunteer. Second, the model does not provide any specification of how an offender will behave as a result of a possible intervention, i.e., a model of offender behavior is missing.

Therefore, the contributions of this paper are as under:

1. We extend the "model of volunteering" [8] so that it may handle more than one volunteers against a single event (a crime).
2. We affirm that the central notion of "responsibility" used in the model [8] can be used to introduce the findings related to guilt as a persuasive factor for volunteering [18]. This has been incorporated into our model.
3. We introduce a new model of the offender behavior whose motivation is the reciprocity of the original VD.
4. Multi-volunteering and guilt-enabled model is integrated with the model of the offender behavior to analyze the co-evolution of volunteering vs. crimes, asking various interesting "what-if" questions.

2   Related Work

A game-theoretic definition of guilt has been presented in [1]. Authors in [1] have defined the guilt as "the size of the gap between the first agent's beliefs about the second agent's expectations of her, and her own behavior." Hence, guilt is a second order measure, i.e. an agent's belief about the belief another agent is having about itself. In game-theoretic terms, the behavior of an agent i results in lower payoff of another agent j against j's expectations. This results in i's guilt dependent on the difference between the i's current behavior and j's expectations of i. Quantifying the feeling of guilt in this way helps in cooperating (volunteering in this case), if agent i is guilt averse, i.e. it acts to live up to j's expectations.

A variation of game theory capable to handle emotions was first introduced in [7]. The concept was used to allow beliefs to be included into agents' utility function [1]. Authors in [1] modified a trust game originally presented in [4]. In the game, both agent A and agent B choose the best response given their perception about each other. The game is played pivoted on the belief of A about B *rolling* the dice and on the belief of B about A choosing to be *in* the game rather then being *out*. An experimental investigation verified that a player will feel guilty if she perform lower than what was expected of her. Also, if she is guilt averse, she would raise her contribution to match the expectations.

Since VD is a collective game, authors in [18] have pointed out a possible extension of the above mentioned two players' settings, i.e. to use average of the beliefs of the bystander group. However, to avoid the complexity of this mechanism, they have proposed to use a special player known as designated volunteer (DV) who will volunteer automatically. This to us is a grave simplification which restricts the game towards a specific situation in which a public good is achieved only if more than one person in a group of bystanders volunteer. This also presets volunteering as the choice of priority thus hindering an inert evaluation (a fairness between volunteering and not volunteering right from the start). Another simplification is about avoidance of diffusion of guilt. This was achieved through a relatively smaller group size (of 5). We in our model not only refrain from introducing a DV (instead we use a behavior-based model of volunteering), but also, the group sizes used are quite flexible. Since guilt is a function of responsibility. Responsibility is the basic ingredient of our model already, would avoid the diffusion of guilt situation.

Although, the logic presented in [18] would be able to avoid the diffusion of responsibility and diffusion of guilt, thus supporting a reasonable number of individual to volunteer. However, at best, this is just one special case of many possibilities that can happen. To analyze all these possibilities, we have opted to use ABM in different settings. Instead of using a designated volunteer, we like the model used in [8], which analytically model a person to volunteer or not based on his own capabilities (beliefs, desires and intentions) and his perceptions (about norms and intensity of violation). However, we introduce a feedback loop in the model transforming it from a one-shot model to a repetitive one. As stated above, we have also extended the model so that it support more than one volunteers. We also introduce a new model of the offender behavior, that operates in conjunction with the model of volunteering. Hence, in our framework, we use a model of "bystanders effect on volunteering" (whether a person will volunteer or not). The model is run in a repeated game manner with a feedback loop, thus able to generate interesting dynamics. Hence, the consequence of volunteering or not volunteering is then integrated with agents' cognition in terms of responsibility to act.

3   Models

3.1   Longuemar's Experimentation of VD

First, we state an experiment signifying the importance of guilt in VD. In [18], it is assumed that, initially, the game played would increase probability of failure in cooperation (a group not volunteering to an extent to ensure public good). Such a failure would incur guilt in agents, thus infusing a sense of responsibility [2], which is assumed to motivate them to cooperate for public good in subsequent runs of the game. The structure of the game is presented in Table 1. A player can either choose to volunteer (cooperate) or defect (free-riding). The players are

Table 1. Game structure of volunteering dilemma.

	Enough players volunteer	Not enough players volunteer
V (Volunteer)	8 points	0 points
D (Defect)	10 points	2 points

informed about required number of volunteers. There is a cost of volunteering equal to 2 points. A player defecting would gain 10 points if, in the group, enough players choose to volunteer. A player volunteering would gain 8 points if, in the group, enough players choose to volunteer, excluding the cost of volunteering. Similarly, if not enough players volunteer, then a player volunteering would gain 0 points, whereas, a player defecting would still gets 2 points.

The game is further enhanced by explaining to the participants that there is one person who will volunteer unconditionally (a designated volunteer (DV)). An experimental analysis was conducted to explore the effect of guilt aversion in the volunteer's dilemma. The following results were found:

1. If the player is guilt averse, then her second order beliefs about the DV's expectations have a positive correlation with her choosing to volunteer.
2. The volunteering rate is proportional to v, where v is the number of volunteers required for public good.
3. There is no significant difference in volunteering rate between situation with DVs and situation without DVs.
4. The players avoid "no-guilt" behavior and "guilt-inducing" situation in the presence of DVs.

3.2 Gerritsen Model of Bystanders Effect on Volunteering

Gerritsen proposed an agent-based model of bystanders' effect on volunteering [8]. The model described the decision-making behavior of one individual using the BDI-model [19]. The agents are of three types; (i) the bystanders, (ii) the intervener (who will make a decision of intervening or not, and (iii) the offender (who performs an action against a norm). In addition to beliefs ('B' of BDI), desires ('D' of BDI), and intentions ('I' of BDI), an intervener will also "observe" and perceive the surrounding. Observations may change the beliefs of the agents. The model is based on rules executed in an order. The following sequence depicts the application of rules:

1. If the intervener observes that there is no intervention from others, it turns its belief that the "intervention-will-be-evaluated-negatively" from boolean value false to true. This corresponds to *social influence* theory.
2. If the intervener believes that "intervention-will-be-evaluated-negatively", then her belief of "audience-inhibition" will be set to number of bystanders who can observe him. If the number of bystanders who can observe him are zero, then there will be no "audience-inhibition". Contrary to belief of audience inhibition (and related theory of *audience inhibition*) derived from social influence theory, the belief of "intervention-cost" (equal to number of bystanders) is a consequence theory of *diffusion of responsibility*.

3. The value of beliefs of "audience-inhibition" and "intervention-cost" will determine the belief that the intervener has "personal-responsibility" to intervene. The value of "personal-responsibility" will be set to true, if both above beliefs justify the thresholds, corresponding to intervener perception of seriousness of the event. The more the values of these thresholds, the more serious the crime is.

4. Next the intervener resets its belief about seriousness of the crime. If he observes no intervention from others in the presence of n bystanders, then the belief of "has-seriousness" is set to previously believed value of seriousness divided by n times α, where α determines the influence of the group. This means that more the value of n, more the decrement in belief about seriousness of an event will be.

5. If the updated value of "has-seriousness" is greater than believed value of "normality", then the intervener believes that there is a "emergency".

6. The belief of "emergency" leads to the desire to intervene.

7. If the intervener has a desire and believes in "personal-responsibility", the desire will be converted into the intention to intervene. However, the actual intervention will only happen if the intervener believes that she is "capable", and "resourceful".

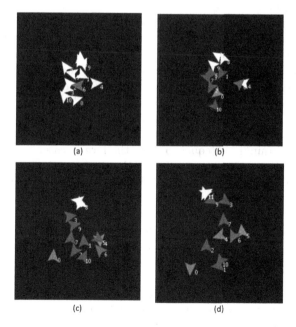

Fig. 1. Simulation environment and screen-shots of a selected case. (Color figure online)

3.3   The Proposed Extended Model of Bystanders Effect on Volunteering

The extended model is motivated from findings of Longuemar's Experiment of VD. Specifically, first, the finding that "If the player is guilt averse, then her second order beliefs about the DV's expectations have a positive correlation with her choosing to volunteer", corresponds to **decrement in the audience inhibition, equal to the difference between the number of bystanders (who are observing) and the number of bystanders who have already intervened.** More explicitly, this extension is realized in extended rule 1 and rule 2 as stated below. Second, the finding that "The volunteering rate is proportional to v, where v is the number of volunteers required for public good.", corresponds to **introduction of sense of guilt equal to difference between the number of bystanders that were required to intervene and the number of bystanders who have actually intervened.** The more the sense of guilt the more the belief about the seriousness of the event is, which increases the possibility of volunteering in the subsequent interaction with the offender. More explicitly, this extension is realized in extended rule 3 and rule 4 as stated below.

The rule 1 restricts the inclusion of more than one volunteers, that may be necessary to achieve a public good (multiple interventions), and will be first extension of the model we have proposed. In our model the number of volunteers needed to achieve a public good is represented as v. If number of bystanders who are observing an intervener are n, and m is the number of bystanders who have already intervened, then the belief that the "intervention-will-be-evaluated-negatively" may have two opposite values; $true$ if $m = 0$ and $false$ if $m > 0$.

The rule 2 has to deal with two possible values of the belief of "intervention-will-be-evaluated-negatively"; being $true$ or $false$. In the former case (as before), the belief of "audience-inhibition (represented as $N1$)" will be equal to n. In the later case, the belief of "audience-inhibition" will be equal to $n - m$. Similarly, the belief of "intervention-cost (represented as $N2$)" is changed to $n - m$ in the later case, while retaining it (equal to n) in the former case.

The rule 3 also changes accordingly. However, we introduce the notion of "guilt" here. Since, the values of beliefs of "audience-inhibition" and "intervention-cost" will determine the belief that the intervener has "personal-responsibility" to intervene or not, which depends on corresponding thresholds (corresponding to intervener perception of seriousness of the event), we incorporate the sense of guilt to raise these thresholds. The guilt infuses into intervener cognition if he had not intervened recently, and is represented as: $guilt(intervener) = v - m$. Hence, as before, the value of "personal-responsibility" will be set to true, if both above beliefs ($N1$ and $N2$) justify the *updated assignments* of thresholds (with attachment to guilt in this case).

The rule 4 also changes. The basic rule as as follows. The intervener resets its belief about seriousness of the crime. If he observes no intervention from others in the presence of n bystanders, then the belief of "has-seriousness" is set to previously believed value of seriousness divided by n times α, where α determines the influence of the group. The extended rule is as follows. Since, m bystanders may have intervened already, the belief of "has-seriousness" is set to previously believed value of seriousness divided by $n - m$ times α. This change has the following consequence. If value of m is 0, the new value of belief about seriousness of the crime depends on n (the more it is the less serious the crime is), whereas, if the value of m is greater than 0, then, the more the value of m, the more the seriousness of the crime is.

Rules 5 to rule 7 remain the same.

3.4   The Proposed Offender Model

This model represents a reciprocating case of VD presented in Table 1.

The offender will have an index, say, $OffenderIndex$, initialized with 1. From this value, the index can only decrease based on intensity of intervention against the offense. After each iteration (run of the simulation), the $OffenderIndex$ will be updated as: $1 - (m/v)$. Hence with, continuous interventions, the index will reach to 0, which would be equal to offender not offending anymore.

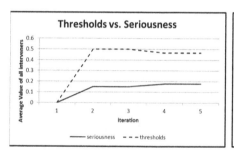
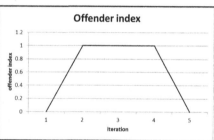

Fig. 2. Quantitative analysis of simulation setting presented in Fig. 1

4   Simulation

The simulation was performed in ABM simulation environment NetLogo [20]. A square space equal to the dimension of 32×32 cells was used. A cell is a spatial representation of a place where an agent can reside. Simulation runs in iterations. In each iteration, all agents "perform" what is modeled in a sequential manner, where, an agent can use the updated state (even in the same iteration, if sequentially preceded, or the previous iteration, if sequentially proceeded) of the environment and the other agents.

Initially, the agents are of two types; an *offender* who will commit a crime, and all other *agents* in the population. For example, in Fig. 1 - (a), agent 6 is the offender, whereas, all agents colored white are normal agents. As we can see that all the agents at the start are very close to each other. This gives ample

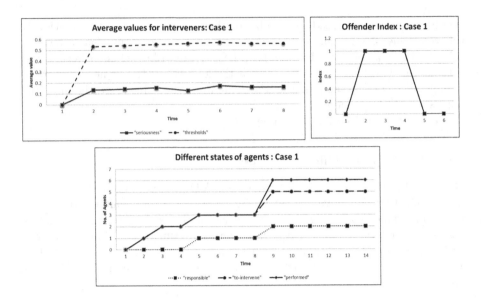

Fig. 3. Simulation results of case 1.

opportunity to the agents for a possible intervention. Although, arguing that such a setting does not depict a realistic situation (of randomly placed agents) seems acceptable, however, this is not the case. We have started with a sample of agents represented by a population. And a population is a set of agents who are within a given radius relative to the offender, at the start. Only the behavior of this sample is relevant for behavioral analysis, even when the neighborhood of the offender would not be same in subsequent iterations. Since, we do not include new agents during the simulation, placing all agents in close proximity at the start of the simulation makes sense.

Three variables, *radius*, *normality*, and α, are not changed between differ-ent cases that are simulated, setting these to 4, 0.2 and 0.5, correspondingly. For the scenario presented in Fig. 1 - (a), the *population* is equal to 12 agents. The *thresholds* are set to 4, and the number of agents required to intervene (v) are 1. Agents perform random walk between iterations. During iteration 1 (see Fig. 1 - (b)), agent 0 (the agent in green) had a contention to intervene. The bystanders of agent 0 are represented in blue color (6 in number). A large pop-ulation of bystanders dropped the perceived value of seriousness of crime from original value of 0.4 (corresponding to the thresholds) to 0.15. However, the value of threshold is increased to 5 due to feeling of guilt as a consequence of non-intervention. Since the intervention-cost and audience-inhibition is greater than thresholds, agent 0 will not feel responsibility to intervene.

A similar behavior during iteration 2 (see Fig. 1 - (c)) was observed (the intervener being agent 4 with similar number of bystanders, while agents in gray represent the interveners in previous iterations). However, during iteration 2 (see Fig. 1 - (d)), the current intervener (agent 5), in fact, performed intervention,

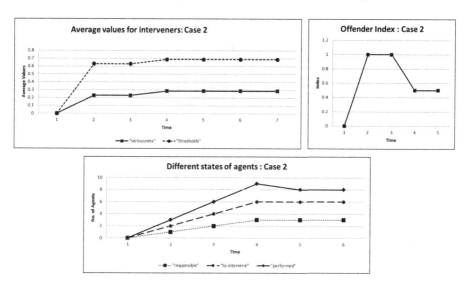

Fig. 4. Simulation results of case 2.

as a consequence of less bystanders. This also increases the value of perceived seriousness of the crime from agent 5 perspective. Since the number of interventions required to intervene are sufficient, the simulation stops. The performance of this simulation is quantitatively represented in graphs of Fig. 2.

We simulated three representative case of the model. These cases explain the change in agents' behavior due to variation in agent population, thresholds and required number of volunteers. These cases are given in Table 2.

Table 2. Interesting simulation cases.

	Number of agents	Thresholds	Required number of volunteers
Case 1:	6	3	1
Case 2:	6	4	2
Case 3:	12	4	2

Overall, the simulation results reveal the following trends.

The threshold plays an important role in volunteering. If it is too low at the start (< 0.3), even the sense of guilt is not capable to raise it to a level where intervention is materialized. This is evident in case 1 of the simulation, described by thresholds equal to 3, population equal to 6 and value of v equal to 1. A represented result of this simulation is shown in Fig. 3.

With population equal to 6, the minimum initial threshold required to ensure volunteering is 3. With increase in thresholds to 4, there is a decrease in number

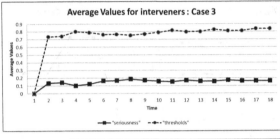
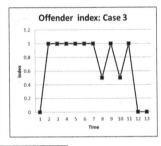
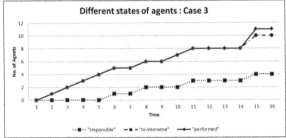

Fig. 5. Simulation results of case 3.

of iterations required to lower the offender-index from 1 to 0 (even when the value of v is raised from 1 to 2). This is case 2 that we represent in Fig. 4.

With increase in population, the time required to realize a successful intervention increases. This is evident in case 3 (see Fig. 5), with thresholds equal to 4, population equal to 12 and the value of v equal to 2.

From many simulations we performed, it was revealed that an increase in thresholds increases the chances of volunteering. Also, an in increase in the neighborhood (with increase in radius) increases the likelihood of intervention. Finally, the more the value of normality, there was less likelihood of intervention.

5   Conclusion

In this paper, an agent-based model of bystanders effect on volunteering in a crime situation is presented. The model is pivoted on the results of a game-theoretic experimentation of the volunteering dilemma [18], emphasizing the role of guilt in increasing the volunteering tendency. An analytical model of bystanders effect on volunteering [8] is extended so that it incorporates multiple intervention and change in agents beliefs to be used in subsequent interactions. However, the main contribution is the model extension including the guilt propagation subsequently responsible for increase in volunteering tendency. We also introduce a new model of offender behavior, that operates in conjunction with the model of volunteering. Through repeated simulation, it was revealed that an increase in thresholds (a value relating the seriousness of a crime with bystander inhibition) increases the chances of volunteering. Also, an in increase in the neighborhood - the bystanders themselves - increases the likelihood of intervention. The sense of guilt enables this unlikely relation, where, the theories not taking guilt as part of people-making loop, just advocate the opposite. Finally, the more the value of normality (a value representing the extent of seriousness of a crime), there was less likelihood of intervention.

References

1. Battigalli, P., Dufwenberg, M.: Dynamic psychological games. J. Econ. Theory **144**(1), 1–35 (2009)
2. Berndsen, M., Manstead, A.S.: On the relationship between responsibility and guilt: antecedent appraisal or elaborated appraisal? Eur. J. Soc. Psychol. **37**(4), 774–792 (2007)
3. Bosse, T., Gerritsen, C.: Social simulation and analysis of the dynamics of criminal hot spots. J. Artif. Soc. Soc. Simul. **13**(2), 5 (2010)
4. Charness, G., Dufwenberg, M.: Promises and partnership. Econometrica **74**(6), 1579–1601 (2006)
5. Diekmann, A.: Volunteer Dilemma. J. Conflict Resolut. **29**(4), 605–610 (1985)
6. Diekmann, A., Przepiorka, W.: "Take one for the team" individual heterogeneity and the emergence of latent norms in a volunteer's dilemma. Soc. Forces **94**(3), 1309–1333 (2015)
7. Geanakoplos, J., Pearce, D., Stacchetti, E.: Psychological games and sequential rationality. Games Econ. Behav. **1**(1), 60–79 (1989)
8. Gerritsen, C.: Agent-based modelling as a research tool for criminological research. Crime Sci. **4**(1), 1–12 (2015)
9. Gilbert, G.N.: Agent-Based Models (153). Sage, London (2008)
10. Groff, E.R.: Simulation for theory testing and experimentation: an example using routine activity theory and street robbery. J. Quant. Criminol. **23**(2), 75–103 (2007)
11. Groff, E.R.: 'Situating' simulation to model human spatio-temporal interactions: an example using crime events. Trans. GIS **11**(4), 507–530 (2007)
12. Hegemann, R.A., Smith, L.M., Barbaro, A.B., Bertozzi, A.L., Reid, S.E., Tita, G.E.: Geographical influences of an emerging network of gang rivalries. Phys. A Stat. Mechan. Appl. **390**(21), 3894–3914 (2011)
13. Latané, B., Nida, S.: Ten years of research on group size and helping. Psychol. Bull. **89**(2), 308 (1981)
14. Lemos, C., Coelho, H., Lopes, R.J.: Protestlab-an agent-based tool for simulation of street protests and violent confrontation
15. Lemos, C., Coelho, H., Lopes, R.J.: Agent-based modelling of social conflict, civil violence and revolution: state-of-the-art-review and further prospects. In: EUMAS, pp. 124–138 (2013)
16. Lemos, C., Lopes, R.J., Coelho, H.: On legitimacy feedback mechanisms in agent-based modelling of civil violence. Int. J. Intell. Syst. **31**(2), 106–127 (2016)
17. Liu, L., Wang, X., Eck, J., Liang, J.: Simulating crime events and crime patterns in ra/ca model. In: Wang, F. (ed.) Geographic Information Systems and Crime Analysis, pp. 197–213. Idea Group, Singapore (2005)
18. de Longuemar, G.: Guilt aversion in the volunteer's dilemma (2015)
19. Rao, A.S., Georgeff, M.P.: Modeling rational agents within a bdi-architecture. KR **91**, 473–484 (1991)
20. Wilensky, U.: {NetLogo} (1999)

Author Index

Printed in the United States
By Bookmasters